Christian Lessons from the Y2K Problem

❦

Chris Haidri

To Margaret and Doug, great church leaders, great friends, and two of the most thoughtful people I know. With love, Chris

Hopewell Press
Crossville, Tennessee

Copyright ©2000 by Chris Haidri.

All rights reserved. No part of this book may be used or reproduced in any form or by any means, or stored in a database or retrieval system, without prior written permission of the publisher except in the case of brief quotations for the purposes of review or criticism. Making copies of any part of this book for any purpose other than your own personal use is a violation of US copyright laws. For information, write to: Hopewell Press, PO Box 177, Crossville, Tennessee 38557.

Microsoft, Windows 95, Windows 98, and Visual C++ are trademarks of Microsoft Corporation. Macintosh and Mac are trademarks of Apple Computer Corporation. JavaScript is a trademark of Sun Microsystems, Inc. McDonald's is a trademark of McDonald's Corporation. Masterminds of Fun, Zeek the Official Y2K Hero, and Y-Rus the Official Y2K Villain are trademarks of Masterminds of Fun, Inc.

Poem credits: "Anticipation" ©1999 by Alissa Barnes. "Y not" ©1999 by Carrie Sauther.

The following publications or news sources have been quoted briefly:

Y2K: The Millennium Bug by S. Feldhahn (Multnomah Publishers, 1998)
Facing Millennial Midnight by H. Lindsey & C. Ford (Western Front Ltd., 1998)
Y2K Family Survival Guide by J. MacGregor & K. Charles (Harvest House Publishers, 1999)
Spiritual Survival During the Y2K Crisis by S. Farrar (Thomas Nelson Publishers, 1999)
Computerworld, The NY Times, The LA Times, The San Francisco Chronicle, CNN, The NBC Nightly News, Civic.com, ZDY2K, Michael Hyatt, *The Washington Post, Y2KNews Radio,* Y2KNewswire, *The Bergen Record,* and *The Orlando Sentinel.*

All trademarks and copyrights affiliated with publications, web sites, software, or any products or content mentioned in this book remain exclusively the property of their respective trademark, service mark, or copyright holders. All material in this book is believed to be reliable; however, due to the possibility of human or mechanical error by our sources, Hopewell Press, or others, the publisher and author do not guarantee the accuracy or adequacy of any information in this book and are not responsible for errors or the results obtained from any use or application of such information.

All Scripture quotations, unless otherwise indicated, are taken from the HOLY BIBLE, NEW INTERNATIONAL VERSION (NIV). Copyright 1973, 1978, 1984 by International Bible Society. Used by permission of Zondervan Publishing House. All rights reserved.

ISBN 0-9676276-0-5
Library of Congress Catalog Card Number: 99-091918
First Printing January 2000

00 01 02 03 04 05 — 9 8 7 6 5 4 3 2 1

Printed in the United States of America

Publisher: *Lynn T. Parker*
Managing Editor: *Timothy Caitlin*
Editorial Assistant: *Sandy Willoughby*
Interior Layout: *Marian Hartsough*
Cover Design: *Scott Fray*

This book is dedicated with love to my mother, who grounded me in faith and who taught me by her steadfast example to evaluate everything from a Christian perspective above and beyond all the world's other filters.

Because of your patient guidance, Mom, I know that when one person views a glass as half empty and another views it as half full, the glass often is being examined from the wrong angles, and actually contains exact and sufficient grace for each of them.

Thanks for teaching me to recognize the relevance of God in every aspect of my life.

Acknowledgments

My heartfelt appreciation goes to those who helped me research and prepare this book, as well as those who offered suggestions or encouragement during its writing. Special thanks to my wonderful wife, Vicki, who throughout the book's completion has allowed me to be even less helpful than usual with household chores; to the volunteers at The Church Computer Project, who have put up with me keeping even stranger hours than usual; to Tim Caitlin, who has become a professional at the sport of spotting my grammatical mistakes and ill-chosen words; and to Marian Hartsough, who has been exceedingly flexible and patient about the ever-shifting deadlines. Every book is a team effort, and you've all been extremely helpful in making this one everything I imagined it could be.

Table of Contents

CHAPTER 1
We'll All Stop Procrastinating Tomorrow 1
Quick Review of the Problem.. 2
Lesson 1   The Need to Adhere to Standards........................ 5
Lesson 2   Everything We Do Leaves a Wake 7
Lesson 3   Building Toward Excellence and Permanence 9
Lesson 4   You Have to Care in Order to Prepare 12
Lesson 5   Long-Term Thinking Is Essential 21
Lesson 6   Acting Earlier Makes Things Easier 22
Lesson 7   Waiting May Mean Missing Out Entirely 25
Summary.. 28

CHAPTER 2
We Can Get Through Anything 29
Lesson 8   Joy and Suffering Go Hand in Hand 29
Lesson 9   A Christian Life Does Not Guarantee
              There'll Be No Hardship 32
Lesson 10   You Never Face Things Alone 36
Lesson 11   God Listens to Our Songs 38
Lesson 12   Fear Is Natural, But Can Be Overcome.................... 40
Lesson 13   Panic Can Make a Situation Worse....................... 42
Lesson 14   Running Away Is Not the Christian Way 46
Lesson 15   You Can't Anticipate Every Trouble 50
Lesson 16   Faith Conquers Fear 53
Lesson 17   Hope Is Derived from Faith 58
Summary.. 59

CONTENTS

CHAPTER 3
Walking at the Speed of Light 61

Lesson 18   I Can't Wait to See All the Patience 61
Lesson 19   Sharing in God's Timelessness 65
Lesson 20   Maintaining a Steady Pace 68
Lesson 21   Figuring Out the Path You Should Take 72
Lesson 22   Standing Firm 73
Lesson 23   The Believer's Forecast—Perfectly Cloudy and Bright 74
Lesson 24   The Central Source of Our Strength 76
Lesson 25   Rest Is Not Optional 77
Lesson 26   Refreshing Ourselves 82
Lesson 27   Shelter Along the Way 84
Lesson 28   "Just Enough" Is All You Need 86
Lesson 29   Don't Forget to Set Up Road Signs 90
Lesson 30   The Finish Matters as Much as the Start 92
Summary 96

CHAPTER 4
The Tangled Web We've Woven 97

Lesson 31   Understanding Interconnectedness 98
Lesson 32   Over-Reliance on Technology 104
Lesson 33   Ouch! Your Moccasins Don't Fit Me 109
Lesson 34   The Benefits of Simplicity 122
Lesson 35   Embracing Complexity of Thought 126
Lesson 36   The Only Limitation Is Your Own Faithful Expectation 128
Lesson 37   The Deeper They're Embedded, the More They're Dreaded 131
Lesson 38   More and Different Problems Are Everywhere 134
Lesson 39   We're All Hooked on Happy Endings 143
Summary 144

CHAPTER 5
What Matters Most 145

Lesson 40   Money Is Too Often Considered the Top Priority 147
Lesson 41   Identifying the Few True Essentials 156
Lesson 42   Recognizing Priorities 166
Lesson 43   Prayer Needs to Become a Priority 170
Lesson 44   Beginning at Home 175

Lesson 45	Priorities That Are Out of Whack	178
Summary		183

CHAPTER 6
Knowing What You Don't Know 185

Lesson 46	Investigating the Value of Initiative	185
Lesson 47	Every Good Siesta Must Give Way to Work	205
Lesson 48	Ensuring Quality in the Face of Adversity	210
Lesson 49	Partial Solutions Aren't Permanent Solutions	216
Lesson 50	It's Kinda Sorta Mostly Pretty Important to Be Accurate	219
Lesson 51	You Can't Let Down Your Guard	225
Lesson 52	So Many Mistakes, So Little Time	227
Lesson 53	Moving from Knowledge to Wisdom	235
Lesson 54	This Is Undoubtedly Far and Away the Best Lesson Ever Written	240
Summary		244

CHAPTER 7
Getting Everyone to Work for the Team (and Vice Versa) 245

Lesson 55	The Benefits of Working Together	245
Lesson 56	Perhaps Some People Think Jesus Taught Us to Prey	247
Lesson 57	Finding the Good Samaritan in All of Us	252
Lesson 58	Do All Requests for Service Deserve Us?	259
Lesson 59	All Parts Matter	262
Lesson 60	The Least... You Should Do	264
Lesson 61	Concern for the Weak	266
Lesson 62	The Nature of True Support	273
Summary		278

CHAPTER 8
Imperfect World, Perfect God 279

Lesson 63	Maintaining Cohesion and a Strengthened Sense of Community	279
Lesson 64	Only in Spelling Should Jesus End With Us	285
Lesson 65	Learning Extends from One Generation to the Next	291
Lesson 66	The Need to Get the Word Out	294
Lesson 67	The Relentless Pursuit of Perfection	305
Summary		308

Introduction

Look out! A flood has arrived! A flood of information, that is. Unless you've been living completely detached from society, you've been swamped throughout 1999 with information about the *Year 2000 computer problem* (commonly called the *Y2K problem*) and the many steps taken to combat this problem. You've been inundated from all directions with viewpoints that often contradict each other and sometimes are extreme. At one end of the spectrum are ominous predictions of impending devastation and chaos, while at the other end are nonchalant assurances that everything will remain business as usual. The actual events will fall somewhere in the middle, with a number of unpleasant mishaps and frustrations arising because people were unable to—or unaware that they needed to—correct certain systems in time.

There have been several other excellent—and many not-so-excellent—books about the Y2K problem, and plenty of attention given to Y2K issues in thousands of shorter pieces in various media. You've seen the Y2K problem move from an occasional spot on the evening news to a far more pervasive topic appearing constantly on morning radio, TV talk shows, and newspaper op-ed pages. The amount of column space and airtime it gets has increased steadily.

At one point or another, it's possible that you've become sick and tired of hearing about the problem, and frustrated by the fact that even after all the stories you've seen, nobody has told you with certainty the exact impact the problem will have on your life and on the world! That's because no one knows the complete extent of the problem—all anyone can do is predict and extrapolate from the research done so far. The good news is that there's now an awful lot of research completed, and a great deal of awareness and information has drawn us closer to understanding the full scope of the problem. Even better news is that many talented people from a variety of disciplines have brought their knowledge and ingenuity to bear on the problem full-time, putting new pieces of the solution in place literally every minute of every day around the globe.

INTRODUCTION

What's in This Book?

There's a great deal you can learn *about* the Y2K problem, but equally as important, I believe there's a great deal you can learn *from* the Y2K problem. The book in your hands now is not a comprehensive examination of the problem from a technical, social, business, or psychological standpoint, although it will address those aspects of the problem. It's not intended to be a preparation guide—too late for that!—and it's not intended to be your only source of information about the Y2K problem's overall impact. That said, however, this book is an important ripple in the flood of information about the Y2K problem, and I think you'll find it's unlike anything else that's available to you. This book is a mixture of several things:

- A Christian perspective on why the problem matters and what extent of concern the average person should be feeling.
- Basic, easy-to-understand explanations of the problem, how it arose, and what's been done to combat it.
- Bible tie-ins for numerous issues that have surfaced during our worldwide efforts to handle the Y2K problem.
- Personal reflections and opinions from me and others about this truly unique moment in time, and some broader lessons for living that come from confronting and studying the Y2K problem.

On a few topics, I've included notes of a technical nature—you can breeze right past those if you wish, or stay and savor the nitty-gritty if you enjoy that sort of thing. For the most part, though, the book is written in casual language for the layperson, because it explains how the Y2K problem impacts *all* of our lives, not just the lives of information technology workers. Business people, government leaders, and technical insiders aren't the only ones affected by this problem—average citizens must learn to filter and sort all the complicated information on Y2K that has been circulated. I want this book to be a very comfortable experience for you, just an informative chat between friends (by necessity, of course, I'll do most of the talking), during which I'll answer some of your questions, share a handful of my opinions, and hopefully leave you with a different, clearer outlook on the Y2K problem.

Who Should Read This Book?

When asked to write this book, I initially felt (as many people do) that society has been overloaded with information about the Y2K problem, and that any other Y2K book published ought to have a title like *Believe It Or Not, Here Comes Yet Another Y2K Book*. I changed my mind, though, after watching friends and family members tossed back and forth by sloppy and contradictory information, seeing the general public whipped into a frenzy of confusion and blurry thinking by all the opinions washing over them, and having a number of pastors tell me that they long for a resource on the Y2K problem that they can easily digest. If I can help to promote some understanding, then adding another book to the imbroglio is worthwhile.

I hope this book will prove helpful to Christians from all walks of life, not just those with a fascination for computers. I also hope it will prove helpful to preachers preparing Y2K sermons after the start of the new year (it's safe to say there'll be *lots* of sermons on Year 2000 topics). Lastly, I hope that some Christian book discussion groups and adult Sunday School classes will take up Y2K as a topic worthy of a short study (perhaps 4-6 weeks) about the Christian lessons that can be gleaned from Y2K. The massive amounts of prediction and preparation may be over, but this decades-long event (remember that the Y2K computer problem has been in the making for over 40 years) offers distinct lessons worthy of being carried away and retained for a lifetime.

Some churches have done wonderfully in terms of preparation and remediation efforts, providing special programs and materials for their congregation members to keep abreast of Y2K issues. Some other churches have remained oblivious to the entire problem. For the most part, though, people (including religious leaders) have been so busy battening down the hatches and taking precautionary measures that there hasn't been much time for the type of Christian reflection that might lead to additional perspective on this significant event.

Even with all the Christian voices discussing Y2K preparations, there's been a noticeable lack of public dialogue on the entire event from a Christian viewpoint. By "Christian viewpoint" I don't mean to suggest that all Christians are of a single mind, but I do think there's a distinct perspective that accompanies a profession of Christian faith, and with that perspective we move through life in a slightly different manner than do people who aren't Christians. This book includes faith-based discussion and draws upon Scripture as a basis for understanding the world, our roles in it, and God's relationship with us as individuals and with humankind as a whole.

Do I Need to Understand Computers?

There's no prior knowledge required for you to benefit from this book. If (although it would be amazing at this point) you know absolutely nothing about the Y2K problem, or even nothing about computers at all, this book shouldn't

INTRODUCTION

lose you or confuse you. If you already know a great deal about the Y2K problem, I promise that this book will offer new ideas beyond the sorts of information you've already gathered on this topic.

Members of the media love to create nicknames, and you'll see lots of references in other places to *Millennium Bug* (an inaccurate term) and *Y2K disaster* (which jumps to conclusions) and so on. I'm sticking with the straightforward term *Y2K problem*, which is exactly what we're facing—a known problem whose ultimate impact is yet unknown. Likewise, the date January 1, 2000 has gotten nicknames—I've seen it referred to numerous times as *D-Day* in various media, but that label has a negative connotation which I wish to avoid. Since it's a unique event, it might deserve its own letter, so I've chosen to refer to January 1, 2000 as *M-Day*. M is a nice, neutral letter that doesn't assume any particular level of doom or disaster will occur on that day.

The use of the term M-Day saves me from writing—and saves you from reading—the entire date January 1, 2000 written over and over again, and prevents a variety of clunky phrases such as "the first day of the year 2000" being used hundreds of times throughout this book. I trust you to know that when I refer to midnight on M-Day it of course means the midnight that marks the beginning of the day, not the end of the day, because that moment when December 31, 1999 turns to January 1, 2000 is when the majority of potential Y2K-related computer problems have their first chance to occur.

Remember as you read this book that it's being sent to the printer on the very cusp of M-Day, during the last week of 1999. Why not just wait another few months and include reports of whatever Y2K problems take place during the early part of the year 2000? Quite simply, the reflections presented in this book aren't dependent upon the Y2K experience resulting in a particular positive or negative outcome. These lessons will remain valid regardless of the exact extent of the Y2K problem's impact on the world. To me, in fact, it's important that the book is finalized after nearly all the preparation is done, but before we find out exactly what amount of trouble occurs. It's too easy for discussions of faith and related issues to become skewed once uncertainty is removed from the equation.

In conclusion, don't fear the flood of information about the Y2K problem that's rushing around you. Be glad the flood exists, because while it contains some rubbish and some whopping fish tales and occasional confrontations with a few crabs, it also carries some life preservers and some schools of beautiful ideas and some well-constructed rafts that provide places to sit and contemplate the full implications of this computer problem. Cast your net wisely into the flood and catch only those opinions which seem well thought out, levelheaded, and impassioned. Beware the uninformed, the biased, or the blasé.

INTRODUCTION

I thank you in advance for your time and companionship as you read this book. Other books were likely your starting point, but I hope this book will be your finishing point in terms of Y2K considerations, a place to gel your conclusions about what the Y2K experience has been, and how this world event—as well as any other challenges you face in the future—can enable significant Christian reflection.

Chris Haidri
December 27, 1999

Note for Readers with Internet Access

The author will be maintaining a set of web pages until at least June 2000 to provide additional or updated information as it becomes available, and to function as a free forum for discussion of the Y2K problem, preparedness efforts, reports of ongoing glitches and repairs, and Christian responses to the problem. Feel free to check out this material at **www.churchcomputer.org/y2k.html** as often as you'd like.

1

We'll All Stop Procrastinating Tomorrow

When I was working on my undergraduate degree in computer science in the 1980s, one of our projects in an advanced COBOL class was remediation of the "two-digit year dilemma" (that's what we called the Year 2000 computer problem, a.k.a. the Y2K problem, back then). We were taught that the practice in earlier decades of not storing four-digit years would cause problems for applications that needed to work with historical data such as dates from previous centuries (1492, 1812, etc.) as well as those that might need to work with data from the year 2000 and beyond. Our instructor said that the greatest need for remediation of such programs, however, would arise in the early 1990s, when any businesses still using programs written in older languages would naturally task their in-house programmers with the job of revamping those programs to be able to handle four-digit dates, thereby accommodating all dates until the year 9999 A.D. rather than just being limited to handling dates in the 1900s. That was great news, he added, because it meant there'd be plenty of programming jobs available for us in the early 1990s. We all chuckled and didn't think much more about it once that class project was over.

Back then, we didn't envision that:

- Most businesses wouldn't actually do anything about the problem until at least 1998.
- COBOL and FORTRAN and other older language programmers would mostly be gone from the programming scene by the time remediation efforts took place, although their code lived on.
- Computer hardware prices would have dropped dramatically, and capabilities increased tremendously, so that just about every business in the world contained computers handling an astounding range of automated processes.
- Certain complicating factors—like the proliferation of embedded chips, which are discussed later—would make the problem much more difficult to fix than simply making line-by-line code changes.

As the years went by, I drifted into academic and publishing jobs and did only occasional work as a database developer and consultant, but always had plenty of friends and colleagues who were full-time programmers, systems analysts, and network administrators. Whenever the topic of the two-digit year dilemma came up in conversation, they'd tell me that nobody in business or government seemed interested in doing anything about it yet. If it didn't bother the leaders, we figured, it needn't bother us, so we put it out of our minds again each time. A few more years went by, then a few more, and suddenly it was 1995 and the Y2K computer problem had just about reached the crisis stage.

Quick Review of the Problem

> ∾ *Note*
> Don't worry—this is the most technical talk that you'll need to trudge through in this book, and I'm not going to go into much detail since there are many excellent sources that explain the technical ins and outs of the Y2K problem.

Throughout the 1960s and well into the 1970s, a kilobyte of computer space could cost tens of thousands of dollars, and a megabyte was just about unheard of (the terms "gigabyte" and "terabyte" which are now commonly used to measure storage capacity in larger amounts didn't even exist back then), and memory was limited not only by physical storage space but also by a lack of caching technologies and transmission technologies that could efficiently move large chunks of data here and there within a computer system.

Data entry also had restrictions. Punch cards contained limited spaces, and every digit was entered by hand. Today the majority of computer applications requiring data entry use auto-extends (where as soon as you type the beginning of an entry the program's "smarts" offer you the complete item they think you're in the process of entering) and picklists (where fields with frequently-entered data offer you a list of options from which you can select the date or other piece of information you want with a single mouse click) and thus on most new software, it takes exactly the same effort to enter the year 1992 that it takes to enter 92. In those early decades, however, the story was much different.

Every action that involved data chewed up precious memory resources, so you pared everything down to its most essential elements—in those days, for example, if you wanted to uppercase an entire sentence, you'd most likely write a procedure in your program to run through it one letter at a time, uppercasing just that letter and then returning it to its original location, then fetching the next letter. These days, programming languages have no problem snatching up an entire sentence (or paragraph, or document, or however much you want at once) and applying a function such as capitalization to all of it at once, because there's plenty of memory capacity available; in fact, most individual computer programming objects are so "robust" (that's a favorite techie term meaning something is full of features and capabilities) that they even contain their own sets of instructions for performing lots of specific actions on themselves without needing outside programs to control all their actions. Alas, back then programmers had to handle everything in tiny pieces, and for this reason many shortcuts were born. The two-digit "blunder" that most now view in hindsight as a tremendous problem was actually quite acceptable—in fact, was even praised as good standard practice—in the days when it was done.

Programmers used two-digit years to save what was then extremely precious memory space. Here's a comparison of how the approximate cost of a single megabyte of RAM has changed over the years:

1970	$3,200,000
1980	$64,000
1990	$120
1995	$30
1997	$5
1999	Less than $1

Translated into the value of today's dollars, companies saved billions by opting to use two-digit date fields up through the mid-1980s, when memory prices finally plunged to truly accessible levels.

Just about everyone in the earliest generations of programmers did things this way! Federal Reserve Chairman Alan Greenspan, in fact, designed computer programs for his firm in the 1960s. As part of his testimony regarding Y2K during an appearance before the US Senate in 1998, he noted, "I'm one of the culprits who created this problem. I used to write those programs back in the 60s and 70s and was so proud of the fact that I was able to squeeze a few elements of space out of my program by not having to put 19 before the year."

> ### ∞ Note
> Not all programs involving dates were written using two-digit dates. There were some (those that dealt with historical data, for instance) where it was absolutely necessary for programmers to use a four-digit date, and the companies that dealt with those sorts of data simply had to accept the extra computing cost of handling four-digit years. Realize, though, that computer applications weren't nearly as wide-ranging as they are these days—companies were selective about the types of things they used computers to handle, and it's only when prices eventually dropped (and when newer programming languages had greater flexibility and extensibility) that many organizations decided to computerize the large majority of their processes.

The two-digit problem was not unique to computers, by the way. We did the same thing with other aspects of our lives—most often with paper forms. Think about checks, which for decades were printed with 19 followed by a short blank line for you to add the two final digits for the year. Remember how funny it felt the first time you received an order of checks that didn't have 19 preprinted, and you had to write the entire year? That was a two-digit year problem very much like the Y2K computer problem in origin, but the check-printing industry solved it simply by omitting the 19 from checks that were printed beginning in early 1998.

Warning: Those who find death too creepy to be amusing might want to skip this paragraph. Another problem not often discussed, but more common than you'd think, is "millennium headstones"—in countries like the US where pre-purchasing headstones has become commonplace, most people who were born earlier than 1910 got their tombstones with 19 pre-inscribed as the first two-digits of the year of death. The more writing one put in place when purchasing the headstone, the less the survivors had to add following one's death—and at roughly $60 per letter (varies by region) for additions following the person's death, putting the 19 in place ahead of time seemed like a smart idea. Recall that the average life expectancy for humans was nowhere near 90 when many of these headstones were purchased, so few people had the foresight (or the optimism, depending on how you look at it) to think that they might end up among the rare lot who make it to such a ripe old age. They put the 19 in ahead of time for the same reason that computer programmers caused Y2K problems—to save money by taking a calculated risk that they thought would not cause any trouble later. Now, though, any people who have unexpectedly lived much longer than anticipated after getting a headstone with a 19 already in place find themselves in the odd position of having outlived their own expiration date. One chipper woman who's in this situation was asked by a TV news reporter what it felt like to face the possibility of scratching out or buffing out the number 19 on her death date when she lived past New Year's Day 2000. She smiled and said, "All I can really say is, having to redo those numbers is far better than the alternative—don't you agree?"

You can see, therefore, that Y2K problems appear in a wide variety of settings, not just in computer systems. What's unique to Y2K computer problems, though, is that computer programs often perform calculations involving dates, so potential problems in those programs don't remain isolated to the single location where a two-digit year is entered. A two-digit year might be used for dozens of calculations that each get passed along and take part in dozens of additional calculations. Moreover, sometimes older programmers would simply add 1900 during a calculation to convert a two-digit year into a four-digit year, but sometimes wouldn't add it during the calculation but instead place a hard-coded 19 in the necessary location on a report (just like the older bank checks) and then would spit out the final two digits after the preprinted 19. The variety of ways in which two-digit dates were manipulated deep within the innards of computer programs is what makes the Y2K problem so complicated to correct.

We saw the overall problem coming, however, and there were a few voices trumpeting all along that something needed to be done in a more timely manner—those foresightful people were largely ignored throughout the 1980s, when it would have been cheap and much more possible to correct the entire problem. Greed and bottom-line concerns, ignorance and denial, arrogance (thinking a quick fix would come along, or that technology would evolve so far that we wouldn't use any of those early systems anymore)—all of these and more were factors.

LESSON 1: THE NEED TO ADHERE TO STANDARDS

Over the years, programs were built atop other programs, and sometimes by many programmers within the same company, each with his or her own coding style! Coding style determines ease of repair. (As used in this book, "coding" is simply another word for "programming"—it means to write lines of programming code in any of various programming languages.) Coding style doesn't get a lot of attention, but is one of my favorite aspects of the Y2K problem. Outside of the central problem of most early programmers using two-digit dates in order to conserve memory usage, there have been plenty of additional problems caused by programmers making individual decisions that in hindsight could be considered quite self-centered. These fall into three areas:

- Lack of concern about coding standards
- Naming or structural quirks
- Insufficient or obscure documentation

In the couple of years before M-Day, there has been much discussion by non-technical people of a desired "magic bullet" or "silver bullet" solution which might greatly reduce the impact of the Y2K problem by having some kind of software tool automatically revise and/or replace two-digit code with four-digit code, thereby updating thousands of lines of code in the time it would take a human programmer to do just a few lines by hand. That notion is laughable to programmers, because it fails to take a few things into account. First, there never have been—and still aren't—coding standards so strict that an automated process could review a strange program and be able to count on having its variables named in a certain way, or initialized in a certain location relative to where they're first used, or any other detail that would be necessary to know in order to implement automated remediation. Even though there are syntactical rules for each programming language, there is plenty of room for variety in the way the rules are brought to bear on any given programming task.

Second, there's tremendous lee-way for individuality when coding—each programmer develops his or her own personal style which can range from a completely obvious, fastidious, highly-organized style all the way to a sloppy, chaotic, cryptic style that delights in its own obscurity.

Third, there's a tremendous disparity in the ways various programmers have used documentation throughout their programs (documentation is information included in a program which doesn't actually DO anything, but rather DESCRIBES something, usually offering a quick insight into what takes place in the current line or the subsequent set of lines). Some programmers never, ever write documentation. Not once in their entire careers! Some other programmers, by contrast, write at least one line of documentation for every line of actual programming code they write, and while you'd think that those long-winded programmers might also care enough to adhere to coding standards better than those with terse documentation, the opposite is often true. If a programmer writes extensive comments throughout his program, he sometimes feels greater license to use atypical coding techniques, since the documentation explains what's going on. No automated tool can evaluate lines of programming code with sufficient brainpower to figure out an individual programmer's style, his set of programming conventions, and his own personal quirks—and sometimes all of that knowledge is necessary in order to revise or rework older programming code. Therefore changing code involving two-digit years to use four-digit years instead—which really is a very simple repair—sometimes has been much more complicated due to an unusual, inconsistent, or murky coding style.

The problems wrought by such individualism serve as a call for the use of some standards in everyone's life—at least in terms of things that ultimately could affect others or the world around you. Think about terms used all the time: "the common good" and "common sense" and "common knowledge." These terms exist because people acknowledge that there's a set of stuff which applies to just about everyone, and that the set of common stuff coexists alongside all the particular things that are good for you alone and the particular sense you bring to decisions and the particular knowledge you've gained throughout your lifetime. The ratio between the general and the particular in your life is dynamic, and you can adjust this ratio as needed from moment to moment. Be sure, however, that you don't indulge your own uniqueness so much that you forget the common sense that keeps people safe, that you fail to contribute to the world of common knowledge that can benefit others, and so on.

"No man is an island," goes the old saying, and it's particularly true that no Christian is an island. There's a small set of standard Christian beliefs—the supremacy of God, the sacrifice of Christ for our salvation, and adherence to the scriptures as guidance for how to live—and you must unswervingly hold to those standards. Beyond that, you're also well-advised to notice and comply with a selected set of societal standards so that you'll be considered a responsible member of your own family, of your local community, of your nation, and of the world. While eccentricity may be tolerated to some extent, you'll find that disregarding standards is usually unappreciated when it works against the common good.

LESSON 2: EVERYTHING WE DO LEAVES A WAKE

A book published in 1998 stated, "Y2K is the result of shortsighted computer programmers who forgot that 2000 follows 1999." That's far from accurate, of course. Programmers knew 2000 was coming and would cause troubles for their code, but they did what seemed right and necessary at the time, accepting in good faith that the next generation of programmers would either rework or replace their code as required. Now those first-generation programmers are taking a bad rap for limited decision-making, and it will forever overshadow all their excellent achievements.

Clearly you must live with everything you've done. Your life is the sum of every action you take, and in this era of inescapable paper trails and computerized accounts, it's all on record. Make sure every small decision you make and every little thing you do will be representative of what you want people to think of you overall. As you move through life, constantly strive to anticipate the consequences of your actions.

There are other Y2K-related problems (embedded systems and so on) which will be touched upon in later chapters. For now, though, you can clearly see the basic unfolding of Y2K computer problems: many people consciously decided to implement systems that they knew would later need to be undone, redone, or discarded—and then the majority of efforts to undo, redo, or discard the flawed systems began too late.

It's not just the Y2K problem where shortsightedness has occurred over the years in computer programming. I've seen many situations where programmers have declared a project finished without every planned feature functioning as intended. My colleagues and I called that a "SWEFT solution," where SWEFT was an acronym for Somebody Will Eventually Find Time. Somebody will eventually find time to finalize the table optimization routine; somebody will eventually find time to expand the error-checking to take care of all the obscure scenarios; etc. In essence, many programmers go live ("live" here rhymes with "hive" not "give"—the expression "go live" means to have users start using an application you've coded) with applications that still have minor weaknesses. These weaknesses are often documented carefully in the code, in the expectation that somebody will eventually find time to completely and properly do everything that the original development team was unable to finish doing. That's a dangerous attitude in certain ways, but one that's surprisingly common not only in computer programming but in any setting where large, complicated projects and inflexible deadlines are the norm.

With anything we do, it's important to think about the consequences of our actions, especially if we might be handing off the results to someone else and never getting a chance to follow through and fix things ourselves later. It's essential to realize that you won't always be the one to clean up your own messes (just as original programmers usually weren't the ones to have to figure out how to revise their code for Y2K compliance).

My father, a pathological pack-rat, had his life filled to the brim with clutter and possessions and files and unfinished projects. Everything he had been involved with personally and professionally for the past 40 or more years was scattered around the house, garage, basement, attic, storage shed, front porch, and yard. In his later years, he often told me (because I tend to follow directly in his pack-rat footsteps), "When I die, don't think twice about this stuff. Just walk away from it all and don't look back." That was easy enough for him to say, but the truth is that when he died—without making a will, mind you, which caused a few complications—there were some legal papers and some memory-filled trinkets that had to be located, and it took me over six months of weekends to go through the mess that he left behind.

Along with giving relatives and charities the things that were decent, I gradually threw away over 800 extra-large garbage bags full of completely unsalvageable stuff. While that big sorting and searching project went on, we were short-staffed at my workplace, and I was working 70-hour weeks to carry my share of our department's increased workload, then commuting six hours and working nonstop every weekend sorting out Dad's stuff. After a few months of wearing myself down, everything caught up with me and I fell asleep at the wheel of my car on the highway, left my lane and crashed head-on into a concrete barricade at 55 mph. By the grace of God, the sacrifice of the car, and the effectiveness of the airbag, my life was spared and my body fully healed after several months. Was that accident my father's fault for leaving behind disorganized things that required exhaustive amounts of attention? Certainly not! But if he had realized the true state of what he left behind, I doubt that he would have left everything in exactly the shape he did. A quick epilogue: Oddly enough, shortly after that whole experience, my mother and my wife's parents and some of our aunts and uncles all began to start giving away and throwing away many of their old things. Just a coincidence? Hmmm...

Lesson 3: Building Toward Excellence and Permanence

Recall that one of the assumptions programmers made three decades in advance of M-Day was that by the time the end of the millennium rolled around, very few—if any—of the programs being written back then would still be in use. Surprise, surprise! Not only did we see them still in use by 1999, but unfortunately in many cases they had served as building blocks for layer upon layer of extensive, integrated systems that had been expanded one piece at a time over the years, whenever company processes changed or whenever new staff came up with different ideas about how systems should operate.

Again, it's not just the computer world that frequently handles things this way. As long as local law allows it, people often deal with the dilemma of outdated wiring in an older home by simply adding a new circuit or two with heavier amperage to accommodate their new oven or whatever appliance requires a heavier line—they do this even though they know it would be in the home's best long-term interest to have a completely new panel and updated circuits throughout the entire house. What they end up with is a mish-mosh of old and new electrical systems combined into one, and if there's ever a problem that requires repair work on only the old system, they may have to dig through layers of added complexity to get at the original setup.

Okay, forget wiring—how'd you like to rid the same old house of its lead-based paint, since we now know the inherent dangers of such paint? Have fun! The average room in a 60-year-old home has had five layers of paint added, with no removal of earlier layers. This is because we're all prone to freshening up, extending, and modifying things which are out of date, but the old stuff usually stays in place. I think it's great—in fact, it's essential—that we're not wasteful enough to completely start over every time we want to update something. Indeed, it doesn't matter whether it's laziness or frugality or lack of time or shortsightedness or conservationism or any other motivation that causes us to operate this way. All that matters is that you realize that no matter how short a time period you think something you're creating will last, it's likely to be around and still in use (or around in a modified or derivative version) for far longer than you anticipate.

I urge people to assume that anything they build is going to be used forever—this means you shouldn't do shoddy work, whether in the workplace or in parenting or in being a friend to someone. Realize that everything you put in place has the potential to stand forever—it may have many layers added to it or extensions built onto it, and it may be corrected or revamped by you or others in the future, but everything you do is undergirding something that will never be completely undone. Make every action something of which you can be proud, and which is a good reflection of God's presence in your life. Whether you're part of a team that's building a marriage or a church or a career or the mindset of a child or anything else of value, the determination to build something that will function properly forever will bring about much better results than an effort that lacks such determination.

Let's discuss for a moment how computers think—or, more accurately, how they don't think. Except for a few advanced artificial intelligence computers that are programmed to fake it, you know that computer programs don't have intuition. To illustrate how this plays out in their behavior, consider a quick example: Assume somehow you've trained a computer program to open doors, and you show it three doors. Your human mind knows that one leads to a bathroom, one leads to a coat closet, and the other leads outside. You give the computer program this instruction: "Open the door and go outside." Unless you've told the program something about the particular door you mean—the one nearest the window, the one that's wider than the other two, the one with the glass panels in it, the one with the deadbolt lock on it, the one with the security peephole in it, or any of the other various ways you or I might easily identify the main entrance door—the program won't know which is the correct door. And, unless you've specifically told it to check all three by opening them to find out which one leads outside, the program won't take the initiative to open any door to check what's behind it—the program will just return an error message along the lines of "I don't know which door to check" or possibly even something less helpful like "I can't move" or "I'm stuck now" without telling you the exact problem.

To get the program to successfully open the desired door, most programmers won't bother to do all the work required to tell the computer every possible way to determine the differences between types of doors, but instead will simply make the first portion of the instruction more specific: "Open the widest door" or "Open the door with glass panels in it" or "Open door #2." The computer program can successfully accomplish that instruction in that circumstance, but still doesn't know much about the door it just opened or why it was opened, except that it was the door to use and the action to take *in that particular moment.*

Realize that the computer programs and embedded systems which have given us the most grief with the Y2K problem still appear to be functioning completely correctly on the surface at the time they're upgraded. They're able to successfully do everything they were instructed to do, so most of these programs can't self-determine that anything's wrong with what they're doing, and they certainly don't know they're approaching a moment in time (M-Day) that might cause them to experience glitches. One of the most insidious variations of potential Y2K problems, in fact, involves corrupt data being passed from non-Y2K-compliant systems to compliant systems in cases where the non-compliant systems don't realize anything at all is wrong (we'll look at this "one bad apple spoils the bunch" problem in Chapter 4).

This makes me think about children, and the fact that we instruct them all the time—if our instructions are incomplete or shortsighted, the kids can get into as much of a quandary as some computers are in due to Y2K. They might end up doing everything correctly that we told them about, but still "messing up" simply because of skills we didn't bother to give them for one reason or another.

To look at drugs as an obvious example of something that can be a problem down the road, many parents think they understand their hometowns well, and say to themselves confidently, "I've done the research and I definitely need to teach Daniel about pot and crack and crystal meth, because that's what people in this town have trouble with. We thankfully don't need to talk about hashish, because that's one my child will never encounter." To those parents, the idea that their child could encounter hashish is as remote as the notion of the Year 2000 rolling around was to programmers thirty years ago. But what happens when hashish makes a comeback as a national fad and reaches even your small town? It's not enough to teach your son just about avoiding specific drugs, even if you mention them all by name. You can warn him about heroin, cocaine, marijuana, LSD, alcohol, and so on, but if you haven't mentioned the dangers of huffing paints or other inhalants, he may be offered those someday and not realize they're also a problem. It would be more effective to teach the child a more general rule—that *anything* he's offered with the claim that it will alter his body temporarily, or make his body feel different than it's ever felt before, is suspect and should be avoided until he consults with you to find out what he's being offered.

We shouldn't trick ourselves into thinking we've satisfactorily programmed our own children with loving information and solid guidance and that they're out there walking around with a *complete* set of instructions—there is probably some area where we haven't been complete enough in our discussion and instruction.

The same goes for thinking "My child won't be lured into sexual activity" and so on. Sometimes, life gets complicated and time keeps rolling along and suddenly you realize that your pre-teen has become a 20-year-old, and you never got a chance to go back and tweak the program, never got to update the initial set of instructions you gave at each step along the way. So in our very first chance to give our children instructions about critical issues, we either ought to give instructions for *every* possible case (including situations that may arise far into the future), or else ought to make our instructions general enough to be effective even in cases where we couldn't possibly predict the details of the problematic situation.

The Y2K problem is a call for all of us to rethink the amount of care and concern we put into giving proper instructions to our loved ones, especially our children, before we send them down a path that will likely lead them past every obstacle we foresee for them and then some! Don't think of a moment in their lives that's 30 years away as something so remote that you don't need to plan for it now. Think of how to instruct them in ways that will remain useful for every moment of the rest of their lives.

Beyond directly building their character and their values, never forget that teaching them to turn to prayer and the Bible in times of decision is essential to help make up for areas you can't foresee. The Bible is a manual of standards, and prayer is a path to obtaining guidance from God, and anyone who learns to spend plenty of time with both won't be easily flustered when an unanticipated problem comes along. All of us are constantly building things, and we have a choice of foundations to use. In the long run, only one foundation will withstand all the tests of time:

> *1 Corinthians 3:11* For no one can lay any foundation other than the one already laid, which is Jesus Christ.

Whatever you build with your life, make sure it is built upon the foundation that never crumbles, and that the result is fit to stand as a permanent reflection of your craftsmanship and care.

Lesson 4: You Have to Care in Order to Prepare

> *Proverbs 22:3* A prudent man sees danger and takes refuge, but the simple keep going and suffer for it.

Some Y2K watchers like Jim Lord made the point early and often that people for some odd reason felt it was pessimistic to prepare for Y2K-related problems, although it actually was exactly like other preparations that most of us accept as reasonable and necessary. For instance, we purchase insurance for our homes, autos, and so forth—and we consider that prudence, not pessimism. Our goal, in fact, is to never make an insurance claim, yet most of us are sensible enough to still take out the policies just in case. With Y2K computer glitches, the potential exists for so much bad stuff (and so varied), it only makes sense to prepare for the worst. Jim Lord directed a few words at those people who don't believe anything at all will go wrong: "If it doesn't happen, declare victory and have a party, but the worst is worth preparing for."

Why not err on the side of caution? In an era of extreme sports and extreme wealth (for some) and extreme information (we're deluged by information morning, noon, and night from so many media sources that it often seems we can find out everything there is to know on the planet), it somehow has gone out of fashion to take measured action to avoid potential pitfalls. We're too on top of things to need to get prepared for problems that might not come to fruition. These days, it just isn't cool to be cautious!

A wise military leader once said, "Those who are good at getting rid of trouble are those who take care of it before it arises." Not surprisingly, public workers who protect and serve were among those who took a real attitude of precaution toward Y2K. The Canadian Royal Mounted Police, for example, canceled vacations for their entire staff from 12/27/99 to 3/15/00, and the Canadian military considered doing the same, just in case any emergency situations cropped up, demanding huge numbers of helping hands. The Pentagon, which is responsible for so much of the US national defense infrastructure, had $1.1 billion for dealing with the Y2K problem written into its fiscal year 1999 budget.

Understanding What Could Happen

It became clear that the following types of things (to give only a few examples) could go wrong if computers weren't fixed:

- Some ATM machines might refuse to give out money.
- A bill due in January 2000 might be mistaken as 99 years past due, and whopping amounts of interest and penalties might be added.
- Improper billing such as that just mentioned, if it takes place on accounts that are paid through automatic withdrawal, might result in certain banks being asked for far too much money from multiple customer accounts, in turn skewing the banks' interactions with the Federal Reserve, which could in turn provide faulty data to all other banks that take action based on numbers they get from the Fed.
- Computers that regulate the flow of electricity, water, or telephone service could become confused, producing isolated cases of erratic behavior or outages in utility services.

- A telephone call or other activity charged through measured-time accounting might start just before midnight Dec. 31, 1999 and end an hour later on Jan. 1, 2000, but be billed as a hundred years' worth of charges.
- Pensions, life insurance, or other age-dependent items might be canceled automatically as certain computer systems suddenly start to think that everyone born in the 19th century has not been born yet.
- Patients on an ongoing physical therapy regimen might show up for an appointment the first week of January to find that all of their previously approved sessions are no longer scheduled.
- Some weapons systems might turn themselves off, unable to resolve a discrepancy between two pieces of date information. While many people have joked that this makes the chances for world peace better than ever on M-Day, that's foolhardy thinking, because the loss or malfunction of weapons attack warning systems might cause added tensions in certain countries, and some country which has been at war with another country for years might see any Y2K-related weakness that arises in their enemy's systems as a great opportunity to attack.

Throughout the late 1990s, tests of computers in many different settings revealed that the Y2K problem was real and would have severe repercussions if left unresolved. Even companies that managed to fix all Y2K-related problems in their main systems might still experience one or more surprising problems that hamper productivity. When Chrysler Corporation simulated the year 2000 during testing at one of its assembly plants, computerized security gates refused to let anyone in or out. Most things that could go wrong due to actual Y2K problems are along the lines of this Chrysler test result—not life-threatening, just inconvenient—but the larger concern in most people's minds is the cumulative effect of numerous tiny problems that might occur simultaneously around the world. Most of us have had to make calls or write letters to correct a single billing error at one time or another, and can easily imagine the massive headaches that would result from even small, spotty malfunctions in the computers that process nearly every aspect of our modern lives.

It took insightful people to understand that the Y2K problem was real and to commit to doing something about it. This reminds us how important it is to be forward-thinking. The wisest and most useful individual in any situation is one who sees what hasn't really become apparent to anyone else yet. That's what wisdom is, really—noticing what hasn't fully formed yet, and sensing the subtle urgency of a situation which seems calm on the surface to most other onlookers. Truly perceptive people accepted quite early the enormous potential ramifications of the Y2K problem, while the average person looked at the simple surface issues and didn't get enough of a glimpse to realize this was a substantial problem. To adequately prepare yourself for whatever troubles you encounter in a lifetime, work on noticing that which is barely noticeable, and on acting quickly to confront issues that have just begun to take shape.

Basic Personal Preparations

We'll be talking much more throughout the book about specific actions that people have taken to prepare for Y2K, so for now let's just quickly summarize a few of the most common ones. Quite a few people bought Y2K books (thank you!), subscribed to Y2K magazines and newsletters, tuned in to Y2K coverage on electronic media, and attended Y2K seminars in their local community or broader geographical region.

In addition, most people stocked up (or flat-out stockpiled, which means a far more feverish version of stocking up) such goods and equipment as: water, dehydrated foods, canned goods, toiletries, medical supplies, flashlights, batteries, candles, generators, wood-burning stoves, oil or kerosene lamps, seeds, grain and hand-powered grain mills, guns and ammunition, animals they had never owned before (chickens, goats—you name it), and even survival shelters.

Basic Business Preparations

The standard Y2K project for businesses has included a few stages:

- **Information/Education:** Figuring out why they needed to act on Y2K, and then convincing those who controlled the purse strings.
- **Assessment:** Analyzing hardware and software to determine everything that's date-dependent, then seeking specific Y2K dependencies (can they function with dates beyond 2000; can they handle leap year in 2000, and so on) to see if they required simple correction, comprehensive upgrading, or complete replacement. Pinpointing which activities are most critical to the business, and fixing the systems that supported those activities first.
- **Remediation:** Revising code, replacing hardware and software, and so forth. Working on critical systems first, then systems that interacted with the critical ones, and so on.
- **Testing:** This was crucial and required a great deal of attention, since new problems might very well have been created during remediation.
- **Contingency planning:** As soon as assessment was completed, safety nets and alternative methods of operation had to be developed in case one or more systems did fail due to Y2K. Contingency plans also needed to be tested through simulations, the more realistic the better.

Areas of Concern for Computer Systems

There are four basic areas of concern regarding Y2K problems on most computer systems, including personal computers (PCs):

- **Infrastructure:** If the power goes out, it doesn't really matter if a computer is compliant. Electrical, cable, telephone, or even satellite network failure can prevent even the most compliant systems from functioning properly.

- **Hardware:** Macintosh computers are expected to function without any date-related hardware errors for tens of thousands of years. Still, it isn't easy for anyone—even Mac owners—to confidently say, "My computer system is compliant." Every PC contains an assortment of component parts that come together to work in particular combinations each time you start a different task. The system's real-time clock might not transition from 1999 to 2000 smoothly. The system BIOS, which houses basic instructions for handling hardware needs, is often non-compliant if manufactured in 1997 or earlier. Free hardware tests for these items abounded (for example, at **www.pcy2000.org**). If hardware fails the tests, purchasing new equipment is the simplest solution for many companies, since prices have plummeted and product improvement cycles have become so short in the PC industry.

- **Software.** Once hardware is compliant, operating system and applications software need to be checked for how they'll handle dates beyond 1999. Even Windows 98 when released had a few date-related foibles that made Microsoft's Y2K web site label it "compliant with minor issues." Most Windows operating systems work atop MS-DOS, which interacts situationally with the hardware. So, even those who never knowingly use MS-DOS might need to upgrade their DOS version for Y2K-compliance.

- **Systems That Interact With Your System.** After verifying compliance in all their own hardware and software, businesses need to review their entire supply chain (physical goods as well as information) for potential problems. Every supplier (and, in fact, every major customer) that's considered key to a company's performance has to be checked out to make sure that they also will be fully compliant and able to continue business as usual after M-Day.

Checking Printers

Almost no printer hardware is affected. Generally, even if a printer becomes confused about the date, it can still print items sent to it. All-in-one peripherals (printers with fax, scanning, and copying capabilities) are more susceptible to problems, because some fax features are date-sensitive, but most functions on those machines should still work fine.

However, some print drivers that connect applications with printers don't support four-digit dates, in which case the following might happen:

- Inability to print (in rare cases)
- Failure in interconnected software, such as faxing software
- Corrupted activity reports
- Date errors when reinstalling a printer driver after M-Day

Virtually all printer manufacturers supply free upgrades for their non-compliant drivers.

> ∞ *Note*
>
> Discontinued products are the only area where hardware manufacturers have left certain customers in the lurch. Generally, if manufacturers are still in business and have technical data available on a given product, they've been very cooperative about helping customers achieve Y2K-compliance.

THE PAYOFF FOR PREPARING

There are undeniably great results from the preparation efforts that have been made. Mitch Ratcliffe, who wrote many opinion pieces on Y2K, is one of my favorite media players to watch because of his relentless optimism. (Later in the book I'll discuss some of my favorite doomsayers, too; I've been equally bemused with the Y2K spindoctoring that occurs at both ends of the spectrum.) On July 14, 1999 he was happy to give a status report on the progress that many companies and government agencies had made, using as the basis for his exhilaration the fact that most states in the US had begun their new fiscal years on July 1 without significant reported problems—that date was long regarded as a litmus test for how things might function on a larger scale when M-Day arrived. Ratcliffe wrote:

"It looks like information technology professionals in organizations that have been diligent about Y2K have successfully answered the challenge. Except for corporate or government systems that have been ignored, it seems, there is no reason to fear a data meltdown.... Now, this is not to say that a company or government that has made no attempt to remediate Y2K problems will get off scot-free. But, it does indicate that effort returns substantially decreased chance of failure. Nevertheless, we still hear constantly that 'no one can know what will happen come January 1st.' While this may be true when attempting to describe the entire globe on the first day of 2000, it is clearly no longer applicable to organizations that have made Y2K repairs. Wherever you are, no matter what systems you rely on, the level of preparation in the organizations that support your life is a good indication of the risk you face."

He went on to say that he didn't mean to minimize the fact that there was indeed a Y2K problem, but pointed out that in his estimation, "If your company or the governments you rely on have made a good faith effort at Y2K repairs, your chances of experiencing a severe interruption in services of any sort is very low."

Notice the only people to whom he didn't extend his happy hope—those who have "made no attempt to remediate Y2K problems" and those who have not "made a good faith effort." He's very correct in his assessment that organizations which have prepared have a drastically reduced risk of experiencing failures—the same holds true for all who prepare well in advance of any potential disaster.

Those Who Have Chosen Not to Prepare

So, who in their right mind wouldn't bother to prepare for Y2K? Well, for starters, all of those who aren't convinced of the need to prepare. Next, those who are inundated with too much hype and decide eventually to tune it all out. Lastly, those who can't cope with the unavoidable uncertainty that's involved in any discussion of the impact of Y2K—people who don't care for solid information that ends in a question mark, but rather expect to be told in concrete terms whether or not they'll be affected and to what extent, even though this kind of information is impossible to come up with prior to M-Day.

A CBS television poll in mid-July 1999 found that less than one-fifth of households were actively preparing or even "thinking about doing anything" to get ready for Y2K.

A poll at the CNN Interactive web site in August 1999 asked: *Are you making preparations for survival in case of a Y2K disaster?* Of the thousands of web surfers who had chosen to participate when I checked the results, about half (49%) had selected the answer "No, I find it comical."

Both of these were non-scientific polls, and one can't assume that the results represent the opinions of the public as a whole. These results do match up, however, with general attitudes that I and other Y2K experts have encountered time and again from individuals. "If you can prove to me that I'm going to be affected," they say, "then I'll certainly prepare." With that sort of attitude, there'll probably be little sympathy for any of those people if they do end up suffering minor inconveniences due to lack of preparation. Contingency planners point out that this is an increasing trend in modern society—we are willing to take preparatory action only if we know that something's going to really hit us.

We saw a prime example of this during September 1999 when Hurricane Floyd was brewing south of the US, and officials urged residents of certain coastal states to evacuate. People waited until the very last minute they could, in order to learn from the National Weather Service if their specific area would be hit or not. I love that we have faster and more efficient communications technology than ever before, and that we can have jets fly in and drop measuring equipment in the middle of a hurricane to bring us amazing details about the storm's activity long before it approaches land. What I don't understand, though, is people's stubborn refusal to be inconvenienced at all for the sake of preparation. There are many events (large natural disasters among them) which you will never get a chance to do over. The end result of the Hurricane Floyd evacuation effort was that over one-and-a-half million people, the largest evacuation of its kind in the US to date, crowded every mile of interstate in the coastal Southeast just about all at once, causing major traffic snarls that lasted in some cases for several hours. Many people in those hundreds of thousands of vehicles were ill-prepared for the evacuation, not having brought water or food along, not having filled their gas tanks before leaving, etc. Relief workers ended up having to treat these evacuating vehicles as the first wave of disaster relief, helping people to survive a traffic nightmare that could have been greatly minimized if all evacuees had actually left their homes when they were told to do so, and with better preparation.

It wasn't just individuals who put off preparing for Y2K for various reasons. In fact, there have been entire countries acting as if they think the notion of Y2K computer problems is a ruse, and they certainly aren't going to fall for it. Italy leaps to mind as a great example of a nation that could have rallied the resources and manpower necessary to do a great remediation effort, but the national government has never really seemed to buy into the idea that it needs to make a concerted effort to understand and deal with the problem.

There are a few countries that simply aren't in a good enough position financially or politically, or have other crises already occurring that far outweigh the less tangible, potential crisis posed by the Y2K computer problem. (Chapter 8 talks about different approaches to the Y2K problem by a number of specific countries.)

A *Computerworld* article in mid-1999 discussed a US Securities and Exchange Commission (SEC) report showing that while most US brokerages had completed most of their Y2K work, foreign ones hadn't. The report cited a study by the Securities Industry Association and International Operations Association, showing that only 22% of foreign financial institutions such as investment banks and stock exchanges had completed Y2K remediation projects. Far more interesting to me was the information that *wasn't* available as part of the study—572 out of 650 foreign brokerages and stock exchanges targeted for the survey did *not* participate in the study. The majority of the 78 institutions who did provide information revealed that they'd completed less than half of their Y2K projects, and it's impossible to know how little or how much the non-participants had completed.

For any individual, business, or government that has had the time, information, and money required to take on a remediation effort and some important contingency planning, why not prepare to some extent? Preparations for any potential problem can only hurt you if you overdo the preparations by going into debt, taking on unwarranted stress, ignoring other daily responsibilities, and so forth.

MORE BIBLE VERSES ABOUT PLANNING AND PREPAREDNESS

> *Proverbs 15:22* Plans fail for lack of counsel, but with many advisers they succeed.

You don't need to get advice or approval from others before every action you take, but in general it's true that a group of well-informed people can make better decisions than individuals. The more critical a given situation is, the more sensible it is to solicit the advice of others who are knowledgeable about the situation.

> *Psalm 20:1,4* May the Lord answer you when you are in distress ... and make all your plans succeed.

The Lord is there for you, but you need to put plans in place yourself and trust him to make them succeed. It's the same whether considering your readiness for Y2K or your readiness for God's kingdom. Once you've prepared, you can carry on with greater confidence. You do the planning; trust him to work things out according to his purposes. In case there's any doubt about who's ultimately in control, consider this:

> *Proverbs 16:9* In his heart a man plans his course, but the Lord determines his steps.

Perhaps at first you think it's pointless to make decisions about your own plans if God has the final say on what will occur. The ultimate outcome of your life and your relationship with God, though, will hinge upon the decisions you make and the plans you implement for yourself. Only limited thinkers are frustrated by the preeminence of God's plans above their own. Mature thinkers take comfort in the fact that God is in control of everything, appreciating that he can overrule their plans when they're inappropriate, and can ensure the success of those plans when they align with his intentions. Because God has provided for our care according to his master plan, we needn't worry about our own occasional missteps.

Proverbs 31:10-31 offers a great description of a wife valuable beyond measure. She knows the Lord, she's watchful, and she keeps food and critical supplies on hand. Wisdom is an integral part of her life, and she's prepared for anything. Many of the behaviors cited in this verse are excellent for telling us what it is like for anyone to be "of noble character" during Y2K or for any other crisis; it's ideal to be "clothed with strength and dignity" so that one "can laugh at the days to come."

Lesson 5: Long-Term Thinking Is Essential

Something (perhaps simply greed, but perhaps more than that) made many large companies decide to benefit their bottom line numbers in the short term by not spending any time and money on Y2K conversion projects early—say, in 1995 when information technology professionals really started getting clued in to what a big deal this was going to be, and started asking their managers for allocations of funds and staffing in order to conduct Y2K remediation efforts. Companies did not want to spend that sort of money—it often sounded like terribly high amounts—to fix what on the surface sounded like a tiny, silly blunder from decades earlier. I don't know if they honestly believed that a simpler solution would be developed as M-Day drew closer, or if they didn't get correct information about the scope of the problem early enough, or thought that perhaps industry-wide solution efforts would be put in place so that their own company needn't foot a hefty bill to convert their own systems. Whatever the factors were, many, many, many companies chose to not interrupt their corporate productivity and not take a big financial hit to do Y2K work early. The result? Far from benefiting themselves by waiting, they hurt themselves, because no new information or products have ever really arisen, and in fact costs of consultants and programmers and everything else have increased.

We all need to strive for long-term thinking as opposed to shortsighted goals. Leonard Sweet tells of a church which in 1998 added a six-million-dollar education wing for their school, with not a single computer hookup. Was that a careless blunder (or just a very clumsy way to avoid the Y2K problem altogether)? Undoubtedly, it was shortsighted. Just one example of short-term thinking in people's personal lives is the willingness of many to live paycheck to paycheck, and even to become comfortable with the idea of constantly carrying high credit card balances. In 1999, we reached a negative average savings rate for all Americans for the first time since the 1930s.

The Christian point of view also requires long-term thinking as an alternative to short-term sin. It's not worth compromising our broader principles to have a small satisfaction in the immediate moment. That's why we give back the extra $10 accidentally given to us by a cashier, and why we forego numerous other temptations that arise occasionally throughout our lifetimes. The short-term pleasure is not worth having abandoned one's long-term principles.

Jesus knew well in advance that he would be overtaken by his enemies and put to death. How's that for pressure? But he lived gracefully with that knowledge, because he knew the importance of doing God's will, and he knew that glory awaited him at the right hand of his father. Don't we know that, also? Why should the potential for some of our modern conveniences experiencing glitches send us into such paroxysms of concern? Our hearts should not be troubled, for we know the utter insignificance of the things of this world long-term. There's no time like the present for Christians to exercise their *faith*. Later chapters will explore these concepts in greater detail.

The ultimate need for long-term thinking, of course, is in making sure we've accepted Jesus' offer of eternal life. He prepares the way for us, not so that we'll have a plush setup and a pile of rewards while still on earth, but so that we'll have a heavenly reward. On this ultimate long-term planning concern, he's done the work for us, by being sent through God's grace and dying for our sins at Calvary.

LESSON 6: ACTING EARLIER MAKES THINGS EASIER

The time to take action and begin remediation of the Y2K problem was at least several years ago, when only a handful of techies were discussing the problem, and the media spotlight was blissfully ignorant of what Y2K meant at all. That sort of foresight was difficult, but with wisdom and discernment it was possible for a few people to see what a giant fiasco awaited us. The first person to begin seriously warning about Y2K computer problems did so starting in the 1970s in narrowly-circulated computer science journals, and a handful of others followed suit throughout the 1980s. Chapter 9 discusses how tricky it was to get the word out about the Y2K problem.

Once the problem was widely known, though, most people still didn't take prompt action. We've all heard and used these axioms:

A stitch in time saves nine.

An ounce of prevention is worth a pound of cure.

Although sayings like this are firmly ingrained in our culture, we apparently don't operate that way. Many people and organizations maintain a "fix upon failure" mindset. This attitude—that it's more efficient to fix something after it goes wrong, rather than waste effort in advance trying to prevent problems that might never occur—doesn't work well in all circumstances, and can open the floodgates to some major messes. Despite a steadily rising awareness of the potential disruptions that could result from Y2K and a steadily rising level of concern about individual industries and nations as M-Day approaches, most people and companies have not done a great job at contingency planning. Beyond Y2K, there will be many other situations that strike individuals and certain communities with devastating force, and it's essential that people learn to have at least basic contingency plans in place at all times in case the unexpected strikes in one form or another. Hopefully Y2K has been instrumental in demonstrating this necessity to at least some people; it definitely has been helpful in the regard that many organizations have made widely available some great checklists and collections of solid, practical advice on how to prepare for and cope with emergencies.

Among the difficulties resulting from delaying Y2K projects is that we've ended up with shortages on some fronts. Survival supplies remain in great demand, and are far less available at the end of 1999 than they were when Y2K awareness first began. As just one example, the waiting time on getting a backup generator from leading sources increased from about one week in 1996 to about 8 months in early 1999; at that point, some vendors simply stopped promising delivery would be possible by M-Day. People with foresight in many fields prospered as they boosted their inventories in recognition of the soon-to-grow demand for Y2K-related supplies, while others who were former industry leaders kept their inventories at typical levels and watched themselves run out of stock and be left behind while Y2K-related shoppers turned to other suppliers. Repair waiting times also have increased for certain items, and backlogs of work for many companies have grown to previously unseen sizes.

Costs have gone up for everything from programmers' hourly rates for code revision to consulting firm fees to the price of certain high-demand replacement chips to personal survival supplies. Chapter 7 will discuss some of the price-gouging and awful profiteering involving Y2K-related products and services; for now, suffice it to say that the longer individuals or companies waited to take action regarding Y2K, the more it cost for them to accomplish the exact same stuff that they could have done more cheaply six months earlier, or *much* more cheaply two years earlier.

Original estimates were that the worldwide cost of repairs would be between 200 and 600 billion dollars. Experts who are well-positioned to make such predictions now estimate that the total cost is ending up around a trillion dollars for repairs and testing of mission-critical systems alone, to say nothing of what it will cost for further less-critical repairs that must eventually be done, not to mention litigation related to Y2K. If total costs end up approaching $2 trillion, that would mean that dealing with this mishap costs about $300 for every living person on the planet—that's an astounding amount! Capers Jones of Software Productivity Research, a Massachusetts software consulting firm, summed it up this way: "The costs of fixing the Year 2000 problem appear to constitute the most expensive business problem in human history."

Many ethnocentric Americans have assumed the US leads the way on Y2K preparation (as you'll see later in the book, the US is definitely among the top five countries in the world in terms of preparedness, but isn't ahead of everyone) and were convinced that at least the world's economic "superpowers" would get the problem completely under control. One of many reality checks, though, came on September 13, 1999 when Bruce McConnell, Director of the International Y2K Cooperation Center, while discussing which countries are most ready, said bluntly: "Nobody's going to get all their systems fixed, not even the US."

So, who did begin early enough in addressing the Y2K problem? In my opinion, absolutely no one did. There *will* be plenty of companies who end up 100% compliant by M-Day thanks to a tremendous effort during 1998 and especially 1999, and it might not faze them to have spent tens of millions of dollars on last-minute repairs, because it's a tax write-off or can be built into the end cost of their products and services. But no major corporation in the world took care of Y2K concerns when it would have been most cost-effective to do so, which means consumers and other taxpayers ultimately have to foot a much higher bill than they should have needed to for most corporate remediation efforts. There *will* be plenty of countries who have hammered on the key players in their national infrastructure and procured enough conversion projects and contingency planning to have their citizens' lives continue without the slightest bump in the road following M-Day. But no country in the world did so much Y2K preparation so early that it could declare to its citizens at any point, "We assure you that there will be no problems in our national agencies due to Y2K computer problems." The extra costs, the supreme effort required during the past couple of years, and the tremendous burden of uncertainty that people have been forced to live with as M-Day approaches, are inexcusable and could have been mitigated tremendously if businesses and governments had simply heeded warnings and taken necessary actions earlier.

> *Ecclesiastes 10:10* If the ax is dull and its edge unsharpened, more strength is needed but skill will bring success.

People can save so much effort with a little forethought! The proper preparation eliminates an enormous amount of labor. Unfortunately, in the Y2K preparation effort, there have been many dull axes around, and sometimes people have had to swing harder than they would have needed to if they had taken the appropriate actions sooner, as soon as they noticed the need to take action. Just as a couple of examples, these blunt axes include:

- People brought in to do programming changes knowing little or nothing about the original programming languages they're working on, simply because all the available workers who do know those languages are already busy working on Y2K efforts that began sooner.

- Second-rate consultants (or some even worse than second-rate) who got into the Y2K game simply because it was a quick way to make a buck during 1998 and 1999, whether or not they had any true expertise in advising companies about critical information technology decisions.
- Products and supplies that aren't best suited for a given purpose having to be bought because all the most appropriate items have already become unavailable or cost-prohibitive.

Anyone forced to swing these or other types of dull axes has found that their Y2K remediation efforts are slower, more costly, and less certain of being done correctly.

In your own life, try to notice situations that require you to be an ax, and make sure you're sharp and honed and ready for the jobs that await you. As a sharpened ax, you'll always be able to accomplish more and be more useful to others than if you let yourself become dull through lack of enthusiasm, lack of training or personal development, lack of spirit, or any other reason.

LESSON 7: WAITING MAY MEAN MISSING OUT ENTIRELY

The tragic deaths of John F. Kennedy, Jr. in July 1999 and Payne Stewart in October 1999 were highly visible examples of how swiftly and unexpectedly life can end, and how completely people's expectations can be overturned. There are many similar examples of completely unexpected events that suddenly flip people's worlds upside-down. In August 1999, Turkey was rocked by one of the most deadly earthquakes in recorded history. In December 1999, devastating floods wiped out entire towns in Venezuela. Let's face it—we never know exactly what's coming, or when or why.

We can speak of tomorrow all we want, but today is the only day that's known for sure, and the only day in which we can take action. Tomorrow may never arrive. Since tomorrow might not arrive, it's tempting not to work on reshaping things on behalf of tomorrow's needs; on some level, this could even be an argument for *not* doing much preparation and contingency planning. But if the future is going to be excellent—and we have to allow for the possibility of the future here on earth lasting for quite some time—it will only be excellent because of efforts people make in the present.

How often do we postpone progress in our Christian walk? How many times have people sat in church hearing "The time for action is now" or "The time to make yourself right with the Lord is now" and said in their minds, "Yes, I know the time is now," but then still not acted to bring themselves into compliance with God's commandments? No one knows when a calamity will strike an individual life, and some calamities allow for recovery, but some do not.

My lifetime lesson in this reality came when I was ten years old and Trudy, one of my mother's closest friends, fell and broke a hip. I resented the time and attention it took from our lives to go visit her in the hospital day after day, and in my 10-year-old misunderstanding of the situation, I concluded that Trudy might not even be injured at all (at age 10, you see, I knew a thing or two about feigning or exaggerating injuries in order to get attention). I was sure that Trudy must be pulling a stunt like the ones I knew I myself was capable of pulling. One day, after Trudy had been in the hospital for about a week, my mother called her and forced me to get on the telephone and say a few words. Grumpy and indignant, I spent the obligatory minute or two making conversation, then when it was time to say goodbye, Trudy said to me, "I don't know if you'll ever see me again" and I snorted, "I don't care if I ever do" and hung up, furious in my young mind that she was trying to milk her injury for more than it was worth.

That night, Trudy died, and a few days later I sat at her funeral—the first one I'd ever attended—bawling my eyes out and feeling lower than the lowest of all creatures for thinking that she had been lying about being sick, and for my awful final words to her. Through the shock of the whole situation, I learned indelibly that nobody can know what lies ahead for them—not one minute ahead, not one hour ahead, not one year or fifty years ahead. More than that, I learned that if there's anything you can improve about yourself, like having a kind thought instead of a mean one, it needs to be done immediately, because to delay the intended improvement at all might turn out to mean never making the improvement.

It is incumbent upon all of us to stay vigilant in self-evaluation so that we know if there's anything that needs to be fixed in our lives, and can take care of the problem immediately. The only thing you can know for sure about the future is that you can't know anything for sure about the future. Don't postpone any opportunities to bring yourself to a state where you can honestly say that nothing is awaiting correction in your life. Don't allow flawed situations to continue if you know that they have the potential of causing trouble for others who might have to deal with them after you're gone.

> *Psalm 90:12* Teach us to number our days aright, that we may gain a heart of wisdom.

We all need to number our days, keeping track of how few they are, how fast they go by, and how unsure we are of what they'll bring. The challenge to gain a heart of wisdom means determining the smartest and most meaningful ways to spend our ever-dwindling supply of days.

Identify what's important, and do it today. Don't postpone! This holds true not only for Y2K preparedness efforts, but for anything in your life that matters—kindness, remedies, declarations of love, apologies, wrapping up loose ends, and many more actions. Don't put off any actions today that you would do if you knew that no more tomorrows were coming. That's a great goal, you might say, but unrealistic. There are many days when you feel you simply can't get around to doing all those goody-two-shoes things you'd do if you knew for sure the end of your time on earth was coming. The truth, my friend, is that one of these days *will* be your last, and nobody is ever going to hand you an engraved invitation telling you the date. Everything you postpone might never be done, and it's critical to make sure you don't put off that which truly matters!

Read Luke 12:37-40 and think about the importance of the fact that the return of Jesus is being compared to a thief in the night. When the time comes, swiftly and completely, there won't be a chance for those who have shunned God and carried on careless lives to suddenly become watchful. Being on alert needs to be done in advance, steadily, and continuously.

> **RELATED VERSE:**
> MARK 13:33-37

Realize that even when the solution to a problem is sitting right in front of people, some won't choose to partake. Just as some individuals and companies haven't bothered to take action regarding Y2K, or haven't done it until the very last minute, so some people won't accept the eternal solution that's available to them through Christ even though it's plain and simple before their eyes, or won't do it until the last minute. Some people who wait for the last minute will be left with nothing but their intentions. Others might attempt to take action but find the effort ends up being too little, too late.

Matthew 25:1-13, which contains another parable speaking directly to that issue, has been mentioned by many Christian books and TV/radio programs discussing the Y2K problem because it's one of the easiest comparisons to make. This parable tells of ten virgins who are waiting to meet a bridegroom. Five wise ones bring extra oil for their lamps, but five foolish ones do not. When the five foolish ones have to go buy more oil at the last minute, they miss the groom's arrival and are locked out of the wedding banquet. They're not just late, but completely locked out.

Think about why they failed—not because they didn't try to prepare (they had brought lamps, at least) but because they didn't prepare by bringing enough of the most critical thing. The most critical thing when you need to produce light is not the container, but rather the oil that's in it (or, to update the tale according to how most of us light things these days, it's not the fixture, but rather having a working light bulb in it). This parable addresses spiritual preparedness, emphasizing that it's not your body that matters most, but the spirit that fills it and enables it to work as needed in a given situation. No life will be without moments of crisis, and it's essential that we be ready for them when they arrive.

At those moments, we'll need to have a supply of that essential oil in place to let our own lamps shine through the darkness of the current circumstance. The bottom-line message for the foolish virgins, and for us, is: "Keep watch, because you do not know the day or the hour."

Summary

Flawed people are as individual in style as the flawed computer programs which require repair during Y2K remediation efforts—we're all unique in our outlooks and approaches to life, and in the types of instructions we've been given by parents and others who have programmed us at various times throughout our lives. We have an advantage over the computer systems involved in Y2K, though—when God sent his son to die for our sins, that *was* the silver bullet capable of repairing us all, no matter what our personal setup happens to be.

God's willingness to provide this solution to each of us doesn't release us from responsibility for our end of the bargain. You have to want and accept the eternal life that's available to you. To be a fully prepared Christian, you ought to have an adherence to standards, a willingness to build in ways that endure and that reflect your permanent goals, an awareness that everything you do has consequences beyond what you can predict, a genuine concern and desire to be prepared, an ability to buck the modern trend of short-term decision-making, a capacity for prompt action, and a realization that one can't wait to take advantage of essential opportunities for preparation, including the ultimate preparation that leads to eternal joy.

2

We Can Get Through Anything

Everyone for decades assumed that M-Day would be a tremendously joyous occasion, a huge travel weekend loaded with perpetual partying and endless enthusiasm. For many people, though, the Y2K problem has turned it into a time fraught with concerns. My opinion is that people should still enjoy it to whatever extent they can; it's clearly a special occasion, and no one needs to feel like the only rain cloud at a once-in-a-lifetime celebration. Being aware of potential problems and taking preventative measures should never preclude you from also moving forward and enjoying the things that are going well.

LESSON 8: JOY AND SUFFERING GO HAND IN HAND

In many communities, Y2K preparedness efforts focused on defending against foolhardy celebrations and reckless partygoers as well as computer problems. Don't think celebrations can turn ugly? Recall the riots in recent years in some major cities that have won sports championships, and events such as the riot and fire-setting by some concert-goers during the final night of Woodstock '99. Celebrations can become horrors instantly if people let overwhelming excitement carry them away. Grief and celebration (or wonderful and horrible, or happy and sad—pick your own favorite pair of extremes) can follow immediately on each other's heels.

> *Proverbs 14:13* Even in laughter the heart may ache, and joy may end in grief.

Rest assured that it occurs in both directions—sometimes joy turns unexpectedly to sorrow, but sometimes when you're burdened with sorrow, joy can be found right around the corner. Indeed, experiences which evoke completely opposite feelings in us are inextricably intertwined throughout the entire fabric of our existence. No matter how good things are in certain places at certain times, they're not good in some other places. Conversely, no matter how bad things are in certain places, they're not bad in some other places. I strive to remember when I feel joy in my life, sorrow and concern still exist for other people, and even as I celebrate whatever's delighting me, I should be attuned to the plights of others. That doesn't mean I need to give up any of my joy. I just need to remember that the world is much bigger and more complex than my own success or satisfaction in any given moment. Likewise, the world is much bigger and more complex than my humiliation or weakness or pain in any given moment.

This is one of the trickiest concepts about life—joy and suffering can coexist. You know this on a small scale, of course. Even as families enjoy purchasing and improving their own homes, they know that tens of thousands of homeless people are trying to outwit the weather each night. For everyone who gets a job, other applicants are disappointed. Every sports victory means that some team has lost. The more you think about it, the more examples you'll find. Machiavelli expressed it matter-of-factly: *Time sweeps everything along and can bring good as well as evil, evil as well as good.*

Many people feel so overwhelmed if they dwell on these complexities that they just decide to block them out altogether. Do yourself a favor—don't ignore the individual threads of joy and suffering that form the tapestry of this world! Realize that God's universe has far more going on in it than your own localized set of emotions at any particular moment. To be a full, compassionate person and a useful player in the game of life, you must empathize with the broader world in order to be truly aware, cognizant, and helpful whenever possible in the ways most appropriate to the talents and resources you've been given.

During the Great Depression, for instance, it's undeniable that many people suffered. At the same time, though, individual hearts and homes opened up in direct response to the banks and businesses that were forced to close down. People learned to help each other in wonderful and creative ways, and wellsprings of personal strength and compassion that had gone previously untapped started flowing freely. Those years form a great example of tremendous suffering that had equally tremendous joy and goodness come trotting along beside it.

Steve Farrar, author of *Spiritual Survival During the Y2K Crisis*, wrote that while studying Y2K issues, something stirred his heart: "I think we are going to see [the Lord] show himself to us in ways that we have never seen. I don't know what he will do or how he will do it. But if there is no food at Safeway in the evening, I'll bet there will still be manna on your grill the next day." Those are the words of a man who has mastered the challenge of trusting that even rough times can be alive with greatness if we keep our hearts and minds fixed on God.

It's clear at the time this book goes to press that suffering due to Y2K problems will vary tremendously by region. Entire countries may be unaffected, but some will have serious messes. No matter how well the Y2K problem turns out for you, most experts concur that there will be some people in some parts of the world who have troubles related to Y2K. In corporate circles, the hurt may be felt severely in one or two industries while others get by completely unaffected. Donald Estes, a Y2K tester, is one of many people who refer to the "Y2K lottery," which he describes this way, "Some will do a lot and still get hit. Some won't do enough and luck out."

You may do some suffering at the hands of Y2K, but odds are that you'll be spared. In that case, your celebration can be unrestrained! Read Esther 9:22, where Mordecai told the Jews to celebrate annually the month of Adar in recognition of the relief that they had gotten from their enemies. He told them they should celebrate their sorrow turning into joy and their mourning turning into celebration. His specific instructions to them were to have days of feasting and happiness and give gifts to the poor and presents of food to people they knew.

If completely spared from Y2K computer problems, what are we going to do to celebrate getting through the challenge? Those of us who thought it worthwhile preparing need to take the next step—an appreciative celebration that involves sharing what we have that hasn't been lost to the Y2K problem with others. Most people doing personal preparation stored extra food and household supplies. Opportunities to do something good with these items are plentiful, because food kitchens and other charitable organizations are always appreciative of donations. Let's make something joyful out of a time that has been, at the very least, inconvenient and worrisome to many people, and actually has caused significant problems for some others.

One more point regarding joy in the midst of suffering. Bear in mind that many types of individuals and companies have found various ways to benefit from the Y2K problem, and will continue to do so after M-Day. Obviously, programmers and consultants and other organizations doing Y2K remediation benefited, but so did many other sorts of people, including those who came quickly to market with Y2K-compliant products, those who still possessed manual skills to do many of the tasks which had been completely automated and temporarily needed to be done or double-checked by hand, and so on. Beyond financial benefits, the Y2K preparedness effort has rewarded people in other ways, including preparedness for many other life challenges, improved introspection, a heightened willingness to help others, and more.

Some whole communities found silver linings in their Y2K clouds. New York City installed a vast new computer and telecommunications network that eventually will let citizens do online just about everything that currently requires standing in line at city offices. Nine outdated computer systems running software certain to crash on M-Day were replaced by the visionary new centralized system. The transition to the new system yielded a few complaints (for instance, from suppliers who received late payments) but city officials consider that short-term inconvenience minuscule compared to the benefits they anticipate from the new system, which came about thanks to the need to address the Y2K problem. New York is not alone by any means—many companies and governments who had the time and resources took advantage of Y2K remediation as a chance to not just apply a duct-tape solution, but to implement brand-new and greatly improved systems and services for their users.

Be glad for those who have experienced these sorts of joys even as you sympathize with those who suffer any Y2K-related ill effects.

LESSON 9: A CHRISTIAN LIFE DOES NOT GUARANTEE THERE'LL BE NO HARDSHIP

Your experiences are not all guaranteed to be good. You may face some incredibly hard times. Y2K is only one of many serious and complex situations that might touch your life, and in the course of living on Earth you may face other challenges that seem daunting or overwhelming when you first consider them, but that reveal themselves to be equally exciting and satisfying once you identify the opportunities nested within those challenges.

Anyone seeing only hardship usually isn't seeing the entire picture. To someone with broader understanding of a situation, God is never-failing and pitfalls can be avoided and enemies can be defeated and obstacles can be bypassed and challenges can be met and righteousness won't fail. The wise Teacher of the Old Testament recognized that both adversity and prosperity remain under God's control, saying:

> *Ecclesiastes 7:13-14* Consider what God has done: Who can straighten what he has made crooked? When times are good, be happy; but when times are bad, consider: God has made the one as well as the other.

Amos recognized the same thing:

> *Amos 3:6* ...When disaster comes to a city, has not the Lord caused it?

The Teacher went so far as to acknowledge God's control over the timing of everything, despite our desire for bad times to pass quickly:

> *Ecclesiastes 8:6* For there is a proper time and procedure for every matter, though a man's misery weighs heavily upon him.

It's very easy for all of us to stumble and feel weakness when problems strike. Even many of the Bible's greatest heroes, such as Simon Peter, failed when certain tough times rolled around. The Bible tells us this, though:

> *Proverbs 24:10* If you falter in times of trouble, how small is your strength?

This verse emphasizes that our true mettle is revealed during tough times, and that the spotlight will shine unfavorably on anyone who seems strong only during times of smooth sailing, but collapses under pressure.

Consider Job, who patiently endured many afflictions. For a stretch of time, in fact, God allowed Job's devotion to be proven by letting Satan hurt Job in every way short of killing him. Job's wife viewed the horrible suffering Job went through and urged Job to curse God in order that Job might then be able to die and end the suffering.

> *Job 2:10* He replied, "You are talking like a foolish woman. Shall we accept good from God, and not trouble?"

Job kept his trust in God, and felt that even misery from the hand of God was better than having joy and comfort without knowing God. Like Job, we ought to be willing to have a full relationship with God. Being "spoiled" by God's favor—without a readiness to accept *whatever* his will is for us—is not a healthy, whole relationship. We must accept good or bad as it comes, and remain confident that God is looking out for our best interests, even when we can't fathom why certain circumstances have occurred.

It's a great challenge as well as a privilege to be in a secure relationship with God. There are responsibilities and expectations by God, and we should be willing to demonstrate that we're worthy of the grace. Asa of the Old Testament demonstrated his worthiness. In a time when unfaithful nations were being troubled by God with many types of distress, Asa was reassured that he would be fine because he remained in God's favor:

> *2 Chronicles 15:2,7* The Lord is with you when you are with him. If you seek him, he will be found by you, but if you forsake him, he will forsake you ... as for you, be strong and do not give up, for your work will be rewarded.

On so many occasions, the people of Israel turned away from God when times were good, and only turned back to him when he made suffering set in because of their arrogance. God recognized and disliked this pattern:

> *Hosea 5:15* ... And they will seek my face; in their misery they will earnestly seek me.

Let's not be like the Israel of old, crying out "Come, let us return to the Lord. He has torn us to pieces but he will heal us; he has injured us but he will bind up our wounds." (Hosea 6:1) Let's instead be in constant relationship with God, drawing nearer in times of goodness when all is smooth sailing, so that we can rest assured of his faithfulness to us in times of storm or strife.

People often wonder why God doesn't alleviate all human suffering and provide joy for everyone. The Bible tells us that even when the church reaches its eternal and perfected state, certain people won't be able to enter the gates of the holy city and share in its splendor.

> **RELATED VERSE:**
> **REVELATION 21:27**

Don't feel bad if it takes significant effort for you to come to terms with the presence of suffering on the Earth, and God's willingness to allow it. This is a truly tough topic for non-Christians and Christians alike, as evidenced by the abundance of books that spend significant time exploring this issue—to name just a couple, *Where Was God at 9:02?* (which looks at faith in the context of the Oklahoma City bombings) and *You Don't Find Water on the Mountaintop* (which examines life's emotional peaks and valleys).

Even Jesus momentarily focused on the same concern:

> *John 12:27* Now my heart is troubled, and what shall I say? "Father, save me from this hour?" No, it was for this very reason I came to this hour.

In any moment of difficulty, we should do the same: not fixate on our trouble, not immediately give in to the temptation of asking to be saved from it, but instead ask that we might willingly and effectively play our part in whatever God has brought about and intends to bring about from that moment. Instead of praying for escape, we should pray to understand our role, for God is able to provide us wisdom and understanding as well as relief.

> *Hebrews 12:7,11* Endure hardship as discipline.... No discipline seems pleasant at the time, but painful. Later on, however, it produces a harvest of righteousness and peace for those who have been trained by it.

Tough times produce endurance. While we certainly don't enjoy or understand most true physical suffering that we go through, we see that there is a history of God strengthening people through trials not just in the Old Testament but even after mankind received redemption through the life and death of Christ. It isn't our place to expect completely smooth sailing just because we're faithful and devoted to God. His plans surpass our understanding, and may bring us down paths we don't want to walk and don't see the value of for ourselves.

> *2 Corinthians 4:17* For our light and momentary troubles are achieving for us an eternal glory that far outweighs them all.

> **RELATED VERSE:**
> ACTS 14:22
> ROMANS 8:18
> 1 PETER 1:6
> 2 PETER 2:9

Jesus repeatedly gave his disciples the message that true treasures and permanent peace await us in heaven, so we should be willing to accept whatever our earthly life brings. While it's terrible to go through certain things, we need to see beyond the present experience to the future promise. We've all heard the trite saying *That which doesn't kill us makes us stronger.* An old philosopher expressed it more fully: *Confront them with annihilation, and they will then survive; plunge them into a deadly situation, and they will then live. When people fall into danger, they are then able to strive for victory.*

Those notions can be very little consolation when tragedy strikes our lives. When we're awash in grief and emotional turmoil, we sometimes don't want to soothe ourselves with banalities about how the experience will refine us and make us stronger. But it is imperative that we find ways to endure. The apostles building the early church faced terrible troubles, but they held to that ideal:

> *James 1:2-3* Consider it pure joy, my brothers, whenever you face trials of many kinds, because you know that the testing of your faith develops perseverance.

The "joy" in this verse doesn't imply you must truly enjoy whatever unpleasant experiences you endure. Just maintain some perspective on them, and try to realize the special pleasure and deep-seated contentment that comes from knowing that God is constantly strengthening and developing us through the entire spectrum of events in our lives.

LESSON 10: YOU NEVER FACE THINGS ALONE

Remember that you don't face any hardship alone. Not only are you constantly connected to God, but there's almost always a set of interconnected factors larger and more involved than you realize at first. Y2K is an extreme example of this interconnectedness, as neighborhood groups and community organizations and even businesses that are historically rivals have come together to work cooperatively on various aspects of the Y2K problem.

In fact, the ways some participants in the Y2K effort behaved, the odd angles at which they found themselves forced to approach things, and the strange couplings of effort required between certain unusual partners who otherwise would never be linked, all in an effort to attain the goal of Y2K preparedness no matter where those preparedness efforts might lead, makes me think of Ezekiel's bizarre vision of God (Ezekiel 1:4-28), a Bible passage that both confuses and fascinates many people.

Ezekiel saw four living creatures, possibly angels, which had four faces each. One of these faces represented man, the others (lion, ox, and eagle) represented the greatest wild, domesticated, and winged animals. There were also mysterious wheels that matched up with the creatures; these appeared to be made "like a wheel intersecting a wheel" (1:16) and followed everywhere the four creatures went. The four creatures, in turn, were following a spirit that represented God. This really is the sort of attachment that man has with God—a wheel locked into relationship with him such that wherever he leads us, our wheel automatically turns. We can aim at things, and we can do the work of moving things along, but the spirit within us—the wheel intersecting a wheel—can move us as easily as we can. The knowledge that God rules over every episode in our lives brings assurance; it's wonderful to realize that even as we make efforts of our own, he is at work both outside of us and within us providing the real turning power that moves our lives along.

It comforts me to realize God's sovereignty, which is expressed in several other verses such as the following:

> **RELATED VERSE:**
> JOB 42:2
> ISAIAH 46:10-11

Colossians 1:17 He is before all things, and in him all things hold together.

Psalm 29:10 The Lord sits enthroned over the flood; the Lord is enthroned as King forever.

This psalm can apply to any flood in your life—emotional chaos, moral turmoil around you, commotion in your family life, upheaval in your church, or anything else that feels like a violent flood rushing all around you and threatening to pull you under. God calmly sits as King while this flood vainly tries to wash away what he has put in place. God never feels under pressure or under siege; he controls everything completely and easily.

If you ever want to understand feelings of pressure and see an amazing example of grace under fire (literally), read the third chapter of the Book of Daniel. In an amazing demonstration of trust in God's control over their lives, Shadrach, Meshach, and Abednego knew that even a fiery furnace pumped to the highest possible heat could not harm them as long as God was with them.

David, whose life was in peril many times, was another firm believer that God would not leave him helpless. He expressed confidence that the troubles he endured were seen and handled by God:

> *Psalm 10:14* But you, O God, do see trouble and grief; you consider it to take it in hand...

God has promised to care for those who love him and humbly keep their hearts turned toward him:

> **RELATED VERSE:**
> PSALM 30:2
> PSALM 34:6
> PSALM 40:1
> JONAH 2:2

> *Psalm 107:13* Then they cried to the Lord in their trouble, and he saved them from their distress.

> *Psalm 121:1-2* I lift up my eyes to the hills—where does my help come from? My help comes from the Lord, the Maker of heaven and earth.

Jesus Christ understood suffering. Though the Son of God, he became flesh to live in this sinful world with all its pressures. Paul makes reference to Jesus' suffering:

> *2 Corinthians 1:4-5* [God] comforts us in all our troubles, so that we can comfort those in any trouble with the comfort we ourselves have received from God. For just as the sufferings of Christ flow over into our lives, so also through Christ our comfort overflows.

The context of this verse is persecution and other difficulties faced in the days of the early church, but the verse can be applied to any troubles. Some face emotional struggles, others face physical duress. Jesus lives within us, though, and shares whatever suffering and frustration we feel. He encourages and comforts us, and that encouragement can spill over from believers and flow to wherever it's needed by others.

Occasionally you might have difficulty feeling Christ's comfort, but at such times you should allow others to offer you comfort and lessen your pain. Their spiritual strength in those moments can bathe your life in grace, just as Christ himself has delivered grace to each of us. Like everybody else, Christians may experience tough times, but are blessed never to have to endure those tough times without the companionship of comforters.

> **RELATED VERSE:**
> 1 CORINTHIANS 12:26
> 2 TIMOTHY 2:3

LESSON 11: GOD LISTENS TO OUR SONGS

We've established that suffering can produce greater life, and we should be grateful for whatever learning or growth comes out of even the most unfortunate situations. The Bible is clear about the need to be in steady communication with God no matter what is happening in our lives:

> *1 Thessalonians 5:16-18* Be joyful always; pray continually; give thanks in all circumstances, for this is God's will for you in Christ Jesus.
>
> *James 5:13* Is any one of you in trouble? He should pray. Is anyone happy? Let him sing songs of praise.

That sums it all up—we must reach out to God in all circumstances, with prayer when we're in need, and with praise when our needs are met. On no occasion is it inappropriate to draw near to God.

People use poetry, song, prayer, and every other form of verbal expression to explore their feelings and ideas and to communicate with God in all sorts of circumstances. Many types of songs appear in the Bible, including praise songs and love songs and so on—my favorite are the songs of rejoicing that various people sing after they recognize that the Lord has done something tremendous on their behalf. Here's just one example, a simple song of rejoicing in the land of Judah because the people had seen God act on their behalf:

> *Isaiah 26:4* Trust in the Lord forever, for the Lord, the Lord, is the Rock eternal.

David composed a lengthy Song of Praise (Psalm 18:1-50) after he had escaped Saul and assumed the throne of Israel.

A teacher at a Christian elementary school asked her students in the spring of 1999 to write poems about the Y2K computer problem after they had learned about it as a current events topic. This problem was created well before their lifetimes began, and they don't bear the same responsibilities and pressure to prepare for Y2K that their parents might, yet I found that many of the "songs" these children created were remarkably insightful and able to balance realistic concern with optimism and an unflinching trust that things will work out as the Lord intends. I want to share two of the poems with you:

> *Anticipation*
> I want to grow up and not grow down,
> but on the hands of time, each finger fidgets,
> and the face of each clock is wearing a frown,
> trying to figure out those missing digits.
>
> If computers see my future,
> and mistake it for the past,
> will they give what we've got coming,
> or take the whole thing back?
>
> The next century was meant to be
> a great one — and it's here at last.
> I want to meet my future,
> so please fix everything fast!
>
> —*Alissa Barnes*

> *Y not*
> Everyone's buzzing, "Y2K"
> I say "Y not."
> It's not the first time the world's been in a tricky spot
> If faith and hope and charity
> Swell strong in each community
> Solutions and smooth transitions will be all we've got
> God uses tough times in his own way
> So take some thoughtful steps today
> Prepare and don't forget to pray!
> And the next time you hear "Y2K"
> Just think "Y not."
>
> —*Carrie Sauther*

In modern times, songs are still written amid depression and difficulty. War, imprisonment, slavery, illness, and other situations of peril have produced some of the finest poetry and songs the world has seen. What song will you sing during this time of confusion and potential crisis regarding Y2K? Perhaps it won't be a song, but rather a conversation with a neighbor, or a letter to the editor of your local newspaper, or a private prayer. Whatever it is, try to find some way to express your trust and gratitude to God about Y2K and what it has meant to you.

LESSON 12: FEAR IS NATURAL, BUT CAN BE OVERCOME

For years sociologists have foretold that premillennial mayhem at the end of the 1990s would bring a record number of religious fanatics and right-wing survivalists to the surface, spreading doomsday scenarios and stockpiling food and weapons to prepare for whatever battles they believe will soon be underway.

Despite what a few folks have suggested, I don't believe Y2K has any direct correlation to the apocalypse coming, and I think specific predictions about modern events signifying the end times are often a futile exercise. It is incumbent upon us as Christians to know what the entire Bible says, including the book of Revelation, and be watchful for what we know will come, but we shouldn't jump to far-flung conclusions about when and exactly how all the events of the end times will play out.

Senator Robert Bennett, chairman of the Senate Year 2000 committee, was generally pretty positive about Y2K readiness efforts proceeding in a steady fashion, but even he had his moments of concern. After he sat in on a number of confidential briefings about the nation's growing vulnerability to terrorist acts by computer hackers, and how some hackers might redouble their efforts following M-Day hoping to pass off such attacks as Y2K problems, he said, "The more I find out about it, the more frightened I become.... The vulnerabilities are there, especially at the Pentagon."

Some average citizens caught a whiff of Y2K fear, too. In September 1999, the *LA Times* reported that emergency preparedness classes in Orange County, California (which in previous years focused on preparing for earthquakes and other natural disasters) had generated so little interest in 1998 that some classes had to be canceled, but by late 1999 the courses, now covering Y2K preparedness, had soaring enrollments.

Many Y2K experts, the people in positions enabling them to know more than the average person about both the extent of the problem and the resources available to correct it, were among the biggest worriers. It seemed to naturally occur that the more trustworthy information people managed to obtain about the problem, the more likely they were to be scared. Steve Farrar, author and lecturer on Y2K, wrote "the more you learn about the facts of this Y2K, the more you wake up with anxiety in your stomach." Carlos Guedes, CIO for Inter-American Development Bank, noted that perhaps all it took to end up with a pessimist about Y2K was "a well-informed optimist."

Peter Wellhuner, a spokesman for KLM (the Dutch airline), said that demand for seats on New Year's Eve flights to certain locations had declined steeply in 1999. When questioned if he thought the decreased bookings indicated that travelers were afraid to fly on New Year's Eve due to Y2K concerns, and whether thin bookings to certain countries could be the result of a lack of confidence in

Y2K preparedness at those locales, Wellhuner carefully said, "That could be a reason.... I can't look into the hearts of people." Whatever the reasons, KLM reduced its schedule to only five intercontinental flights at midnight on M-Day, compared with 35 flights scheduled at the end of 1998. Several other airlines also canceled some or all of their New Year's Eve flights, some openly acknowledging Y2K concerns as a motivating factor.

People who know God have a way to control fear:

> *Psalm 34:4* I sought the Lord, and he answered me; he delivered me from all my fears.

THE GOOD AND NECESSARY FEAR

One more point before we leave the topic of fear: Just about every Christian has heard the expression "fear of the Lord" from time to time. We are told to maintain a fear of the Lord, but sometimes we don't get a good explanation from clergy or fellow Christians about what that really means. I call this the "good and necessary fear" to distinguish it from the crippling and undesirable types of fear discussed throughout the rest of this section. To have a fear of the Lord doesn't mean to live in terror that he's going to punish you, stop loving you, withdraw his gift of grace from you, or unleash his mighty wrath upon you the moment you mess up in some way. God does have that sort of power, but he has mastery and control over his own anger and vengeance, just as he has mastery over his all-encompassing love, grace, and every other aspect of his nature. The Old Testament describes in various places the special relationship that God has with those who have learned to fear him, and this simply means those who respect him and trust him completely and seek to do his will and do not turn a hardened heart toward his presence in their lives. A fear of God requires an obedience of God, to be sure, but not an obedience based on fear of punishment, but rather based on an enthusiastic commitment to remain in a covenant relationship with him and to accept the many responsibilities and rewards that come from that covenant relationship. It's a concept no emotional formula can perfectly express, but let's try: take relentless respect multiplied by unwavering devotion raised to the power of limitless love, and the result resembles what it means to fear the Lord.

The promise of this willingness to remove fear was given to Israel directly by God:

> *Isaiah 41:10* So do not fear, for I am with you; do not be dismayed, for I am your God. I will strengthen you and help you; I will uphold you with my righteous right hand.

The promise that allows us confidence in daunting moments was extended through God's gift to us of his son, who now serves as an intermediary for us:

> *Hebrews 4:16* Let us then approach the throne of grace with confidence, so that we may receive mercy and find grace to help us in our time of need.

No story illustrates the process of eliminating fear better than that of David and Goliath (1 Samuel 17:1-54). Learning to convert our fear to courage can help us overcome Y2K or any other Goliath-size problem with the stones that are at our disposal. Notice that a steady conviction and a disciplined temper provided David all the backbone he needed to face a challenge that made other men tremble.

Lesson 13: Panic Can Make a Situation Worse

During the years of Y2K readiness efforts, there have been people who are oblivious, people who downplay the problem, people who are panic-stricken, and people who are knowledgeable and prepared. The latter, of course, are the most useful type. The panic-stricken ones are the most dangerous type, because panic is either crippling or else motivates people to make hasty moves that aren't rational and aren't in their overall best interest.

Panic is when fear makes you lose your head. It sets in when you move past fear to a feeling of complete helplessness. Throughout history we've seen national panic, individual panic, panic affecting entire industries, consumer panic, and spiritual panic—in the Y2K problem, all these forms of panic have found a meeting place.

Dr. Michael Dertouzos, an engineer and Director of MIT's Laboratory for Computer Science, has said, "It is in the nature of human beings to go crazy about potentially apocalyptic events that have no basis in rationality. Y2K is a fully rational bug; we know it's going to be trouble. So now we have the apocalyptic tendency of human beings, with a real bug that could hurt a lot of things. I take the position that, yes, we are going to have a few bad cases, but the bulk of it is going to be mostly a nuisance. The minute I took this position, I heard from a large number of people who said, 'How can you say this? The world is coming to an end!'"

We'll survey just a few skirmishes in the ongoing war against Y2K-related panic.

PREVENTING PANIC BY HEALTH CARE CONSUMERS

The drug and health care products industries have been worried that panicky consumers could cause shortages by clearing pharmacy shelves in a last-minute prescription filling and product hoarding frenzy. The industry is confident that its systems are in good shape, but considers the consumer the ultimate unknown. If even a moderate percentage of people on prescription medications buy extra supplies to last a few months, the appearance of an artificial shortage could easily be created, which in turn might prompt other, previously unworried customers to also feel the need to stockpile medications for themselves.

"Once the medications are in somebody's medicine cabinet, they're obviously not available to anybody else," says Mark Grayson of Pharmaceutical Research and Manufacturers of America, a drug industry trade group. He offers some specific detail about how little actual stockpiling consumers can do without causing problems: "If everyone were to get an extra month, it would throw (the system) out of whack."

There's an industry-wide plan by pharmaceutical manufacturers and distributors to try to prevent hoarding, consisting of an informational brochure with the advice that consumers should refill prescriptions only as often as usual, stay informed about Y2K, maintain health records, and keep a first-aid kit well stocked.

In Canada, the government has taken some very active steps to insure consumer confidence that medications will be available after M-Day. For instance, they've inspected for Y2K readiness at all plants that are the sole facility in that country producing a particular drug. In return, the Canadian government feels it has the right to expect calm from consumers, and it appears this strategy has worked. People appreciate the extra lengths that Health Canada and other relevant government agencies have gone to on their behalf, and polls conducted in Fall 1999 indicate that Canadians in general have no intention of stocking up extra medications prior to M-Day.

PREVENTING PANIC BY INVESTORS

In September 1999, federal regulators of the securities industry, along with stock market executives, held a press conference explaining that there was wholesale Y2K readiness in the securities industry, but that their big concern was investor ignorance and the panicky reactions it might cause. They stated that the greatest Y2K risk still facing the securities industry lies in the individual investor's behavior. Securities and Exchange Commission Chairman Arthur Levitt said, "The worst [thing] we have to fear right now is public misperception, public fear."

As their method of boosting investor confidence, the SEC has fined and filed actions against investment firms that failed to do sufficient Y2K remediation on the schedule established by the SEC, and has taken action to shut down a handful of investment firms that couldn't present adequate proof of their Y2K readiness by November 1999.

Once it was confident it had the industry itself ship-shape, the SEC turned its energies toward educating investors about Y2K and how the SEC hopes they'll behave. There's printed information and a web site telling individual investors to avoid making changes to their usual investment habits, stay informed about Y2K, keep good records, and invest for the long term.

Preventing Panic by Other Consumers

Did you notice a pattern in the information being given to consumers by the pharmaceutical industry and the securities industry? Let's be honest—virtually the same formula is used for the Y2K information campaigns of every major industry trying to prevent consumer panic. They hold one or more press conferences and then put out a booklet and/or web site making the same points:

1. Remediation in that industry is complete and there's confidence that no major failures will occur.
2. Consumers should behave in a business-as-usual manner. The between-the-lines meaning of this is: If there's any problem in our industry, it's going to be your fault for giving in to worry and behaving erratically either by trying to stock up too much (in product-based industries) or else by decreasing your usual level of participation or withdrawing your business (in service-based or financial industries).
3. Consumers should stay informed about Y2K developments in that industry. This means: We might have to admit there's some trouble later.
4. Consumers should keep good written records appropriate to that industry. This means: If there's a problem, be forewarned that you may need to prove it to us.
5. Consumers should perform whatever minor contingency planning is relevant to that industry. This means: In case we're wrong about being fully prepared, you'll never be able to say we didn't tell you to put safety nets in place. This is the first-aid kit recommended by the drug industry, the long-term investing outlook recommended by the brokerages ("long-term investor" is code for "someone willing to persevere through a short-term loss if things do go wrong in individual companies or the market as a whole").

Preventing Panic about Things That We *Should* Stock Up

Even with items that people have been encouraged by government officials and Y2K experts to stock up in reasonable amounts—for example, money, gasoline, and groceries—government and industry leaders have concerns about panic setting in at the last minute. At the time I'm writing this in late November 1999, the majority of Americans still have not gradually built up an extra supply of groceries, a tankful of gas, and extra cash throughout the preceding months. There's a lot of buzz circulating that people will rush out and try to stock up, even on December 31, if they see any Y2K problems occur in the 17 time zones that reach M-Day before the US does. Listen to the recurring theme: Kelly Johnston of the National Food Processors Association says, "We'll be fine as long as there's no mass panic." A representative of the petroleum industry trade association says, "Our supplies will be fine. We just can't handle everyone pulling up to the gas pump on New Year's Eve."

The banking industry cares very much about heading off any possibility of a bank run by panic-stricken customers, and the government has heeded their concerns to some extent. Over $50 billion (and later $120 billion) in extra currency was approved to be placed in reserve in government vaults to be held through the initial timeframe when Y2K glitches might occur. Even with those additions, less than $3.00 in actual cash is available for every $100 that's on deposit with financial institutions in our country (if you don't know how our fractional reserve system works, ask your local banker—it's fascinating and they'll be happy to tell you about it . . . at least, I think they'll be willing to tell you about it). The extra cash placed in reserve due to Y2K concerns will allow a certain amount of money to be withdrawn by customers who want to have it on hand when M-Day arrives, as long as everyone doesn't want to take large chunks of their money out. The banks have nowhere near enough cash available to handle things if, say, 70% of depositors requested 20% of their deposited funds back in cash, so there's been a huge effort by bankers to convince people that money should be left in the bank. In fact, I'll tell you later in the book about a ready-to-preach Y2K sermon the bankers wrote which they sent around to priests, ministers, and rabbis, hoping they'd convince their congregations to leave money in the banks. It's highly amusing!

The ultimate perspective on panic was provided by a first-grader in a church Awana club who had difficulty memorizing John 3:16. Following several unsuccessful tries, he was certain he had it down pat, and triumphantly said, "For God so loved the world that he gave his only begotten Son, that whoever believes in him should not panic but have everlasting life" (as told by Betsy Shook in *Christian Reader*, Sept/Oct 1999). As much as we all find tremendous assurance in the more accurate version ("not perish") I like this new rendering, also. All the information about fear and hope and worry and faith and everything else covered in this chapter can be boiled down to exactly the notion that the young man so confidently expressed about Jesus: "whoever believes in him should not panic."

LESSON 14: RUNNING AWAY IS NOT THE CHRISTIAN WAY

Back in Old Testament days, who ever had more reason to panic than Jonah? He had run from the Lord, and was in terrible fear for his life. At the heart of the crisis, though, he finally found the cure for his panic:

> *Jonah 2:7* When my life was ebbing away, I remembered you, Lord, and my prayer rose to you...

Even in a situation of panic our awareness of God can break through the fear that grips us, and we can see a way out of the peril. The whole story of Jonah is a tremendous lesson in not running away from troubles. The escape Jonah sought was a refusal to do the work that God expected him to do.

A surprising number of people who never felt any survivalist tendencies in other circumstances took a very nervous posture toward Y2K, some fearing that chaos and looting and lack of utilities and supplies might result in such bad crises that martial law would be instituted in certain countries (even normally peace-filled countries like the US) for a short time after M-Day.

Suppliers indulged the survivalist mentality with products ranging from sensible items like candles and freeze-dried foods to mid-size purchases like generators all the way up to prebuilt survival shelters. Some industrious people even developed entire communities for people who wanted a place to attempt a complete escape from Y2K concerns. One such community was God's Wilderness, a Minnesota operation marketed toward Christians, selling complete package deals including land, cabin, water well, greenhouse, outhouse, and storage shed.

In late 1998, the London *Sunday Times* quoted a senior executive at Barclays Bank as saying, "The average man or woman does not appreciate what is going to happen. I'm going to plan for the absolute worst. I am talking about the need to start buying candles, tinned food and bottled water from mid-1999 onward. People think that I am mad, but a [US] company director I met last week is intending to set up a commune and buy a shotgun because the potential for looting is also quite high." He also advised stockpiling cash and buying gold in case Y2K results in economic collapse. When the newspaper asked another banker to comment on those seemingly extreme remarks, he said investing in gold might not be a bad idea. Prime Minister Tony Blair moved swiftly and announced the very next day that the British government would recruit 20,000 more programmers to work on Y2K remediation. He knew, as most government leaders know, that it's unwise to let the average citizen reach the point of panic.

Many companies cashed in on people's panic by encouraging them to leave behind paper money and move at least partially into hard currency, pushing the idea that gold sovereigns, silver dollars, and other "permanent currencies" would be more trustworthy in a crisis than paper money with dubious government backing. These companies usually ran carefully targeted print, radio, and TV ads (Christians, by the way, were among their favorite target audiences) hinting at the fallibility of paper money and bank or brokerage accounts, but the trustworthiness of cold, hard coinage. These ads either indirectly or directly mentioned Y2K as something that was "likely to cause a global recession" or similar implications. Camino Coin, a company in California, saw 1999 sales of precious metal coins double their 1998 sales numbers thanks to Y2K worries. The company advertised, among other products, a "Y2K Life Preserver" collection of gold and silver coins selling for about $3,500 which was marketed as a sort of insurance policy against Y2K's possible impact on the economy. Company owner Burt Blumert said, "When people buy gold, they're dropping out... the institutions themselves aren't working."

Some people decided to go completely mobile, figuring they could relocate if their current location experienced any Y2K problems. Entire extended families went in together on boats or giant RVs and loaded them with enough supplies to be able to carry the whole group of people as far as necessary to get away from whatever disasters Y2K might unleash on their home region.

Even some whole churches literally dropped out of society because of Y2K concerns. Several churches had their members pool resources and purchased land in a new location (usually someplace rural) where they felt they'd be able to avoid negative outcomes of the Y2K problem.

Escaping from a problem is not my idea of fixing it. I recently saw a strategic planner's list of various stages in which people can choose to take action to fix a problem. The list began with prevention, of course, which is the best way to avoid a problem. Once it's too late for prevention, however, several stages of remediation and repair were listed ("Immediate," "Mid-Term," "Late-Term," etc.). The final category of effort was the one I found most interesting. It was named "Abandonment" and its description was "to declare a situation unfixable and walk away from it completely, rather than working in some degree toward resolution or repair." It's not planning for, fixing, or coping with the problem in any way shape or form—it's simply walking away.

I've been amazed how many individuals, groups, and businesses have chosen the abandonment route concerning Y2K. I've been disappointed in the churches that have packed up and gone. If nothing comes of Y2K in their area and the general perception is that Y2K was a big non-event, then at best those churches have wasted tremendous resources and have disrupted many lives, and at worst those churches might look foolish and faithless. If something unfortunate does result from Y2K in their home area, more people than ever might need to turn to a church for physical and spiritual support. Think of all the services a church could provide in such an event. But those churches will be nowhere to be found, at precisely the time when they're needed most. In the midst of any potential crisis, even with an entire society momentarily on unsure footing, I believe churches should do their best to stay put and stay anchored in the communities where they've established a presence, rather than turning themselves into moving targets that no seeker or person in need could possibly hit.

Running surely isn't what God wants most of us to do when challenges confront us. Check out Paul's description of performance under pressure in 2 Corinthians 1:8-11. The church leaders he describes in that passage had seen God's grace at work for them, had benefited from God's protection, and it had enabled them to stand firm and accomplish the work that needed to be done. They had felt frightened and unsure of their own endurance, but had placed their trust where it belonged, and God had brought them through the hardship. Paul wasn't looking for sympathy or congratulations by recounting what they'd been through. He was celebrating God's care for them and appreciating the ability to stand strong. We all need to work on noticing God's grace and comfort throughout Y2K and any aftermath there turns out to be, and then recounting it to others, rather than focusing solely on our personal survival and on escaping from trouble. Use this opportunity to give the glory to God as is fitting!

That wasn't the only occasion when Paul had to promote the idea of endurance and perseverance despite fears and concerns. Listen to what an imprisoned Paul writes to Timothy when he's trying to recharge Timothy's batteries and get him to hang tough in the fight against the church's enemies and to keep working to surmount the obstacles in the road ahead:

> *2 Timothy 1:7* For God did not give us a spirit of timidity but a spirit of power, of love, and of self-discipline.

Beyond data problems and miscues with machines, services, and so on, there have been numerous Y2K fears related to thoughts that some people's behavior might be criminal, cruel, or uncompassionate in the midst of any Y2K troubles that result. The Bible is clear in its outlook on fearing our fellow man:

> *Psalm 56:3-4* When I am afraid, I will trust in you. In God, whose word I praise, in God I trust; I will not be afraid. What can mortal man do to me?

Proverbs 29:25 Fear of man will prove to be a snare, but whoever trusts in the Lord is kept safe.

Hebrews 13:6 So we say with confidence, "The Lord is my helper; I will not be afraid. What can man do to me?"

Worry is the worst way to spend your energy. Not only for Y2K, but in general, most actual afflictions don't live up to the level of anxiety that people pour into a given situation in advance of seeing what will really happen. There's an old British saying: *I have had many troubles but most of them never happened.* My father was fond of quoting a Persian saying about people's silly tendency to try to take on every possible care and concern: *We have gathered troubles lavishly unto ourselves using both arms, and still many of them have escaped.*

The Bible punctuates the point with these verses:

Luke 12:25-26 Who of you by worrying can add a single hour to his life? Since you cannot do this very little thing, why do you worry about the rest?

Matthew 6:34 Therefore do not worry about tomorrow, for tomorrow will worry about itself. Each day has enough trouble of its own.

Here's a key question: In the face of any potential disaster, if everyone becomes worried and puts their energy into contingency planning and preparedness efforts geared toward coping with disaster, who's working on preventing or correcting the actual or potential problems? A balanced effort is needed, some aimed at preventing problems and some aimed at coping with the potential aftermath. One form of effort without the other isn't good enough, so in every individual home, business, or government agency working on Y2K preparation, people needed to emphasize both remediation and contingency planning. People who allow panic to cloud their judgment to the point that they feel the need to seek escape are usually giving too much emphasis to contingency planning, which detracts from their ability to help work on combating the actual problem, which in turn might result in a sort of self-fulfilling prophecy where more goes wrong than would have if the preparation had focused on solutions as well as escape.

Many great opportunities are accompanied by fear or discomfort—everything from heading off to the first day of school when you're five years old to introducing yourself to a stranger who might become your best friend (or whom you might lead to Christ) to giving a public speech. You're allowed to be fearful at first—new and imposing situations naturally cause this—but you can't let the fear cause you to run away. You need to dispel fear in order to be ready in time to do the work that God requires of you.

Lesson 15: You Can't Anticipate Every Trouble

Psalm 119:50 My comfort in my suffering is this: Your promise preserves my life.

We have solutions for all our problems—God's care and Jesus' sacrifice have overcome our problems, and the Scriptures dwell on descriptions of solutions. We know that whatever spotty or widespread disasters occur in the future, the Lord will provide for us and not forsake us.

Remember that we have disaster areas declared every year—in late summer 1999, drought caused disaster areas in parts of Pennsylvania, Maryland, and other states. A few weeks later, floods in North Carolina caused disaster areas. There's always a fire, tornado, earthquake, typhoon, or other disaster popping up somewhere on the planet. People constantly compare the Y2K problem to natural disasters, and aptly so.

The Y2K problem and its potential for disastrous impact stand out because none of us have ever encountered a technological fiasco so widespread before, and because of the possibility of far-reaching problems impacting every plugged-in country in the world. Left completely unremedied, Y2K would have been the equivalent of tens of thousands of local disasters all occurring simultaneously around the globe. With the remediation and contingency planning that has been done prior to M-Day, it's uncertain exactly what problems will arise from Y2K,

---

Which Natural Disaster Is the Best Analogy for Y2K?

By now you've probably heard people compare Y2K to every other type of disaster known to humans. In case you're burning with the need to know which metaphor is most accurate, I feel the most appropriate comparison is to a hurricane, for experts identified Y2K as problematic and watched it brewing and gathering momentum long before it became a full-blown threat, and watchers have been able to take measurements and make highly educated estimates about its potential impact, but we can't pinpoint exactly where—or how many times—it will achieve landfall.

Also, while there's one huge central mass of problems to face, the Y2K turmoil has the potential to spin off other types of tangential problems, in the same way that a hurricane can spawn tornadoes, deadly waves, flooding, and other devastating side effects.

but the possibility for it to cause significant inconveniences in many places certainly still exists.

> *John 14:1* Do not let your hearts be troubled. Trust in God; trust also in me.

This passage, which in a single verse sums up the eternal promise that Jesus Christ embodied and the salvation that we have been given through his death, is applicable on a daily basis. When you know that you're saved, what can truly trouble you? When you know that all episodes in your earthly life, no matter how wonderful or horrible they seem at the time you go through them, are fleeting and will eventually evaporate and amount to barely a drop in the bucket of universal history, what can reach into your heart of hearts and trouble you?

Nothing can!

When Jesus spoke these words, he was comforting his disciples because he knew that his departure from them was imminent, but he promised he wouldn't leave them alone. The Holy Spirit came and stayed with them—and is with each of us throughout our entire lives—to be a steadfast companion. No matter what you ever go through, God has not deserted you. The Spirit is with you; the Word lives within you; and the Father watches over you.

> *John 16:33* ... In this world you will have trouble. But take heart! I have overcome the world.

Jesus makes the point even more directly in John 16:33. He's saying farewell to his disciples, knowing that they'll each abandon him and be scattered apart soon to face the tough times of the early church. He knows that to get through all their upcoming challenges they need to know that there's a reason—and he is the reason—for them to take heart.

> *Luke 12:22-23,31* Therefore I tell you, do not worry about your life, what you will eat; or about your body, what you will wear. Life is more than food, and the body more than clothes. ... But seek his kingdom, and these things will be given to you as well.

This doesn't mean that you need to suffer while on earth to demonstrate faithfulness to God, but that you need to place your focus fully on commitment to God, and trust that your earthly needs *will* be provided for. Can we actually practice that sort of thinking in our lives? I believe so, but it's not easy to do, because in general we live highly comfortable and trouble-free lives, and we do form attachments to our creature comforts, sometimes forgetting who truly provides them.

Most of us don't even know how it feels to be hungry or cold. We like to think we know what hardship is, but most of us really don't have a clue. Some schoolteachers take their classes to spend a night experiencing what it's like to be homeless, and while I think such an exercise can be useful, it's usually structured so carefully as to not really give a true idea of the horrors of life on the streets. I've been along on some of these field trips. The kids usually have blankets, local police have been told what they're doing so that they can keep a protective eye on them, and the children have the comfort of a good meal at both ends of the experiment.

About four years ago, I decided to try something more authentic: I spent an uninterrupted 18-hour period on a sidewalk in downtown Philadelphia with several homeless men, having armed myself with no equipment other than a healthy dose of prayer, and the experience was miserable beyond description. Bathroom facilities—you don't want to know. Getting quality sleep in an even remotely healthy position was out of the question, and when I awoke from what little sleep I managed, I was covered with hundreds of small bugs—fleas, lice, and more—and was lightly coated with soot from the exhaust of passing buses. Ironically, I had appreciated the buses when they passed for the momentary bursts of warmth they shoved my way. I learned an awful lot about my own comfortable life that night, and about how far removed the average person is from an understanding of what constitutes true hard times.

There hasn't been a single day in the lifetime of my generation in the US that foods like sugar and butter have had to be rationed, that products like soap have been in short supply, that good-paying jobs simply haven't been available somewhere in our country. To be completely honest, most of us these days think that an outage in our cable television for a full day is an inconvenience worth complaining about. Don't get me wrong—I think it's okay to be comfortable. It's not okay, though, to let comfort lead to complacency and a lack of appreciation for the tremendous blessings that most of us find lavished in every aspect of our lives.

The average person also doesn't know how difficult it can be to achieve simple physical survival without many modern advances. Some people preparing for Y2K have planned to raise grains and veggies as a solution in case Y2K impairs present-day food production and distribution methods. They've bought seeds by the thousands, along with hand mills or self-powered mills to produce flour and cereal from the food they'll grow. That's a fine plan, but before you think growing food is easy or a sure thing for anyone who acquires seeds and an area of land, listen to the words of a Texas farmer, someone who has farmed his entire lifetime, who lost all of his crops during 1999's early summer drought. "Farming is a matter of faith," he says. "You need to have faith that certain biological processes are going to take place." If the weather doesn't cooperate, there's no food, despite all your best efforts. I'm sure you feel sorry for his total crop failure due to drought in 1999, but wait until you hear more of his story. He also lost most of his crops in 1998 because his fields received *too much* rain too early in the year, and he couldn't get his seeds to germinate without rotting.

Add to these unfortunate sporadic and localized problems the fact that global warming increases yearly, plus the fact that computers are our key to understanding the global warming trend and figuring out ways to deal with it, and you'll rightly conclude that there's no reason to expect continued success from professional farming endeavors in the new millennium, let alone amateur efforts. So, people can't assume that everything they plan as a defense against an opponent like the Y2K problem will work out. Even in a task as traditional and straightforward as farming, there can be many more complicating factors than one might imagine, including completely nontechnical problems like the wrong weather at the wrong time, or an infestation of a recently migrated insect, or a brand-new strain of crop-damaging fungus.

Another example points out the fruitlessness of thinking you can avoid every disaster. Throughout 1998 and 1999, the state of Idaho was one of the favorite places for those with Y2K concerns to move because land there is plentiful and reasonably priced, the environment is healthy, and the state is relatively shielded from most types of natural disaster. In early August 1999, though, I turned on the news one day to learn that surprise wildfires had wiped out nearly 100,000 acres in Idaho.

It's clear that actions, no matter how extravagant, to protect oneself from potential Y2K disasters couldn't possibly make one immune to all other sorts of disasters that might arise. Forget about anticipating trouble-free spots and trying to hide from all of life's uncertainties in order to stay safe. Keep your eyes focused on the goodness of God and what he can do to help you endure.

LESSON 16: FAITH CONQUERS FEAR

Several Christian greeting card companies came out with "millennium greeting cards" and this was the verse most often used on cards related to the uncertainty of how things would play out with the Y2K problem:

> *Psalm 46:1-3* God is our refuge and strength, an ever-present help in trouble. Therefore we will not fear, though the earth give way and the mountains fall into the heart of the sea, though its waters roar and foam and the mountains quake with their surging.

Faith is the most important tool you have for conquering fear. The authors of *Facing Millennial Midnight* compared Y2K to the Egyptian army marching down on the Israelites as they stood at the Red Sea. It took relentless faith from Moses to pass God's test and bring about God's saving grace via the parting of the waters. With Moses-like faith, they suggest, we can look forward to God's grace sparing us from the army of Y2K bugs marching down on us. Other than a few rare exceptions like that, discussions of Y2K—even by Y2K experts who claimed a Christian perspective—did not give a lot of detailed attention to issues of faith. For the most part, their tip of the hat to Christianity consisted merely of repeating phrases such as "don't forget that the most important thing you can do is put your faith in God and trust him to see you through this crisis" over and over again. It's clear that faith is crucial in the face of impending trouble—so what exactly is faith?

> *Hebrews 11:1* Now faith is being sure of what we hope for and certain of what we do not see.

In the New King James Version the same verse says, "Faith is the substance of things hoped for, the evidence of things not seen." I love the word "substance" used in that version—it emphasizes that faith requires us to treat as *substantive* (as *real* and *weighty* and *consequential*) those things which are not here yet!

Faith allows moving forward confidently without specific assurance of the exact outcome of certain situations. This largely conflicts with how the secular world today works—people have become spoiled and used to having facts. We've raised knowledge of trivia to a place of high importance through the games we choose to play and the pace we choose to live our lives and the way we've reduced just about everything to soundbytes. News, business correspondence, and personal communications all used to be the equivalent of a five-course meal—now they're more of a snack pack. While we've reduced the depth of the ideas we communicate, we've increased the breadth, all but eliminating silence in our lives by creating hundreds of new media outlets and endless variations on ways to bring sound and light and words and images to our eyes and ears all day and night. Because we have tidbits of information pushed at us constantly, we tend to think that we know it all, that we truly understand everything.

Modern news reports have become ridiculous, often trying to predict news in advance, rather than waiting until it happens and then objectively reporting on it. Just a few quick examples: legal correspondents often tell us what verdict a jury (sequestered in closed session, mind you) is expected to return; financial networks now often report the "whisper number" disclosing the quarterly earnings figures a company is expected to report the next day; most networks and newspapers confidently declare election results days or even weeks in advance of the actual voting, rather than waiting to declare winners after most votes are tallied on election night as they used to do; and it's only in the past couple of decades that we're being told who's expected to win the gold medal in Olympic events, who's a shoe-in to win an Oscar, and so on. There has been a tremendous slippage and gravitation toward predetermination instead of waiting and then objectively reporting. This sort of predictive approach to news is perhaps unavoidable given the glut of airtime to fill, and given the speed of information transmission these days. In my opinion, though, it's not good. Even in situations where the predictions turn out to be wrong, some modern consumers of news act upon the predictions as if they were already established fact.

Facts and faith are often at odds with each other, and people who abide by faith don't feel much sway from what this world claims are facts and people who abide by facts don't usually place much stock in faith. As people of faith, we must be willing to move forward without needing to get a handle on every detail of how things are going to work out—we know that God is going to enable them to work out as they should. There are advantages to a faith-based approach. In science and romance and so many areas in addition to religion, you need to believe much more than you currently can see or know. To invent something new, you need to believe that what you envision in your mind can somehow be created in the lab, and then work feverishly on proving it. To end up with a spouse, you need to believe that a person who initially doesn't even know you exist will not only take notice of you but then grow to love you and spend a lifetime together with you. Faith in the unseen, and a willingness to work toward securing that which has not yet been seen, is what brings about amazing discoveries and accomplishments in all walks of life.

The best faith of all doesn't even need to be rooted in specific goals—the very faith itself is enough to keep you going. For the Christian, faith is an absolute necessity. For many of us, our decision of faith stems from a personal encounter with God that we know in our hearts is absolutely real. In the typical secular world view, though, God's not real enough to know—God requires 100% faith. It's pointless to conduct a campaign to convince any non-believer that a person's relationship with God can be real and can transcend mere faith. Be quick to tell anyone who asks, though, that what overcomes your fears is faith, and that your faith comes from knowing Jesus:

> *1 Peter 3:14-15* Do not fear what they fear; do not be frightened. But in your hearts set apart Christ as Lord. Always be prepared to give an answer to everyone who asks you to give the reason for the hope that you have. But do this with gentleness and respect...

A key thing faith does is help you to stand firm in the face of tribulation. That applies to when your spirit is tested as well as when your physical body is tested.

> **RELATED VERSE:**
> 2 CORINTHIANS 1:24
> 2 CORINTHIANS 5:7
> HABAKKUK 2:4
> ROMANS 1:17

Galatians 2:20 ... The life I live in the body, I live by faith in the Son of God, who loved me and gave himself for me.

Many Old Testament heroes such as Abraham, Isaac, Noah, and Joseph had strong beliefs about *unseen* realities concerning their present circumstances, and were rightly convinced that God would uphold them if they remained steadfast in their faith. Many in the New Testament also demonstrated such faith.

You might sometimes think you don't have enough faith, or wonder where faith comes from. Paul asserts in Romans 12:3 that God has given *everyone* a measure of faith. Paul encourages us to use our faith to honestly evaluate our abilities and figure out how we can be as effective as possible when we face the challenges before us. If you read 2 Corinthians 11:24-30, you'll see that Paul himself went through horrible situations, and felt the pressure of caring about others who were facing the same troubles. He had every reason to feel weak and worried, yet his faith remained. Here's another place where he sums this up:

> *1 Corinthians 10:13* God is faithful; he will not let you be tempted beyond what you can bear. But when you are tempted, he will also provide a way out so that you can stand up under it.

Notice this important assurance—God is also faithful to us. Our faith can actually lead to help and healing, as seen in Jesus' statement to the only one of the 10 lepers who returned to praise God:

> *Luke 17:19* "Rise and go; your faith has made you well."

Related Verse:
Proverbs 14:14

The gospels include dozens of miracles done by Jesus, but no consistent cause triggers them all. God does attend to our needs when we ask him, but there's no particular thing that people can say or do to procure healing from God. Faith is what God requires of us, and if we have it, we know our needs will be met in the most appropriate ways. Just as Lesson 9 explained that God's protection does not exempt us from all suffering, our faith does not entitle us to healing and repair of everything that's sick or broken in our lives. There's no guarantee we'll never face uncertainty or fearful situations, but God is stronger than that fear and than whatever we have to overcome.

Perhaps the most famous example of Jesus emphasizing the importance of faith is found in the story of the calming of the storm found in three gospels. We'll look at Matthew's version:

Related Verse:
Luke 8:22-25
Mark 4:35-41

> *Matthew 8:24-26* Without warning, a furious storm came up on the lake, so that the waves swept over the boat. But Jesus was sleeping. The disciples went and woke him, saying, "Lord, save us! We're going to drown!" He replied, "You of little faith, why are you so afraid?" Then he got up and rebuked the winds and the waves, and it was completely calm.

Faith means knowing we're not alone. God is nearby and available whenever a bad storm rages in our lives; he's well-rested and untroubled and able to help us. If we know we can rely on him to handle things that strike us "without

> ## FAITH AND PRAYER ARE INSEPARABLE
>
> There was a boy with a demon whom Jesus healed, and his disciples asked why they hadn't been able to remove the evil spirit from the boy when they had tried. Here's Jesus' answer:
>
> > *Matthew 17:20* He replied, "Because you have so little faith. I tell you the truth, if you have faith as small as a mustard seed, you can say to this mountain, 'Move from here to there' and it will move. Nothing will be impossible for you."
>
> The exact same story is told in Mark. When the disciples asked why they hadn't been able to remove the evil spirit themselves, here's Jesus' answer:
>
> > *Mark 9:29* He replied, "This kind can come out only by prayer."
>
> I have no difficulty at all handling the difference in answers, because I've always considered faith and prayer to be basically inseparable. The disciples did not have sufficient faith and they did not deploy prayer. Fixing one problem or the other would most likely fix both, because those who are faithful enjoy actively praying, and nobody genuinely prays except when moved to do so by faith.
>
> Here's another verse about prayer:
>
> > *Philippians 4:6* Do not be anxious about anything, but in everything by prayer and petition, with thanksgiving, present your requests to God.
>
> You see here that the replacement for anxiety is prayer, and you get to control the replacement. You can erase concerns through prayer. Prayer can wipe out any worries that are weighing you down. Prayer is not a lobbying effort to get God to change things, but a way to move ourselves into the realm of trust and confidence. Take special note of the fact that prayer is appropriate "in everything"—no situation is excluded.
>
> It's great to realize that faith defeats fear, but bear in mind that you can't exercise faith effectively without using prayer to set your faith squarely before God.

warning" we should be much more at ease when we face situations like Y2K where we actually have some warning. You know at least the basics of so many terrible things you'll face in this life—temptation, illness, death of loved ones, etc.—so be prepared to rely on God to get you through those things.

If any Y2K-related problems that arise are hard for those of us with faith to go through, think about how much harder they must be for someone who lacks such faith! At the same time as we stock up on food provisions and other physical necessities, we must make sure we have a storehouse of faith. We want to have not only enough faith for ourselves, but enough faith on hand for those around us who might need to borrow a little in the midst of rough times.

Lesson 17: Hope Is Derived from Faith

Hope is discussed often throughout the Bible. It appears several times in Psalms alone (for example, see the following verses: 33:22, 62:5, and 147:11). In fact, Romans explains that all scripture is meant to serve as a major source of hope:

> *Romans 15:4* For everything that was written in the past was written to teach us, so that through endurance and the encouragement of the Scriptures we might have hope.

Here's my favorite verse about hope for times of weakness:

> *Psalm 42:5* Why are you downcast, O my soul? Why so disturbed within me? Put your hope in God, for I will yet praise him...

This psalm explains where to place your hope: "in God." Why? He is completely able when we are not. He is willing to be faithful to us. He has promised us complete assurance and future care. This verse nicely captures the truth that it's both an obligation and a privilege to put our hope in God.

> *Proverbs 23:18* There is surely a future hope for you, and your hope will not be cut off.

Why is this hope essential during a situation like the Y2K dilemma? It brings perspective and outright courage:

> *2 Corinthians 3:12* Therefore, since we have such a hope, we are very bold.

It's important to be aware that there are people without hope—many of them—in this world:

> *1 Thessalonians 4:13* Brothers, we do not want you to be ignorant about those who fall asleep, or to grieve like the rest of men, who have no hope.

Notice in this verse from Thessalonians that hope is portrayed as an antidote to grieving. Clearly, hope is a wonderful thing to have, so I'm sure you want to get your hands on some. Quickly! Well, we learned earlier that hope can be found in scripture, but there are definitely other ways you can generate hope. Start with this chain of events:

> Romans 5:3-4 ... we also rejoice in our sufferings, because we know that suffering produces perseverance; perseverance, character; and character, hope.

Yes, it's all that stuff we discussed earlier about suffering making people stronger. The suffering leads to perseverance, the perseverance builds character, and within our own strengthened character, we can find hope. Did you know that you were equipped to be your own little hope factory? Just wait, it gets better:

> Romans 15:13 May the God of hope fill you with all joy and peace as you trust in him, so that you may overflow with hope by the power of the Holy Spirit.

Notice the simple emotional recipe that's at work here—as God fills you with joy and peace, you can overflow with hope. Joy and peace, therefore, are components of hope, and we're meant to end up with enough hope not only for ourselves, but to overflow and be available to others. Combine joy and peace and faith and the Spirit and you'll always be able to keep hope flowing out of yourself and toward those around you who need a glimpse of hope, but who don't have their own relationship yet with the God of hope.

Summary

We should seek joy in all situations, even miserable ones. Joy and peace inspire hope, all three of these qualities require faith, and faith and prayer go hand in hand. God is with those who are hopeful, faithful, and prayerful. In all circumstances, carry out the instruction of Romans 12:12: *Be joyful in hope, patient in affliction, faithful in prayer.*

When you are facing hardship of any sort, you can count on all of these: God, who oversees everything even in times of adversity; Jesus, who understands your suffering; the Holy Spirit, your constant comforter; yourself, the round-the-clock hope factory; and other people, who can offer you reassurance in your moments of need.

The Y2K problem did not sneak up on God, and he is not flustered by it. Realize that whatever comes of it—whether there are disasters everywhere, minor problems here and there, or no problems anywhere—will be exactly what

God allows to happen. Seemingly bad events and seemingly good events resulting from the Y2K problem are all under his watch. Any Christians who rise to the challenge and achieve tremendous things in the context of this potential crisis are doing so for him. Any non-Christians whose lives are touched by this challenging event are also watched over by him. His overall intentions for us are unfathomable, but his constant preeminence in deciding how life goes is unmistakable. As you gather your wits, gather information, and take action during any challenging time, God is in control.

Just as joy and suffering can go hand in hand, so must your feelings of sobriety yet excitement, objectivity yet optimism. For faithful Christians, there's nothing incongruous about feeling the enormity or seriousness of a given challenge, yet simultaneously feeling positive about rising to the challenge on the wings of a power far stronger than us.

3

Walking at the Speed of Light

Even once people have committed to getting through the Y2K event with courage and confidence, they face plenty of decisions about how to travel through the experience: what mood and mindset to stay in, how quickly things need to be done, which order is best for completing the many tasks they face, which path to take when multiple routes are available, how often to remove their attention from Y2K to handle other important projects, what types and amounts of resources to give to Y2K, and so on. This chapter looks at various aspects of the journey toward Y2K compliance which are equally important during many of life's other significant journeys.

LESSON 18: I CAN'T WAIT TO SEE ALL THE PATIENCE

On October 12, 1999 the Associated Press newswire carried an article that simultaneously amused and worried many people. A computer in the Maine Secretary of State's office had suffered a Y2K problem and misinterpreted the model year 2000 as if it were 1900 for about 800 passenger cars and over 1000 tractor-trailers. Unfortunately, the incorrectly interpreted year 1900 didn't trigger any sort of error awareness and intervention, because Maine has a registration category for vintage vehicles built prior to 1916, so the computer issued titles as usual for the brand-new vehicles, listing the vehicle type as "horseless carriage" and the model year as 1900. This goofy output occurred after the State of Maine had spent millions of dollars to prepare its computers for Y2K.

Since most people finance new vehicles, most of the faulty titles went to banks rather than vehicle owners. Secretary of State Dan Gwadosky said the recipients of the faulty titles were largely understanding: "Most of them chuckled and said we need a clean title as soon as possible."

Maine Governor Angus King did not know about the problem until reporters asked him about it, but a spokesman for him said that any problems that might result from state computers on M-Day weren't expected to be any worse than the minor title mishap, explaining, "We're pretty sure if there is a problem, it will be this kind and not something serious."

The slip-up with those vehicle titles is typical of the sort of mild, almost laughable Y2K problem that will be turning up time and again throughout the year 2000 and beyond as older systems reveal interesting Y2K problems that were never fixed or were fixed incorrectly. A couple thousand misprinted vehicle titles don't ruffle any feathers—people merely request new, corrected copies. Wait, though, until there are payroll problems (and there will be) or billing errors of any sort (and there will be). In those cases, people's tolerance will be a bit more limited, and the phone calls to the offices issuing the incorrect items will be more urgent and probably less patient. The average person will be willing to write letters or make calls to straighten out a few small problems, but imagine the irritability that's likely to set in if many people find themselves forced to take steps to correct numerous little errors from multiple companies with whom they do business.

As frustrating as that could be, it's critical that people and businesses try to stay patient and cooperative in sorting out the inevitable small Y2K problems that will crop up. You know as well as I do that some people will be short on patience, that certain tempers will flare, that business will be taken elsewhere, and that threats and lawsuits might fly because of some Y2K problems.

If you find yourself one of the victims of Y2K mishaps, the best thing you can do is to exercise tremendous amounts of patience. Take action to clear up the mess, of course, but don't lash out at those who have inconvenienced you. Impatience and nastiness only make trying times worse.

Patience, in fact, is a large part of the Christian experience. The ever-popular Beatitudes (Matthew 5:1-12) may be viewed as a variety-pack of instructions about being patient. Jesus reversed the thinking of the day, which previously had been that being healthy and wealthy and wise indicated someone had won God's favor—kicking out that old notion, Jesus said that even those bereft of worldly advantages were loved by God, and if people were faithful and patient, things that they were lacking would be theirs eventually. The writer of Luke records a few of the same ideas from Jesus' teaching:

> *Luke 6:20-21* Blessed are you who are poor, for yours is the kingdom of God. Blessed are you who hunger now, for you will be satisfied. Blessed are you who weep now, for you will laugh.

Indeed, the eternal hope given to us by God through the sacrifice of Jesus Christ requires patience:

> *Romans 8:24-25* For in this hope we were saved. But hope that is seen is no hope at all. Who hopes for what he already has? But if we hope for what we do not yet have, we wait for it patiently.

Sometimes when we feel life is difficult, it takes a while for God to reveal to us the answers we need. David advocates patience as follows:

> *Psalm 27:14* Wait for the Lord; be strong and take heart and wait for the Lord.

That's fine, you say. We can be patient waiting for the Lord—after all, we have no right to be pushy when such great things are given to us by him. But do we really have to remain patient and forgive a bunch of human bozos if they cause Y2K problems that fill our lives with chaos? Yes, we do—here's the scoop:

> *Proverbs 19:11* A man's wisdom gives him patience; it is to his glory to overlook an offense.

If there are things we have to endure post-Y2K, let's endure them graciously. Let's be eager to get them straightened out promptly and correctly, but not punish those in charge of the situation who themselves are also victims of the problem, even if their own negligence somehow contributed to it. Let's demonstrate the patience expected of us by God.

There's another way in which Y2K has required patience during the past couple of years. I want to quickly address this because it's required in many similar situations where people are working on finding a solution to a significant problem. It's the need to be patient and understanding about the inconveniences and interruptions caused along the way by researching, fixing, and testing efforts.

For example, the city of Atlanta shut down its central mainframe computer for 36 hours on Labor Day weekend in 1999. This gave Y2K remediators time to put Y2K-compliant hardware and software together in the city's entire centralized network for the first time. The mainframe they took down for the fix usually controlled business functions and criminal justice activity, so some people, including a city councilman, worried that the shutdown would be problematic in terms of arrest bookings and court procedures, the sorts of things that often increase on holiday weekends.

Herb McCall, Atlanta's Administrative Services Commissioner, made sure all city departments had contingency plans in place to continue functioning without the computer during that weekend, and bluntly explained the necessity of the shutdown that was trying some people's patience. "We either cause some inconvenience and disruption now to get it fixed," he said, "or we're in a world of trouble come December 31."

Anyone feeling put out by Atlanta's repair work would have had a much worse time tolerating the broad-based Y2K test conducted in the metro Washington, DC area on September 1, 1999 involving hundreds of agencies and officials from several cities and counties. They did it up right, with dozens of worst-case scenarios (some pure Y2K problems, plus some other troubles to complicate matters) put into place, monitored, and responded to from a set of local command posts across the metropolitan region.

They began with a fake news report of civil unrest in certain countries where M-Day had arrived at earlier hours. Problems with foreign currency had caused bank shutdowns, and televised reports of the mess overseas had frightened many Americans, who were now stampeding stores and attempting to hoard supplies. Isolated incidents of violence had occurred in at least one US city so far. A pretend snowstorm approaching plus fake freezing temperatures complicated DC's unfolding troubles during the test: some pipes burst, power went out in certain areas, and chlorine gas began leaking in one neighborhood. Then the Y2K problems really started kicking in: direct-deposit paychecks to city workers never made it into their accounts; electronic debit cards from the food-stamp program weren't working, so some people who wanted to stock up food couldn't do so; hospitals experienced Y2K problems with certain medical devices, including kidney dialysis machines; trains full of passengers got stuck; traffic signals malfunctioned; some electrical problems occurred at the White House; and an annoyed customer pulled out a gun and shot a Y2K-troubled ATM machine when he couldn't withdraw money.

To complicate the test scenario, more than a million imaginary New Year's Eve partiers were out on the pedestrian mall, a helicopter crashed into an important bridge, a prison riot broke out, and reports came in of terrorist activities—suspected bombs had been found, and one county's water system might be poisoned. The DC mayor had done what any of us probably would do in such a situation—asked the President to declare a state of emergency in DC—but he hadn't gotten an answer yet. The phones went down sporadically throughout the region, and so on...

Michael Rogers of the Metro Washington Council of Governments, which sponsored the test, explained the reason for the relentless onslaught of troubles:

"This exercise was not designed to ensure success, but to push people to the breaking point." They wanted to do everything possible to test both the responsiveness of the cities and counties and the cooperation among local jurisdictions in solving various emergencies. It was an exercise for both the computer systems and the people systems throughout the region. By the end of the day-long simulation, Rogers and other officials declared their agencies ready to roll past M-Day.

Hundreds of participants spent a lot of time planning and then had to dedicate another full day for the test. They bore expenses and disrupted their usual workflow and prioritized the tests above some daily business of the cities and counties involved. They also went through a harrowing day full of adrenalized crisis management that was physically stressful and emotionally draining. They endured the testing patiently, though, for they realized its critical importance.

All of us at various times in our lives need to be patient through activities that are going to achieve something that will help us have a better future (although good luck trying to tell your kids that the next time they complain about going to school). For those with a mature outlook, keeping a long-term view is a way to sustain patience through trials.

As you go through any sorts of inconveniences related to Y2K, try to dress for the occasion in what I like to call the "love garment" which Paul described:

> *Colossians 3:12-13* Therefore, as God's chosen people, holy and dearly loved, clothe yourselves with compassion, kindness, humility, gentleness and patience. Bear with each other and forgive whatever grievances you may have against one another. Forgive as the Lord forgave you.

Lesson 19: Sharing in God's Timelessness

We're all so busy and so time-oriented these days! I try hard not to be—in fact, during college I stopped wearing a watch because I had reached the point where I felt it controlled too much of my life (it's been over ten years and *not* counting since I've worn a watch, although I sometimes have to carry a pocket watch during speaking engagements, Sunday School class, and so on to help me know when to shut up). From my point of view, it's great not to always know what time it is, and to have finally become attuned to my mental and physical needs as far as eating and sleeping and waking and working are concerned, rather than doing everything by the clock. That doesn't work for everyone, and I certainly advocate keeping track of time as much as you need to in order to show up for all your necessary appointments.

Remember, though, that our human notion of time is not the final take on time. We've come up with many different ways to measure time (everything from nanoseconds and milliseconds all the way up to millennia and eras) and we think to some extent that we've mastered time through fancy day planners and time-management courses and successfully juggling all the obligations and activities that fill most of our lives. But of course time is the one thing over which we truly have no ultimate control. Each of us has a limited time on earth, and no one knows how long his or her earthly life will last.

The most important things, like visiting with loved ones, being in prayer, cuddling with your spouse, reading to your children, volunteering to help worthy causes, and so on, are activities that don't have an appointed time and don't have any time limits. More and more these days, however, counselors of all sorts are having to tell people to schedule even this essential stuff into their lives. People have to be encouraged now to do things that most used to make plenty of time to do, back when there weren't as many constant distractions competing for our time. I know a couple who lost their marriage to time pressures. The wife was a store manager working crazy hours to be present when the place opened and closed each day, the husband was a college teacher and wrestling coach often kept very busy with practices and workouts and road trips, and their two young children were taken care of mostly by a combination of day care, the assistance of other family members, and at best—on a good evening—one parent managing to spend time at home. The husband and wife kept in touch mostly through notes and cell phone calls from their respective vehicles, and this gradually took its toll on their marriage. They had to schedule appointments for romance and togetherness, and even those meetings started to feel more like an inconvenience than a blessing. They eventually divorced, and at that point the wife decided to leave the job that had been keeping her so busy, and started spending tremendous amounts of time with her children. It was too late to save the marriage, but she probably spared herself and the children a lifetime of bitterness and hurt by finally adjusting the ways that her time was being spent.

Time as measured by humans repeats itself in cycles. That's how the 1972 fix came about. Some people doing Y2K remediation of various systems at home or work have decided that rather than repair or replace certain appliances, programs, etc., on certain systems that misinterpreted 00 as 1900 rather than 2000, they simply will set the two-digit date to 72 so that the system continues functioning and any calendar functions will be accurate in terms of days of the week. Every year that we live through matches particular previous calendar years, and the most recent year matching the weekdays of the year 2000 is the year 1972. Is this a true solution? Not really—it's a "workaround," a technique that keeps something working despite a known problem. Still, the 1972 workaround for the Y2K problem is going to be used on many older VCRs and other devices where people's main concern is not for total accuracy, but simply continued performance. The sorts of people who are comfortable with the 1972 solution for certain Y2K problems are the same sorts who are comfortable leaving the time 12:00 blinking on their VCRs, coffee pots, and so on after a power outage resets the clock. They just want to watch a movie or make some decaf, and don't care what time the machine thinks it is as long as it does its primary job.

The truth is, it hardly matters if we have a few appliances sitting around that must be set to 1972, or that think it's 1900, or any other strange date-related phenomena that aren't critical. By all means, let's fix the Y2K problems that matter greatly (and there might be a number of those), but let's also realize that for other reasons such as laziness and cost, some of us already have things in our lives that are operating in a less-than-perfect condition that we have decided are "good enough" for our own personal standards, and Y2K may simply introduce a few more of those "not perfect, but at least it works" items into certain households.

Another key concept to bear in mind regarding time is that we are each the sum total of all our actions over time—all our transgressions and failures and moments of weakness and problems, as well as all our successes and achievements and glories and solutions. None of us is defined by just one moment in time, so no matter how large and wide-reaching the ill effects of the Y2K problem might be, they're minuscule in the overall scheme of the universe and God's master plan. Let's not get too caught up in our own illusions about time, and instead remember the tremendous scale on which time truly operates.

When time is mentioned in the Bible, it's most often presented as something we don't know. We don't know the moment that our own mortal lives will end, or when any particular good or bad season of our lives will end. We don't know when Jesus will return and when the world as we know it will end.

> **RELATED VERSE:**
> PSALM 90:4

Ecclesiastes 8:7 Since no man knows the future, who can tell him what is to come?

Matthew 24:42 Therefore keep watch, because you do not know on what day your Lord will come.

2 Peter 3:8-9 With the Lord a day is like a thousand years, and a thousand years are like a day. The Lord is not slow in keeping his promises, as some understand slowness...

We don't understand exactly how time works from God's point of view, but we know that each of us has been given a precious allotment of time for our earthly journey, and must make wise decisions about how to spend it. The Y2K problem may be a great chance to rethink our perceptions of what time is and how it should be spent. A mind and heart unencumbered by time pressures and by constant capitulation to the measurement of time can feel free to engage in activities that are truly important, for whatever time length is most appropriate.

LESSON 20: MAINTAINING A STEADY PACE

We are a hurried-up world, with just-in-time deliveries of many items that we consider fairly essential to our lives. We've seen that one strike or scheduling problem with a single key supplier can lead to factory shutdowns, grocery store shortages, fuel shortages, and the like. This happens occasionally in various industries for reasons completely unrelated to Y2K, and causes some degree of inconvenience whenever it happens. One of the central concerns about Y2K is that even if manufacturers are in good shape, some middlemen involved in transportation or distribution of goods might experience computer trouble, and therefore not be able to deliver the just-in-time shipments that other companies like supermarkets or gas stations need to receive to continue business as usual. When things are going fine, a large city grocery store which thousands of people depend upon for most of their food will turn over its entire in-store stock about every 3 days. That's not a problem as long as shipments are not delayed. In fact, the trend in most businesses has been gradually to move the scheduling of just-in-time deliveries to as close before the moment of actual need as possible.

This faster pace with complete expectation of convenience and with little contemplation of error has found its way into every aspect of business and personal life: fast food, overnight package delivery, and so on—all of these things have become commonplace as the pace of the world has increased. And we've now reached extremes. The fax outdid the postal service for getting messages delivered, but now e-mail and FTP transfers have supplanted the fax. Overnight delivery seemed the ultimate speedy method of product delivery, but in 1999 two rapidly growing Internet-based companies began offering one-hour delivery of over 60,000 consumer products—video tapes, flowers, sports equipment, you name it—so there's no more waiting until tomorrow morning to have that pink flamingo you've been craving for your lawn. A couple of clicks, and a courier will deliver it to you in under an hour—guaranteed! For a price, we can have gratification almost instantaneously. These services are currently available only in the several largest US cities, where bike messengers are readily available, but give them time and those companies vow they'll find a way to deliver virtually anything to anywhere in the US in under an hour. Usually I leave my personal behavior out of a book, but I must confess that as I'm writing this, I'm literally scratching my head and wondering, *Why?!?* I can wait a couple of days to receive any product I ever need to order—anything! Yet these hyperactive delivery services are surging in popularity.

The speed at which we live is like a race, and it's usually more a sprint than a marathon. But hurrying up typically doesn't produce excellence, and might even cause unfortunate results:

Proverbs 14:16 ... a fool is hotheaded and reckless.

Proverbs 19:2 It is not good to have zeal without knowledge, nor to be hasty and miss the way.

Y2K experts worldwide have constantly advised people not to be rushed, for reasons such as the following:

- Someone suffering injuries from an accident during a regional (or even very local) crisis following M-Day could find it difficult to get medical attention that normally would be easy to obtain.
- Rushed repairs of programming code or embedded systems could mean overlooking something or making an incorrect change. (Chapter 6 will describe some of the many unfortunate mistakes that have been made during Y2K testing and remediation.)

In this already busy world, Y2K has been an interesting added pressure. Those who waited the longest to begin their work have had to immerse themselves far more deeply in their remediation projects as M-Day approaches. Many people have gotten into situations where they're forced to work overtime and weekends on a regular basis to keep their companies' Y2K plans on schedule. The squandered time earlier means that they need all the more time later, and of course it's the one thing that they can't come up with any more of at such a late date.

Rep. Constance Morella, chair of the House Science Committee's technology subcommittee, at a hearing on the Y2K problem in March 1998, referred to it as an "impending catastrophe," and Rep. Stephen Horn reported that to attempt to fix even just mission-critical systems, "we have no choice at this point but to double our rate of progress, and then we must double our rate of progress again." Companies throughout 1999 have announced increased staffing, additional shifts, and more subprojects being sent out-of-house in an attempt to get more done in the ever-declining number of days.

The same unfortunate bind can occur in many ways in our lives. For instance, it applies to being in debt—those who have already borrowed lots of money are at a disadvantage for all future transactions related to money. If they need to borrow more, it's often only available at increasingly exorbitant rates, and their early debt is a hindrance to obtaining and repaying any later loans.

Another area where early negligence causes later magnification of the problem is that the consequence of slipping away from God a little bit (the casual "backsliding" that so many people think it's okay to occasionally do) is often that they get into circumstances that can move them even further away from God. The longer anyone participates in what he knows to be flawed behavior, the more costly and difficult it usually is to achieve a fully repaired state when he finally decides to do so. Coming to the Lord is easy—his mercies are always available in abundance, if one sincerely asks. What may prove much more difficult is exiting the sinful life. The people one knows, the places one goes, the objects that fill one's home, the decisions one makes about how to spend time—all of these things can contain remnants of the same sinfulness, so the further a person has slipped, the more difficult it may be to extract himself from the maze of problems. A constant pattern of backsliding and then surging forward with renewed Christian dedication is not the way to go.

I wonder how much of a setback Y2K preparation has been to the forward movement of our personal and business lives. A number of companies have reported a slowdown in innovation and implementation of new ideas the past two years as they focused instead on Y2K preparedness. A number of individuals have put all their extra money (or even borrowed money) into buying supplies and equipment for Y2K readiness at home. After M-Day, will we enjoy a super surge forward as everyone achieves everything that has been on hold, or will we simply witness a slow, methodical trudging through the backlog of projects and ideas and unpaid bills that have been waiting for Y2K concerns to get out of the way? The first year or two of the new millennium might be a chaotic repair effort with many lives and businesses in shambles, or by stark contrast could end up being a huge sigh of relief accompanied by a boom time of tremendous advances and exciting new possibilities being brought to fruition.

People are already more overextended and running along more recklessly than ever. I feel that this time of slowing down and refocusing attention due to Y2K may be just what some people need to realize that they haven't been good stewards of what God has provided them, and that they haven't done a great job of maintaining a steady pace in certain aspects of their lives.

During the past couple of years, I have seen a few excellent examples of disciplined people who have worked on Y2K preparation at a steady, successful pace, keeping it a fixed priority and not being distracted from the task at hand. David Tulis is one of them. He's a newspaper editor from Chattanooga, TN who has stocked his pantry and made other home preparations gradually for over a year. Some days he gets a little cash, some days he gets dry goods, and so on, but no matter what, he says, "I try to do a little every day."

Evonne Rogers is another great example. She's the Y2K project manager for the State of Wyoming and has been working on the readiness of state government computers since 1996. The task never lets up, but she never lets it get her down. She participates in conference calls with the president's Y2K council, monitors the schedule of the consultants working on the state's computers, gives many community presentations to inform the public about Y2K in Wyoming, is responsible for spending a large portion of the $10 million budgeted by the state legislature for Y2K, and works closely with FEMA offices in their state on a series of Y2K testing exercises. She and over 100 other employees in her division will not be allowed to take vacation from December 27th to January 15th. Her gigantic dual challenge has been to make sure that state systems become and remain compliant, and that the public develops and maintains confidence in the state's Y2K preparation efforts. "I'm actually very positive," she says, and keeps working steadily toward the goals she intends to meet.

Our Christian walk also benefits from a constant, controlled pace:

> *1 Corinthians 14:40* But everything should be done in a fitting and orderly way.

What good would it be to start out an enthusiastic new convert who ends up drifting and falling into a lull of disinterest in our faith? What good would it be to exercise one's faith in alternating spurts of total immersion and then total avoidance? A steady attention to faith ought to be our goal, just as a steady attention to solving Y2K has proven the best way to reach the goal of readiness for M-Day.

One fun thing to me about Y2K has been watching people move personal preparedness from being a special consideration occupying a tiny space in their home to a constant consideration taking over larger and larger areas of their home (one drawer or cupboard, then a spare closet, and eventually a whole room or basement). That reflects the way Christian preparedness works, too. New Christians often focus their attention to the Christian life in a limited space—their Bible, their prayer time, and their church worship each week. Later, they expand to additional spaces and times—start attending Sunday School as well as worship service, start reading Christian books or devotional guides in addition to the Bible, start spending a private daily devotional time with the Lord each morning. Then they program a Christian radio station or two on their car radio. And, just like those who started out preparing for Y2K in a very small space and ended up letting the satisfaction of preparedness spread throughout their entire lives, those steadily growing Christians find themselves letting the joy and ultimate preparedness of being a Christian spread throughout all the space and time of their lives. I'm not saying that God needs to squeeze out everything else in your life, but that for the joyful Christian, there's a standing acceptance of God in every compartment and in every moment of life, and it naturally broadens and deepens.

I've seen this progression in the lives of fellow Christians time and again, and by witnessing the same phenomenon popping up during Y2K preparations, I realize now that it's a letting down of boundaries that comes with maturing of faith, and that causes a godly life to become all-encompassing and ever-available, rather than something we seek only in an emergency. If you recognize now that you're locking away your Christianity in only certain small places in your home, certain brief moments in your week, and so on, think about decompartmentalizing a little and becoming an ever-ready Christian with your spiritual preparedness steadily finding its way into more nooks and crannies of your life.

Lesson 21: Figuring Out the Path You Should Take

We know that even in situations of problems and frustration, the future is wide open and available for us to move forward in any way we choose. We have learned that our pace should be steady, but which direction should we be moving at any given moment?

When selecting your path, remember scriptural guidance. The book of Proverbs, for instance, offers principles for living wisely and in accordance with God's wishes, commenting on the way life typically proceeds, and helping us to stay away from common pitfalls and to proceed along smart, safe paths.

Dr. Henry Blackaby explains three ways in which Christians must respond to any crisis, which certainly apply to Y2K: by fully turning their hearts toward God, by adjusting to God in readiness, and by obeying God's call. If you walk in a state of submission to the Lord's leadership in your life, the best path will become clear.

> *John 9:4* As long as it is day, we must do the work of him who sent me. Night is coming, when no one can work.

Night *is* coming, and we need to seize opportunities to do everything we can for God in our lives before night arrives. Confusing and overwhelming times are often when we feel most unsure about which path to take. In the course of learning about Y2K, it wasn't uncommon for people to move through stages of denial, anxiety, frustration, and so on because of their tremendous uncertainty about what might come. Each of these feelings could cause someone to take a different path of action, and the only solution for such shifting emotions is to count on God to help you sort it all out and help identify the most appropriate path.

Chapter 2 discussed some people and entire churches who felt that their necessary path during Y2K was to pack up and move to safer places. I don't think for the most part that God wants separatists, and a time of any level of crisis is perhaps the worst possible time for believers to remove themselves from the eyes of unbelievers. That said, though, if those people were sure that God wanted them to move, then it was the right thing to decide to do. The disruption and stress of moving, in that case, would be a small price to pay for following God's call. Remember that the Israelites were forced to wander 40 years in the desert (Numbers 14:34) and many were brought to a bitter end. Those who ignored God's command and went up to the high hill country (Numbers 14:40-45) were destroyed by their enemies. God's plan may send us down paths that sometimes don't make sense to others or even to ourselves, but every day brings fresh chances to fill life with an unwavering commitment to serving God by choosing right paths and pursuing right actions at right times.

On another occasion, the Israelites were led to cross the Jordan River, and Joshua trusted God to lead them safely through the flood-level waters. Joshua 3:4 says "... you have never been this way before" and that surely was true for the frightened people facing the rushing waters, but when they ventured forward, God created dry ground for Joshua and company to cross the waters, reminiscent of what was made possible for Moses and his followers at the Red Sea.

We all sometimes have to go ways we've never gone before. When you are led down any new path, go with the knowledge that you have divine protection, and that unknown or intimidating paths often turn out to be just variations on roads you've safely traveled before. The details might be slightly different, but the steady and confident steps you need to take are often the same.

Lesson 22: Standing Firm

Sometimes the action that God expects of you is to simply stay where you are and not go anywhere. Y2K saw this manifested in a number of ways, including:

- People choosing to continue working in jobs related to Y2K remediation, rather than pulling their talents away from the pool of available remediation resources in order to pursue a less stressful way of making a living.
- People scared that some troubles from Y2K glitches might befall them, but being courageous enough to not run away from their current house, job, community, etc.

How do we find a firm place to stand? God provides it.

> *Psalm 40:2* He lifted me out of the slimy pit, out of the mud and mire; he set my feet on a rock and gave me a firm place to stand.

Faith anchors us, and the love shown to us through Jesus Christ supports our stance:

> *1 Corinthians 16:13-14* Be on your guard; stand firm in the faith; be men of courage; be strong. Do everything in love.

> **RELATED VERSE:**
> 2 CORINTHIANS 1:24

Many challenges have required God's people to prove themselves unshakable:

> *Exodus 14:13-14* Moses answered the people, "Do not be afraid. Stand firm and you will see the deliverance the Lord will bring you today. The Egyptians you see today you will never see again. The Lord will fight for you; you need only to be still."

> *2 Chronicles 20:15,17* Do not be afraid or discouraged because of this vast army. For the battle is not yours, but God's.... Take up your positions; stand firm and see the deliverance the Lord will give you...

Every significant effort is God's. When he needs you to move down a path, be prepared to step lively; and on other occasions when he needs you to remain in place, be prepared to stand firm.

LESSON 23: THE BELIEVER'S FORECAST—PERFECTLY CLOUDY AND BRIGHT

> *Psalm 48:14* For this God is our God for ever and ever; he will be our guide even to the end.

> **RELATED VERSE:**
> PSALM 37:23-24

> *Isaiah 40:11* He tends his flock like a shepherd; he gathers the lambs in his arms and carries them close to his heart; he gently leads those that have young.

> **RELATED VERSE:**
> PSALM 23

Has God ever guided people through a massive project of problem identification, repair work, and contingency planning comparable to Y2K computer problems? Absolutely! Here's one example:

> *Isaiah 58:11-12* The Lord will guide you always; he will satisfy your needs in a sun-scorched land and will strengthen your frame. You will be like a well-watered garden, like a spring whose waters never fail. Your people will rebuild the ancient ruins and will raise up the age-old foundations; you will be called Repairer of Broken Walls, Restorer of Streets with Dwellings.

In that situation, God was embracing the people of Israel who had finally returned to faithfulness, and Jerusalem (which lay in ruins) needed to be rebuilt to serve as evidence for everyone to see that God had restored the people of Israel. The restoration of the city was a tremendous challenge, but God guided them through it.

Our key responsibility in receiving guidance from God is to not be distracted from his loving leadership:

> *Proverbs 4:25* Let your eyes look straight ahead, fix your gaze directly before you.

This need to not lose focus from the goal applies in our Christian commitment as well as in Y2K work. Having an awareness of the ultimate goal keeps us on a steady path without straying.

> *1 Corinthians 9:26* Therefore I do not run like a man running aimlessly; I do not fight like a man beating the air.

Read Numbers 9:15-23, in which God presented himself to the Israelites in a cloud that was positioned over the tabernacle whenever he wanted them to stay encamped, and lifted when he wanted them to set out. In the Old Testament, God often appeared as a cloud to lead the Israelites to safety or victory from a tough situation.

> **RELATED VERSE:**
> EXODUS 13:21

They didn't always believe the promise he had made to guide them. In one case, he became angry because they wouldn't acknowledge his love for them by trusting him to lead them to safety:

> *Deuteronomy 1:32-33* In spite of this, you did not trust in the Lord your God, who went ahead of you on your journey, in fire by night and in a cloud by day, to search out places for you to camp and to show you the way you should go.

Many people have trusted God, though, and noted his ability to flood light into a situation in which they initially could see nothing but darkness:

> *2 Samuel 22:29-30* You are my lamp, O Lord; the Lord turns my darkness into light. With your help I can advance against a troop; with my God I can scale a wall.

> **RELATED VERSE:**
> PSALM 18:28
> PSALM 43:3

You probably know that you shouldn't hide your own lamp under a bowl (Matthew 5:15-16), but do you know why? Because it's more than just an expression of yourself—it's actually God's light shining through you. In the New Testament, we learn that God is not the sort of cloud that blocks light, but the sort that produces it. Since he allowed his son to shine down into the world, everyone who comes to know him has their internal light switch flipped permanently to the On position.

> *1 John 2:8* I am writing you a new command; its truth is seen in him and you, because the darkness is passing and the true light is already shining.

John's new command for us mentioned in this verse is to allow God's light to shine through our lives by living as Jesus lived, and by helping others to see their paths clearly. Jesus understands the types of guidance we need, for he has shared the experience of human weakness and bewilderment:

> *Hebrews 5:2* He is able to deal gently with those who are ignorant and are going astray, since he himself is subject to weakness.

Christ rules this world pervasively, is within and around everything at all times, and we don't ever need to feel as if we're moving forward without him.

LESSON 24: THE CENTRAL SOURCE OF OUR STRENGTH

Either standing firm in the face of challenges or following the correct paths we're supposed to travel requires strength. We all fall short of some goals. We all get tired and slip backwards occasionally when we know we should be surging ahead. We know we need to keep going ... but how?

You learned in Chapter 2 that hope in God can lead to renewed strength. As you walk the paths required of you, don't lose your connection with God, because he's the central source of our strength.

> *Isaiah 40:31* Those who hope in the Lord will renew their strength. They will soar on wings like eagles; they will run and not grow weary; they will walk and not be faint.

He has provided strength to his followers even in the worst of times, reassuring them and giving them fortitude even when their physical strength is depleted:

> **RELATED VERSE:**
> EXODUS 15:13
> PSALM 28:7
> 2 TIMOTHY 4:17

> *Psalm 18:32* It is God who arms me with strength and makes my way perfect.

> *2 Corinthians 4:16* Therefore we do not lose heart. Though outwardly we are wasting away, yet inwardly we are being renewed day by day.

> *2 Timothy 2:1* You then, my son, be strong in the grace that is in Christ Jesus.

God expects to find in us a personal strength of character that will keep going even under adversity. We are led with *God's* strength, not our own, and he expects us to carry on with our journey. We have no right to complain that the path should be made smoother. When Jeremiah griped about the easy life some unfaithful folks seemed to be living while the faithful struggled through tough conditions, God's response was:

> *Jeremiah 12:5* If you have raced with men on foot and they have worn you out, how can you compete with horses? If you stumble in safe country, how will you manage in the thickets...

Just like many other aspects of man's relationship with God, the way that we can manage in any thickets we encounter underwent a fundamental change through Jesus Christ:

> *John 14:16* And I will ask the Father, and he will give you another Counselor to be with you forever.

Whether the road is easy or rough at any given time, the Holy Spirit is available just as Christ promised—a truthful, faithful companion to accompany and support us on our earthly journey.

LESSON 25: REST IS NOT OPTIONAL

The Y2K problem has caused more overtime to be worked than any other computer-related event, and possibly any event in the business world ever. From the time most companies and individuals developed true awareness of the situation, there's been an ever-dwindling number of days in which to complete gargantuan amounts of work, so many companies have had to use nights as well as days to prepare. Some instituted second and even third shifts for their Y2K projects, and working every weekend was a given for many Y2K-related employees. The end result has been a lot of tired people.

The *Virginian-Pilot* ran a story introducing its readers to Roz Jones on Sept. 28, 1999. Roz hasn't taken any vacation during 1999, rarely takes a lunch break, and continues many workdays at home through e-mail and phone calls while her boyfriend sits by and waits for the business to be over. She's the Y2K coordinator for the City of Virginia Beach, handling city-wide remediation of thousands of computers across many departments, plus loads of backup planning. Most of the remediation chores are done, but she's heading the effort to double-check all the repair work and upgrading. Her life is a series of meetings and deadlines; even her smoke breaks can include Y2K discussions with coworkers. She interfaces with a wide range of people, from engineers to librarians to civic groups, resolving highly technical issues and simple questions with equal ease.

Whenever she finds a free moment, she surfs the Internet for more Y2K info. A former programmer, she knows her stuff, and has found a cooperative city to work for—Virginia Beach is one of very few cities its size with a person dedicated entirely to Y2K. She is relentless in her quest to make the city compliant, and has earned a reputation for keeping the pedal to the metal in the race toward readiness. David Sullivan, the city's chief information officer (and her boss), has reportedly referred to her as "The Nag" during city council meetings. Thanks to "The Nag," most city workers in Virginia Beach have a thorough understanding of the importance of preparing for Y2K thoroughly and diligently, but without panicking. Roz is now waging war against public indifference or misperceptions about the problem, making herself available to talk to groups of citizens about Y2K, and also helping to create an informational video for local cable TV.

How does Roz feel about all the multitasking she has to do? "I wouldn't be happy doing just one thing," she says good-naturedly. Up until September 1999, it was Roz who constantly reached out to other people to bring Y2K issues to the table; as M-Day has gotten even closer, though, her phone rings more often with people seeking information, and her appointment book for speaking engagements is fuller than ever. Roz is prepared to hang tough all the way through New Year's Eve (she'll be at work that night, of course); she's aware life might get even busier than it has so far, noting that she has now come through "the lull before the storm."

Roz is not at all atypical. Diane Lambert, a systems manager involved with Y2K repairs, has said that she considers herself lucky if she can answer "Yes" when her teenage daughter calls her at work and asks, "Will you be home before midnight?"

Many people who are heading up Y2K efforts for government or corporate entities have essentially put their lives on hold and have been eating, sleeping, and breathing Y2K issues for a couple of years now. Worldwide, the enormity of the problem is staggering. While most of us have been able to seek repose and renewal each night, the Y2K problem has kept people working around the clock in just about every time zone, trying to fend off a global nightmare. Y2K conversion projects are scheduled to continue into the year 2005 and beyond for some companies and governments. (Remember that hundreds of millions of lines of code have been categorized as non-mission-critical by people who had to decide what needed fixing prior to M-Day and what could wait until after M-Day; many of the less-critical systems are still slated to be revised eventually in order to get those companies fully Y2K-compliant for the rest of their company's future, beyond just the "Y2K-ready" state they're trying to achieve for M-Day itself.) Keep these dedicated workers in your prayers, if you will, because God can provide the proper balance of rest and stamina needed to complete their Y2K projects.

I know an IS manager who never before had experienced stomach distress, but as a result of his company's Y2K preparedness effort has developed an ulcer which caused his doctor to recommend significant dietary and other changes. Some people who aren't even working on any remediation efforts have reported having sleepless nights about Y2K because they've been badly troubled about glitches that might occur. A restful sleep can only come when troubles are removed from your mind, and renewed strength and vigor to accomplish things with your days will result from getting quality sleep. It's crucial to try to obtain rest for your body even when your mind is restless and full of concerns. God can facilitate rest even when you're in the middle of stressful events:

> *Psalm 4:8* I will lie down and sleep in peace, for you alone, O Lord, make me dwell in safety.

Besides sleep, occasional times of relaxation and renewal are important as well. There are biblical examples of people devoting time to meditation:

> *Psalm 39:3* My heart grew hot within me, and as I meditated, the fire burned; then I spoke...

David's meditation here was part of his personal plan to keep from taking wrong actions and speaking wicked thoughts about the tough situation God had placed him in. After his meditation, he did voice his thoughts, but he begged God for mercy rather than lashing out at God as he had initially felt like doing. As exemplified here by David, the most productive meditation isn't just shutting off the senses and mentally escaping—it has a goal: to prepare us to return to the demands of the world, to give us a deepened knowledge of situations around us and how we fit into them, and to equip us to discern the best steps to take in a given situation.

People who are tired or well on the way to being completely burned-out are often cranky and prone to snapping at others. They run down their immune systems. They become less productive over time because sleep-deprivation makes them think less clearly. No matter how important a challenge you're tackling, it's unwise to carry on without reasonable amounts of rest.

Two friends of our family illustrate extreme examples of failure to rest, and they're both good-natured enough to let me tell the tales:

- Gary was a family friend. His career as an engineer was far from flashy, but several years ago his company was working on a project that generated quite a bit of media attention. Gary was interviewed by several newspaper journalists, and excitedly called one night to tell us he was going to be a guest on a national network news show the following morning to discuss the project. It was going to be his first time on TV. Since Gary had been working long hours, my father advised him to get a good night's rest, but Gary said he needed the interview to go perfectly so he was going to stay up all night and practice over and over the things he was going to say. He practiced once on the phone with Dad, too. The interview was at 6:45 A.M. and since Gary didn't have to go to work afterward, he planned to return home and sleep during the day. Well, the next morning came and we looked for Gary's interview on the appropriate channel, but it never appeared. Dad called Gary a day or two later and he downheartedly confessed that he had stayed up all night rehearsing, but about 4:45 his body had finally given out and he'd fallen asleep and slept right through the scheduled interview time. The news show never extended a second invitation.

- Jake was one of my housemates during college, a biology/pre-med major with plenty of smarts. He postponed signing up for his MCAT exam (the admission test for medical school) until the final time it was offered during the academic year. The evening before the MCAT, he and I grabbed dinner with some friends, and he met up with some other people he knew and stayed out most of the night visiting with them. When he got back at about 4 A.M., he set up the ironing board and pressed the clothes he was going to wear to take the test. Then he sat down to study a few last-minute things for the exam. By about 5 A.M., I was done with all my homework and went off to bed. The next day I was out in the living room about noon when Jake came stumbling out of his bedroom, having just woken up. "What time is it?" he asked in a panic. I told him it was noon, and asked what time the MCAT started. "8 A.M.," he said quietly, then returned to his room. Jake could have taken the MCAT the following year, but he never did, and never again talked of going to medical school.

Whenever I have a big event coming up and I'm torn between staying up and fighting through until morning, or else going to sleep in order to rest, I can't help but think of Gary and Jake. The Y2K problem has shown me plenty of people like them who are trying to fight through until M-Day with flagging energy levels, and I hope that these folks take enough time out to revitalize themselves so that they're able to actually follow through and finish the necessary work, and be refreshed enough to do it correctly.

Some people have cheered the need to prepare for the Y2K problem as a great chance to return to a more focused, less frenzied lifestyle. We all know how good it feels to clear our heads once in a while—some do it with a walk along the river, some do it during a round on the golf course, some do it when they take the time to bake bread or another favorite dish that takes more time than is usually spent in the kitchen. Most of us do this kind of mental and physical resting on the weekends, if at all. These days, though, more and more kitchens contain an extra TV set, and many vehicles (especially family vehicles such as minivans) are being sold with a TV/VCR combo in them besides the now-standard radio and CD player. In these days when it's harder than ever to separate ourselves from the influx of media, it's also harder to spend time alone with God and our private thoughts without additional incoming clutter.

In his landmark book *The Cross and the Switchblade*, Rev. David Wilkerson told of a turning point in his life and his ministry, when he felt the need to give up his television time and instead spend that time in prayer and visitation with God. The results were remarkable, and that time each day became more fruitful than Rev. Wilkerson ever could have predicted. In fact, the importance of what happened during that non-television time eventually spilled over from a mere handful of hours each week to change what he did with his entire life. Many of us who have had to take our TV set in for repairs can see the difference that even a few days without that powerful distraction in the house can make; for many people, the day seems longer without TV, and after overcoming the initial shock of all that extra silence, it seems possible to achieve more with each day.

It's not just TV that barrages us with mind clutter. Video games, the Internet and other computer-related distractions, cell phones seemingly attached to people's ears in the car, at the grocery store, even at the mall—all of these high-tech toys can become so much a part of our lives that we lose track of how much time and attention we sacrifice to them.

> *Hebrews 4:10* For anyone who enters God's rest also rests from his own work, just as God did from his.

Related Verse:
Matthew 11:28

Many churches or groups within churches hold annual retreats to serve as a time of rest and renewal both physically and spiritually. I'm a huge fan of annual retreats, and in addition to endorsing those as a technique for you to withdraw into a brief period of spiritual renewal, I'll go so far as to say you should try to take a weekly retreat, even if it's only a half hour. And you should take a daily retreat, even if it's only five minutes.

Make special time on a regular basis to clear your mind and step away from your ongoing cares for at least a moment. I assure you that if you do it wholeheartedly and with a willing attitude, that personal retreat time will quickly move from being a strained, funny-feeling exercise to being an inspiring time that you treasure and look forward to, a revitalizing experience putting you back in shape to rejoin the daily grind.

LESSON 26: REFRESHING OURSELVES

At the beginning of September 1999, Ravi Rajan, Vice-President of Information Technology at Citibank N.A., warned business leaders at a conference on the Y2K problem that companies needed to start looking out for "Y2K fatigue" among both in-house staff and hired consultants, who easily could burn out as the work burden increased closer to M-Day. "It is important that in the next 122 days you don't break down," he said. "Y2K fatigue has to be carried on . . . at least till the end of January." According to some other experts, Y2K fatigue must be guarded against well into 2002 or even beyond, because employee morale and determination are likely to taper off even more sharply once M-Day comes and goes, and the workers realize that there are still hundreds (or thousands, depending upon the company) of programs which were deemed non-critical prior to M-Day but will still require correction sometime down the line.

The book of Proverbs repeatedly tells us to trust God and also maintain our own spirit so that we can do what's required of us. Well, how do we maintain our own spirit in the face of a potential or ongoing crisis? A lot of it begins with attitude:

> *Proverbs 17:22* A cheerful heart is good medicine, but a crushed spirit dries up the bones.

A well-respected psychologist offers these suggestions for how to overcome the gloom and fatigue that can impair your ability to cope in an extended emergency situation:

- Establish a routine pattern for the actions required of you
- Achieve a positive attitude
- Cling to a healthy concern directed at finding solutions rather than unproductive fears

- Take care of your health with rest, nutrition, and exercise
- Keep busy, because idleness promotes wallowing and worry
- Work on cooperating with and finding ways to help others, because teamwork in an emergency produces strength and support

I feel those suggestions go hand in hand with the Bible passage 1 Kings 19:1-21 in which Elijah is fleeing for his life after Jezebel's death threat. This passage presents the following cures for bleakness and discouragement in the face of a challenge:

- Standing before God on a regular basis with prayer for a pattern of action
- Looking on the bright side
- Recognizing God's quiet, unseen control over the situation
- Physical renewal through food and rest in order to carry on
- Always having a task to do
- Finding another person to help carry on your work

Every one of the psychologist's suggestions is directly addressed in this passage! Make sure to remember that all of these methods of refreshing yourself are available for you to utilize whenever you're in a rough patch.

The concept of deriving support from working with others appears in several other Bible verses which depict situations where people gain strength and encouragement from other believers. In 1 Thessalonians 3:2-3, for instance, Paul is following up after having sent Timothy to bolster the attitude of the Thessalonians, who were being persecuted. Even more than I like the notion that you can be bolstered by receiving help from others, I enjoy the lesser-known secret that your own attitude can be bolstered by giving away some of your precious energy and resources to help others:

Proverbs 11:25 ... he who refreshes others will himself be refreshed.

This is an example of God's mysterious mathematics. In the math we've all learned in school, when you take a portion of a positive quantity away, the result is always a lower quantity (in other words, positive stuff is finite) and if you take enough of it away, you have nothing left at all. In God's marvelous math expressed in this verse from Proverbs, though, taking something away means that you end up with more positive stuff on *both* sides of the equation.

There's one more way to become refreshed that deserves to be mentioned. At the same time that we enthusiastically work for God in the ways expected of us, we need to sometimes slow down and just take time to be with God so that we're nourished and rejuvenated and better able to get back to the tasks that await us.

Don't forget the occasion (Luke 10:38-42) when Jesus went to the home of Martha and Mary, and Martha ran around doing everything she could to make the Master feel at home and honored as a guest. She prepared the meal and dashed this way and that doing everything she thought was required to serve the Lord, while Mary simply sat and listened to Jesus speak. Martha thought Mary should be joining her in doing the work that needed to be done, and rebuked her for not helping. Jesus, however, pointed out that what Mary was doing was essential. This is true for all of us who want to serve our Lord—it is good to spend time and effort doing what needs doing, but we also should spend some time simply abiding with and learning from him.

LESSON 27: SHELTER ALONG THE WAY

For many people, Y2K preparation has raised issues of personal safety, and some extremely concerned folks have built or purchased places to seek shelter and relief, such as ranch land, prefabricated "survival domes" that come completely stocked with food and supplies, or other places suitable for weathering any eventual Y2K storm. Not surprisingly, several companies have chosen to spoof this behavior, including a contest at the end of 1999 in which **PowerStudents.com** and **InsideGuide.com**—two web sites aimed at high school and college students—are giving away a fully stocked "Y2K Bunker." The grand prize winner gets, among other things, the following: sleeping bag, mountain tent, solar radio, batteries, year's supply of SPAM™ or Twinkies™, bottled water, US Navy Seals Watch that's virtually indestructible, time capsule, two-way radio, year's supply of underwear, "I survived Y2K" T-shirt, and "plenty of toilet paper." Kelly Tanabe, director of the web sites, says that the sites are known for "preparing students for what's ahead . . . and you might say our Y2K Bunker Contest is the ultimate exercise in preparation."

That contest is strictly for fun, but some of the items being given away ring true with the sorts of supplies being assembled by those who have set up actual "Y2K bunkers" in anticipation of ill effects once M-Day arrives.

There's a better bunker available at all times to Christians:

> *Psalm 18:2* The Lord is my rock, my fortress and my deliverer; my God is my rock, in whom I take refuge . . .

> **RELATED VERSE:**
> PROVERBS 30:5
> 2 SAMUEL 22:31
> PSALM 62:1

There is no disaster from which God cannot protect those who seek his assistance, but the key is that you must actively seek:

> **RELATED VERSE:**
> PSALM 18:16
> PSALM 34:7
> PSALM 61:2
> PSALM 62:8

Psalm 32:6-7 Therefore let everyone who is godly pray to you while you may be found; surely when the mighty waters rise, they will not reach him. You are my hiding place; you will protect me from trouble and surround me with songs of deliverance.

Psalm 57:1 ...I will take refuge in the shadow of your wings until the disaster has passed.

Even on occasions when God was wrathful against humans who disobeyed him, he sheltered those who remained faithful to him. God simultaneously can be a safe place for the faithful and a storm raging against the unfaithful. For example, when Nahum delivered a message from God about his anger against Nineveh, the message mentions that those who trust God will still have him as a place of shelter:

Nahum 1:7 The Lord is good, a refuge in times of trouble. He cares for those who trust in him...

God provides the Holy Spirit to be with us constantly, and also provides us personal tools with which to take care of ourselves in stormy times:

Proverbs 2:11 Discretion will protect you, and understanding will guard you.

God is the ultimate policeman, protecting and serving in all circumstances. He shelters us and acts as a fortress to block out our enemies and protect us from ambush by the evil forces of the world, at the same time as he strengthens and restores us:

Psalm 71:3 Be my rock of refuge, to which I can always go; give the command to save me, for you are my rock and my fortress.

The protective guarantee of God is general, not specific to any particular physical circumstance. Spiritual safekeeping is always available even if physical safety is sometimes not. The Bible tells of some people who were not saved from physical threats as well as some who were. Jesus warned his followers that some would be killed, and indeed they were. Jesus himself suffered and died in keeping with God's plan. If you focus on God and goodness and trust, though, you can cling to the promise of protection from God. He doesn't guarantee that we'll escape all the trials of the world, but that he will never abandon us in even the most unfortunate situations.

We know that it's easy for anyone to appear strong when everything's going well. It's easy for Christians, though, to be strong even when things are shaky or downright dangerous. When calamity threatens, Christians have a key advantage over non-Christians. Realizing our inability to save ourselves, we need no safe place besides God. As soon as we're aware of impending danger or affliction on the road of life, we must run to that safe place and make sure we're fully availed of its protective walls, because to only be somewhat close to God isn't enough. People in Old Testament times had designated "cities of refuge" where people could escape whatever battles and conflicts raged outside the walls of those cities. That's what God is—a perpetual city of refuge available at every step along our life path, always easy to find and always perfectly equipped to take care of our current needs.

We have a tremendous capacity to recover from surprises and setbacks. It is a very Christian capability to bounce back from troubles. Those of us who understand the refuge and perpetual care that God provides should be the first to respond in appropriate ways when there's a crisis.

Lesson 28: "Just Enough" Is All You Need

An overriding concern throughout the last couple years of Y2K computer problem awareness has been determining how much preparation is necessary. Most people won't be left without power or food, but some will. Y2K is potentially disruptive, but in localized ways. So how much precaution is really required?

The Red Cross recommends keeping 3 to 5 days' worth of food and water on hand, but some organizations at the other end of the spectrum say that having six months' to a year's worth of food is necessary. Clearly nobody knows, but one noteworthy point is that as this book goes to print in the last weeks before M-Day, more people are moving toward higher cautionary tones than are moving the other direction. Several experts who originally said people did not need more than a week's worth of food and water have begun recommending during late November that people store up two to three weeks' worth. That's not a drastic change in outlook, but it's a slight shift toward greater precaution that has taken place among both government and private sector experts. To me, it stands to reason that Y2K is so unpredictable that it's prudent to have at least 3 to 4 weeks' worth of food and water for every member of your household, plus at least one refill of any required medicines. Beyond those things, it's also a no-brainer that anyone in an area that gets chilly temperatures in the winter needs to make sure that they have definite ideas about how they're going to stay warm if they have to make it through a significant power outage. This matters not just for Y2K, but for any severe problem that occurs in the future. Within recent memory, a horrible ice storm kept a large area of Maine powerless for the better part of two weeks—and there are plenty of other occasional incidents that require some basic emergency planning to be in place so that people can stay warm and fed.

In 1998 there was a moderate amount of concern that by 1999 there would be shortages of many supplies, and that whatever was left would be unaffordable. The predictions proved only mildly true, with some isolated shortages and very gradual price increases occurring—certainly the Y2K hoarding and complete breakdown of normal market pricing that some pessimists predicted has never occurred. That's probably a function of the fact that, in America at least, we're such an overconsuming society that manufacturers have been producing and distributing ever-larger quantities of goods, so any increased purchasing that people have done for Y2K has blended right in with our usual tendency to consume more and more stuff each year anyway.

There are some companies who *have* stocked up lots of goods, taking a chance that there will be Y2K problems, and standing by with a view to cashing in. In the city closest to my home, a company has rented 100,000 feet of warehouse space and filled it to the brim with pallet upon pallet of bottled water, canned and dehydrated foods, kerosene heaters, batteries, and other items specifically meant to be useful in the event of a Y2K disaster. Did they do this back in 1997 or 1998, trying to cash in on the entire Y2K preparation period? No, they just started this warehousing effort in October 1999, with less than ten weeks remaining before M-Day.

Even later—on November 2, 1999—the Chicago Tribune ran an article about warehouse space being sought by several companies for the time period from November 1999 through February 2000. A spokesman for National Distribution Centers, a N.J.-based warehousing and distribution firm, said his company was increasing storage space during that time period in anticipation of increased storage needs related to Y2K problems, adding that they've received requests from "major food industry clients" to have extra space available to handle any emergencies that might require the storing or movement of additional goods. "Overall, our inventory levels are peaking right about now," he said. "Everybody is hedging their bets." It's uncertain whether those companies are gearing up for possible increases in consumer demand for certain items, or whether they are just contingency planning in case their own supply chains somehow end up compromised by computer problems.

David Pals of Grubb & Ellis Co., a commercial real estate services firm, has talked with logistics firms (companies that arrange storage and freight transport for just about everything that ends up in consumers' hands) about possible warehousing deals. "My take on it is that they must expect Y2K not to be a nonevent," he said. "They want to store materials [such as] air compressors, generators and dehydrated foods." He said, "In real estate terms it's a curiosity," but also pointed out that the companies might need the extra space after M-Day to accommodate massive returns from consumers who don't end up needing all the stuff they've stockpiled.

The extra warehousing that's taking place in cities around the world might very well prove to be a stupid gamble on the part of the companies doing it, or it might turn out that a few people in a major metropolitan area end up sitting on the largest available stashes of much-needed resources.

In terms of Y2K's impact in your life, there's a far bigger likelihood of having headaches sorting out a few paperwork problems than actually having something threaten your physical well-being. Still, there's no way of knowing exactly what will occur, and there are quite a few outspoken Christians who have found media time to discuss their view that God might use Y2K to test people in the same way that he tested Job and Abraham and others, placing them in a position of losing just about everything except their hope in God, in order to confirm the strength of that hope.

People sometimes see the abundance in their lives start to diminish for various reasons. Job layoffs, injuries, and other events can throw a household quickly into a tailspin and start eating away at their available resources. Even if your supplies dwindle for any reason, there's no limit on the supply of God's love, care, and grace. All who want these things can have as much as they want, can have everlasting life and have it abundantly.

God doesn't necessarily give us all we'll ever need for a lifetime right up front—he provides on an ongoing basis according to our changing needs. We need to pattern ourselves after the viewpoint of Paul, who thanked the church at Philippi for gifts and financial support they sent him at a moment of severe need, but at the same time expressed his willingness to carry on even if such gifts weren't available:

> Philippians 4:11-14 I am not saying this because I am in need, for I have learned to be content whatever the circumstances. I know what it is to be in need, and I know what it is to have plenty. I have learned the secret of being content in any and every situation, whether well fed or hungry, whether living in plenty or in want. I can do everything through him who gives me strength. Yet it was good of you to share in my troubles.

He's appreciative of what they've done for him, but he's willing to bear whatever God expects him to, even if it means watching his own physical needs not be met.

What Paul's fellow believers did was wonderful, though. They recognized that no matter how much was available to each of them, the collection of their resources as a whole wouldn't be optimally useful until placed in the hands of those with the greatest current need. Although some of them had meager amounts for themselves, they still helped their fellow man, and that willingness to empty their own storehouse actually resulted in the betterment of everyone's situation. The writer of Luke recorded Jesus' teaching of the same concept:

> Luke 6:38 Give, and it will be given to you... with the measure you use, it will be measured to you.

Now, since many Christians cite Abraham as a classic example of trusting the Lord, let's talk about Abraham for a moment. He was faithful to the extent of being willing to put his only son's life on the line when God asked him to be willing to do that (Genesis 22:1-18) and was unfailing in his belief that God would see to everything in the most fitting way. When God provided a ram to be sacrificed instead of his son, Abraham named that spot using a special name for God: Jehovah-jireh, which means "the Lord will provide" or literally "the one who will see to it"—it's a name with a character description built directly into it. Some people still use that name today when they're referring to God and want to place special emphasis on his provisionary care for us. There are plenty of Christians who have never used the name Jehovah-jireh, but rest assured it isn't something outlandish and isn't reserved only for the scholarly set attending seminary. It's a special name that any of us can call the Lord when we're appreciative of what he gives us.

As with most disaster preparedness efforts, we all hope not to actually need to utilize the Y2K plans we've put in place. We're all aiming for 100% leftovers of everything we've stocked up, so that means we need to have a solid idea about how much extra we're buying, and how it's going to end up being used if all goes well and Y2K has no physical impact on us.

Do you know who takes it on the chin pretty badly when hard times strike? Charities and churches and other institutions that provide key services to local communities. When a crisis occurs, their intake of contributions often declines. If an organization of that sort hasn't stockpiled and planned carefully, it can be in big trouble, finding its services requested most often at the very time when the fewest donations are coming in.

Y2K saw its share of both for-profit and not-for-profit organizations struggling to stay afloat as their resources were depleted, and whatever advertising or sponsorship deals they started out with usually went down the tubes as the public became less and less interested over time in learning about the Y2K problem.

John Anderson, who produced Y2K booklets, videotapes, and a radio show (Y2KNews Radio), was frustrated in the fall of 1999 that his radio show nearly went off the air due to financial trouble, and stayed on only because some caring sponsors intervened and helped out. At the same time, Anderson said, public perception was that gobs of money kept rolling in to all Y2K experts hand over fist. "I lost $25,000 last year trying to warn the general public," he said. "So much for making a fortune."

Disappearing resources also undid **y2ktoday.com**, a web site that for many months worked hard at focusing attention on Y2K issues and providing a range of useful information for its site visitors, but which was forced to completely shut down by October 1999 because the site owners could no longer afford to keep it going. Nobody ever stepped forward to help keep them operational all the way through to M-Day.

Even though it boils down to guesswork exactly how much we personally need to have on hand when M-Day arrives, let's at least learn from this experience that some reserves must be available to us at all times. Contingency planning is something many of us don't do enough of on a regular basis. It's great to think positively, but it's also important to know exactly how you're going to handle anything that goes wrong. Larry Burkett, a Christian financial planner, has many callers to his radio show who tell him that they're budgeting for the first time and would like to work on building savings or investments. He immediately advises them that the first priority should be to have a couple of months' worth of expenses in a fairly liquid asset, such as a money market fund. This is a basic contingency fund that everyone ought to have on hand in case something unexpected occurs which requires money to remedy.

Aside from money, we also need contingency plans in place for other types of unexpected demands we might face. Have you got emotional reserves at all times so that you can cope with an illness, injury, death, personal betrayal, or other traumatic event that might suddenly strike your life? Work toward happiness daily, stay balanced, keep your relationship with God solid, and avoid stress to make sure you do have those emotional reserves. Have you got energy reserves so that you can cope with additional responsibilities within your family, at your church, or on the job if such responsibilities should quickly crop up? Don't bypass chances for vacations, even if they're short ones taken close to home, because they can be tremendously rejuvenating; don't shortchange yourself on sleep; and take whatever other steps are necessary to make sure you do have those energy reserves.

In ancient times, when it was often possible to defeat enemy lands just by interrupting their food or water supplies, everyone knew the importance of keeping extra provisions on hand. It meant you were less vulnerable, more able to survive a negative surprise. We don't face the same sorts of crises that people in those times did, but we might face equally challenging circumstances of various sorts, and it's important that we make sure we're proactive in trying to have enough on hand to not leave ourselves vulnerable. With a conscious effort to keep your reserve levels where they need to be and a constant reliance on Jehovah-jireh, you'll find yourself ready to cope with any problem situation that ever does strike your life.

LESSON 29: DON'T FORGET TO SET UP ROAD SIGNS

If you have any doubt that Y2K assessment, repair work, and testing are going to add up to a very lengthy process, simply review the report issued in late 1998 by the US House subcommittee studying the Y2K problem which described the progress that federal agencies and departments had made toward Y2K compliance so far, and gave expected completion years for each agency or department.

Here's a tiny sampling of the target completion years specified:

Social Security Administration	1999
Department of Defense	2001
Nuclear Regulatory Commission	2001
Department of State	2027
Department of Justice	2030+
Department of Education	2030+

∞ Note

All right—I've been writing "Y2K problem" throughout the book, but I just have to write it out fully here to emphasize the ridiculousness of the mess we've ended up in. These target dates are provided in all seriousness for fixing the *year 2000 problem*, which as we all well know is a problem related to the year *2000* that has the potential for causing tremendous trouble if not corrected by the year *2000*. Somehow, though, the government managed to issue these expected completion dates for year 2000 remediation all the way up to the year 2030 and beyond with an absolutely straight face. Anyway, employees in certain departments clearly will be staying saddled up for an awfully tiring ride.

On the long trip to Y2K compliance—or any other long trip—you'd get dejected or lost very easily if you didn't have something to look at along the way and measure your progress. One of the roughest trips taken by anyone in the Bible was the trip into exile of the Israelites that took place after God decided that Babylon would be allowed to defeat Judah and keep the chosen people of God in captivity for 70 years. For much of the prophet Jeremiah's lifetime, Israelites were trapped in foreign lands or wandering aimlessly, and Jeremiah for a long time was unsure that they'd ever be restored in their relationship with God and returned to their homeland. The Lord finally gave Jeremiah the word, though, that the time definitely would come for the children of Israel to be allowed to return home, and one of his instructions for them was this:

> *Jeremiah 31:21* Set up road signs; put up guideposts. Take note of the highway, the road that you take...

This verse reflects the fact that a displaced Israel needed to keep track of guideposts figuratively, to be able to find the way back to the Lord, and literally, to be able to find the way back home whenever the time was right. The King James Version of the same verse begins "Set thee up waymarks"—when travelers in those days tagged a path for the benefit of themselves or anyone else who came along later, those waymarks truly mattered because wayfarers didn't have the luxury of a road atlas—or better yet, a AAA Trip-Tik with mileage estimates and construction zone advisories—to guide them from start to finish. These days, we can take all of life's journeys from point A to point B and never bother to establish any road signs or guideposts of our own, because most of what we do these days—and I don't just mean actual traveling, but practically *everything* we do—occurs in a pretty standard way, and we take for granted that everyone knows how it goes.

If you start thinking in new terms about the significant experiences of your life as you go through them, though, I believe you *can* still come up with reasons to set up road signs and guideposts once in a while as you move along. Set up spiritual guideposts for yourself and others. They show an awareness of history and a willingness to provide information for those who come after you; they keep your most precious experiences fresh and easy to find again; they help memorialize anything in your life that's worth revisiting.

You can put up guideposts for acts of kindness you've seen or done. You can establish waymarks warning of dangers you've run into. You can set up road signs for those special places where God has shown you his grace, displayed evidence of his perfect partnership with you, or carried you through some difficulty. I hope this book even serves as a guidepost of sorts, and I hope that you notice plenty of other guideposts in the Y2K melee, and think about setting up a few of your own before M-Day fades to just another insignificant point along life's path. It's a guarantee that in many future situations, other people who have made mistakes will need direction, other people gripped by worry will seek reassurance, and tired workers will need to know where to turn for re-energizing—if our experiences and shared remembrances can serve as waymarks for them to more easily complete that later trip, then something marvelous will have resulted from our journey through the Y2K problem.

Lesson 30: The Finish Matters as Much as the Start

In August 1999 Dennis Grabow, a business consultant on Y2K issues, described the need for companies both large and small to vigorously work toward achieving full Y2K compliance, "We will all need to get there: government regulators will demand it, suppliers will dictate it and, in the end, internal inefficiencies will require it or the market will compel it."

Unfortunately, 1999 was full of press conferences by various companies announcing that they had achieved Y2K compliance. Why do I say "unfortunately"? Because to think that Y2K compliance was ever achieved sometime during 1999 was a mistake. Those companies have gotten all the latest information and revamped every mission-critical system they could find, so as of their announcement they're Y2K-compliant. What about the following day, though? And the one after that? Although Y2K remediators use the most current information during their Y2K projects, that information changes every day. Leading manufacturers are continually testing thousands of products for Y2K compliance, and some new problems arise every week. Products previously thought to be Y2K-compliant suddenly might require a patch to work properly after M-Day. No corporation can be sure it's Y2K-compliant, because key manufacturers aren't even completely sure whether their products are Y2K-compliant.

Greg Holt, who gave some excellent attention to this issue on ZDY2K (the Ziff-Davis Y2K information web site), wrote in a June 1999 article, "The IS manager who completed the job three months ago and is on vacation until January is in for a surprise. So is the guy who finished last week. In fact, any corporate-wide declaration of total Y2K compliance at this point is premature." Holt supported his conclusion by pointing to the ever-shifting information available through Infoliant, the most popular fee-based Y2K information service for IT professionals.

Since 1997, Infoliant has maintained a highly-trusted database of Y2K compliance information on over 35,000 hardware and software products from more than 600 manufacturers. Its monthly Compliance Tracker Delta Report ("delta" is used in many scientific fields to represent change) describes which products from the database have had a recent positive or negative compliance status change. About 1/3 of the status changes in the second quarter of 1999 were negative (the manufacturer released new information identifying a previously unknown Y2K problem making that product non-compliant, or announced complete discontinuation of support for that product). As of mid-June, nearly 3000 products in the database were non-compliant and over 5000 required corrective action to function correctly after M-Day. About 1800 products hadn't been tested for Y2K compliance yet, and manufacturers had determined that more than 1500 would not ever be tested. The upshot is that any corporation claiming Y2K compliance in summer or fall of 1999 and thinking it was safe to close the book on Y2K efforts subsequently missed out on status changes in hundreds of products from leading manufacturers like Hewlett Packard, 3Com, Lucent Technologies, and more.

In addition to the compliance status changes, manufacturers of some products whose status simply remains "action required" have made thousands of changes to the specific instructions for how to achieve compliance in those products. Certain products have had their official set of corrective actions changed more than ten times since 1997—sometimes this means a new patch has replaced a patch which was earlier believed (mistakenly) to make the product compliant. Some products ended up with a series of patches that needed to be used sequentially to achieve full compliance, so any repair efforts using an earlier patch that claimed to be the final fix for that product would now have fallen out of compliance again. Holt noted, "There will be a lot of overtime for IS employees both before and after January 2000. The most important advice for a

Y2K team is to get the newest information available, and then keep on looking for even newer information."

Companies can think they're fully caught up and Y2K-compliant at one moment, then new problems may face them the next day. Likewise, as a Christian you may be fully compliant with God's commandments and the lifestyle you know you should be living one day, but there's no time for resting on your laurels. There may well be new challenges, new temptations, and new pitfalls waiting for you the next day, and you have to A) recognize them and B) be willing to correct them in order to continue your claim that you are a compliant Christian.

Besides pinning down what total compliance actually means, there have been difficulties in simply keeping everyone going through these seemingly endless Y2K projects. When there were about 120 days left before M-Day, the managing director of NIIT Ltd., a software training firm, spoke at a conference and advised Y2K project managers to not only help keep their programmers energized and motivated, but also light fires under their companies' top executives so that they would be willing to move fast to tackle obstacles to Y2K remediation that might occur as the companies approached the finish line. He said, "At the CEO [level] you need to create panic, but to the programmer . . . give support. This is the most important time to do it."

The US Social Security Administration has been working on overcoming their Y2K problems since 1989, but they've still got people working on contingency planning right up until M-Day. The Canadian government has reached a state where they're satisfied with the remediation of critical systems across the entire federal government, but they still recognize that the finish line isn't yet reached. Linda Lizotte-MacPherson explains that their attention remains on backup systems and contingency plans, saying, "We certainly don't intend to relax. There is still a lot of work left to do."

> *James 1:4* Perseverance must finish its work so that you may be mature and complete, not lacking anything.

On the personal level, if you've planned well and are unfazed by Y2K, but people in your area actually are hit by some degree of problems, you might be the hero of your family or your neighborhood—people who didn't prepare as well might come out of the woodwork and ask you for favors. Isn't it better to be in that position than to be the one who has to go around doing the asking? Do you know Aesop's fable "The Grasshopper and the Ant" in which the grasshopper hops happily along without a care in the world as winter approaches, but the ant diligently stores up at a steady pace to make sure he has enough? When winter hits, the grasshopper needs to come begging to the ant.

The ant in that fable is a great example of steady, sober attention to the ethics of work and preparedness. Where else can one find the same fine lesson taught? In the Holy Bible, of course:

Proverbs 6:6 Go to the ant, you sluggard; consider its ways and be wise!

The ant has foresight and a willingness to work on preparation. He'll never need to abruptly struggle to resolve a shortfall later, for he does what's needed along the way. He is released from the fear of the future that an unprepared creature feels. Anyone who's lazy and short-sighted, and knowingly opts to be unprepared, shows no respect for his role and responsibilities in the future.

Linda Lewis of the Limited Stores saw the impossibility of her company finishing everything on its Y2K agenda by M-Day, but she kept her determination to work at a steady pace and achieve everything possible, including the implementation of even better systems than the company previously had. "Y2K is a big challenge," she said. "Our strategy is even bigger. We're not just patching old systems, we're developing new systems that are better, faster, smarter—and Y2K compliant. We can't implement every new system before January 1, 2000. The idea is to get blueprints in place so that after that date, we can implement our plans quickly. We're building systems that go way beyond Y2K." And since she sounds like she has kept the excellent outlook of an ant, I have a feeling her company will get there as intended.

The last thing I want this lesson to encourage you to do is to never stop striving, not even in the very last moment that something can be done. This is as true for Y2K as it is for any other circumstance. Since most people have started their personal preparations for Y2K too late, it's important to *never* stop finding ways to prepare a bit more. To take a minor example, people who have not accumulated extra water in their homes—and even those who have—are urged by most experts to take the basic precaution of filling bathtubs and sinks and large pans with water on the night of December 31, 1999 in order to have as many extra gallons on hand as possible in case of a problem with a local water supply.

We as Christians should never stop preparing, either. There's no point at which we've done enough to fulfill what God asks of us. Jesus paid our debt, but we bear the responsibility of living our entire lives in a way that shows our gratitude for that gift, and in a way that shows we adhere to God's commandments and biblical blueprint for our lives. How do you reach the finish line as a Christian? First, you make sure you find ways to remain encouraged during the long trip, as early believers did:

> *Hebrews 10:25* Let us not give up meeting together, as some are in the habit of doing, but let us encourage one another—and all the more as you see the Day approaching.

Second, make sure that you direct yourself toward the goal rather than just drifting aimlessly:

> *Philippians 3:14* I press on toward the goal...

The direction you're headed reveals itself in even the smallest decisions and concerns in your life, not just in major events. The ultimate goal is the calling of Jesus for our lives, and you mustn't forget that it outshines any interim marks we set for ourselves along the way, no matter how important those are.

> **RELATED VERSE:**
> 2 TIMOTHY 4:7

1 Corinthians 9:24 Do you not know that in a race all the runners run, but only one gets the prize? Run in such a way as to get the prize.

Summary

The more that people have learned about the Y2K problem, the more worried they've typically become. Experts disagree about the extent of problems that might arise, but nobody who has spent significant amounts of time studying the problem ever has dared claim that *no* problems will result. I have heard from a few people uninformed on Y2K issues that they feel no problems will result, but one must consider the source. Even the most optimistic experts who have computer backgrounds always temper their optimism with the realistic view that the world will see at least isolated problems in certain systems, due to the inescapable likelihood that things will be overlooked or corrected poorly, or that time will run out on certain remediation efforts.

Unfortunately, what has happened to a number of people is that they've become burned-out on details about the Y2K problem and have been so swamped with the story week after week throughout 1999 that they've started to tune out the details just when everything is becoming most critical.

It's easy for us to become so overloaded with information about a certain topic or event that at some point we decide we know all that there is to know about it. Once we reach that point, just try to tell us anything else about it—it's like talking to a wall! Sometimes good Christians are like that—they've practiced religion for many years, they commune daily with God, and they've grown absolutely secure in their faith. I feel that they, more than anyone, need to make sure they don't get lulled into missing out on further growth in their Christian lives. Christ spoke out against complacency and arrogance a number of times, and those messages have trickled down into many of our favorite fables. Don't forget the hare who assumed he'd already won the race because he had steadily completed most of it, but then became so complacent that the prize actually went to the tortoise who never wavered or lost focus.

As you work on maintaining a steady pace, it's critical to refresh yourself along the way. Make it a point regularly to conduct a personal revival and renew your purpose and dedication so that you're capable of going through the emotions as well as through the motions of your Christianity!

4

The Tangled Web We've Woven

Phones went out, beepers went silent, ATM customers went away empty-handed. The National Guard mobilized, emergency shelters opened, and public-safety workers scrambled around the clock. There was anger and resentment, and a host of politicians and other folks were pointing fingers and placing blame. It was a chaotic scene right out of the worst conceivable Y2K nightmare. More than 1 million people and businesses were affected.

That was the lead to an article in *The Bergen Record* on September 26, 1999 describing what had happened in Northern New Jersey because of flooding and wind damage from Tropical Storm (formerly Hurricane) Floyd. Dr. James Pruden, chief of emergency services at St. Joseph's Medical Center in Paterson, said, "It lets you know how important it is to stand alone without depending on outside capabilities, and also gives you a sense of the level of cooperation you can get all around when crises occur," adding that by comparison to Floyd, "I've heard people say Y2K will be a piece of cake." His hospital was forced to communicate with ambulances using police radios, and had to have police cars fetch some doctors and bring them in. Some police departments themselves were affected—the Bergen County police had worked hard to make their department

100% Y2K-compliant, but all their upgraded equipment was useless when floodwater poured through their headquarters. Bell Atlantic, which since 1995 has spent over $300 million preparing for Y2K, had declared itself fully compliant in June 1999, but that was no help at all when floodwater soaked equipment in an important switching office. The storm destroyed a segment of the local phone network, and caused considerable problems elsewhere—injuring people, destroying homes, and so on—making the lack of phone service even more of an inconvenience than if it had occurred on an otherwise uneventful day. Critics were mad at the phone company for not doing more to prepare for the flood, placing a crucial switch in a flood zone, and not having a backup system to reroute calls.

The manager of a supermarket explained the problems he experienced. He was unable to contact suppliers, which made running the store extremely difficult. Luckily, suppliers eventually started guessing what products the store might need and sending things over, but that proved tricky for the store manager, too. He said, "We were completely in the dark about what they were bringing and when the trucks would show up." Fortunately, customers reportedly demonstrated great patience, making the whole event go as smoothly as possible.

Many people in Northern New Jersey now feel, rightly or wrongly, that they're ready to face anything Y2K can bring, since they've endured the consequences of Floyd. That storm taught them a tremendous amount about how various problems can strike in many places at once, and how great numbers of people can pull together with flexibility and ingenuity to overcome a very complicated set of challenges.

I told you in an earlier chapter that a hurricane's a wonderful analogy for the potential problems that Y2K can cause, and Floyd was a perfect example of the futility of trying to predict specific problems that might result. Over 1.6 million people were evacuated and 17 deaths resulted from that storm, but Florida and Georgia, which spent more time than any other states battening down the hatches to meet Floyd's wrath—and were even declared disaster areas ahead of time by the President—actually ended up having fewer problems than states much farther up the coast. The storm produced plenty of inconveniences and woes here and there, as people had expected, but the problems turned up in some of the least expected places and least expected ways. This chapter will look at the complicated nature and tremendous unpredictability of the Y2K storm that's currently within striking distance of every shoreline and soon will have its moment in history, however mild or wild it turns out to be.

Lesson 31: Understanding Interconnectedness

We live in a world of tremendous interconnectedness, not only in obvious ways like the Internet or global satellite systems, but also in pervasive, subtle ways that most people probably don't think about often. Y2K brought many of these normally quiet relationships screaming to the surface for some long overdue attention.

The securities industry found this out quickly during their Y2K testing. To make the first huge industry test of market trading in July 1998 manageable, some major systems had to be omitted, including those that manage margin trading, interest, and client account records. Only the most common types of trades and securities were tested at first. Donald Kittell, an industry executive, explained how complicated a market transaction can be: "People don't realize that a trade may go through 40 to 50 steps from start to finish." US securities companies have spent over $4 billion resolving potential computer problems, but on M-Day the ability of Wall Street to do business as usual is still unknown, because it depends on the preparedness of overseas markets as well as New York City's utilities and numerous other systems outside of its own testing ability. Even the best Y2K test plans of any industry manage to check only a fraction of the overall situations that their computers might encounter in real operations during the new millennium. Doing business in a big city like New York should be pretty safe—they'll have everything under control by M-Day, right? Quite possibly, but only after addressing their own local web of complexity—at the outset of its work on the Y2K problem, New York had 43 city agencies using 687 different major computer systems programmed in dozens of computer languages.

It was critical for banking in the US to get straightened out, because much of the business banks do is based on Fed Reserve information that goes back and forth between banks and the Fed. One bank feeding faulty numbers to the Fed could result in other wrong numbers being widely distributed to other banks, and a whole nation of banks making incorrect calculations and significant business decisions based on the incorrect numbers.

Banks always have led the way in computer safety issues anyway, due to dealing with hacker attacks, high pressure from customers to assure safety and security, and so on. Banks all can be prepared, but what if they don't have telecommunications abilities? Likewise, hospitals can have their internal systems prepared, but what if they don't receive supplies and medication, or can't get approvals from insurance companies to proceed with patient care? An important part of Y2K preparation by any business is working with outside vendors and partners to verify that those systems also will be prepared.

It's astounding how many sectors of the business world rely upon each other. For example, many maritime shipping companies depend upon airlines to deliver replacement crew members to various ports around the world where they'll meet up with the ships that need them to replace tired crew members who have been aboard for long stretches. Many airlines are slowing their flight schedules for the first few days of 2000, so maritime shipping companies have needed to develop contingency plans for having fresh crew members available at the ports where they need them.

The North American electric power grid has four main "interconnections" including one which covers a chunk of Canada, a chunk of the US, and a tiny piece of Mexico. These interconnections generally help to improve reliability. When all the generators are working together, the failure of one is like a single person in a large choir who stops singing—the choral performance as a whole continues nearly unchanged. Unsure about trusting their choirmates on Y2K, however, some utilities have contemplated going solo on M-Day. That would be a last resort, but the utilities—which usually start power plants only when necessary, and in the order that's cheapest—are definitely planning to operate differently as M-Day hits. Each area will have at least a few generators running, regardless of cost, so they can cope better and take action more swiftly if any transmission lines fail or segments experience trouble. If some generators have problems, it will be easier to manage the entire system if other generators are already at partial power.

In Germany they're planning the same way, and some large industrial manufacturers are cutting back production at the end of the year to insulate themselves from the impact of any abrupt power disruption. BASF AG, a huge chemical conglomerate, has decided to take down a number of its systems on New Year's Eve and power the remaining systems solely with electricity from its own on-site power plant. In fact, so many German manufacturers are planning to reduce their power consumption that night, the utility industry has begun to worry about possible momentary power dips (the converse of power surges) or other disruptions being caused by an abrupt *decrease* in demand.

The complexity of each individual business is multiplied many times over when the company interfaces with its business partners. Many companies do business with, or have reporting obligations to, the US Government, which will not have all of its mission-critical systems fully compliant by M-Day (let alone the tens of thousands of systems which have been categorized as non-critical).

Even little pockets within the government have turned out to be remarkably complex. For over two years, the Federal Aviation Administration has been coordinating the debugging of the National Airspace System, which consists of 297 interrelated computer systems used by 20 air traffic control centers that monitor long-distance flights. The software changes alone cost around $100 million and involved about 22 million lines of code. Yet the FAA felt this set of systems to be so critical that it didn't know if it could trust the fix alone. According to George L. Donohue, associate administrator of the FAA for research and acquisitions, "Some of the software people now say that even if you think you've fixed all the microcode, there's no way to be sure." So the FAA decided to replace a number of aging computers that were at the center of it all. In other words, this one large system was so complicated that to be completely sure everything would keep working on M-Day, they simultaneously worked on two different approaches: repairing the old version and also replacing much of the same stuff they were repairing. The repairs were necessary, they felt, because it wasn't certain they would have enough time to complete and test all the replacements of the aging computers before M-Day. Drucella Andersen, a spokeswoman for the FAA, said, "We're trying to do both because it gives us the highest assurance and insurance."

Okay, perhaps the airlines and the flying public can rest easy now. The planes are reportedly safe and the air traffic control system is fixed with tremendous care. Will air travel be completely trouble-free then? Well, are the airports all fully compliant? Are any of the flight schedules confused? Is every travel agent compliant? You get the idea. It's not simple to conclude at any point that an entire industry is prepared for Y2K.

Let's talk about the petroleum industry. One problem there could cause problems with trucking, passenger buses, and other transportation businesses, as well as impact airplane flights, reduce the ability to manufacture certain goods reliant upon petroleum products, and so on. Bear in mind that Y2K compliance for any system that interfaces with other systems must be viewed in terms of the readiness of those other systems as well. Any set of interconnected systems can only claim to be as Y2K-compliant as its weakest link.

It's no wonder that throughout late 1999, companies which have already fixed their own systems have been scrambling to come up with ways to fend off disaster that might be caused by the failures of others. "An increasing number of organizations are recognizing the inevitability of date change related problems occurring early in the new millennium," says Peter Barnes, General Manager of Survive! International, an independent user group which advises businesses on problem preparation. "Whatever the state of readiness and compliance you have achieved with your own applications and software," he says, "it is to be assumed that you will be affected by the failure of a trading partner somewhere up or down your supply chain or within the environment in which you operate."

Following everyone's best Y2K remediation effort, data from some noncompliant systems (either those which have been overlooked or those which nobody has thought to fix or those which have been fixed incorrectly) could be passed to compliant systems, thereby corrupting the data. It's a classic case of one bad apple spoiling the barrel—the entire world is a big networked barrel these days, and while one bad computer system certainly doesn't ruin all the computers in the world, it can spread corrupt data gradually through many systems outside of its own home location. The problem is exacerbated by the fact that today's programming languages and smarter-than-ever applications often interact in ways that are much more than merely handing a packet of data from one machine to the next—lots of times the data is passed along in a software "container" that has its own smarts, and that will make decisions and take actions based on the status of the system to which it is passed. In other words, some data could not only be faulty, but could be faulty and also full of capabilities to take a variety of actions within a previously uncorrupted system that it enters.

The cascading effect of corrupted data works like the parlor game "Telephone" in which one person tells some slightly complicated information to another person, and that person tells the next person, and so on until the info has traveled from system to system (person to person) many times. Invariably, especially with a bunch of kids playing, some faulty information creeps in and is distorted repeatedly so that the story you end up with from the last person is far off from the correct story you began with. Even if most exchanges of the information along the way occur perfectly, it takes only a single faulty system to corrupt the data and in many modern business transactions, as in the game of Telephone, there's no way for faulty data to be corrected once it has been accepted as trusted data from a sending system.

Yes, faulty data and the resulting business problems can be identified and straightened out later (as soon as the problems are identified by clients, consumers, or whomever), but that's not always easy. You know how hard it is to straighten out little problems—imagine a whole world full of people and companies trying to straighten out many problems at once. Moreover, with consolidation that has occurred in many service industries, even one isolated problem can affect hundreds of thousands of customers. Our home mortgage, for example, is held by a lender that has about 700,000 mortgages. The largest brokerages in this country handle hundreds of thousands of accounts each. So if there are any unexpected problems with data concerning those accounts, it might not be a matter of needing to undo just a couple hundred wrong numbers—it can take tens of thousands of employee hours to manually review and correct a problem on that scale.

You know all the ways that you're interconnected with other people, don't you? If not, do a quick analysis. You have relationships with family members, of course, and friends on whom you depend for various types of information and services. What if there's a fault in you or in one of them—does it transfer through the interfacing you do? You bet—the Bible puts this directly into human terms, mentioning several times the importance of keeping an eye out for bad data coming your way from other people, and the importance of passing along valid information yourself:

> *Proverbs 13:20* He who walks with the wise grows wise, but a companion of fools suffers harm.
>
> *Matthew 15:14* Leave them, they are blind guides. If a blind man leads a blind man, both will fall into a pit.

2 Timothy 2:2 And the things you have heard me say in the presence of many witnesses entrust to reliable men who will also be qualified to teach others.

Now focus for a moment on your interconnectedness with God. Remember the passage in the first chapter of Ezekiel describing very special wheels which consist of one wheel joined with another wheel. A general take on this is that we're all connected to God and he steers us to successfully go places in our lives according to his will. God can both live within us and allow us to find rest within him, just like oxygen is the sustainer of our life both within our bloodstream and in the environment outside of us.

Next, think about your relationship with Jesus Christ. It's as fundamentally intertwined as any corporate connections in the world today:

John 15:5 I am the vine; you are the branches. If a man remains in me and I in him, he will bear much fruit; apart from me you can do nothing.

A partnership with Jesus is different than a business partnership during the Y2K crisis in one crucial way—his preparation and remediation efforts were extended to benefit others, not himself:

Matthew 27:42 "He saved others," they said, "but he can't save himself!"

The problems that Jesus helped people avoid through both his living and his dying are plentiful: disease, danger, death, and sin. In a way, "he can't save himself" is an outright lie, for Jesus is almighty, but in another sense it's a wonderful truth—he couldn't save himself because he was dedicated to be, and willing to be, the savior of others. Notice that we are exactly complementary with Jesus. He saved others and would not save himself. We have the power and choice to save ourselves through him, but although we can introduce others to Christ, we ourselves truly cannot save any others. Christ is willing to be in perfect teamwork one-on-one with every person to overcome the perils of this world, if each of us agrees to ally with him.

RELATED VERSE:
ROMANS 14:7-8

Last but not least, consider the ways in which you're connected to the church. This relationship is so important that a problem which occurs with you alone can cascade into the life of the rest of the church and become a problem for the whole body of the church:

1 Corinthians 12:26 If one part suffers, every part suffers with it; if one part is honored, every part rejoices with it.

The diversity and wide-ranging organization of the church has unity through God, and this shared spirit makes for a great interreliance in which the failure of one member doesn't need to bring the entire church crashing to a halt; rather, the continuity achieved by millions of fully compliant members can work together to lift and sustain the member who's having problems in whatever ways are necessary until that member's troubles are resolved.

It's wrong to respond to problem members by cutting them off completely—they are part of the larger, interconnected system, and if one suffers, we *all* suffer. Every component part is critical to the church as a whole. In the parable of the lost sheep (Luke 15:4-7) Jesus made the point that if only one sheep out of 100 has problems, the entire flock has problems until that sheep is restored. The church must exhaust all possible means to try to improve and renew a member who has problems rather than lose him or her for good.

LESSON 32: OVER-RELIANCE ON TECHNOLOGY

A forward-looking Star Trek episode in the late 1960s involves a computer falsely accusing Captain Kirk of an offense he did not commit. The computer has had faulty programming and has made a mistake, but a council of elders is trusting the computer's flawed information. Kirk is finally vindicated thanks to an impassioned defender who begs the council to mistrust the computer before mistrusting the human, saying, "A machine does not have rights. A man must... In the name of humanity, hanging in the shadow of a machine, I demand it!"

Here's what Mike Adams of Y2Knewswire (y2knewswire.com), one of the more worry-prone Y2K watchers, wrote on October 26, 1999 about his expectations of what Y2K will bring:

> The computer-generated problems will be extremely difficult to trace, track and repair, because the people on the other end of the phone will **assume everything the computer says is fact.** Furthermore, they will have no workarounds. Go back to manual? Forget it. That phrase is only believed by the ultra-gullible. Sure, you can go back to manual in a low-tech **cement factory.** But not in a bank. Not in a cell phone company. Not in the IRS. Not in the federal government. You don't go back to manual without re-educating an **entire generation** and changing the way they work. And the first obstacle? Convincing them the computers aren't gods. The trust in computers is near-complete. Our population has made the transition from **overseeing** computer operations to **surrendering** to them. People have divested themselves of the **responsibility** of making sure things work correctly.

One of the reasons the Y2K problem could have such a great impact on our lives is that we're extremely reliant (I dare say overly reliant) on computer technology. I've made a fine career out of working with computers for many years, and I appreciate very much their capabilities and flexibility, but I'm fortunate to also have the perspective of people such as my wife, who refuses to touch a computer except when forced by a few critical tasks at work, and my dear friend Barb, who has been known to shout with glee while yanking computer plugs from the wall when the machines don't comply with her instructions.

Even for a computer lover like me, there's no denying that we've become too dependent upon them in certain ways. Many people have graduated from carrying laptops to carrying Palm Pilots, and examples of the next logical development—wearable computers built into clothing and eyeglasses and jewelry—are expected to be increasingly common by the end of the year 2000. Teams of researchers have even considered the idea of implanting babies with chips to be able to, for instance, easily track down a child if someone kidnaps him. Some people in the religious community see technological initiatives such as that as setting the stage for people to be given the mark of the beast—and if you extrapolate that the implications of not having such a chip if it ever became commonplace might be consequences such as being unable to purchase things or being unable to vote, I suppose the comparison is adequate enough to sustain some people's fears. I don't fear computer technology that much—at least, not now—but we surely need to keep our eye on technology and make sure that it doesn't ever trounce our humanity and free will.

Some psychiatrists have remarked lately on the fact that growing numbers of people are reporting having dreams, often nightmares, about computer technology. Here are a couple of examples recently given to me:

- A request for a three-page printout turns into an endless print job that fills an entire office building with paper until all the employees are swimming through a sea of printouts.
- A computer comes to life and starts biting its user.

I'm not going to get into a discussion on what dreams do or don't mean in psychological terms, but it's clear that the settings and context for a dream often come directly from things we're involved with while awake. An increase in dreams about computers at the very least means that we're a world of people who increasingly have technology on the brain.

Worse yet, society as a whole seems to have decided it's necessary to love computers. Politicians in the past few years have used school computers as a campaign issue, everybody and his dog has gotten a web site, and people who don't understand computers are made to feel completely uncool and out of touch. Becoming a mass of techno-heads leads to a decline in individuality, a fact bemoaned by people from many walks of life. See how this sentiment found its way into Amy Spindler's fashion article reviewing the European Fall collections for 1999:

> Some of the more dim-witted designers tried to tie themselves in with the Y2K bug, as if it were an event like the Fourth of July or Mother's Day. But sharper minds are cutting themselves loose from the cyberworld completely, having grasped that fashion's computer virus has been much more destructive to the industry than Y2K could ever be. With collections beamed onto the Internet within minutes of being shown and factories copying ideas quicker than even designers themselves can produce them, the computer hasn't exactly been a friend to original thinkers.

Even if you don't have a home computer and have never had to use a computer in a workplace, many aspects of your life are currently dependent upon computers in ways you probably didn't even realize until Y2K problems came up for discussion.

The more technologically advanced we've become, the less manually capable we've become. Some places might not be able to accept charge cards (one of the very first chances for the Y2K problem to grab headlines was when this occurred at a store in Michigan two years prior to M-Day). Availability doesn't necessarily equate to accessibility anymore. What if gas is available, but the pumps won't pump? What if the drugstore actually has medicine on hand, but is unable to sell it to you?

Within a one-week stretch in April 1999, my wife and I experienced two amazing episodes relevant to this lesson. On the first occasion, we were turned away from a fast food restaurant drive-through window because their computers were malfunctioning and they didn't have any way to ring up the charges. I saw numbers displayed on the digital cash register's screen and couldn't bite my nerdy tongue, so I asked if the registers were still doing anything. "Oh, yes," came the reply. "They work if you type in numbers, but we're supposed to ring things up by pushing the picture buttons." The young man working the window was all too happy to explain to me that beside the numbered keypad (which *was* functioning) was another keypad where every key contained a small picture of a food item—french fries on one key, a milkshake on another, etc.—and those pictures were linked automatically to a database of prices, which is what was having trouble at the moment.

"Couldn't you enter the prices using the numbered keypad?" I asked.

"I guess we could," said the cashier, "but our manager won't let us." He wished us a nice afternoon and we drove off to find a place where the picture pads were still working.

On the second occasion, we were in a grocery store checkout lane and suddenly everyone in the lane heard the cashier tell the customers at the front of the line, "I'm sorry; the computer just went down, so we can't sell you anything." According to an apologetic manager who came out to explain things to the upset customers, their store system was set up so that the cash register drawers could not even open without their central computer functioning, and there was no way to use a key or manual override of any sort, so the cashiers couldn't even conduct any manual transactions with customers. When asked if she could accept exact change for a few items that one of the customers needed pretty badly, the manager said that it would be a violation of store policy, and refused to let the person purchase any items. Most of the customers walked out of the store muttering things to themselves and deciding which other store to patronize. I have to wonder whether, if the whole city's power were out following Y2K and that store held a large portion of the fresh food supply in the city, the manager would continue the strict company policy and not sell the much-needed food, preferring to give up the sales rather than figure out how to be flexible and meet customers' needs.

It's insane that thanks to computers, we have not only dumbed down our workforce, but also removed many chances for flexibility in terms of customer service.

Some companies may have employees who possess the manual skills to do their jobs without computers, but no longer have the correct equipment (think about the many newspapers now produced via a computerized process by companies that no longer own actual typeset machines) or not have enough manpower to manually complete their normal business workload (think about a bookkeeping firm that handles payroll on computer for thousands of clients—they might have the manual skills to do only a severely reduced version of that workload).

We've got increasing amounts of technology in our homes, too. Most experts expect the Y2K problem to have minimal impact on the home, but consumer groups warn to expect some home-based surprises. Any products using calendar year data may be affected; certain older camcorders, VCRs, fax machines, PCs, and home automation and security products are most likely to malfunction. The greatest concern at home, of course, is the readiness of local utility companies. It doesn't matter whether your appliances work if you lack electricity. Another concern involves smoke alarms that are hard-wired into a home's electrical system (according to the Red Cross, most new ones are), in which case you should make sure there's a battery backup for the smoke alarm. People with home offices typically have additional Y2K testing to do in terms of office equipment and software. Even most of our everyday tools—drills, saws, etc.—have become electric ones. Many people who wanted a cutting tool around as part of their Y2K preparation had to go buy a handsaw again. (Fortunately, some of us who are notorious pack-rats didn't have to worry about that sort of purchase! We just needed a trip to the back of the garage.)

Y2K preparation has helped us to realize how truly fundamental computers and technology in general have become to the operation of most aspects of our lives. Frank Martinez, executive director of the Los Angeles Y2K Project Office, says, "No one can predict with certainty what will happen. We live in a very complex society technologically and there's too much reliance on systems that we can't control."

During a CNBC interview in August 1999 regarding Y2K and investors, Jeanne Terrile, Director of Strategic Research at Merrill Lynch, imparted lots of good news about progress in the financial sector, and cited only one key remaining area of concern—unknown aspects of systems. "We all spend a lot of time pushing a button and making things happen," she said, "and not being sure *why* they happen."

We've seen minor examples of what an inconvenience it can be when the everyday technology we rely upon fails temporarily:

- A power outage struck Auckland, NZ in January 1998 and lasted several weeks; it took nearly six months for everything to be completely restored to its previous working state.
- On September 24, 1999 a computer that monitors every train in the Washington, DC subway system failed (an error in a graphics generating program, not a Y2K problem), stopping all service, delaying the opening of subway stations, and delaying tens of thousands of morning rush-hour commuters. The subway system handles about 380,000 passenger trips per day, including commuters from Virginia, Maryland, and DC, plus tourists visiting national monuments and museums. The computer failure required subway personnel to spread out along nearly 96 miles of track with two-way radios to monitor trains themselves until the computer system was fixed.

Realize that potential problems exist outside of Y2K, and that all the Y2K remediation efforts in the world haven't necessarily changed the perilous nature of our growing dependency on tremendously sophisticated computers and communications technologies. Consider a couple of other examples that have nothing to do with Y2K, but that clearly demonstrate how complicated operations can go haywire when glitches occur:

- When one satellite in orbit above the earth failed in May 1998, a handful of television broadcasts were interrupted or postponed, and over 30 million people with pagers were temporarily without service.
- Hong Kong opened a beautiful new airport in mid-1998, but some hastily-completed software contained errors that caused their baggage-handling system to act improperly, which in turn led to the collapse of a synchronized network that involved almost every system in the entire

airport. For two days, this brand-new airport with the highest of high-tech amenities had blank flight information terminals, passengers missing planes, hundreds of delayed flights, thousands of pieces of lost luggage, rotting food, and other incidental problems. The estimated cost of the mess was over a billion dollars, but there's no real way to measure the damage done as far as angry customers (remember that the customers of an airport include its airlines and shopkeepers as well as passengers), frustration among their own partners (airport employees, customs officials, and so on), and looking foolish at the precise moment when the airport management had invited the world to pay attention to their brand-new facility and how it functioned.

Canada is highly prepared for Y2K. As early as 1988, the Treasury Board of Canada Secretariat recommended the use of a four-digit date standard by federal government departments. In 1996, they established an office to coordinate and monitor Y2K readiness work by nearly 11,000 people across the government. They've kept Y2K a top priority, and have reported 100% compliance on all essential federal government services. Their web site still admits honestly, though: "Y2K is so complex that no matter how ready organizations are, it is likely there will still be glitches."

For anyone worried that we've built a golden calf of technology, it's safe to say that even if Y2K doesn't melt down the calf completely, at least some of its imperfections are being revealed! There's no reason to shy away from all technology, but let's never be so in awe that we deify it; let's make sure we always control technology rather than allowing it to control us.

Lesson 33: Ouch! Your Moccasins Don't Fit Me

Remember how Floyd knocked out phone service in much of Northern New Jersey? Well, many people thought that wireless phones would come in handy when the old phone system went down. Unfortunately, the traditional phone network's failure disabled wireless customers in the region, too, proving that wireless is still somewhat dependent on the old infrastructure in a couple of ways: first, because many cell phone users are attempting calls to people with traditional phones, and second, because even cell-to-cell calls often travel on land lines in spots where the wireless network has gaps. Many people's belief that wireless phones weren't subject to the problems that strike land lines had to be revised, and unfortunately that change in perspective didn't occur until a crisis was already at hand.

I'd like to spend this lesson discussing different perspectives. You know that it's easy to get locked into a perspective and not want to adjust it—that's why they say "you can't teach an old dog new tricks." I urge all of us to keep the attitude of a young pup throughout our lives. That means remembering to take frequent romps in the park (remember the need for retreats and times of refreshment discussed in Chapter 3) and also remaining on the lookout for new ideas and outlooks that can add to our existing life experience in important ways.

Perspective Can Shift over Time, Usually Improving in Clarity

As time ran out for many companies to complete their remediation efforts, each company had to decide what was mission-critical and what wasn't. They also had to decide which aspects of contingency planning would be made top priorities and which would be sacrificed. Their views on what constituted the most essential parts of their business operations shifted as their Y2K projects rolled along. This brings up the question of whether it's ever possible to claim that you have a correct perspective.

Almost everyone, whether they're pessimistic or optimistic by nature, and whether they're truly seeing the big picture or not, believes that he or she alone is the epitome of what it is to be a realist—and one psychological test after another has revealed that most people feel they have more common sense than the average person. This is even trickier for people of faith, because one not only can fall victim to the apparent human trap of thinking oneself more sensible than others, but can compound it with the certainty that comes from knowing God's sovereignty—this combination of confidence factors can lead to self-assurance and even cockiness. It rarely pays to act like a know-it-all, and certainly not when facing a complicated challenge. A willingness to let one's perspective shift and improve is essential sometimes.

We've seen shifting perspectives occur in the overall recognition of and attention given to the Y2K problem; people began by being completely unaware, then most grew somewhat aware yet unconcerned, then some grew much more aware and much more concerned, and a few even became far more concerned than the extent of their awareness merited.

Some people came to a conclusion about the seriousness of the Y2K problem quickly. For example, Senator Robert Bennett in June 1998—after he had really been introduced to the broad nature of the problem—said, "Worldwide problems are now inevitable from the glitch.... Don't panic, but don't spend a lot of time sleeping either." But through several hearings and numerous statements to reporters over the course of many months, a careful observer could tell that Senator Bennett's perspective shifted slightly over time. In fact, Y2K showed plenty of people the importance of being willing to let your perspective shift and improve. It worked in both directions. A number of authors of Y2K preparation books wrote that they began with very little concern, but after reading thousands of pages of research material and conducting interviews with people in many areas of the programming and business worlds, they developed a more concerned outlook.

Many other people who became deeply immersed in Y2K issues, though, found their perspective shifting in the other direction—most of these were people who started out at the end of the spectrum that was highly fearful, and then once they developed a more balanced outlook over time, they stopped fueling the climate of fear about Y2K and started instead being a useful part of the solution. Richard Bergeon, a business consultant in Seattle, is one of them. Working on Y2K to some extent since 1992, Bergeon had grown somewhat worried that so little was being done about it. "I was predicting a catastrophe up until about six or seven months ago," he said in early 1999, adding that the increase in awareness and the actions he saw people start taking in 1998 had reassured him that the outcome was not going to be as devastating as he had felt it might be all the way through 1997. I applaud everyone who left their eyes and minds and hearts open throughout the years prior to M-Day and made adjustments to their outlook as appropriate.

Sometimes the differing perspectives had minor skirmishes with one another. There was a week in mid-1999 when four separate industry associations announced that the companies in their industry had achieved 92% Y2K compliance across the board. Four leading industries, all suddenly claiming to have moved from varying states of unpreparedness to a point where 92% readiness could be paraded in front of the general public, had the cynics in the Y2K community up in arms. The cynics were always on guard for discrepancies and misinformation being given out by various government officials and corporate spokespeople (later in the book, you'll see some examples showing that plenty of that sneaky stuff actually has happened). Some skeptical experts felt that a public relations firm or government advisor must have suggested to these industry associations that they needed to get their compliance numbers to a point where the public felt they were well on the way to completion (i.e., something above 90%) but also needed to keep the claims realistic by showing a small portion of work remaining (hence the decision to go with 92%). A few critics actually accused industry reps of falsifying the numbers, while others merely tried to call the public's attention to the fact that compliance percentages, like so many aspects of the Y2K problem, are extremely complicated to pin down and can be packaged many different ways. A Brazilian economist reminded people how Y2K numbers can be skewed by saying, "Statistics are like bikinis—they let you see a lot of things, but not necessarily relevance." So, anyone who has wanted to draw conclusions about where we truly stand on Y2K at any given moment has needed to maintain a healthy sense of perspective regarding the information that's in circulation.

The bottom line is that no opinion, as valid as it might be, is ever an excellent opinion unless it's accompanied by a willingness to remain open to additional input and to be subject to revision if that ever proves necessary. It is possible to be staunch about your beliefs, but not become stagnant. You can stand firm on your ideals without being closed off to at least acknowledging and evaluating whatever new information comes along. In fact, people tend to lose respect for those who lock into an idea and never revisit it with newer information in hand to confirm that they still believe the same thing they decided long ago.

While we're on the subject of perspective, let's examine a Bible verse that elicits different perspectives from different people:

> *Ephesians 3:4-5* In reading this, then, you will be able to understand my insight into the mystery of Christ...

Okay, what's "the mystery of Christ" exactly? People's opinions differ, but one school of thought goes something like this—it doesn't mean there's an actual puzzle to solve, but rather a spiritual revelation is presented in scripture in that the life, death, and resurrection of Jesus comprise the mysterious method by which God has made eternal life available to not only his original chosen people, the Jews, but to Gentiles as well. If we embrace the mystery of Christ, we all can receive the inheritance that God has provided for us through Christ. I'm going to accept that perspective on what the mystery of Christ means, because it lets me discuss a couple of other examples of shifting perspective. First, the gift of his son that God made to this world redefined the solution to a problem that many people had been studying and thought they were mastering for many years—faithful Jews prior to the arrival of Jesus thought that they had the whole solution to their spiritual needs and were doing their best to maintain an appropriate relationship with God, but the rules for having a fully-compliant relationship with God changed when Jesus walked the earth. The full extent of what we must do to bring ourselves to God has changed throughout the course of human history, just as the full extent of what people must do to reach Y2K compliance has changed throughout the course of the Y2K event.

∞ Note

I need to give you a disclaimer here—these analogies are not drawn to scale. I'm not by any means trying to say that anything about Y2K is of identical scope and importance to the issue of God's saving grace for mankind. I'm merely pointing out that the shifting perspectives we've seen as people realize there's more to Y2K work than they initially realized naturally makes me think of the ways in which God's people over time have had to be flexible and shift their perspective about what it is that God requires to be successfully in relationship with him.

Christianity is complicated enough for modern believers, but can you imagine how much more so it was for the earliest followers of Christ. First, Jesus started tossing around newfangled concepts about how those without the things of the world were actually rich, and how evil should be repaid with love. Next, he hung out with sinners and tax collectors and lepers and all sorts of other people previously considered outcasts. He managed to shift his disciples' perspective on those sorts of things, but his biggest challenge was convincing them that his kingdom would not be a physical kingdom established on earth. They all started out thinking that the victory Jesus would bring would be primarily a political solution so that the Jews could overcome the Romans who had been oppressing them. Jesus had to tell them repeatedly in greater and greater detail that his work was far more complicated than that, and would have a broader impact than what the disciples were seeing as the goal.

Even all the way up through his final discussions with them before his arrest and crucifixion, Jesus had to correct some of their limited thinking and emphasize that they weren't grasping the true purposes of his life and work. Some members of the Group of Twelve and other followers of Jesus only managed to fully shift their perspective after Jesus was crucified, resurrected, and appeared to them again to show them in person that he had overcome the things of the world, even death, and that their true victory celebration was not going to be in Jerusalem or Damascus or somewhere else right down the road, but in heaven.

CHRISTIAN PERSPECTIVES CAN BE APPLIED IN EVERY SITUATION

There were definitely separate camps of Christians and non-Christians discussing the Y2K problem—and this separation held up even though most of the Christians were mainly interested in secular aspects of the problem: how to protect PCs, what stocking up to do, and so on. Thus, one of the things I enjoyed keeping an eye out for was the decision-making various people did about whether or not the Y2K computer problem had religious implications.

I've already told you about some people who feel that God is going to use Y2K to judge a wicked world that has been straying for too long. There were others, mostly non-Christians of course, who purposely separated religion from Y2K discussions by emphasizing the relationship of the problem to science and mathematics. A.S. Byatt said, "Somebody said [the millennium] was a tribute to the decimal system, which is a very clever thing to have said, because, of course, it is, even if it is the thousandth anniversary of the birth of the founder of the Christian religion. Why is the ten times tenth anniversary particularly important? It's simply to do with our counting system, which is what has caused the Millennium bug, or what is here called Y2K, to cause us such anguish. It's because we're not quite in control of the decimal system."

Now, don't pick on the fact that it's the two thousandth anniversary, not the one thousandth . . . or the fact that "ten times tenth" only equals hundredth . . . or the nuances of whether Jesus *founded* the Christian religion. . . . My point in including this quote is only that quite a few people spent energy separating religion from Y2K, often thinking that eliminating the entanglements of religion would help bring the problem into more precise focus. I, on the other hand, embrace the entanglements of my religion, and have found myself rooting for those occasions during the past couple of years when religion wasn't given the boot from discussions of the Y2K problem.

During my involvement with the Y2K problem, I've seen a couple of things which many Christians will find disappointing. One is that some people are starting to refer to everything prior to the year 2000 as the "pre-Y2K" era, setting the stage for a fresh start at measuring time in the new millennium in a new way. There have been small stirrings of movements suggesting that we take this historical opportunity to start measuring time from Y2K instead of from Jesus' birth—as you know, most scholars now concur that A.D. time measurements are off by a few years from the exact year of Jesus' birth, but even if it's not perfectly accurate, surely most Christians think as I do, that it's a wonderful thing that throughout most of the world time is measured in relationship to the life of Christ our Lord. It would be a real adjustment for me, and not a very happy one, to see us adopt a different moment in world history from which to measure our years.

Another fascinating thing is the newly-built Millennium Dome in Greenwich, London, which is positioned to be a huge tourist destination throughout the year 2000. A focal point for the Dome's year-long celebration is its Hall of Faith. When I first heard that, my mind quickly projected my own concept of faith, and I walked around for a couple of days thinking how nice it was that Christianity was being linked to the millennium celebration in that way. I learned soon after, though, that through programs changing daily, the Hall of Faith's goal is to depict humankind's interaction with the religious experience through many world religions during the last 2,000 years. A spokesperson explained, "This emphasis on the totality of religions rather than on Christianity alone was largely a contribution of Britain's increasing Asian community." My excitement at learning of another opportunity for religion to be showcased in a secular setting tapered when I learned that the specific desire of the exhibits is to shift focus away from Christianity to include "the totality of religions"—again, one's perspective on things constantly shifts, and the year 2000 has given ample opportunity for me to watch shifting perspectives in action (even my own) and to watch Christian perspectives meet up with non-Christian ones, just as they do in the context of any other situation in life.

I admit that I don't always think Christian thoughts first when I'm evaluating things. I do evaluate using a Christian filter eventually, but don't always remember to do that first and foremost. So I don't know why I get surprised at all when non-believers make a concerted effort to push aside God in the thinking that such a move creates greater clarity. Even many believers often think of God later, or even last, when they're assessing a situation—but of course that's the very first filter we should apply to our thinking on any topic. As I explained in the introduction to this book, I don't feel Christians are at all constrained to a robotic adherence to one particular way of handling everything in life, but I do feel that the unity of thought that exists among Christians on the central tenets of faith will naturally inform our varying outlooks on life.

Plenty of room remains for disagreement within our agreement. For example, some Christian speakers and writers have expressed their fear that Y2K could give rise to the beast spoken of in Revelation 13. I've mentioned elsewhere in this book that I think that's extreme, and that the challenges of Y2K, while significant, aren't apocalyptic.

Some others at the opposite end of the scale didn't even focus on Y2K as the computer problem that it is, but instead used its moment in the spotlight as a platform to express other ideas. Here's a letter to the editor that appeared in *The NY Times*:

> **Y2K Bug? A Simple Fix** The doom and gloom you reported... concerning the millennium bug seemed to suggest that a 19th-century "wild West" approach is the best solution. I believe, however, that a simpler solution exists for the Year 2000, or Y2K, bug. I propose that by common consent, or through a declaration of the United Nations, we follow the lead of our computers and begin the 20th century over again on the day after Dec. 31, 1999. I hope that this time around, we can avoid the countless genocides, the Holocaust and two atomic bombings. Furthermore, it buys us another century in which to fix the millennium bug.
>
> THE REV. EARL KOOPERKAMP
NY, April 6, 1998

That's unrealistic and mostly tongue-in-cheek, but the writer made a bold statement that put additional food for thought on the national table. So, what's your perspective on his perspective? In fact, what's your perspective on any of the varying perspectives you see cited in this book or in other Y2K discussions going on around you lately? Go ahead and decide—and be ready to adjust your thinking again later if needed.

On Any Complex Topic, Different Perspectives Exist

Numerous types of people are following the Y2K problem closely: logicians, psychologists, economists, software developers, business people, stress management experts, problem resolution experts, disaster and recovery teams, and many others. It's a rare and special opportunity for all those sorts of people to learn things that apply to their respective fields. It's no wonder that there's been tremendous diversity in points of view about various issues.

First and foremost, you have the TEOTWAWKI set versus the not-TEOTWAWKI set. You've probably seen the acronym TEOTWAWKI in newspaper or magazine articles about Y2K; it means "The End Of The World As We Know It" and has been in common vernacular ever since the corresponding REM song was huge, but in the past few years has really found itself a permanent home in Internet chat rooms, where acronyms are favored over full words any day of the week. During Y2K discussions both online and in the "real world" there have been surprising numbers of people who feel that Y2K will be TEOTWAWKI and bring complete chaos, and a strong movement of those rising up to protest that it clearly won't be TEOTWAWKI and will be about as important as a car odometer reaching 100,000 miles.

A classic TEOTWAWKI attitude is visible in the words of the Y2K author who suggested, "65% of people might lose their jobs or have a salary reduction due to Y2K... and the unemployment rate might skyrocket from below 5% to above 50% in the space of a few months."

A classic "not TEOTWAWKI" attitude is shown by Bruce McConnell, director of the International Y2K Cooperation Center, who on September 1, 1999 said about the economic impact of Y2K, "For the most part, the fears are unfounded. I'm not saying there won't be problems, but the kind of problems will really be a blip."

The extent of preparation needed brings out its own battles. The American Red Cross and others call for preparations akin to those for a severe winter storm, but others argue that unlike a winter storm, Y2K is capable of striking everywhere in the world at once. As many countries have made great progress toward the end of 1999 and disclosure of preparedness status remains an ongoing event for most companies and government bodies, we've begun to get a more streamlined sense of the possible problem scenarios. The uncertainty factor has stayed in effect for every single locale in the world, but the level of problems one can honestly expect has become almost negligible in certain places while the level remains fairly high in certain other places.

Levels of cynicism about the Y2K information available from corporate and government sources have differed. John Westergaard of Westergaard Broadcasting Network has discussed a "collage" of information being put together that might prove misleading to people who don't examine issues carefully enough, warning against "accepting information at face value." Immediately, some contrary thinkers rebutted his view in various forums; Howard Belasco, for example, wrote an opinion piece for an online news service stating that Westergaard's perception was "based on ignorant although well-meaning intent" and saying "With this 'collage' it would be just as easy to prove that the earth is flat, that the holocaust never happened, and that the moon landings took place on a sound stage in Hollywood." Belasco urged people to believe that some items presented as fact truly are factual, or else we'd be unable to learn anything useful about worldwide progress on Y2K preparedness.

The next area of disagreement in perspective is deciding which particular systems are "critical" and which are "non-critical." These decisions are so particular to each organization that one company might decide some of its systems are non-critical without regard for the fact that those same systems are critical to some other company with which it shares data. Wherever two companies do business together but don't cooperate fully on their Y2K efforts, one of the companies can undermine the ability of the other company to carry on in the way it desires following M-Day, simply by having a different outlook about the order in which certain business systems deserve to be fixed.

The choices of comparisons have always been interesting. Some people say the Y2K problem is unlike anything we've ever seen before, and don't even try to compare Y2K to anything earlier in our history. Many people use a storm analogy or the analogy of a complicated building project (you'll see elsewhere in this book that whenever I'm not on a biblical bent, I'm big on home renovation metaphors), but way up at the other end of the spectrum a few people compare the Y2K problem to the Great Depression or even to the Holocaust. The latter's a tremendous stretch, but just the fact that they make such a comparison says something about how important they think Y2K is, and how hard they want to promote a sufficient amount of concern about the problem. All these different spins aren't just from casual citizens having private conversations. The entire gamut of comparisons from "I don't know what it'll be" to "it's gonna be just like Armageddon" have been made in public by the diverse crop of Y2K experts, in everything from books that became bestsellers to town council meetings to thousands of radio and TV interviews.

There have been those who feel that without hard currencies like gold and silver on hand after M-Day, you won't be able to buy groceries or anything else for a while until the economy recovers. More experts, however, have advised strongly against moving assets into gold or other precious metals, pointing out that even when paper dollars are beaten down, they're still among the best monetary assets you can have for use anywhere in this world. Gold (especially in coin form), on the other hand, has been a very poor investment in recent years, and the potential Y2K crisis up through Fall 1999 has done little to give hard currencies a boost. Jim Griffin, chief strategist for Aeltus Investment Management, wrote on **TheStreet.com** that the advice to invest in gold "has always struck me as having been derived from nine parts emotion and one part analysis. Gold hasn't been able to hold its value even against a loser such as oil has been during the 1990s."

The amount that should be spent on Y2K gets different perspectives. You've seen that willingness to spend has been a big factor in when (and how) businesses have tackled the problem. It has been an issue on the personal level, too. A surprisingly large number of people of all ages have cashed out their IRAs during 1999, feeling that paying a 10% penalty to have the security of the available cash was well worth it. Many financial advisors, though, find this heartbreaking, and say that wasting money to prepare for an epic disaster that might never arrive—whether through unnecessarily giving up 10% of retirement savings, or going into debt on credit cards to buy more food and supplies than are needed for your pantry—is a terrible thing to do, and can leave you in worse straits later than if some disaster had actually hit you. Y2K might not be within your control, they say, but stupid spending decisions are, and preparation for any disaster must be done with some fiscal responsibility.

Most of the banking industry, as discussed elsewhere in this book, has fought tooth and nail to get depositors to leave their money in bank accounts and not make large Y2K-related withdrawals, especially at the last minute. A sudden surge of withdrawal requests can destroy a previously stable bank, and a nationwide rush to liquefy the majority of assets held on deposit by financial institutions could lead to collapse of a system that was otherwise steady. You want sufficient liquidity to be able to cope with problems that arise, and to be able to take advantage of opportunities for service to others, investments in rebuilding any families or churches or businesses that you see weakened by Y2K problems, and that you feel you're meant to help—so that means having some money on hand. But bankers have for the most part urged people to use a great deal of restraint when considering how much cash to withdraw prior to M-Day. Even some bank industry reps, though, have been willing to respect the viewpoint of even the most nervous customers, while still urging them to be sensible. Brian Smith, director of policy and economic research at America's Community Bankers, said, "We'll tell customers not to do dumb things," and he suggested that if people insist on closing their accounts, they should at least put the money in a safe deposit box rather than carrying it home with them.

Some business people saw Y2K as a reason to worry about their business going under, because billing foul-ups alone could drive some small and mid-size companies out of business by destroying their cash flow. Other business people saw it as a grand opportunity. Michael Erbschloe, director of research at Computer Economics, said, "People see an opportunity to get a year or two ahead of competitors they think will have trouble with Y2K." Never forget that when some companies falter, other companies may thrive in response. Sometimes it's because they're direct competitors of the companies who have problems, and can step in and take over market share. Other times companies thrive in such a situation because they provide services that suddenly become much in demand due to whatever problems occur.

Many organizations and web sites, such as **wdcy2k.org**, have conducted surveys on people's concern about the Y2K problem. The results of any such survey, though, have to be weighed against what the person's point of view is on what constitutes the Y2K problem. If they respond with a level of concern that's 7 on a scale of 1-8 but they think it's only a problem with mainframe computers that will happen entirely on M-Day, they're not indicating that they think it will be as troublesome as someone who responds with a level of concern that's 7 on a scale of 1-8 and also realizes the broader potential for problems in embedded systems and with other dates like February 29, 2000 and so on. It has been very difficult to create surveys that gauge anybody's Y2K outlook precisely because of the complexity of Y2K issues.

One more comment on perspective: Sometimes we see things and don't even realize the implications of what we're seeing, and sometimes we're told about things that others see but we're slow ourselves to figure out that we agree with that viewpoint. My wife, Vicki, was seriously involved with another guy for years before she dated me, and everyone who knew them assumed they would get married someday. The whole time that she was his girlfriend, I saw both of them at parties and other events because we had several mutual acquaintances. One day her boyfriend saw a photograph that had been taken at a picnic, which showed Vicki and me standing together talking. "You two look really good together," he told her. "You probably ought to go out with him instead of me." I don't know if a touch of jealousy or tremendous insight made him say that, but it was laughed off at the moment—yet, three years later, when all of our perspectives about who belonged with whom had changed for many other reasons, Vicki and I were getting married and starting a lifetime of happiness together. I'll never forget that remark of his, though, and how far ahead of its time it was. None of us should ever bypass the chance to notice truth even in the perspective of those whose viewpoint we normally wouldn't think we'd benefit from paying attention to.

Now, let's take a look at a perfect example of how tricky the arena of Y2K information can be, because of people's different perspectives. Mitch Ratcliffe in July 1999 wrote this description of his view about Y2K: "It strikes, when it is visible, in non-critical ways." John Anderson, speaking on the Y2KNews radio show a few weeks later, said, "The only time people are told a Y2K problem has occurred is when it's something non-critical."

Notice that the exact same point was being made by both men, and it's valid: Most news of Y2K glitches so far has been about relatively trivial—often even whimsical—problems. It takes work to see that each made the same point, though, because of how each spun it to suit his own viewpoint. Ratcliffe, who believes Y2K problems will be few, far between, and of controllable consequence, introduced an element of all-encompassing certainty and reassurance into his statement. Anderson, who believes Y2K problems will be widespread and that companies and government agencies have refused to own up to the severity of the situation, introduced an element of cynicism and mistrust into his

THE MELEE OVER THE MILITARY REPORT

No situation exposes the differences in Y2K perspectives better than the episode involving a US military report in August 1999. The report received lots of attention when it was summarized on a web site run by Jim Lord, a Y2K author in the camp that predicts more wide-ranging problems than the average expert. The report, though, really made people sit up and take notice. Put together from information from Navy and Marine Corps base commanders worldwide, it predicted widespread "probable" or "likely" failures in key power and water systems for a number of US cities due to Y2K problems; it presented a far more negative outlook than the White House ever had presented to the public. The cities with probable utility outages, according to the report, included Orlando, FL (electric); Dallas, TX (water); Nashville, TN (water), Columbus, OH (natural gas), and a few dozen other cities. The White House had released its own report a few weeks earlier saying that electrical utility failures would be "highly unlikely."

John Koskinen, head of the President's Y2K Council, moved in quickly to refute the report and declared its conclusions overly pessimistic, saying that the military was assuming major utilities would fail unless proved otherwise, and that the worst-case scenario in the report would only exist until more information could be gathered and better contingency plans could be put in place in all those cities.

Sure, Lord replied, but don't we all need to assume utilities will fail unless proved otherwise? He immediately fired back a volley through the national media, saying, "The military has to work from the worst case, but so do we. It's reprehensible for them to know this and keep it from us."

Koskinen defined the lines between the camps of perspectives strongly by saying to journalists about the report, "It's not nearly as interesting as the world coming to an end." (Remember that bringing up TEOTWAWKI is a tactic that has been used repeatedly by anyone who wants to further the idea that those in the doomsaying camp are extremists near the lunatic fringe.) Koskinen denied that the information had been withheld from anyone, noting that the report had been available on a Defense Department web site as recently as a couple of weeks before Lord released it to a broader audience on his web site.

statement. What started out as the exact same point ended up being made in two completely different ways. These sorts of distinctions in the way different people presented the same exact information about Y2K have made for amazing discrepancies in average people's opinions about what the Y2K problem amounts to, and whether there's any need for concern and action.

Indeed, as hard as I try to present objective information about the Y2K problem in this book, it's all reflective of my outlook on the whole matter, a decidedly Christian outlook (which clearly I have no desire to downplay—just look at the title of this book) but hopefully one that's as objective as possible about what's certain and what's uncertain about Y2K. You mustn't forget that your perspective as a consumer of information is always informed by the angles, textures, and nuances of material that comes from others, which you take in and assimilate with your own thinking. Don't let the clang and clatter of differing perspectives prevent you from distilling all the information, drawing your own conclusions, and taking advantage of this moment of rare opportunity to learn many great things.

Y2K Work Brought Some Particular New Perspectives

We've seen quite a few unique changes in perspective completely based on the Y2K problem. When Kathleen Adams, who led the Social Security Administration's impressive Y2K project for a number of years, was moving to a new job, a reporter asked her what Y2K has taught us, and among the things she listed, she cited these shifts in perspective:

- We always tend to think of programming and IT as being very creative, and it should be, but the application of it should be more methodical and disciplined.
- Y2K has really made people realize the extent to which we depend on automated systems and computers to do business.
- It has brought the Chief Information Officer (CIO) more to the table in a number of corporations and governmental agencies.

Many others agreed with her that Y2K can give a boost to the importance of techies in the corporate world. CNN quoted Anthony Paoni, an IT professor at Northwestern University, as saying, "We're going to have a huge wake-up call at the year 2000. CEOs are suddenly going to move their CIOs to the strategy table. I think it will really accelerate the growth of technology."

Even everyday words have experienced a shift in perspective. There has arisen the use of a new term, "date dumb," with very positive implications during Y2K remediation work, because it means that a system isn't aware of the date and therefore won't have any problems functioning when M-Day arrives. This entire crisis has been one of the first times that large quantities of people have publicly acknowledged that in some situations, being "dumb" or underequipped in certain ways can be an advantage.

The simplicity that comes with being behind the times has been praised by many in the context of Y2K. Andrew Eristoff, chair of the New York City Council's task force on technology in government, happily pointed out that the city's systems were somewhat antiquated, which meant the city might have less to worry about than many companies in the private sector. In his words, "Government, being not at the technological vanguard, stands to benefit."

This applies on a much bigger scale than you might imagine. Entire countries that are behind in terms of acquiring technology actually have had much less to worry about regarding potential Y2K distress than those countries which have been on the cutting edge of technological advances for the past couple of decades. Japanese nuclear plants, for instance, had been highly thought of for being run on completely digital systems, as opposed to many countries where manual systems (or hybrid systems that are part manual and part digital) still exist. Well, as you might imagine, that envy turned to pity rapidly during Y2K studies, as everyone realized the Japanese nuclear plants not only required more complicated Y2K assessment programs than older nuclear plants in other countries, but also did not allow officials to do any contingency planning involving reverting to the use of manual systems in the event of a computer-related mishap.

LESSON 34: THE BENEFITS OF SIMPLICITY

We have so much extravagance, we could stand some simplicity. Look at the size and complexity of most newly constructed houses. Think about the options on your latest automobile; you certainly don't need all of those features to drive from point A to point B. Even modern camping is full of comfort items that people have come to rely upon.

You know what an overdone world we've become in some ways. The travel industry originally hoped M-Eve would be the biggest party in the history of the world. The extravagance of millennium hotel packages reflects that expectation. Millennium reservations usually require minimum stays of three to six nights at rates much higher than usual. Numerous and unusual extra touches are often included. Many Ritz-Carlton hotels, for example, are offering one couple per hotel the "Millennium Experience" for $100,000 for a three-day stay, including such amenities as chef, housekeeper, masseur, butler, chauffeured Mercedes-Benz during the stay, keepsake diamond wristwatches, commemorative photo album, and more. Entire hotels (staff included) are for rent from December 31, 1999 through January 2, 2000. $3 million gets the 627-room Millennium Broadway in Times Square, a mere $1.5 million gets the 155-room Fitzpatrick Grand Central, and the 92-room Fitzpatrick Manhattan is practically a steal at $1 million.

New Year's Eve for 2000 seems more a competition than a celebration. Kiribati, a very small island nation in the Pacific Ocean, officially changed its time zone just so that it can arrive at New Year's 2000 before its neighboring islands.

Capitalizing on Greenwich, London being home to the Prime Meridian Line (the exact point from which time is measured), the British Tourist Authority is luring tourists to the country. New Year's Eve plans include a fireworks show to end all shows, then the Thames River will be "engulfed in flames," an optical illusion created with 2,000 pyrotechnic devices.

For those who like to celebrate in more reflective ways, many churches and cathedrals are hosting prayer programs or full services on New Year's Eve. And for the traveler who's truly averse to celebrating, the Four Seasons Hotel in London is offering one suite that allows its residents to block out all partying on that night—for New Year's Eve, it will have soundproofing, blacked-out windows, and all clocks and calendars will be removed.

Columnist Frank Rich comments that he's not sure anyone can escape the festivities for 2000, and look what he says he's willing to use as an escape tool: "What New Year's Eve activity could possibly offer enough fun to usher in 2000? ... The mob demands we be festive, or else.... Given the dire alternatives, those of us who dread millennial New Year's Eve are left with little choice but to root for apocalypse now."

Do we need all this action in our lives, and all this fancy stuff? Of course not. Y2K preparations have taught us in general exactly how minimal our needs really are. One gallon of water per person per day is all it takes to survive. Bathing used to be a weekly event. As scandalous an idea as it is to our modern minds, we all actually could stay healthy without a daily shower and shampoo. Of course, people used to reuse bath water (and toothbrushes and all sorts of other things) for person after person, too—we don't necessarily ever want to step that far back in our thinking.

The *Y2K Family Survival Guide* commented, "Much of what we are calling an emergency situation is really more a circumstance creating discomfort than threatening a life. In many areas of the world these unfortunate and uncomfortable conditions are part of the daily routine. We late 20th-century Americans have become spoiled with luxuries and have begun to think of telephones and televisions as 'necessities.' We not only want our MTV, we expect it. Our grandparents and great-grandparents certainly didn't enjoy the lifestyles most of us do these days, yet they survived very well. You can too."

Plenty of people craved simplicity amid the cumbersome complications of Y2K issues. You saw in Chapter 2 that the Lord helps us when we're in distress, and here's one of the specific ways that he helps:

> *Psalm 118:5* In my anguish I cried to the Lord, and he answered by setting me free.

And here's a verse asserting the same idea:

> *2 Corinthians 3:17* Now the Lord is the Spirit, and where the Spirit of the Lord is, there is freedom.

God can set a person free. What kinds of freedom does he provide? There are many: freedom from stuff, freedom from sin, freedom from troubles, freedom from bad influences (thus freedom from Satan), and ultimately freedom from death. Y2K has been a great chance to at least think a little about freedom from stuff.

A lot of folks have embraced Y2K as a chance to break free of the conspicuous consumption and ambition that society has tended to focus on for decades now, and instead work on a frugal, simple, constructive lifestyle that still has everything it needs, but doesn't have everything it greeds. Some people even picture that if Y2K causes significant problems, we'll see a quick return to food-growing cooperatives and neighbors helping neighbors and windmill-powered grain production and so on. The way they look at the equation, no electricity might equal fewer distractions which in turn might equal more time to spend with loved ones and friends. The long-lost feeling of community might be back again.

Rev. Steve Wilkins of Monroe, LA has bought a water purifier and a mill for grinding flour; he's been advising his Presbyterian congregation since mid-1998 to reduce their debt, plant a vegetable garden, and do other activities to prepare for a lifestyle that will work in the event of significant Y2K problems. His church in Monroe has produced a 90-minute Y2K survival video urging people to, among other things, buy non-electric hand tools and obtain emergency medicine to keep on hand. Hundreds of the videos have been sold.

Y2K has helped boost sales 40 percent during 1998 and even more during 1999 for Emergency Essentials, a distributor of emergency supplies packed in gallon-size cans that don't rust. Alternative energy items like solar panels have been selling well, too, according to several companies that carry those products.

Lots of people are taken at least to some extent with the notion that we might be forced to return to a simpler lifestyle one of these days for one reason or another. Best-selling author Tom Wolfe during a 1999 interview discussed teaching his son to hunt, saying, "The day will come, inevitably, maybe it's the Y2K, when only the grandmothers will have the skills to deal with life on another basis: no computers, hunting for food. It's not going to happen anytime soon, but it could happen. What if two weeks from now the food supplies were all cut off? People are throwing their hands in the air, saying: 'This can't happen! Where's my congressman?' And it turns out he's out in the woods somewhere."

I'm certainly not going to root for Y2K problems to occur, but in the meantime I'm appreciative of whatever benefits the whole mixed-up situation has had in terms of getting people to slow down and take a good look around and decide what's important, and simplify so that those essentials are taken care of in their lives.

Many families have practiced for Y2K problems by staging a "Y2K Practice Day" during which they don't use anything that might have an outage due to a Y2K-related problem. That means no electricity (no TV), no water (no flushing toilets), and no natural gas (no cooking on the range), as well as no trips to the store, no filling up the vehicle's gas tank, and no phone calls to pass the time with far-away friends. News or entertainment could only come through a battery-powered or self-powered (wind-up) radio. Some people limited the exercise and allowed themselves a few comforts, like continuing to run the refrigerator, while others did it all the way by taking all their spoilable food to a neighbor's or relative's house and then depowering their own refrigerator along with all the other appliances in their home.

I think about the people who have packed up and headed for the wilderness and I hope that even if they didn't need to head out there (as most people suspect they don't), they'll benefit from the experience and that the time will be exceptionally good quality time as they're alone with God and their thoughts and the wonders of nature. Remember that the Israelites, John the Baptist, and Jesus himself spent time in remote areas, sometimes by choice and sometimes not. Isolation from the mainstream world can yield tremendous personal growth and change. I don't know anybody who believes in God who can take a good look around when they're spending time in a rural setting, taking a walk in the woods, sitting near a secluded lake, or living off the land to some extent, and not feel moved by God's wondrous handiwork.

Likewise, I hope everyone who has been practicing a simpler life in case it's necessary to survive without resources after M-Day really gains many things from the experience: confirmation of the fact that materialism is not all it's cracked up to be, self-confidence and belief in their ability to make do in trying circumstances, and so on.

Even the small taste of simpler times that has been available through Y2K preparations has been more than welcome in many homes. The presence of camping items in our home for Y2K intrigued my wife enough that she agreed to go camping with me for the first time in over ten years of dating and marriage. A stay-at-home mom recently told me how happy she was that she was able to use their family's preparations for Y2K as a chance to teach her children to bake bread and make candles, things she had enjoyed learning from her own mom thirty years ago, but that had seemed completely unnecessary in the lives of her own children until Y2K concerns arose. This could be beneficial for many families—canning and drying your own foods and similar tasks can be fun, and more importantly, tasks of this sort require many hands and significant chunks of time spent working together. Regardless of whether or not those "throwback" skills prove necessary, many people will have shared warm moments together doing teamwork activities that they otherwise might never have gotten a chance to do.

By the way, since so many people have decided to stay home for New Year's Eve 2000, those elaborate (and expensive) cruises, hotel packages, and so on haven't been selling anywhere nearly as well as the companies organizing the events had originally believed they would. As this book goes to print, there are many last-minute specials available, offering the very same packages for discounts of as much as 80% off the original prices from 12 or 18 months ago. If anybody wants to participate in one of these grand celebrations, it's downright cheap to do so now, because certain companies highly overestimated the demand. I won't be surprised, though, if the huge majority of people in the entire world want to do nothing more on New Year's Eve leading into 2000 than be with as many people they know and enjoy as possible, sharing this once-in-a-lifetime moment without tons of hoopla and hysteria.

Lesson 35: Embracing Complexity of Thought

At the same time as I speak of the importance of simplicity of lifestyle, I feel we shouldn't be scared of complexity of thought—it's essential, in fact. Dr. Frank Bonn, one of my political science professors many years ago, warned wisely of the ongoing shift toward what he called a "bumper sticker mentality" in which most ideas, no matter how important, are reduced to the lowest common denominator and given an easily remembered handle for widespread distribution at the grassroots level. A beneficial aspect of this is that it's easier than ever to achieve broad following for an idea; the downside is that many adherents who are drawn to an idea in its bumper-sticker version won't bother to learn enough about the details of what they're touting. I see this happening in Christianity often these days. The most glaring example is the spread of WWJD paraphernalia, which though based on a concept in a hundred-year-old book, really peaked during 1999 and became so ubiquitous that even a number of secular youth were buying and wearing WWJD stuff just because it was "the bomb" without knowing (or at least without adhering to) the dynamic power that underlies the acronym. It's unavoidable that in our fast-paced, sound-byte society people often find it easier to latch onto a simplistic, reduced version of most major ideas that are floating around in the world.

In some ways, I really like what items like the fish symbol and the WWJD accessories and similar iconizations of Christianity are doing in terms of helping believers proudly display their conviction. I hope two things, though: first, that we all work hard to make sure that all the "quickie" expressions of Christianity which become popular are clear, accurate, purposeful, and truly reflective of the essence of what it means to be a Christian; and second, that everyone who feels an initial or heightened attraction to the Good News through a simplified bumper-sticker version will eventually be inspired to pursue increased information and will delight in acquiring enough details to be an ever-maturing Christian.

Nearly every book on Y2K that had a predictive bent used fictionalized scenarios to speculate about what life might be like following M-Day. Most of the authors felt we needed to connect abstractions such as the Y2K problem directly to our everyday lives in order to understand the concepts. Jesus realized that God's grace and complex relationship with us are also abstractions that might not be understood without stories. That's why we find the gospels full of parables and word pictures. While those are a gateway to understanding and are easy to remember, let us never forget that it's the underlying principles that matter, and we shouldn't get caught up in the "easy" version of Y2K issues or of Christianity. Sure, you should latch onto the handles that allow quick passage into God's courtyard, but don't forget to knock at some of the important doors of his kingdom which have neither a simple handle nor any attractive bells and whistles.

People outside of computing seemed to expect a whiz kid to come along and provide a one-size-fits-all-systems software solution that would zip through various computer systems and solve the problem—that desire showed a complete lack of understanding of the complexity of the problem. The challenge doesn't lie in a single focused setting, but is distributed worldwide in billions of individual systems. People's desire for a silver bullet fix, though, is typical of our tendency in recent times to think that there's an easy, technologically-advanced solution to everything. We expect to cure cancers, we aren't as bothered as we should be about the ecological damage we do because we trust ourselves to come up with ways to manipulate the environment back into balance. We think we'll have at least a hundred years warning before any significant asteroid with tremendous destructive power comes close enough to strike the earth. We know that global warming is en route to making it impossible to live on the planet, but polls show that the average person is convinced we'll find ways to avert the problem. For problems such as those, hopefully we'll get started in a more timely manner and make a more concerted effort to fend off potential disaster than we did as a world for the Y2K computer problem. We need to remember that we're not smarter than everything, despite the fact that we sometimes achieve such scientific advances that we start to think so.

Many people with Macintosh computers mistakenly thought that they were completely in the clear concerning the Y2K problem. Derek Rowan, president of a computer consulting firm, wrote in a column in *The Alexandria Journal*, "Do *not assume* you are compliant just because you have a Mac! The hardware may be, but your application software and the *data you put in* may not!" It's true that the oldest Mac hardware and OS were able to deal with dates from Jan. 1, 1904 to Feb. 6, 2040, and Macs running System 6 or later can handle dates from earlier than 30,000 B.C. up to 29,940 A.D., but Mac software isn't Y2K-proof, and users still have needed to inspect their applications and seek information on Y2K compliance from software manufacturers.

> ### Note
> For anyone interested, the October 1999 issue of *MacWorld* contained a great article and two sidebars on Y2K, outlining a good testing procedure for Macs and detailing possible problems with various Mac software.

Even seemingly simple topics can house more complexity than we usually pay attention to. Through the Y2K problem, many of us learned for the first time the differences in types of seeds. Hybrid seeds (the type sold in most retail stores) grow well, but can be sterile. Non-hybrid seeds, which don't run the same risk of not germinating, were favored by the majority of people who decided to stockpile seeds as part of their preparations for Y2K. Dave Smith of Seeds of Change in Santa Fe, NM, which sells non-hybrid seeds, says that as Y2K awareness grew, his company started "getting calls about bulk seeds and buying in quantities and packing them for storage for some period of time."

We also focused for the first time on the differences between types of water. There's the obvious distinction between drinkable and non-drinkable water, and most people quickly learned to add a few drops of bleach per gallon to tap water they wanted to store so that it would remain safe for drinking. We also were introduced to various classifications of the water that wasn't fit for drinking. "Gray water," for example, is post-bathing water or untreated rainwater that in a non-crisis situation most of us typically throw away. In the context of considering how life would be during Y2K problems or any other crisis, we started to think of this gray water as extremely useful—it can be used to water a garden or do any of a number of other tasks that we typically use fresh, clean water to do in untroubled times when there's an "endless" supply of clean water.

In every aspect of life, a time of crisis can make us start thinking in more complicated ways about topics we usually gloss over or about which we usually settle for simple conclusions.

LESSON 36: THE ONLY LIMITATION IS YOUR OWN FAITHFUL EXPECTATION

In view of some of the splashy New Year's Eve celebrations being planned and in view of the horribly complicated Y2K remediation projects some people have had to go through, I've learned to delight in my own simplicity and smallness. Don't ever confuse smallness and limitation, though. Even in smallness, there's often great opportunity—in some of the Y2K consulting I've done, and while working on this book, I've seen great things arise from situations that seem frustrating and limiting at first. I therefore want to spend one of these lessons quickly looking at limitations versus possibilities.

You probably know the story of the feeding of the five thousand. Read John 6:5-13 to refresh your memory, giving special attention to the dialogue exchanged between Jesus and his disciples about feeding the crowd. In any situation which at first seems to demand more than what you have, don't misjudge your own smallness and ability to rise to the challenge. Don't be like Philip, who saw only limitations, but instead be like Andrew, who at least brought the small amount of available food to Jesus' attention, asking if anything could be done with it. With whatever fishes and loaves you find available, enter into a partnership with Jesus. We all can conquer our challenges as the disciples conquered theirs.

Remember what Jesus told the disciples after they had failed to heal a demon-possessed boy on their own (Matthew 17:20): "... if you have faith as small as a mustard seed, you can say to this mountain, 'Move from here to there' and it will move. Nothing will be impossible for you." In other words, through faith everything moves from being a possibility only for God to being our own possibility! Chapter 2 discussed the concept of faith in greater detail. There are plenty of additional verses that focus on the boundless possibilities of God:

> *Luke 18:27* Jesus replied, "What is impossible with men is possible with God."

> **RELATED VERSE:**
> MARK 10:27
> LUKE 1:37

Let's review one of the few occasions when Jesus seemed to bristle a little at someone's doubt:

> *Mark 9:23-24* "'If you can?'" said Jesus. "Everything is possible for him who believes." Immediately the boy's father exclaimed, "I do believe, help me overcome my unbelief!"

The scene was the healing of a boy possessed by an evil spirit. The boy's father had just said to Jesus, "If you can do anything, take pity on us and help us." This is one of my favorite exchanges in the entire Bible. Jesus could have been angry at the man's disbelief, but my sense of the situation is that Jesus was rather bemused, and sort of cocked his head and repeated the guy's words back to him: "'If you can'?" It must have vexed Jesus that anyone could question his capabilities. But he didn't only mock or criticize the man. With Jesus' following breath, he instantly gave the man encouragement and a path to a solution. "Everything is possible for him who believes," Jesus told him—faith produces possibilities!

What believer today can't relate to this situation? The boy's father is representative of so many of us in our moments of confusion, anxiety, distress—we *do* believe, but we still need some help overcoming the encroaching disbelief which creeps in on wicked little feet and nibbles away at our sense of assurance. Fortunately, we have Jesus with us at all times, and should catch ourselves every time we are tempted to doubt, and picture Jesus giving us a stunned look and asking us, "What do you mean, 'If you can'?"

Now, here's another brief verse that talks about what Jesus was able (and willing) to do:

> Matthew 26:39 Going a little farther, he fell with his face to the ground and prayed, "My father, if it is possible, may this cup be taken from me. Yet not as I will, but as you will."

The place is Gethsemane, and the time is just before Judas Iscariot betrays Jesus into the hands of those who will crucify him. Jesus has a group of disciples with him, but he leaves most of them at one spot and goes a little farther with just his inner circle of closest followers—Peter, James, and John. Then, Jesus leaves even those three and goes a little farther down the path so that he can converse with God alone. What Jesus says is that he doesn't necessarily want to have to go through the pain and death that await him—if it's possible, he suggests, maybe the cup can be taken from him without him having to drink it. Jesus wonders, just for that moment, *Isn't there any other way?* But there isn't any other way, and the little bit farther Jesus went at Gethsemane to have that talk with his Father is nothing compared to what he willingly went through afterward. Realizing that the cup could not be taken from him, Jesus allowed Judas to deliver him into the enemies' hands.

It's important to remember that although we have limitations, Jesus doesn't. Jesus went farther than anyone could have expected him to, and did more than those around him could envision he would. With everything he did, he went farther than Jewish law or ceremonial religion, farther than personal self-importance, farther than any human could contemplate going, and farther than most people's compassion and love today seems willing to go. Let's strive to recognize opportunities where we can go farther than our initial expectations for ourselves; the Y2K problem might provide many such opportunities. If we sometimes need to go farther down the path, as Jesus did, and spend time with God determining what our role must be, that's okay. But then let's go farther by taking the actions that we must take.

Lesson 37: The Deeper They're Embedded, the More They're Dreaded

Here is the first thing that hurt most people's brains about the Y2K problem: Most computer chips are not in computers. Sets of chips—or even a single chip at a time that can do one or several preprogrammed tasks—have been used to provide functionality to an amazingly wide range of products. These chips are called embedded microprocessors or embedded microcomponents, and there are billions of them worldwide. Nobody knows exactly how many there are, but estimates range from 100 billion to over 700 billion, with most experts agreeing that the US is home to about 20% of them.

Several billion new microprocessors per year are used in embedded systems—for the sake of comparison, only about 2% of that quantity of microprocessors is placed in personal computers each year. When you say computer chip, though, the average person thinks of the ones that are actually in computers. Some of the reasons the chips inside of computers get more public attention are:

- They have names like Pentium II or Athlon that consumers can latch onto. If manufacturers could convince you to buy other products based on a preference for the particular microchip that's inside, you'd start seeing those names splashed all over advertisements (a few manufacturers *have* tried to build name recognition for chips embedded in their microwave ovens and washing machines, but haven't been as successful yet as PC manufacturers).

- They are centrally defining components in a computer, and are used as the necessary basis for comparison during purchase decisions. While few people wrangle over the details of processing capability of the new electronic xylophone they're thinking about buying their toddler, most consumers do consider processor speed, caching capability, and so on when they're thinking about buying a computer, which means they need to pay attention to the particular chip inside the box.

- The cost of the chips used in computers is tremendously higher than the cost of most embedded chips involved here, there, and everywhere throughout our lives. The ones in computers cost hundreds of times more than, for instance, the ones that control keyless remote entry systems on vehicles. (Speaking of vehicles, the average new car for the model year 2000 has about 15 computer chips in it, while luxury vehicles have as many as 75 or more, doing things such as adjusting the speed of windshield wipers based on the strength of the rain or adjusting radio volume whenever the speed of the car changes and engine noise goes up or down. Notice that hardly any of these things are date-related, so Y2K has never been much of a concern for vehicle owners, no matter how fancy the cars.)

Embedded chips by the billions are quietly, cheaply, humbly doing many things that most of us barely notice.

An engineer in IBM's Advanced Computing Systems Division in 1968 was discussing the development of the microchip; while acknowledging that it could work, he added, "But what . . . is it good for?" Little could he imagine the types of jobs they'd eventually do. They're most often used in industrial settings, but here's just a sampling of the ways they're used:

- In automobiles for tasks such as fuel mixing, airbag deployment, and anti-lock brakes
- In many types of medical equipment
- In newer automatic toilets
- In sprinkler systems
- In systems that control factory operations
- In many new toys and stuffed animals (chips are how Furby gets his attitude problem, and how Tickle Me Elmo knows whether it's time to giggle or shake)
- In various systems throughout the space shuttle and other scientific endeavors

They're used in millions of other places, from auto-focus cameras to VCRs to many major home appliances sold today. Only 1% to 2% of all these chips might malfunction due to Y2K-related problems, but even that small percentage could be billions of faulty chips, and you can't tell which ones will fail without checking every one of them. Prior to Y2K awareness, very few manufacturers kept great records on the brands or production dates of chips they used in their products, and chips used in a single manufacturing run might have been purchased from several different chip makers.

Are there any Y2K concerns lurking in your own backyard because of embedded systems? Possibly. A Congressional report in September 1999 said, "There are Y2K vulnerabilities in traffic signal systems," and cited Chicago, Columbus, Detroit, and San Jose as four of the largest examples of cities that didn't have their traffic signals ready (based on data from a mid-1999 survey of Y2K readiness in the 21 largest US cities done by the General Accounting Office). The report also cited a GAO survey in August 1999 which found that only half of the largest cities' subway and rail systems were ready for Y2K. Transportation Secretary Rodney Slater issued a statement in September 1999 that preparing for Y2K safety was the US government's top priority, and the DOT published some travel tips regarding Y2K concerns. The advice was basic: "At a non-working traffic light...most states require a four-way stop" and "Stop, look, and listen at all rail crossings. Always expect a train." Most Y2K watchers have interpreted this to be an acknowledgment of the likelihood that many localities will not manage to ferret out and test all their embedded systems prior to M-Day.

In many cases (especially industrial or civil engineering situations), the location of hidden chips wasn't exactly known prior to Y2K assessment, and some of the ones with known locations were in places that made them very difficult to retrieve, test, and replace. Chips built into huge tanks, now filled with stuff. Chips built into massive drawbridges and other structures. A lot of Y2K teams have had to go to great lengths to locate and work on these embedded systems, and it makes for slow going, which of course is bad because time has been of the essence for Y2K remediation efforts.

The scope of some of the Y2K concerns that have had to be dealt with—or at least looked into—is almost unfathomable. A Boeing spokesperson told the press that while older Boeing planes have only a few microprocessors, a more recent Boeing jet, the 777, has more than 1,000 processors in it. Most of them are what we'd all agree are non-critical, making telephone service and entertainment options available at each passenger seat. Some, though, aren't quite as frivolous: on these new planes, digital signals are sent through wires to microprocessors which then activate local hydraulic systems to control the flaps and rudders, rather than the older system of cables and hydraulic systems throughout the whole plane. This newer fly-by-wire system doesn't involve dates, but the very fact that it involves embedded chips meant that it had to be looked into, and the same sort of requirement to at least investigate billions of embedded systems has made Y2K projects around the world extremely complicated and cumbersome for the people doing the work.

The embedded-chip aspect of the Y2K problem has concerned the US government. In March 1998, Representative Stephen Horn said that "uncounted millions of embedded computer chips" would eventually need to be fixed. By way of example, he noted that the Department of Defense alone has 600,000 computer chips in various equipment items, many of which are date-aware. The embedded-chip aspect also has stunned many companies. International Paper ended up doubling its cost estimate for Y2K repairs (an increase of around $60 million) once it zeroed in on electronic controls in its mills that were at risk. At PSE&G, New Jersey's largest utility, Y2K workers scoured 250 locations (substations, power plants, and offices) searching for hidden chips. That took about a year. Then they realized they had not inspected a reservoir that releases water into the Delaware River for environmental reasons. It turned out that a device is used to check creepage at the reservoir's dam, and that device contained a processor which needed to be fixed. At the bottom of the dam they found a control system that monitors how much water is released. You guessed it—that also wasn't Y2K-compliant, and required some work.

Those experiences are quite typical of how Y2K work on embedded chips has gone. In some regards it's a giant, frustrating scavenger hunt with nobody on earth possessing a complete list of exactly what's hidden where. Normally we never even realize many embedded chips are there, and it's easy to overlook them. This is how Christianity works, too—when someone wants to convert to Christianity, they think right away of major areas in their life that need correction. But there are many tiny things hidden deep inside a person that it's easy to forget are also in need of correction until either A) a complete and thorough period of self-examination takes place and uncovers these faulty parts of the person, or B) an external situation arises that causes the person to act in a way that exposes the faulty parts and some of the potentially bad consequences.

LESSON 38: MORE AND DIFFERENT PROBLEMS ARE EVERYWHERE

You've already learned in this book how the Y2K problem is both software-related (programming code) and hardware-related (embedded systems), and have seen that the quirks of individual programmers and several other factors add to the complexity of the original software problem. The complexity of working through Y2K issues doesn't end there by any means.

The problem definitely was not restricted to just mainframes and languages like COBOL. The programming community originally put this problem knowingly into software written in only a few languages that could have been corrected line by line fairly easily. Eventually, though, the repair work amounted to billions of lines. Then people willingly moved the problem inside smaller and more complicated boxes by bringing it into the world of PCs and PC networks, including desktop applications and server hardware components. Then they moved the problem into even smaller, more complicated places by increased use of Y2K-vulnerable embedded chips. After all that negligence, people finally tried to eradicate the problem, a challenge much like trying to fight cancer after allowing it to affect all of the body's systems, even the most difficult to reach and most fragile spots.

EVERYTHING ABOUT Y2K WAS MUCH MORE COMPLICATED THAN FIRST THOUGHT

Chapter 6 discusses some situations in which Y2K testing and remediation efforts have caused some results that in themselves are a problem. Sometimes the Y2K testing has gone well, but still served as a real eye-opener to how the unexpected can occur, and how the situation is more complex than the people doing the testing originally thought. One power company had a plan for remediating several nuclear power plants—they would get things completely fixed at one plant, then use it as a model for how to fix the others. They finished up what they thought was a complete remediation effort on the first power plant, then shut off its nuclear capabilities and ran a live test. Lo and behold, an unexpected shutdown occurred. The cause was determined to be some noncompliant sensors they hadn't identified during their whole Y2K study and identification process.

Organizations have needed not only to face the physical task of assessment and repair, but also to come up with initiatives to minimize risks of problems occurring and devise contingency plans for dealing with anything that does go wrong. Many Y2K teams, overwhelmed by the complexity, have switched from talking about "Y2K compliance" to talking about merely achieving a state of "Y2K readiness." In general, this means that the goal has moved from full correction to simply doing essential repairs and putting contingency plans in place to make up for any remaining noncompliance; the definition of Y2K readiness, however, differs for particular industries and organizations.

It's a mistake to think that everything will go wrong on M-Day alone, because in reality an extended failure curve exists, which began several years ago and should continue well beyond M-Day. Some failures won't be obvious until the end of January, the first time after M-Day that consumers review monthly bank statements or similar paperwork. Problems might pop up well after M-Day, possibly as late as ten or more years into the new millennium, when rarely-used systems are used for the first time or when cascading problems are eventually noticed.

Additional Problems and Danger Dates That Cried Wolf

Y2K problems could involve computers freezing completely, or could involve them creating and passing along faulty information. A third possibility, perhaps the most insidious, is that they could create problems (for example, with stored data) that will go unnoticed for years or decades, until the next time that the particular data is accessed to do a very infrequent task. At that point, if people aren't paying attention, the corrupted data might have such subtle problems that nobody notices anything is wrong—and if it's far enough in the future, it's very likely that even if a problem is noticed, it might not be correctly attributed to a Y2K problem, which might delay or prevent it being resolved.

A number of dates besides M-Day were identified as having the potential for Y2K problems to arise. Here's a quick rundown:

- March 31, 1999: Deadline for federal agencies to be Y2K-ready on mission-critical systems. Nearly half of the agencies didn't make it and neither did the White House.
- April 1, 1999: Fiscal year began for NY state and countries like Japan and Canada
- April 6, 1999: Fiscal year began for Great Britain

- April 9, 1999: A "9999" date, explained later in the chapter
- July 1, 1999: Fiscal year began for 46 US state governments and many corporations
- August 22, 1999: GPS satellite network rollover occurred (explained later)
- September 9, 1999: Another "9999" date
- October 1, 1999: US federal fiscal year began
- February 29, 2000: The leap year that many programmers neglected to treat as a leap year (explained later)

Different Clock Problems That Y2K Has Put in the Spotlight

A number of computer problems have gotten significant attention because of the Y2K problem, which makes us take a good hard look at how prone to pervasive errors the entire computer arena can be. These may pile additional irritating burdens atop any Y2K problems that occur.

Leap Year 2000

The year 2000 does not match up with the simplest mathematical formula for determining leap years, and not every programmer was aware of that. Therefore many software programs in use now have an incorrect method for handling certain leap years. Because 2000 is divisible by 400, there will be a Feb. 29 in the year 2000 even though there was not one in 1700, 1800, or 1900. Programs with the leap year 2000 bug will assign wrong dates every day after Feb. 28, 2000.

> *Note*
>
> You're confused about the leap year rule, huh? The short version we all learn is that they come along once every four years to make up for the extra one-quarter day the earth takes to travel around the sun each year. When Pope Gregory XIII established the Gregorian calendar, his rules actually were a bit more involved: Leap years do not occur in years ending in 00, unless that year is evenly divisible by 400. Many programmers have handled this wrong, and since 2000 is the first year in the computer age that this will be an issue, their code is in need of Y2K remediation along with all the two-digit problems.

The Nines Problem

April 9, 1999 was the 99th day of the year, and because certain programmers used a string consisting entirely of the number 9 to represent an upper-limit date to signify the end of input or to terminate procedures, some people feared the date might be stored in some places as a count of the number of days since the first of the year, so that April 9, 1999 would be read in some places as 9999, the terminating string, thereby causing processing errors.

September 9, 1999 as the ninth day of the ninth month is stored as the string 9999 by some programs, so some people felt it could cause the same sorts of problems just described. These problems would only result from extremely sloppy programming, and for the most part were few and far between, although there were limited reports of Nines problems within certain systems.

GPS Rollover

The atomic clocks inside Global Positioning System (GPS) satellites rolled over to zero in late August 1999 because the system was designed to count time in weeks and seconds beginning on Jan. 6, 1980 for 1,024 weeks. At that point, the internal clocks of the satellites making up the system returned to 0. Sticking to such a simple 1,024-week calendar allows the satellites to communicate very quickly, but also made the August rollover necessary, and will require future rollovers as well.

The GPS is a network of satellites that, among other things, guides ships and airplanes, provides data to electronic mapping systems for cars, keeps cellular networks coordinated, and helps surveyors lay out property lines. GPS can pinpoint the location of a radio receiver to within 50 yards or so, and with support from ground stations, can pinpoint within inches. The system also specifies time down to fractions of a second.

Just like a car odometer rolling over to zero or the hands of a clock sweeping past 12, the satellite clocks moved back to their starting point of Week 0 and the satellites themselves continued working without noticing that anything had changed. The potential for problems rested entirely with the receiving equipment. Some confused receivers stopped working; others generated bad data or displayed 1980 dates; and others looked for a satellite at the location where it would have been in January 1980 and couldn't find it, and were therefore unable to obtain satellite transmissions.

People naturally have been curious how the GPS rollover problem stacks up with the Y2K problem. At most companies, the same teams in charge of Y2K repairs also dealt with the GPS rollover, and many pundits called the GPS rollover weekend a "dry run" for how Y2K's arrival would be. Many telephone hotlines, community agencies, and web sites devoted to Y2K also provided GPS rollover information to the public. Other than the fact that both problems had the biggest potential to start causing trouble at midnight during a weekend, the comparison ends there. On the whole, GPS rollover problems were much more limited than Y2K problems, were easier to isolate, and were much simpler to overcome. For example, about 40 percent of the faulty GPS equipment could be fixed simply by turning it off and starting it up again after the rollover. And there really was very little faulty equipment to be found. Because the government began publicly discussing the rollover date as early as 1993, almost all GPS equipment made since 1994 took the issue into account. Even among systems older than that, professional-quality systems were mostly okay, and problems mostly occurred with relatively cheap personal GPS receivers that were sold to electronics consumers or boaters. All in all, it was smooth sailing for over 98 percent of the estimated 8 million receivers in existence.

The government did warn that the rollover posed "serious hazards" and many experts emphasized in advance of the rollover date that no one should rely on GPS in situations that could pose risk to life, property, or crucial data. It can't be determined, though, exactly how many receiver owners with older, problematic equipment ignored or missed the warnings to prepare for the rollover. Recreational boaters foolish enough to rely solely on GPS navigation in foggy conditions or at night could have run aground, and businesses silly enough not to upgrade their equipment could have ended up with faulty or lost data. Fortunately, there was a safety net in place for many major users of GPS navigation systems, in the form of older technologies—airplanes, cargo ships, and so on had other tools like radar on-board, and thus could have functioned safely even if the GPS rollover had somehow caused them difficulties.

So, why is this book discussing the GPS problem at all? Mostly because so many people have tried to force a comparison between the satellite clock rollover and Y2K computer problems, and have chosen to draw conclusions about Y2K from what happened with the GPS event (more precisely, what didn't happen). The fact that we breezed through the GPS rollover date without widespread problems made some of those Y2K watchers happy, but according to John Gribben, spokesman for the President's Y2K Council, that might be reading too much into the GPS event. In his words, despite a lack of major GPS rollover problems, "People shouldn't get a false sense of security about the Year 2000. They're two separate issues."

Other Time-Related Problems

"As long as there's been programming, there have been date-related issues," says Uche Ogbuji, co-founder of a company named Fourthought. "Y2K has gotten the most attention, but the rest are not going to disappear." Ogbuji is right—there are many date-related computer problems already around and rarely discussed; almost all of them result from using a limited number of digits to store a number representing the time and date. Whenever the limit is exceeded, the date wraps back to zero, making some date data suddenly zoom backward to a moment in the past. Since many aspects of applications and operating systems need time to move forward steadily, such a regression can cause problems. Here are a few examples of such problems in existence today:

- The programming language Visual C++ measures time as seconds elapsed since Jan. 1, 1900, and that time measurement will roll over to zero in the year 2036. Visual C++ is among the most popular languages, so many applications developed today could fail in 2036.
- A well-known Y2038 problem affects computers with the Unix operating system, including many Internet servers. Unix stores time as the number of seconds elapsed since Jan. 1, 1970, and some Unix-based computers will run out of space to store these seconds at 3:14 A.M. on Jan. 19, 2038.
- Microsoft acknowledges a less-forgiving Windows 95/98 glitch that causes computers to "stop responding" (hang and do nothing) after running nonstop for 49 days, 17 hours, 2 minutes and 47.296 seconds. A counter beginning when Windows starts up can only go to 2^{32} milliseconds, which is 49.7 days. Instead of rolling over to 0, unfortunately, this counter problem stops the entire operating system. A fix is available from Microsoft, but few people know to ask for it; fortunately, even fewer people leave their computers running continuously for 49 days.

Why worry about problems that are nearly 40 years away? First, look what waiting on Y2K problems has done. Second, we have some events in our lives that encompass long stretches of time—for example, payment dates on a 30-year mortgage or 30-year Treasury bill issued as early as 2008 will extend past the Unix Y2038 problem date, so it's wrong to think of the moment of problem *activation* (2036 for Visual C++, 2038 for Unix) as the deadline for addressing the problems.

> ∞ *Note*
>
> New products have taken these problems into account, just as many newer products avoided Y2K problems once manufacturers realized what needed to be done. For example, the newest generation of Unix machines has clock capabilities that won't reach a forced rollover for—are you ready for this—200 billion years. I think we'll have encountered bigger events than computer clock problems by then.

There are even some timing problems unrelated to digit limitations. For example, in December 1998, Microsoft admitted that several minor Y2K problems had been found in Windows 98. According to the company, they're so obscure that most users are unlikely to encounter them. A patch is available on the Microsoft web site to correct the problems, which include:

- If a computer is started at the precise fraction of a second when the date changes, the system clock can display the wrong date/time.
- One technique for resetting the date to Feb. 29 for a leap year can result in Feb. 29 thereafter being displayed for non-leap years.

In another infamous time problem that isn't based on digits, a missing equal sign causes an error with Windows operating system calculations of the beginning of daylight savings time, resulting in a problem that will appear on April 1, 2001. It will cause applications to think it's one hour earlier than the correct time, but for only one week—on April 8, 2001, they'll move to the correct time again.

> ∞ *Note*
>
> Here are the geeky details, for those who care: April 1, 2001, falls on a Sunday, which confuses part of a dynamic link library (a very important type of computer file that contain instructions and data that can be shared by any number of different programs written to run on Windows) that checks for the start of daylight time. The file contains a less-than symbol (<) where it needed a less-than-or-equal symbol (<=), causing the one-week delay in daylight time being recognized. Tens of millions of computers could be affected by this problem. It's corrected in Windows 2000 and it's usually possible to fix the problem in older versions of Windows by obtaining a new version of the flawed library, MSVCRT.DLL, from Microsoft.

The flaw could be bothersome for programs that need extremely precise time information. "What happens in a hotel when 50 people don't get their [automated] wake-up call on time?" said Richard Smith, the programmer who discovered the error. "Multiply this by 10,000 hotels and you're going to have a lot of angry people." Also, legal and financial firms that need to create accurate time-stamped records of various transactions can find it costly to have applications record mistakes for a single transaction, let alone for an entire week.

The Crouch-Echlin Effect

A great example of how tremendously complicated Y2K remediation efforts have become is the debate surrounding the Crouch-Echlin Effect, also known as time dilation or simply TD. Supposedly, computers with a certain type of real-time clock (a battery-powered chip which tracks time even when the computer's external power is switched off) might experience malfunctions including faulty calculations, lost data, or computers that won't start following M-Day regardless of

BIOS fixes being done correctly. This problem was first reported in August 1997 by Jace Crouch, a liberal arts professor from Michigan, and then explored in depth by Michael Echlin, a programmer from Canada. Their findings received loads of attention in computing forums and newsgroups on the Internet and were the subject of a very lengthy article in the *NY Times* (11/9/1998) and other international coverage, after which a wild technical debate raged in various laboratories and online. Compaq Computer even agreed to resell the fix developed by Crouch and Echlin at one point, but were slammed by critics who eventually convinced Compaq to stop selling the fix pending further testing. This emphasizes the amazing intricacies involved in the ways that computers keep time.

Critics have admitted that TD is something strange that deserves further research, but many have a gut feeling the claim is just a ploy to sell software. "They are selling a fix for something they can't even explain," said Thomas Becker, chief executive of Rightime Co., a software company specializing in products that regulate timekeeping on personal computers. "They are trying to capitalize on fear." Though TD has reportedly been encountered in places like Cambridge University and MIT, nobody understands exactly what's happening. Large corporations have called their Y2K consultants wondering what they should do about it. If TD proves to be a real problem, it might take billions of dollars more to replace equipment that has already been through an expensive Y2K conversion and is currently thought ready for the new millennium.

Several labs offered to work with Crouch and Echlin on further testing, but claimed they "couldn't get their cooperation" and therefore opted to disbelieve the validity of the claims. Echlin has never backed down, saying that he and Crouch "have been hoping ever since we found this that someone would come along and prove us wrong. No one who has followed our test procedures has." Intel Corporation has several pages of information about Crouch-Echlin in the Y2K area of its web site, but makes it clear that it "cannot confirm or deny the existence of this anomaly" and moreover goes on to mention that Intel's own experts identified a problem with the TD repair toolkit developed by Echlin's company, which they reported to him, causing him to issue a corrected toolkit.

So, people who don't believe that a problem exists are pointing out errors with the software that has been developed to fix the supposedly nonexistent problem. It's surreal. The whole mess typifies how Y2K has caused dilemmas among corporate America and individuals about what an expert is and how much an expert can be trusted. And it makes me wonder if we'll ever realize that it's unrealistic to think we can develop machines that control everything accurately down to the millisecond or even smaller time units when our own brains can't even register things on that time scale. We've reached the stage where we have to build super-duper-machines to try to test our super-machines, and so on, but fallibility will always be there, even in the latest, greatest thing we've ever built.

Piracy

One thing that exacerbates the Y2K problem is that there are hundreds of thousands—perhaps millions—of illegal copies of software programs in use throughout the world. Some software piracy occurs domestically, but the majority of it involves software from US manufacturers being pirated overseas. This practice is condoned or even facilitated by certain foreign governments. Since any vulnerability to the Y2K problem in original software gets transferred to all pirated copies, an immeasurable cascading effect of potential Y2K problems has been transmitted through the underground software market.

Some US software industry executives predict that piracy might be the leading cause of eventual and long-standing Y2K computer problems, because official updates and patches from software manufacturers have been important tools for preventing Y2K trouble. Since most users of pirated software aren't even known, and the volume of pirated software existing in any particular company or nation can only be guessed, there's an inestimable number of Y2K problems waiting to happen beyond the problems that are being tackled in above-board ways.

Pirated software users have found themselves in this situation before; for example, a nasty computer virus named Chernobyl had its nastiest impact in several Pacific Rim countries where software piracy is particularly rampant, because illegal users did not receive notification from manufacturers about how to detect and eliminate the virus.

Software industry execs can't be sure, though, about the impact Y2K will have on users of pirated software. When this topic came up at a "technology summit" run by the Joint Economic Committee of the US Congress in June 1999, Jeff Papows, President of Lotus Development Corporation, surmised, "They can always steal the updates."

WHAT DO ALL THESE OTHER PROBLEMS MEAN?

My bottom-line analysis of the various additional Y2K problem dates and other clock problems is this: I think the amount of focus we've given to these issues, especially things like the Nines Problem which really had very little chance of causing widespread problems, have backfired in that the general public started to think each of those minor possible problem dates was really representative of the overall Y2K problem, so when not much happened on these dates, people who were yaysayers went "HA! Nothing's happened so far, so all of Y2K must be overblown." It's a "boy who cried wolf" thing—if you waste people's time and attention on stuff that isn't critical, they might not believe you when you actually have something critical to tell them.

Let's all learn from this. Measure your requests carefully when you ask people for attention, and wait until there's a real reason. Save your requests for favors until you have a true need. Measure your words of criticism, so that you stand a better chance of having the person listen when there's an absolutely essential criticism to be made of them. Whenever you're in the privileged position of discussing the message of the gospels with someone, measure your words about Christianity carefully, because if you flood people with trivia or apocalyptic talk that's unsubstantiated, they may be less receptive to the core teachings that are so important for you to share with them.

LESSON 39: WE'RE ALL HOOKED ON HAPPY ENDINGS

The possible negative events that Y2K might cause have concerned many Y2K experts, not only because of the actual bad stuff that might occur, but because they aren't sure most people are equipped to cope with any downturns in the economy or other aspects of their lives. The last decade of the twentieth century has seen many new investors enter the booming stock market, and to date most of them have not yet seen a dip in the markets or experienced a tremendous blow to their portfolios. Economically and most other ways, we've all become accustomed to happy endings.

Most action/adventure films, dramas, and even horror films reach reasonably happy conclusions. In real life most of our crimes are solved, most of our medical conditions are treatable, most personal problems have a support group or twelve-step program that can move people steadily toward improvement once they identify that they have a problem, and so on. The general perception is that the wheels of justice in our country turn slowly, but that they at least usually turn in the proper direction. In other words, most things in our lives work out very well at best, or merely okay at worst.

Y2K, though, does not offer the possibility of a simple, happy ending to those who have found out lots of information about it. It offers the potential for surprises and unexpected twists. That's why those who prefer neat and tidy plot lines with predictable conclusions haven't enjoyed learning a great deal about the Y2K problem. Steve Farrar in his Y2K book touched upon the fact that most people shy away from accepting worst-case scenarios as genuine possibilities, noting, "Quite frankly most people don't have the foresight or the vision to think strategically."

My personal hope is that everyone *can* think strategically by making a concerted effort to do so, and that everyone can manage not only to be realistic about things possibly going wrong during Y2K or any other challenge that the world ever faces, but also to see far beyond all anticipatory scenarios, and understand that whatever occurs—regardless of its exact nature—is truly small potatoes in the overall scheme of things. I've tried to point out throughout most of this book how things can be viewed from a Christian perspective, and while to some that might sound like a call to simplify your outlook, I feel it's just the opposite. It's a call to study and understand the various viewpoints that exist in the world for any complicated issue, and to embrace that complexity while relying upon scriptural guidance, wise counsel from others, and God's presence in your life to help you sort the complexity into something manageable.

This makes me think of some Christians I know who shy away from learning about Christianity in all its complexities. When you mention that the four gospels disagree with each other on some minor points, they start to get a little twitchy. When you mention that different denominations disagree about certain aspects of how to be a practicing Christian, anxiety creeps in. When you suggest they study the book of Revelation, they start a full-fledged spasm. Revelation, they think, is a book of tortuous complication, wherein the world is put through the wringer more than once, the Antichrist sits in dominion over the earth for a long period, many folks are made to walk around with undesired tattoos, and so much more that doesn't seem anything like a happy ending. Wars and destruction are unavoidable, and everything as we now know it is going to be obliterated in stages. But that's only some of what you'll find in Revelation, which is one of my favorite books of the Bible. For all Christians, there is an ultimate, untarnished, unrestrained happy ending. The New Jerusalem is established and everyone who is saved is welcome to enter.

The complexity encountered along the way is a necessary part of God's plan for the world, and in fact the end times, whenever they occur, are going to require the same things that *all* times require from those of us who call ourselves followers of Christ—faith, love, patience, perseverance, and perspective.

Summary

Y2K has brought us an amazing realization: The world's reliance on technology has reached a level of layering and interconnectedness so complex that nobody—not even any team of experts you could assemble—understands exactly how it's all hooked up. Whenever you're gauging the complexity of a particular situation, or searching for perspective on it, don't leave God out of the equation. In all circumstances, recognize the value of simplicity but also be ready to embrace complexity as much as is needed so that you don't limit your potential role by limiting your understanding.

On a personal level, realize that we can work as hard as we'd like to fix all of our own inner flaws and make ourselves into a "clean system," but that a later association with one or more other bad systems (bad people or corrupt environments) can make us flawed again. Let's determine to always go farther, as Jesus did, and work toward achieving the possibilities that we know can be actualized whenever we're willingly in partnership with God.

5

What Matters Most

A leading Y2K consultant told me that the first and foremost instruction he gave to businesses was this: Prioritize. You don't need to fix everything to be ready for Y2K—just systems that are absolutely critical to your business operations, and the systems with which those systems share data. If there's one thing the Y2K problem has clearly done for organizations, it's that it has helped them to prioritize.

In March 1998, US government auditors warned a House hearing that it had become too late for federal agencies to fix all the Y2K problems in their roughly 5,000 "mission-critical" computer systems, and that some government functions would likely be disrupted. The Office of Management and Budget had determined that with two years of effort completed and 21 months remaining until M-Day, only 35 percent of the computers categorized as critical for government agencies to perform their missions had been checked and fixed, and about 3,500 such systems remained undone.

> **Note**
> Earlier, US government officials had distinguished levels of importance among computers. "Mission-critical systems" are computers that an agency must have to continue its day-to-day work; "non-critical systems" are those that are not immediately crucial to carry out the agency's mission—for example, a system compiling data for use in government reports will be required to work eventually but not necessarily immediately, so it can be considered non-critical. About 5,000 systems had been categorized as mission-critical, and about 60,000 as non-critical.

It was necessary at that point to set priorities even for repairs within the group of mission-critical systems that previously had all been considered essential to the functioning of government agencies. No one knew how to make those decisions, but they knew they had to be made. John Koskinen, head of the President's Y2K Council, was asked by Rep. John Sununu which agency concerned him most, and Koskinen replied that they all did, saying, "If the IRS or Social Security doesn't function, that's a big problem, even if the FAA runs properly." He went on to discuss the thorny nature of the problem, explaining that identifying which computer systems are actually critical is not simple. A minor system may turn out to be critical if it turns out that some bigger system will not run without it, and a system thought to be critical to the day-to-day operation of a secondary agency that needs output from it might unfortunately be considered non-critical in the day-to-day operations of the primary agency that manages the system and would be responsible for deciding when and to what extent the system gets its Y2K repair work.

The military also felt steadily increasing pressure to prioritize. In mid-July 1999 the logistics branch of the Department of Defense conducted a huge test of the logistics information systems for the armed forces. The test, however, focused on only 44 of the 1,000 DOD logistics systems. Zach Goldstein, director of logistics systems modernization under the Secretary of Defense, explained, "We identified those information flows so essential to supporting military operations and so hyper-dependent on automation that not being able to get the information within 72 hours of needing it impacts your mission." The top priorities included systems that ordered spare parts and food. They also conducted a few dozen vendor interface tests with commercial trading partners and carriers such as FedEx who can impact DOD's supply chain. More than just a programming problem, Y2K for many organizations was a huge operational management headache in terms of figuring out what to test—and when—to keep the most important systems going past M-Day. Nancy Peters, head of an IT industry task force on Y2K, praised DOD's approach, saying, "The selection of an area is the only way to do end-to-end testing, so selecting an area like the supply chain is a good, sane approach." The decisions DOD made in July weren't easy ones, but they knew the time had come to select the most critical systems and processes to focus upon. Another testing phase later in the year focused on fixing systems that failed during the July testing and also tested other systems that hadn't been ready for testing in July, but all along the way, priorities still had to be set.

"The silver lining is that for many organizations this is the first time they've taken a hard look at their information systems," said Jack Gribben, communications director for the President's Y2K Council. "What they have, what is a priority, whether they need what they've got, all that. It's a good opportunity for them to do an inventory."

As early as mid-1997, some companies seeing the limited time remaining to M-Day were forced to make decisions to abandon the notion of fixing certain systems still vital to their overall operations in favor of completing the repairs on certain other vital systems. These were terrible decisions, and hopefully were made with much deliberation and wisdom. In July 1997, IBM held a conference call about the Y2K problem with analysts, and one of their key points during the call was "Triage is upon us," meaning that following thorough assessments, it was necessary to prioritize and aggressively renovate mission-critical systems first, while working on non-critical systems only with extra available resources, or when those non-critical systems bumped up to critical status for one reason or another.

This chapter is about prioritizing and identifying the most essential elements in our lives. When you boil it all down, there are very few things in our lives that truly matter, and the rest is only so much extraneous trivia.

Lesson 40: Money Is Too Often Considered the Top Priority

Too much of the discussion about Y2K has revolved around money—to some extent, that's by necessity, because it has taken money to fix the problem and it has taken the threat of losing money to make certain people bother to fix it. We're pretty spoiled by our prosperity here in the late 20th century, and that makes us focus first and foremost on financial concerns in many situations. So we'll devote this first lesson of the priorities chapter to our old pal, money.

Money as Both Delayer and Motivator

Concern about losing large amounts of money is the only thing that made some people and businesses take any actions at all in terms of Y2K preparedness.

∞ Note

Just for the record, here's my general outlook on money as morality: Money in and of itself doesn't have good or bad qualities, but certainly is capable of motivating evil actions, and it gets any ethical or moral twist from the people who handle it. Some people use their money in tremendously uplifting ways, while others allow themselves to be poisoned by the money they handle.

COST OF THE REPAIRS

In addition to ignorance and refusal to admit the severity of the problem and simple procrastination, there have been many hesitations about cost. Other aspects of the world economy, the rate at which companies are expected to grow to please shareholders, and numerous other factors competing for corporate energy and funding have kept some companies from addressing the Y2K problem in a more timely manner.

With each passing year, the cost of repairs has steadily increased and possibility of repairs has steadily lessened. The eventual cost of not fixing the problem, though, will likely run even higher for some companies in terms of inventory interruptions, lost revenue, customer dissatisfaction, and a number of other problems that could occur. $1 trillion to $2 trillion are the current estimates of the global cost to deal with the Y2K problem. There's a huge difference between one and two trillion, so obviously no expert can predict for sure the extent of problems that might arise and how much the overall dilemma will end up costing.

There's one more cost that has come with Y2K—the postponement of other information technology projects. Y2K-related adjustments in spending patterns showed up first in increased orders for enterprise software (software that coordinates major business functions across a company) as many businesses decided to overcome the Y2K problem by replacing as many antiquated programs as possible. By the end of 1998, when it was no longer feasible for many companies to implement new enterprise software before M-Day, manufacturers of desktop computers enjoyed booming orders from companies upgrading local area networks as part of departmental Y2K projects. Lastly, there was a shift to purchasing testing products, and only now that Y2K is just about completely handled are some companies finally attending to IT projects that have been on hold because of Y2K. After the gray days of working on Y2K, many companies are looking forward not to blue skies, but to getting back to a touch of green. "People see an opportunity to get a year or two ahead of competitors they think will have trouble with Y2K," says Michael Erbschloe, director of research at Computer Economics. "After diverting so much attention to Y2K, management is hungry for applications that will add to revenue."

How Individuals and Banks Feel about Money

The good news is that the federal government expects to successfully deliver unemployment insurance, government pensions, veterans benefits, SSI, and Social Security in January 2000. The bad news is that some recipients aren't sure if they should put those funds in the bank. That's the picture painted by financial industry representatives in the weeks leading up to M-Day.

A few short-term, isolated disruptions in financial services are possible, but consumers' main financial concerns—checks, direct deposits, ATMs, credit and debit cards—will mostly be okay. There's also reason to believe international fund transfers won't be in danger of failure, which is good for the world's financial infrastructure. In mid-June 1999, the computer systems that move trillions of dollars' worth of currency per day among different countries successfully completed a test that involved 34 payment systems in 19 countries, including the CHIPS system in the US, which handles international transactions like foreign exchange trading and import/export payments. Most of the testing checked how computers would deal with Jan. 3–4, 2000. According to George Thomas, a representative of the bank consortium that owns CHIPS, "This test demonstrated that the basic plumbing of international finance is ready for the Year 2000."

Still, many Americans are expected to withdraw extra cash before M-Day (about 64% of those surveyed in a Gallup poll in Fall 1999 have said that they will), so banks and other financial institutions have worked overtime to try to make sure that those withdrawals are in conservative amounts. The Federal Reserve's banking system transactions involve more than $2 trillion daily, and a shutdown could be catastrophic. The Fed has stockpiled over $200 billion to guard against Y2K-related hysteria, enough to support the nation's financial system even if every adult in the population withdraws $1,000 at year's end.

Legislation was approved in September 1999 to expand the types of collateral a bank can use to obtain credit from the Fed (borrowing amounts needed to cover daily operations of financial institutions is usually done against top-grade collateral like US Treasuries, but these special terms allow lower-grade collateral to be used). This should help any banks who need to deal with an unusual demand for year-end cash. The special terms went mostly unused for several weeks, but in the first week of November 1999 the Fed reported that several financial institutions had taken advantage of the more lenient collateral requirements to pad their pockets a bit. That week, banks borrowed $210 million, which Fed officials called the first "significant borrowings" under the new policy.

As discussed earlier in the book, though, even with all the extra cash the Fed has made available for Y2K, those cash reserves still equal just a tiny fraction of the amount that's on deposit, so there's really no allowance in the system for many big depositors suddenly deciding to convert all of their electronic money into cash. Therefore, it has been critical for banks to convince people not to indulge in exorbitant withdrawals in preparation for M-Day.

∞ Note

It's not just individuals who seek extra cash from banks in preparation for Y2K. *USA Today* reported in August 1999 that according to a quarterly Fed survey of senior loan officers, about 20 percent of firms such as mutual funds and brokerages had asked their banks for a special Y2K credit line. Those percentages had doubled from three months earlier, and were expected to rise toward the end of the year. "In some cases, [the amounts requested were] substantial," the Fed said when releasing the survey results.

Fearing a run on the banks by panicky customers, the banking industry's major trade group, the American Bankers Association (whose members represent 90% of US banks), has made marketing efforts a big part of its Y2K campaign. The idea they've needed to sell the public is simple—money is safer in a bank's hands than in yours. It's true, of course. Depositors risk a total loss of their cash in the event of a house fire, and if someone mugs you and takes your ATM card, you're better off than if he mugs you when you're carrying $8,000 in cash.

In early 1999, when TV and radio commercials about Y2K were just becoming fashionable, the ABA was hawkish on any commercial that predicted bank glitches due to Y2K—even obvious jokes, like the Polaroid commercial in which an ATM after midnight on M-Day shows a man an incorrect balance (much higher than what he knows he has in the account) and he snaps an instant photo to have later as proof for the bank of his supposed balance. Whenever ads presented banks' Y2K preparedness in a bad light, the ABA brought pressure to bear, until some were actually taken off the air.

The ABA has worked on achieving its goals from many angles, but the most remarkable in the context of this book is a sermon written in summer 1999 to enlist help from religious leaders to get ABA ideas across to individual customers. An ABA speechwriter crafted a prewritten Y2K sermon, which the group called "a sample" despite the fact that it was fully ready-to-go with chosen scripture and illustrative examples. The sermon drew on Old Testament examples so it could be sent to Jewish rabbis and Christian clergy alike. It compared the challenges of Y2K to the journey of the Israelites from Egypt to the Promised Land

and the challenges therein, such as crossing the Red Sea. It portrayed fearful, old thinking as Pharaoh's men who are swallowed by the waters.

It urged keeping faith in God, and keeping money in the bank. In a set of segues from Bible to banking, the sermon encouraged preachers to remind their congregations, "Whatever you do, don't bury your money in the backyard," and "Banks will keep your money safe. They're backed by the Federal Deposit Insurance Corporation."

"We want to go into the next century as God intended, with hope," the sermon said at one point, and elsewhere said, "We don't want to be crouched in our basements with candles, matches, and guns." Despite telling about the need not to be fearful, the sermon planted a little fear of its own, suggesting that taking cash out in large quantities might make people targets for theft and scams.

While the ABA justified their creation of the sermon for distribution to religious leaders nationwide as a helpful gesture meant to be an outreach by bankers who truly cared about the welfare of their customers' money, many Y2K experts and casual observers alike found it offensive, condescending, and above all, manipulative. Several experts mentioned the sermon in interviews as indicative of the desire by certain government and industry officials to hand people a string of meaningless, feel-good reassurances rather than significant disclosure of Y2K-readiness efforts in measurable terms. My favorite reaction to the ABA's sermon (at least, my favorite one that I can repeat) came from Frank Hayes, a computer industry veteran and columnist for *Computerworld*. He called the sermon "bland, canned, nondenominational pseudo-religious pabulum" and said about the ABA's decision to send it out, "Just when we thought Y2K cynicism and contempt couldn't run any deeper, it breaks through to a whole new subbasement."

In a delightful column titled "Nothing Sacred" still viewable in the archives at *Computerworld Online*, Hayes gave a rousing defense of religious leaders' knowledge and initiative on Y2K, pointing out that many churches and synagogues had already done contingency planning and provided balanced information on Y2K to their members. He gleefully noted that many churches were ready for Y2K long before banks and wrote, "Maybe those bankers would have a little better luck with their own Y2K efforts if they didn't assume most people are hapless, helpless dimbulbs who have to be saved from themselves." For the knockdown punch, he used a biblical allusion more effectively than any I saw in the ABA's sample sermon, saying, "as for the bankers... with any luck, we'll see the money changers driven out of the temple all over again."

At any rate, for reasons that are mostly understandable, it's clear that the banks don't want to let much money leave their hands, no matter what's looming on the economic horizon. In many people's eyes, it's now easy to see where we get the term "piggy banks."

Anyone who thinks bankers are wrong, though, about the concerns they voice about muggings, etc., should listen to the warnings of public officials who specialize in crimes involving the elderly. Whether it's because they recall the Depression, because they depend so heavily on their savings to live from, or because they're the age group least familiar with computer technology, many senior citizens have been withdrawing large amounts of money from banks. People who run senior centers around the nation have reported the perceived need to withdraw money due to Y2K being discussed frequently by seniors during 1999.

Aileen Kaye, who works in Oregon's state senior services division, thinks the withdrawals mostly stem from fear of technology, saying that seniors "are worried that these electronic devices are going to fail." Police say some seniors already have become victims of crime because they have too much Y2K-related cash on hand. "It's a total nightmare," says Paul Greenwood, a prosecutor handling elder abuse cases in the San Diego County DA's office. Jamie Mortensen, a police investigator also covering elder abuse, says, "We have a lot of seniors who are withdrawing large amounts of cash. They are terrified of this Y2K thing. They think everything's going to come to an end." She tells of a woman in Vallejo, CA who withdrew $12,000 (all cash), stopped at a store with it, and was promptly mugged and stripped of her money. In Texas, an amazing act of treachery is taking place—rings of con artists parading as concerned community activists have been giving elderly people free safes that look like Bibles with the pretext of helping them to protect their Y2K cash, but law enforcement officials say that as soon as the safes are used, they're stolen from the victims' homes—and the thieves know exactly which container the money is in, because they provided it.

One company made a full-time occupation out of tracking banks' Y2K readiness. Weiss Ratings, Inc. issues ratings on Y2K readiness and overall financial safety of banks, S&Ls, and insurers. A survey done by Weiss found that 870 of 1,316 banks and S&Ls (66.1%) reported having completed all necessary Y2K remediation and testing. There were 386 (29.3%) whose reported completion dates were rated Average (in line with regulatory standards); 36 (2.7%) were assigned a Below Average rating, and 24 (1.8%) were assigned a Low rating. Most of the largest banks in the nation received the highest Weiss rating; Citibank of NY was an exception, rated Average.

The survey was completed in July 1999 by about 12.5% of the 10,434 federally insured depository institutions asked to respond, and responses were judged using standards established by banking regulators. "Most banks appear to have lived up to the challenge," says Martin D. Weiss, chairman of the ratings company. Regarding the response rate of the survey, he points out that "due to the voluntary nature of our survey, it is safe to assume a tendency for the better-prepared institutions to come forward more readily." Results from this and previous Weiss surveys contradict FDIC figures, which in Summer 1999 indicated that more than 99% of the insured institutions had achieved a "satisfactory" rating in Y2K compliance evaluations. "This discrepancy remains a mystery to me. We are using the regulators' exact guidelines," Weiss said. "Therefore, regulators are either basing their statistics on old data or are giving banks some leeway in their evaluations. Either way, the end result is that consumers are not being given an accurate picture."

Although Weiss Ratings itself makes money selling consumer reports on the Y2K readiness of these institutions, Weiss has repeatedly urged government regulators to require free public disclosure regarding the Y2K readiness of the institutions they supervise, but despite such urgings from Weiss and some consumer groups, that sort of mandatory disclosure to consumers has never been required. Call around, though—banks will be happy to tell you "we've made significant progress" and "we're comfortably confident" and "any disruptions should be manageable" and other loose reassurances; unfortunately, that's the best any consumer can expect from financial institutions prior to M-Day.

THIS CHICKEN LITTLE WENT TO MARKET

Since the beginning of 1998, Edward Yardeni, chief economist of Deutsche Bank Securities, has been warning Wall Street what a threat the Y2K problem truly is. Yardeni has felt unpleasant earnings surprises due to Y2K issues might drain confidence from the market. "I don't think Y2K is [accounted for] in the market at all," Yardeni said in August 1998. "In [a booming] market, people are looking for risk and uncertainty. One of the biggest threats to earnings is the year 2000." He saw a real likelihood of a recession following M-Day.

Indeed, it was unsettling when big companies announced along the way that things would be much more difficult and costly to fix than originally anticipated. Merrill Lynch, for example, disclosed that it would spend $375 million repairing its computer systems, $100 million more than was targeted, which caught people off guard. In Spring 1998, nobody was sure what to think about Y2K's potential impact on the stability of corporate concerns and financial markets. An April 1998 survey of Y2K remediation managers showed that two-thirds of them believed Y2K would result in an economic slowdown and in select locations a few corollary problems such as public rioting or worker protests.

Everything has gone much more smoothly than expected, though. Economists who expect Y2K to send the US into recession have grown scarce (although most of them acknowledge that certain other countries may suffer setbacks to their national economic infrastructure related to Y2K). An informal CNBC.com poll in September 1999 showed economists forecasting economic growth in the first quarter 2000 that would keep the country nowhere near a recession. "I think people were grossly overestimating the effects of Y2K," said David Jones, chief economist at brokerage firm Aubrey G. Lanston, regarding earlier projections of severe economic slowdown. In mid-1999, forecasters started building in a unique inventory cycle for year-end to reflect companies' pre-Y2K stockpiling and consumers' hoarding of certain types of supplies for Y2K. Now that the time has arrived, we've seen that some companies have beefed up production prior to year-end, and the increased inventories might have artificially boosted gross domestic product slightly for the most recent quarter, but not enough to scare the markets. After M-Day, people and businesses shouldn't have to buy much, so the economy might contract. Experts have also allowed for that, and projections are still positive.

The only significant negative market activity directly attributable to Y2K issues in late 1999 has been one episode when IBM stock prices tanked by 20% overnight after the company's third-quarter earnings announcement on October 20, 1999 in which company head Lou Gerstner admitted:

> "On the negative side, we saw a Y2K slowdown toward the end of the quarter, particularly in our large servers, and to a lesser extent in services and operating systems software. Looking forward, we believe we will continue to feel the effects of the Y2K slowdown in the fourth quarter and into early next year."

Gerstner went on to say:

> "Even though it is difficult to make predictions, next year has the potential to be a very good year for IBM, once we get past any lingering Y2K effects."

That was little comfort for investors, though, and they punished the stock momentarily. Shares of IBM are rebounding, however, and as this book went to press in early December had recovered nearly half that loss.

Individual investors in general seem to have heeded the Securities Industry Association's Y2K advice for individual investors released in May 1999:

- Keep paper records of transactions, but *do not* demand stock certificates to be sent to you.
- Do not sell off out of panic.
- Check your credit report for any computer-generated errors about four months after M-Day (in case, for example, you're indicated late for payments you actually made on time which have gone temporarily uncredited).

After six months studying the Y2K problem in depth, the SIA felt it wasn't worth the risk of financial institutions coping with Y2K complications at the end of the year (always a busy time anyway), and issued a report recommending that mutual funds make year-end payouts to investors before Christmas rather than after, and that all US financial markets close early on the afternoon of New Year's Eve, to make it easier to attend to any Y2K glitches that might occur. The major US exchanges have decided not to close early, by the way, but exchanges in some other countries have decided to. I see the US exchanges' viewpoint that added volume won't create Y2K problems, and having a full day on New Year's Eve will simply increase volume; I'd remind them, though, that if there's a problem, the fewer transactions that need to be gone through and manually resolved, the better.

The Securities and Exchange Commission has been a better watchdog on Y2K concerns than just about any other regulatory agency in any industry. In October 1998, in the federal government's first major Y2K enforcement action, the SEC charged 37 relatively small brokerages with failure to fully disclose their Y2K preparedness. 21 of the 37 firms settled the charges by promising to refrain from future violations, being censured, and paying penalties ranging from $5,000 to $25,000. In January 1999, the SEC accused nine stock-transfer agents (companies responsible for keeping records of shareholders and issuing or canceling stock certificates when shares are bought and sold) of allegedly failing to adequately disclose their Y2K readiness.

Moreover, brokerages were required to notify the SEC by August 31 if their systems weren't Y2K-ready, and those which weren't were put on a sort of probation, then those still not ready on November 15 were shut down and their investors' accounts were transferred to other, compliant brokerages.

Billing Mix-ups

How about the billing problems some people are anticipating due to Y2K glitches? It's easy for me to be confident that no one will take my home away despite the worst-case scenarios that some worriers have imagined, and any homeowner with proof of the purchase price and an ability to reconstruct a payment history should share that confidence. But, how about a mistake on one of your credit accounts (even the department store charge card with that pesky little $80 balance) finding its way onto your credit reports? While some Y2K experts think there's only a 10–20% chance of some faulty credit reporting taking place as a result of Y2K problems, others have concluded the likelihood is as high as 90%.

Although the US has a decent system in place that allows consumers to dispute items in their credit files, the process is certainly not flawless (about five years ago, I had to make multiple efforts over a significant time period to have a single mistaken item removed from my credit file and my wife's credit file, and I know several others who have been through the same experience). Moreover, it takes some legwork and written communication, and certainly is miserable when you have to do it for more than an item or two. Just ask the folks who have been victims of identity theft, who have to go through tremendous effort over a span of months or years in order to get their credit files to even approximate a correct picture of their own actual creditworthiness.

The credit file correction process definitely could get bogged down if there's ever an onslaught of corrections all requested simultaneously because of some widespread event such as the Y2K problem. While the burden of proof about alleged late or missing payments rests on the company to whom you've made payments, don't forget that most of those companies are increasingly dependent upon computer systems for their customer service interactions, and have grown so used to trusting the data they pull up on-screen that it can take tremendous effort to force a detailed review of your account in which human eyeballs and brainpower actually get involved and are able to straighten out a computer error.

LESSON 41: IDENTIFYING THE FEW TRUE ESSENTIALS

For starters, I'm going to quickly review some interesting Y2K tidbits from a few of the areas that I feel are important. I'm neither sounding alarms nor shouting praises here—you can draw your own conclusions about what these industries have done. My only goal at this point is that we all start figuring out which things we think matter most for us as individuals and as nations and as the world.

NUCLEAR/CHEMICAL HAZARDOUS MATERIALS

In July 1998, workers at one of Sweden's 12 nuclear power plants did a simple Y2K test and discovered a problem that would have resulted in an automatic shutdown of the plant on M-Day if unremedied. The necessary repair was made at all the Swedish nuclear power plants, which provide about 50% of that nation's power supply. Most potential problems with nuclear plants worldwide fortunately are of this type—they might cause a shutdown or require a return to manual control, but not trigger a leak or temperature regulation failure or anything else catastrophic.

According to findings reported to a Senate panel on Y2K, 85 million people in the US live within 5 miles of a plant handling potentially deadly chemicals. The likelihood of problems is very low, but even a single accident, of course, could cause tremendous damage. As of September 1999, only about 600 out of 55,000 chemical manufacturing companies in the US had reported achieving Y2K compliance. Also in Fall 1999, a Texas A&M survey of 300 small- and medium-size chemical plants in various states found that less than 14% are ready for Y2K. The study showed that most smaller plants have never even been surveyed for Y2K readiness.

Medical
Devices

Many medical devices such as X-ray machines, life-support systems, defibrillators, and even some hospital beds, contain embedded chips, but most are not date-sensitive and are unlikely to pose any direct risk to patients. Certain devices, like IV pumps and other drug-dispensing devices, may be clock-dependent, but typically deal with minutes and hours rather than dates.

There are a few areas of concern with medical devices, though:

- **Number of Devices**—Large medical centers have had to access and test huge numbers of devices to be certain about Y2K readiness. To take just one example, New York Hospital-Cornell Medical Center has had to consider the readiness of over 15,000 medical devices.
- **Cost of Replacement Equipment**—Medical equipment isn't cheap, and each flawed machine can sock a budget pretty hard. The Veterans Health Administration tested a $150,000 machine used for conducting radiation therapy for cancer patients and learned it had a slight chance of calculating wrong dosages after 2000 because it uses the current date to calculate both patient age and radiation strength (radiation decays over time). Wrong dates in either of those bits of information could result in incorrect dosages. With equipment costs like that, hospital administrators aren't always enthusiastic about the findings of their Y2K projects. One administrator told me that repairing expensive medical equipment, some of it manufactured as recently as 1996, "feels like needing to put a new engine in a Rolls Royce after it's only been driven 2,000 miles—it's just painful."
- **Date-Stamping Problems**—While the chances of a glitch with a medical device directly ending a life are minimal, software and chips are sometimes involved in activities such as conversion and storage of data from medical tests or conversion and storage of medical images. If these are hit by Y2K problems—for instance, if a new set of diagnostic images is never seen by a doctor because it gets date-stamped as nearly 100 years old instead of one day old, and therefore isn't pulled up during a request for the most recent image, patient care decisions might be made without access to the latest information.

Prescription Drugs

The debate has raged about whether or not to stockpile prescription drugs. Those who advocate doing so have expressed worry that potential interruptions in the drug distribution system, glitches in the manufacturing process, or problems with telecommunications (essential to everything from shipments of raw materials to pharmacy computer records and the HMO approval process) could occur in the days or weeks after M-Day. Those who say stockpiling would be problematic point out that a drug recall early in 2000 could be much more complicated and expensive if patients had large stockpiles. Are they planning to have a recall, proponents of stockpiling wonder? And even if there is a recall later, what's the big deal about extra cost as long as patients have the security of going into M-Day knowing they'll be able to stay alive?

Laurene West, a nurse turned IT professional turned government expert witness on some aspects of Y2K, has steadily encouraged Congress and health care officials to address these concerns seriously. She's not only the leading voice in the struggle to find solutions for potential Y2K problems with obtaining drugs, but is a brain tumor patient who herself requires daily doses of multiple drugs to stay alive. West has maintained her stockpiling advice to consumers in the absence of health care providers devising any better alternatives. She has expressed a willingness to discuss alternatives such as creating regional supplies in secure locations like National Guard armories, but neither the government nor the health care industry has moved on any initiatives like that.

She argues that people who cannot survive without drugs would be foolish not to plan for the worst regardless of promises from government and industry officials. What might seem like minor glitches to the officials, she says, could produce suffering or death for some drug-dependent patients (tens of millions of patients in the US take insulin, anti-rejection drugs following organ transplants, and many other critical medications). "It's not just the chronically ill we need to consider," West reminds people. "If you have a terminally ill patient, you have to have enough narcotics to allow them to go humanely."

Paloma O'Riley, co-founder of the Cassandra Project, which joined with others a year or so in advance of M-Day crafting proposals for new laws to, among other things, guarantee poor citizens will have medical supplies if a Y2K crisis results, says authorities made it clear the government wouldn't foot any portion of a bill for medication stockpiling. She says officials basically told them "not to propose anything that would cost more money."

In fact, the federal government largely handed off the problem, with the Department of Health and Human Services explaining that the entire issue of drug distribution was a state issue, since states regulate pharmacies. West asked the federal government to provide a one-time waiver allowing patients to buy 90–day supplies of drugs for which prescriptions are currently restricted by law to 30 days, but that idea never made it into law or regulatory policy of any kind, largely due to lobbying efforts against such stockpiling by pharmaceutical manufacturing and distribution industry leaders. They say patient stockpiling could create shortages of certain medicines, which would hurt the poor or anyone else who didn't manage to stockpile their own prescriptions. Moreover, they say, studies show that patients often fail to consume an entire supply of medication sold in quantities greater than 30 days, because they switch to new drugs or simply quit taking meds—so allowing consumers to build up large drug supplies could be very wasteful. To most advocates of stockpiling, that's a nonsensical argument, because the drugs would have been paid for (thus, no loss to the drug companies or pharmacies) and there would have been immeasurable value simply in having sufficient quantities of life-sustaining meds on hand at a time of such uncertainty.

The health care industry's next idea was that health care providers, rather than consumers, should be the ones allowed to stockpile in a responsible manner—when pressed for details, they said that this meant a few days' worth of drugs for each consumer with a current prescription. Burned consumer rights advocates took this as a sign that corporate America didn't trust consumers to level-headedly look out for their own best interests. The entire issue has remained at an impasse all the way through December 1999, with nobody knowing for sure the extent of potential problems in drug availability that might result when the new year arrives, and with neither side ever having changed its tune about the importance of stockpiling or not stockpiling, respectively.

Medicare

I can't say anything more about the Y2K status of Medicare providers than what Rep. Stephen Horn, chair of the House Government Reform subcommittee on Y2K, has said: "The outlook is alarming." As of the end of September 1999, he said, less than 2% of the 230,000 doctors, hospitals, nursing homes, and other health care providers who submit claims to Medicare had tested their computer systems with Medicare contractors.

Problems in those systems might mean that nearly 7 million people in Medicare HMO programs who need preauthorization for their care from specialists wouldn't get the required care, which Joseph Baker of the Medicare Rights Center says would lead to "potentially devastating consequences."

Hospitals

A mid-1997 study by the British Government found that hospitals in that country had made so little progress in reprogramming their systems that in January 2000 they could be forced to close to all but emergency cases, risking as many as an estimated 1,500 unnecessary deaths. Luckily, they put their nose to the grindstone at that point and have made a great deal of progress since then, but here in the US we haven't had a fire lit under us like that, and haven't achieved comprehensive readiness in terms of medical facilities.

A March 1999 Senate Y2K panel report, the most comprehensive single assessment ever of the overall Y2K problem, criticized the 6,000 hospitals and 50,000 nursing homes in the US and noted that about 50% of small- and medium-size ones had failed to work on remediation at all yet.

Fred Brown, chairman of the board of the American Hospital Association, said in September 1999 that large US hospitals have spent $8 billion to upgrade their computers and will be ready for the new year. The concern remains, though, that thousands of physicians, nursing homes and small inner-city and rural hospitals either have not addressed the problem yet or haven't thoroughly tested their systems after completing a Y2K project.

As this book goes to print, for some reason hospitals largely remain focused on excessive partying being more of a concern for M-Day than computer readiness. An *LA Times* article in September 1999 described an emergency medical services Y2K drill held statewide in California that month. Bruce Haynes, director for emergency medical services for the Orange County Health Care Agency, said, "The big unknown is the volume factor. There is a lot of belief that there will be these large parties, but I don't think anyone knows for sure." The drill was helpful beyond Y2K concerns; for instance, it offered state officials a method to tally hospital bed availability statewide for the first time, something that will help with any future disasters.

Critics point out a few limitations of the drill as preparation for Y2K:

- The drill was not mandatory for hospitals across the state.
- Ambulance services across the state weren't required to participate (they were invited, but not required).
- Hospitals didn't have to report to the state their own contingency plans for making sure continued patient care is possible on M-Day; instead, follow-up self-reporting by the hospitals was filed anonymously with the California Healthcare Association, and summary information was passed along to state and local agencies; an association spokesperson defended the anonymity of the reporting, saying, "The purpose is not to identify specific hospitals with specific issues but determine statewide on an aggregate basis how hospitals are progressing."

Even in states where information is made available to the public on a hospital-by-hospital basis, some institutions have been accused of not disclosing enough information about their Y2K readiness. Florida hospitals, which report their own information, were over 90% finished with their Y2K preparations the last time I checked the web site of Team Florida 2000, the group created by the governor to oversee readiness of government and important industrial sectors in Florida.

To get to that stage of readiness, though, according to *The Business Journal,* a scheduled Team Florida report on hospital Y2K readiness had to be delayed to allow hospitals more preparation and reporting time. Team Florida initially described 108 hospitals statewide as being of "critical concern," but most of those hospitals subsequently improved their computer systems and re-reported data to Team Florida showing that they're ready for Y2K. Critics say these self-reported numbers mean little without independent verification from outside inspection teams, something very few hospitals in any state have gone through.

Doctors' Offices

The March 3, 1999 Senate Y2K panel report indicated that over 80% of the nation's 800,000 doctors' offices had not upgraded their computers, meaning that doctors could potentially lose access to medical records temporarily or lose functionality of certain equipment. Larger hospitals in affluent areas will be in pretty good shape, Sen. Dodd said, but "we are very, very worried about what happens in the rural or urban situations."

The Senate Y2K panel later re-emphasized in its 100-day report in September 1999 that while HCFA and most large hospitals have been doing well, there's real concern that doctors and smaller health care centers like community clinics haven't prepared adequately. Whitney Addington, president of the American Society of Internal Medicine, said he and other doctors are very aware of Y2K issues and that many of them have acted on remediation work. He added that few offices have tested their systems, though, which could cause a "last minute debugging demand that could overwhelm available resources."

PERSONAL OR NATIONAL SAFETY

Sen. Christopher Dodd has suggested three places people might not want to be when M-Day arrives: elevator, airplane, hospital. To that I'll add a couple of my own situations it's wise to avoid: absentmindedly crossing a railroad track (the US rail system is thoroughly computerized and responsibilities for maintaining various aspects of it are widely distributed) or traveling in any country described as having poor Y2K preparedness on the US State Department's travel advisory web site (those who do have to travel should review the individual consular reports at **http://travel.state.gov/y2kca.html#specific** which cover countries from Albania to Zambia and indicate specifically which countries face the greatest risks of disruptions in telecommunications, in distribution of electricity and water, and so on). After that comment on personal safety issues, Dodd went on to say that he was "concerned that we are going to face serious economic dislocations" and the ensuing discussion took the direction of worrying about the readiness of businesses.

This was typical of the plentiful government attention given to Y2K—in the US, personal safety in general seemed somewhat less important to most government officials than what might happen to manufacturing, corporate earnings, and so on. I understand that having certain industries in jeopardy can translate to personal safety concerns for US citizens, but I wish more attention would have been paid to the sorts of things that might endanger the safety of the average person besides the things that might endanger corporate bottom lines.

Here in the US there's wide variance in the readiness of Emergency 911 systems. The *LA Times* reported at the beginning of August 1999 that according to the President's Y2K Council, only 37% of the nation's E–911 call centers were Y2K-ready. The biggest and smallest cities are mostly okay, since big cities have had access to money and personnel to conduct Y2K projects, and small cities often don't have a fully automated system. Medium-size cities, however, often have automated systems but not enough staff or extra funding to perform upgrades, so those cities make up the biggest area of concern. Since that time, progress has been made steadily by E–911 directors around the nation; in fact, at the end of August 1999 my own home county (total population only around 45,000) announced that it would purchase an entirely new computer system for its E–911 operations and would have the new system installed by the end of the year. There haven't been additional reports on the nation's E–911 systems, so there's no general assurance of preparedness—it's only safe to evaluate the readiness of local systems on a case-by-case basis.

Y2K readiness for prison security systems is a big concern for many people who live near a prison. Security at airports and federal buildings and other heavily-trafficked public places is a concern as well. One airport testing its emergency and fire alarm systems for Y2K readiness during 1999 found a problem that caused all security doors in the airport to be unlocked for an unspecified amount of time—clearly any place that has a computer-controlled security system needs to be checked carefully for any impact Y2K might have on the functioning of the security system.

Only about 3% of the world's water is drinkable straight without purification. Fresh water and threatened public health are concerns during any disaster, because disease wipes out societies quickly. The major earthquakes in Turkey and Taiwan in 1999, for example, brought immediate requests from those governments for world health agencies to provide thousands of body bags so that health problems wouldn't result from corpses remaining in the open. In any situation of extended power outages, disruptions in transportation systems, or water utility trouble, waste disposal (bathroom waste as well as garbage such as items spoiled due to loss of power) can easily become a very important issue.

Last but not least on the safety front, the military and defense infrastructure also seems highly important. The Pentagon alone has about 10,000 computer systems. A US military official told reporters on New Year's Eve 1998, "If we left things as they are right now, the military would shut down at the stroke of 2000." Fortunately the military has made tremendous strides throughout 1999, with very good efforts made on remediation and testing. The Pentagon has declared a "date transition period" from Sept. 1, 1999 to March 31, 2000, to allow for any leap year problems that might cause trouble. Marvin J. Langston, the Pentagon's top Y2K official, estimates the Defense Department will have an extra 5-10% of personnel on duty on M-Day to handle any surprises. The military has steadily missed deadlines set for its Y2K repair work, though; for example, a deadline at the end of March 1999 saw a number of systems not fixed by their planned Y2K repair date, including command and control networks for the Ballistic Missile Early Warning System, a critical part of the nation's air defense system, and computers used to plan missions for the F–117A Stealth and F–15E fighters. Estimates for total completion of planned Y2K remediation work in the Department of Defense range from 2002 to 2007, depending whom you ask, and absolutely nobody's foolish enough to think 100% compliance by M-Day is an attainable goal for our defense infrastructure.

UTILITIES

The utilities group was farthest behind of all major industry groups in December 1998 based on percentage spent so far of entire budget allocated to Y2K remediation efforts. With several months left before M-Day, Senator Dodd said, "We're no longer at the point of asking whether or not there will be any power disruptions, but we are now forced to ask how severe the disruptions are going to be."

The utilities have come on like gangbusters, though, and are ready to greet M-Day in a position of high preparedness.

Concerns about power problems due to Y2K aren't all hinged on total outages. There's a real risk of damage to expensive equipment from spikes, surges, or even bizarre line noise that can occur when funny things occur on electric lines. These sorts of events happen with power lines all the time—that's why millions of dollars are spent on surge suppressing equipment each year—but some people believe that these electrical anomalies might happen in greater numbers if Y2K creates an unusually chaotic environment within the power grid.

In the first week of August 1999, the North American Electric Reliability Council (NERC) issued its final 1999 statement on the readiness of North American power grids, showing things had come a long way. 99% of bulk electrical supply systems and over 96% of local distribution systems are Y2K-ready. Even 91% of rural electric cooperatives have completed their entire Y2K projects. At the time, only 35 of 108 reactors in North America still had Y2K work remaining. Problems for the most part have been found exactly where they were predicted to be, in places not crucial to the actual control of the reactors, and as I'm sure you'll be glad to hear, utilities say misrouting of bills is unlikely to happen (it figures they'd make sure to fix the billing systems completely). NERC's final report on Y2K readiness stated that the scattered outages that occur due to Y2K will be short, and that NERC would not release another report prior to M-Day, because as of that August statement it had met all its reporting obligations to the Dept. of Energy.

WITHOUT THE DAILY BREAD, YOU'RE TOAST

Walton Feed, a bulk food company, doubled its workforce to 125 people and opened a new warehouse in 1998 thanks to Y2K orders streaming in and piling up. Walton Feed makes a product especially favored by Y2K stockpilers—a sealed 50-pound drum of food with the oxygen removed, which fends off spoilage and keeps varmints out. "I'm falling further behind every day," complained owner Steve Portela. Peaks in demand are nothing new—the Mount St. Helens eruption, earthquakes, and other events have caused flocks of people to order from Walton Feed in the past, helping the Idaho company to become one of the country's largest bulk food suppliers. But other events were nothing compared to the jitters about Y2K. "Add it all together, and Y2K surpasses everything," according to Portela. It's not only survivalists stockpiling grains, rice, and other dried foods, he said, "It's common everyday folks . . . we're not talking about any radical people."

Tamera Toups, office manager at Montana-based Peace of Mind Essentials, has had a similar experience. "The demand is amazing," she said. "99.99 percent of the people we deal with are preparing for Y2K." She estimated sales volume leapt 500 percent during Y2K preparations; if your order wasn't in with Peace of Mind by April 1999, it couldn't be guaranteed to be filled by M-Day. As I write this book, big, impersonal food distributors still have plenty of food for sale, but most of the smaller companies that gave Y2K preparers individual attention are completely backlogged.

The US Army has made great strides in delivering palatable meals to soldiers, refugees, and others, so the Pentagon has taken aim at some home shoppers, too. Meals Ready to Eat (MREs) have very low moisture content and sophisticated packaging that allow them to stay fresh for up to three years without refrigeration, and a water-activated heating element enables them to be cooked with ease just about anywhere. MREs are available in bulk, and sales have risen about 1000 percent since 1997, thanks in part to Y2K stockpiling. In April 1999, William Grimes, a restaurant critic for *The NY Times*, reviewed a few of them and noted, "It could be a lot worse. The newfangled MREs probably won't be turning up at a Martha Stewart picnic anytime soon [but] for the grunt on the ground, this food should pass muster." He praised certain small touches, but disliked particular items, pointing out that the beef teriyaki "looks like raw sewage" and that the noodles "were limper than a civilian's handshake."

As amusing as that is, the people who ordered MREs or any other food to store up for Y2K will not care what it tastes like if a true Y2K crisis develops in their area. They will be grateful to God to have food on hand. It's possible that during Y2K-caused difficulties in isolated locations, "Give us this day our daily bread" will ring truer than ever before for those praying it, that it will be bursting with meaning instead of being a blasé recitation in the robotic way some people have fallen into when they pray the Lord's Prayer each week at church or pray it daily with their children.

At one point in Acts, a crowd in Lystra mistook Paul and Barnabas for Hermes and Zeus, and Paul tried to explain that earth is ruled over by the one true God. This confused the crowd even more, and eventually some Jews came by and convinced the crowd to stone Paul (which they did—just short of death, in fact, and only left him because they thought he *was* dead). Here's why I bring the scene up—in Paul's impassioned explanation of what God does to take care of his people on earth, food was featured prominently. Paul emphasized that God provides the essentials of life to his people:

> *Acts 14:17* He has shown kindness by giving you rain from heaven and crops in their seasons; he provides you with plenty of food and fills your hearts with joy.

Even when temporarily deprived of everything but the barest essentials, believers in the early church stayed committed and did not give up their hope:

> *1 Timothy 6:8* But if we have food and clothing, we will be content with that.

> *2 Corinthians 4:16* Therefore we do not lose heart. Though outwardly we are wasting away, yet inwardly we are being renewed day by day.

Remember that the first and foremost goal (as expressed in Luke 12:22–31) is to be part of Christ's kingdom; in other words, to put the needs of our soul ahead of the needs of our earthly bodies. This is difficult, especially for anyone who has ever tasted my wife's decadent German chocolate cake, but it's the goal nonetheless.

To the essentials of food and water, you certainly must add medicine for those who require it. Outside of that, however, you're beyond basic needs and into the realm of adding extra comfort. While we all enjoy our daily bread with butter or jam on it on a good day, don't ever forget that we can get by on far less than we're used to, if for some reason that ever becomes necessary. Celebrate whatever you do have, regardless of how spare or flush your circumstances seem in any particular moment, and realize that the quality of a meal doesn't determine the quality of the person eating it, but the other way around:

> *Proverbs 15:17* Better a meal of vegetables where there is love than a fattened calf with hatred.

FINAL THOUGHT ON ESSENTIALS

Really, if the worst things that happen due to Y2K are that the Chiropractic Board in some state has a mix-up in sending out renewal notices for licenses to practice chiropractic, or the US Postal Service web site is somehow unable to sell electronic postage to update customers' postage meters, or a major car manufacturer has to shut down an assembly line for a month because one of its small suppliers didn't come through with an important order of brake pads, then things are really okay. Mix-ups like that can be manually sorted out in the space of a few weeks. If, however, there are nuclear radiation leaks or crime sprees that involve injury or death to many victims because 911 service and police communications are on the fritz or a number of other scenarios too ugly to even imagine, then there's no amount of manpower or time in the world that's going to be able to undo or mend those situations.

LESSON 42: RECOGNIZING PRIORITIES

Does everybody in a top priority profession realize it? Are they willing to bear that responsibility? Are we as Christians willing to bear the responsibility for the role we claim? We are morally grounded, spiritually sound, vital and God-fearing. Are we willing to accept the constraints of being Christian and the obligations that come with God being a priority in our lives?

While many industries recognized Y2K as a top priority, the health care industry clearly did not recognize early enough—if ever—that Y2K needed to be among its top priorities. On September 27, 1999 the General Accounting Office in testimony to a House subcommittee said that hospitals, doctors, and other health care providers in the Medicare program "still do not appear to be doing all that they must" to prepare. Congressional auditors also expressed worry that Medicare contractors (mostly insurance companies) will likely run out of time before finishing exhaustive Y2K tests targeted at finding flaws in data systems. Medicare processes about a billion claims and pays out over $250 billion in benefits annually. According to the testimony, 40 out of 69 Medicare contractors have tested with less than 2% of all the doctors and other health care providers who need to submit payment claims accurately. This came on the heels of other findings that the entire health care industry is behind on Y2K fixes. Just a week earlier, the Senate's Y2K committee voiced concerns about the readiness of doctors' offices and nursing homes. Senator Dodd said that in a lot of areas in the health care industry, "it seems as though not much has been done." Congressional auditors have concluded that it appears hospitals, doctors, and nursing homes have been hesitant to conduct Y2K tests and demonstrate their level of compliance. Gary Christoph, chief technology officer at HCFA, the agency which oversees Medicare, testified, "Virtually all of the surveys of provider readiness have fairly low response rates. . . . We continue to have serious, ongoing concerns about the ability of some Medicare providers to successfully meet this challenge." Keep in mind that this was said with only three months and one week left before M-Day!!!

A US military official in a story on *NBC Nightly News* on 12/31/98 said, "Someplace, there will be people who die because of the Y2K problem." He was one of many government officials who, fortunately, realized how much of a priority the Y2K problem needed to become. In October 1998 when several key technology bills were waiting for attention but Congress needed to recess for the session, members of Congress put in the extra effort to pass only one of those bills—the Y2K liability disclosure bill, to encourage companies to share information about methods of solving the problem by protecting them from lawsuits based on the data they disclose. On another occasion, the Senate took the unusual step of devoting a whole day to addressing the Y2K problem. That day, they voted 99 to 0 to authorize government-guaranteed loans for small businesses to fix Y2K problems, and voted 92 to 6 to extend the Senate Y2K panel's work through February 2000 with a budget of roughly $800,000. The C-SPAN networks broadcast many congressional hearings about Y2K during 1999, and Congress was very diligent about never abandoning its focus on the problem. They did everything in the standard way, of course—huge hearings that moved at a tedious pace in which expert witnesses got only brief statement periods and limited Q&A time to try to tackle the highly complex issues involved in the Y2K problem. Some members of Congress were more proactive than others, though, and worked hard to make sure that as much as possible was accomplished with each hearing that took place and each report that was issued.

If you could have only one light on in your house, it wouldn't be the one lighting your carport or driveway, would it? If you could have only one working appliance, you wouldn't choose your toaster, would you? Sort out what is a critical need and what is just being "spoiled" and carry this awareness with you far beyond Y2K, regardless of what does or doesn't occur as a result of Y2K computer problems. The pitfalls of Y2K have been very useful for causing many people to examine their priorities, and I hope it can do the same for you.

Imagine there's a fire in your home. As you wake up and realize what's going on, you have the opportunity to grab a few things on your way out the door. There's no time, strength, or composure to gather up everything that you like; you can only take the most essential things and they must be in a particular place where you know you can get at them quickly. So, what items do you grab? If you immediately thought of saving cash or anything else with high value that you wanted to preserve, think about where that places your priorities. Of course, those of us who are sentimental types and would go for objects of the heart probably didn't name truly essential things, either. Once the residents of the burning house are safe, what really matters? Family photographs? Wedding keepsakes? A child's favorite toy? Those are all precious to us here on earth and they're fine choices, but in truth none of them are essential for continuing life as the gospel teaches us. Very little actually matters, and you should make sure that the little which does matter always has a place of primacy in your life.

> *Proverbs 18:10* The name of the Lord is a strong tower; the righteous run to it and are safe.

This fits in with everything discussed in Lesson 27 about how God is a place of shelter for us, but I like this particular verse and the way it emphasizes that all it takes to access this tremendous refuge and strength of the Lord is his name. Just his name! Consider this in terms of my suggestion that you prioritize God as the first place to turn for help—let's say for some terrible reason you suddenly have one second left, in which you can manage but a single breath, a final thought. What do you do with it? Hopefully it's something good—maybe uttering the name of God in a fitting way, maybe mentally focusing on something in your life that's representative of the blessings you've had and your awareness of them—and hopefully it's a natural extension of the excellent way you've chosen to live prior to that moment.

To be basically prepared for Y2K, it has made sense to store up not only essentials to keep us alive (food and water and medicine and heat sources), but also the things that matter most for our lives: birth certificates, deeds, bank account statements, etc. Notice that when you start to make such a list, much of it is financial. In fact, the various checklists that Y2K experts have given people to follow in order to prepare during the past couple of years have focused on so many things that are financial, it has really made me think about where our values lie, and about some other things in our lives that matter every bit as much but aren't on some of the checklists because they don't have monetary value. What about photographs? They're not in danger due to Y2K, are they? Well, not for most of us, because we still keep them on our walls or in photo albums stored on a bookcase or in a drawer somewhere, but a few people now have all of their photos archived on computer systems in their homes or housed on a web server for use within their web sites.

So if you had all your photos of great memories, good times, and beloved family moments on the computer, would that be your top priority to protect and save from harm in the event of a technological glitch, or would the money stuff still come first? I doubt that everyone's answer would match up, but as computers become involved with more and more aspects of our lives, we all either have to do tremendous amounts of backing up and contingency planning, or we have to be ready to suffer losses of stuff that used to only be vulnerable to threats like theft, fire, and flooding.

As you take steps to accumulate the most critical items of your life in preparation for Y2K or the next big computer mishap that comes along, notice what those critical items are and evaluate how much they matter in the big picture (I mean, the really big picture). Let's try the fire drill again, but in terms of computers. If all things in your highly computerized life were in danger of being damaged, lost, or doomed to malfunction due to a computer error, and you only had a limited amount of time and energy and resources to save things, what would you save first? What would you abandon completely because you wouldn't really care if it were destroyed? Most importantly, once you've answered these hypothetical questions based on your current lifestyle and interests, do you like your own answers?

Y2K is not going to be the end of the world. In fact, for most of us it isn't even going to be a slight inconvenience. But it's a good chance to think about what matters most, and make sure your life is arranged in such a way that you get to spend plenty of time and energy working with those things that matter most, instead of the insignificant fluff we often allow to creep into our lives at the expense of what really matters.

I can carry on without anything except my Lord and my wife and a few morsels to eat and a little water to drink. In fact, physically I really only need the first and the last. As much as any of us depend upon our spouses and other family members, we carry our own individual body through this world, and we could physically get by to some extent without our loved ones. God never leaves us. We sometimes might leave him or let our attention wander a bit, but he never leaves us. The reality of my life is that it has been years since I've ever spent a day unemployed, I've taken for granted the luxury of having my wife around all the time to share life with me, and it's only fair to say that I've taken the Lord for granted a time or two as well. While most of us would offhandedly say with a great deal of confidence that we could live without many of the amenities to which we've grown accustomed, the chances of that being tested are so remote that we don't really know. We don't know our true mettle. We don't know the tenacity and ferocity of our faith, because for the most part we live comfortable lives, and our faith has not come under fire. Count your blessings when everything's well, but strive to develop an awareness of what matters most in your life, and let that awareness guide your decision-making so that your actions always sustain your established priorities.

LESSON 43: PRAYER NEEDS TO BECOME A PRIORITY

While many people and businesses were focused on how much they would need to *pay* to overcome Y2K, my heart was uplifted to see that many others were focused on how much they would need to *pray* to overcome Y2K.

Don't forget that prayer is appropriate before a challenging situation arrives, during an unfolding dilemma, and after an important event is over! It's also appropriate on the quietest of days when everything's going well and specific reasons for needing to pray don't seem close at hand. There's a booming Christian prayer movement in the world today. Mission America is just one of many groups leading the way; their Lighthouse Movement (**www.lighthousemovement.com**) is an evangelical mission urging prayer for the nation and the world. In three words, the movement can be described: Prayer, Care, Share. They're addressing some physical needs as part of the care portion of the goal—for instance, they're coordinating a far-reaching care resources directory that can direct any individual to the types of help that he wants to find in his local area. And they've got a specific end goal in mind in terms of sharing the gospel—to share it with every person in the US by the end of the year 2000. The movement begins with prayer, though, and keeps prayer steadily at the heart of all it does. Over 350 denominations and ministries are coming together to mobilize over 100,000 churches and missions groups to establish several million lighthouses of prayer (which can even include tiny Bible study groups or an individual home) from coast to coast, each of which lets its own light shine, but the end result of which is one large glow with a shared recognition of the importance of prayer. At their web site you can find resources such as "prayer coordination tools" which are designed to facilitate local and national coordinated prayer both on an ongoing basis and for special situations.

This concentrated effort and attention to prayer by the Lighthouse Movement—and by other coalitions of all sizes that keep prayer as a central purpose—has been useful for our world during Y2K preparation and will be useful during future challenges as well. And these movements are also useful when there's nothing physically threatening the world, on what most of the world considers a good day, when the only crises looming are spiritual ones. In all circumstances, and at all times, prayer truly matters.

A tremendous Protestant revival arose in the late 1850s after a financial crash brought a time of prosperity to a screeching halt. Another wave of Christian conversion (not to mention a great groundswell of human kindness and warm fuzzies being passed from heart to heart in simple acts of decency and human teamwork) took place after the Great Depression hit. Tens of millions of Christians are actively praying for another such revival to occur today, no matter what the impetus might turn out to be. Nobody wishes for financial catastrophe, of course, but it seems to many Christian leaders that people in times of prosperity don't seem to have the same motivation to welcome God into their lives that they do in times of dire straits and despair. Many Christians feel the Y2K problem might be enough of a crisis—or even enough of a threat of a crisis—to bring people to God. Other Christians feel the need to pray for minimized damage due to Y2K, or for restraint to win out over rash behavior in the event that rough times do strike certain locations and cause emotions to start running high.

Take a quick trip to Doylestown, PA with me. Throughout 1999, the Central Bucks County Evangelical Churches have held dozens of prayer gatherings and other programs to seek God's help overcoming the Y2K computer problem. Goals of the coalition of 16 churches include informing parishioners and others in the community about Y2K issues and asking God to give humankind the knowledge to solve the Y2K problem. A couple dozen people at a time, in gatherings at one church after another, they've asked God to make leaders give truthful information about Y2K, to help foreign countries solve their Y2K problems, and to take special care of the weaker segments of society. Dan Collison, minister of Doylestown Community Fellowship, is one of the clergy involved. He recommends spiritual preparation along with physical preparation. He calls the Y2K problem "man-made" and doesn't see it as God's plan for the end times or as any other biblical sign. At least one service has opened with Collison saying, "We're here to pray about Y2K, not to create fearmongering," and DCF's web site emphasizes that the worst thing someone can do during Y2K is to remain ignorant of the problem, but the second-worst thing is to panic. Participants at these services sing hymns and pray, as they diligently keep track of the days left to M-Day and the prayerful role they can have both before and after this time of uncertainty, just like many other churches throughout the world have been doing.

Note

Anyone who wants to add their own prayers to the ongoing prayer effort in Bucks County is invited to do so by visiting the DCF Y2K information page at **http://www.dcf.org/DCF/y2k.htm** and then clicking the link to join the "Online Y2K Prayer Meeting" e-list.

Remember Psalm 32:6, which tells you that when we need deliverance from trouble, we should pray to God while he may be found.

> ∞ **Note**
> After reading this discussion, you might also want to review the sidebar *Faith and Prayer are Inseparable* in Chapter 2, which talks about how prayer is linked with faith, which in turn produces hope and joy and perseverance and strength and all the other good stuff discussed in this book so far! There is literally no aspect of your relationship with God that can't benefit from the involvement of prayer from beginning to end.

> *Matthew 6:8* Do not be like them, for your father knows what you need before you ask him.

In this verse from Matthew, Jesus is explaining that there's no need to babble and put on airs during prayer with the mistaken notion that lots of fancy words will impress God. You just need to pray earnestly on all occasions, as is described elsewhere:

> *Ephesians 6:18* And pray in the Spirit on all occasions with all kinds of prayers and requests. With this in mind, be alert and always keep on praying for all the saints.

The Y2K problem in all its uncertainty has been a baffling situation for many people, some of whom have felt that they don't even know where to begin in terms of understanding Y2K, the role they can play in it, or what sorts of needs might arise because of it. Even when you don't know exactly what to pray for in any situation, though, you still must pray. Paul explains that there's a place even for prayers that aren't articulated well:

> *Romans 8:26–27* In the same way, the Spirit helps us in our weakness. We do not know what we ought to pray for, but the Spirit himself intercedes for us with groans that words cannot express. And he who searches our hearts knows the mind of the Spirit, because the Spirit intercedes for the saints in accordance with God's will.

That's a beautiful concept. Forget about Y2K completely for a moment—maybe you're a technical whiz who understands the ins and outs of Y2K issues and feels certain about which specific aspects of Y2K require prayer. There will be something in your life, though—if you have a typical human existence—that will so stun you or bewilder you or knock the wind out of your sails that you don't even know what to pray for.

I've had times when the Spirit has had to groan for me. When I was in college, one of my best friends, Frank E. Shalaty, died in a car crash. I was 21 and he was just three years older than me, and I don't think I managed to pray with a single coherent word in the months immediately following his death before the shock finally dissipated to something bearable. But without a doubt, the Spirit did some groaning for me, and I was able to take an active role, not through my power but through God's, in organizing a memorial tree planting ceremony for Frank on our campus and taking other steps that helped me manage to move forward with my life.

Earlier than that, when I was still in high school, I was dating a great girl; she and I thought we were on top of the world, having good grades and someone nice to go out with, many friends at school, and good homes and families. We thought nothing could end our proverbial magic carpet ride.

One evening when I walked her home, however, that carpet was swept right out from under us. We turned onto her street to the sound of approaching sirens, and found that her family's home was completely up in flames (later determined to be arson committed by their landlord). A neighbor was badly injured in the fire, and my girlfriend's family lost every possession they'd owned. Family members were standing around watching the fire, completely helpless and overcome with loss.

I was praying for them and thinking surprisingly lucid thoughts until I saw a small boy—my girlfriend's cousin—kneeling over the body of the family dog, which had suffered from smoke inhalation. The boy lost his composure, pounded his tiny fists against the lifeless dog, then removed the dog's collar and threw it with all his might into the raging fire in front of us. Something about that action, the complete frustration he felt, and the flash of the shiny collar disappearing into the flames, tore at my heart and made me suddenly feel every ounce of their whole family's loss. I didn't know what to pray for anymore, and my head swarmed with chaotic thoughts—it was too complex, and I couldn't understand why anyone's life had to contain moments like that. But I know that the Spirit groaned for me that night, too, because even with our minds muddled and our hearts heavy, everyone standing there needed to be in communion with God. There are times when you need to pray even though there isn't a single word that makes sense to say.

Paul was constantly celebrating prayer's many possibilities. Even when he was away from his core support group of fellow believers, Paul knew that they could lend him their support from afar through prayer. Here's his outlook at a time when he was besieged by unbelievers in Judea and was struggling to maintain hope that his work in Jerusalem was worthwhile:

> *Romans 15:30* I urge you, brothers, by our Lord Jesus Christ and by the love of the Spirit, to join me in my struggle by praying to God for me.

Let's see one more aspect of prayer through Paul's eyes. He knows it's not only something we can do on our own behalf, and can have others do for us, but that we must also be willing to do for others. Here's a situation in which he's praying for the Colossians to have their strength renewed by God:

> *Colossians 1:11* ... being strengthened with all power according to his glorious might so that you may have great endurance and patience ...

Never forget that one of the things you can (and should) pray for is that God strengthen others so they can endure any difficulties they're going through.

Don't ever postpone a prayer for any reason, and never hesitate to unload a prayer in God's direction even when you're despairing, or angry, or in pain, or feel unworthy of his favor. Jeremiah felt all of that and worse after seeing Jerusalem fall to Babylon and become a pathetic, disgraceful, utterly defeated place instead of the thriving land it had been just a short time earlier. Jeremiah felt the sins and shame of the people of Judah, but knew it was necessary even in that miserable time to turn to God in the following fashion:

> *Lamentations 2:19* Arise, cry out in the night, as the watches of the night begin; pour out your heart like water in the presence of the Lord.

It is never too late to cry out to God even when the darkness of night has begun. Pray passionately, earnestly, intensely. Cry out with your entire soul and pour out your heart before him. What kind of prayer is required for a pouring out of your heart? It's simple, it's direct, and it's complete. Think about how water flows when a full pitcher is poured—the water cascades and rushes and tumbles to get out the fastest way it can. That's the way your heart should be poured out to God in prayer, and when it's purely and completely poured out before him, he'll fill it right back up for you. Don't hold back anything from God when you pray!

Make sure that you devote energy and time to prayer to determine what God is offering to you as revelation and insight through the entire Y2K problem and your encounter with it. Praying isn't limited to you presenting things to God in one-way communication. Listening to what God says in return is part and parcel of the activity of praying:

> *John 8:47* He who belongs to God hears what God says ...

In all circumstances prayer should be a priority, and Y2K has given us great opportunities to pray—for our own wisdom and diligence in preparation efforts, for strength and reassurance in the face of an unseen outcome, and for all of those around the world who might suffer problems as a result of Y2K.

> ### A Y2K Prayer
>
> The following prayer is a simple one I began using in 1998 and have shared with others who have asked what sort of prayer might be appropriate on a daily basis during the time both prior to and after M-Day. This prayer doesn't try to address every possible way we might want to request God's assistance during Y2K remediation projects, or every possible way we might want to share our needs and request his mercies during any possible Y2K-related problems, but it expresses a few things that I personally have brought to God on a regular basis during the time when so many people are working frantically toward Y2K readiness:
>
>> *Lord, be with each individual throughout the world who's doing work related to the Y2K computer problem. From preparation to reparation, inspection to correction, information to inspiration, assist people to handle their various challenges well. Guide our decisions daily, and by your Spirit restore energies that are depleted and strengthen those who feel defeated. Help the Christian church around the world to take an active role in problem identification and resolution, as well as contingency planning to handle any ill effects that do result. Help us to remember that what impacts one human life has the potential to impact all lives, and that whatever service we do for the benefit of even one other person, Lord, we do for your benefit. We know that our faith is well-placed in you and must not waver; we find comfort in the knowledge that in all circumstances you're in complete control and will steer us down appropriate paths of discernment, wisdom, and action as required. Amen*

Lesson 44: Beginning at Home

For most people, it has been important to take care of personal readiness and household readiness first. An Agriculture Department representative complained during a meeting of the President's Y2K Council in December 1998 that the agency's most frequent telephone inquiry had become: "How many cans of food should I stockpile for my family?"

People care mostly about the local level, which is understandable because everyone in the world lives at the local level. We can't be of any use to any other person or place unless we first make sure that everything's going okay on the homefront. The Bible tells us that it's a requirement for someone of faith to take care of the needs that exist at home:

> *1 Timothy 5:8* If anyone does not provide for his relatives, and especially for his immediate family, he has denied the faith and is worse than an unbeliever.

Experts feel that out-and-out Y2K concerns are far fewer at home than in business settings. One area needing attention at home might be appliances that have electronic clocks—if they malfunction at all, they'll likely display the wrong date but keep working. "If anything, it's a nuisance not a catastrophe," said Donald Mays of *Good Housekeeping*. The Consumer Electronics Manufacturers Association and American Home Appliance Manufacturers Association offer extensive web sites with Y2K information and manufacturers' Y2K links for home electronics and home appliances, respectively.

∞ Note
Anyone with a home office, of course, might face the same Y2K challenges as any business, and should take steps accordingly to remedy problems and/or put contingency plans in place.

Safe Sitter, Inc., a not-for-profit organization that since 1980 has trained more than 200,000 babysitters, has been urging parents who have a New Year's Eve sitter in 1999 to take into account possible household emergencies that might arise due to Y2K, and has been advising sitters to come prepared for the usual challenges of babysitting plus the unique challenges that Y2K might offer. The group recommends approaching the subject of Y2K at the time of the initial job offer, so that sitters understand the potential problems and household preparations that have been made.

Dr. Patricia Keener, founder of Safe Sitter, says that problems such as blackouts, unsafe drinking water, disrupted phone service, or loss of a heating source might cause anxiety or panic in teen sitters as well as young children. She recommends that parents identify a nearby adult willing to assist teen sitters if necessary. Before leaving for the evening, parents should allow extra time to review emergency procedures with the sitter. Parents should not promise their children "there's nothing to worry about" but should acknowledge uncertainty and reassure the children that they will be safe even if they have a "bit of an adventure."

Some millennial hotel packages have been aimed at those afraid of losing electrical power at home. It somehow has never appealed to me to be at a hotel on New Year's Eve 1999—I'd rather be at home with no power but people I love, than in a strange place with the power still on but without any of the people around who energize my life. When I did the exercises described earlier in this chapter, trying to figure out what I'd do in the event of a fire and what I'd do if I had one breath left, all of my answers somehow involved other people. To me, there are certain people who matter more than anything else in my life, and one of the things I'm always struggling to keep as a priority in my life is spending time with them. Perhaps we all ought to make a point of being with as many loved ones as possible on M-Day, and spending thoughts and prayers on all our loved ones who are in other places.

I'm convinced more than ever that this is an occasion I want to spend at someone's home with people I care about, rather than in a public setting being bombarded with what newspaper columnist Frank Rich calls New Year's Eve "force-fed fun." Apparently the same goes for many of us; a *Newsweek* article described some people's plans for New Year's Eve 1999, and concluded that most have little desire to indulge in the extravagant once-in-a-lifetime celebrations being marketed so feverishly throughout 1999, but instead want to remain at home with a few friends or family members and try to make it a truly meaningful experience.

The very act of preparing for possible fallout from the Y2K computer problem at home can be a bonding experience. One woman is gathering rain water and has given everyone she knows packets of seeds and bottles of rain water in the expectation that they'll need to grow their own food in the year 2000. She says it has pulled her family together and strengthened her friendships because people know she cares about them, even the ones who think she's going a little overboard in her Y2K planning.

While subsequent chapters will discuss the importance of helping your community and thinking about the entire world, it makes sense for most people to begin at home, and we should take on all work God sets before us in the same way. Following Jesus' ascension, historical accounts tell us that the apostle Andrew traveled and preached to people in southern Russia, Ephesus, and Greece, but first he spent several years in Jerusalem doing the work that needed to be done there—and don't forget his very first act after meeting Christ: He went home and told his brother Simon that the Messiah had been found (John 1:41–42). This recruiting act by Andrew was momentous because the recruit was Simon Peter ("the Rock") who not only went and met Jesus and decided to follow him, but went on to serve as one of the most fundamental leaders of the early church. Sometimes a tremendous opportunity is waiting directly under our noses, right there at home.

Lesson 45: Priorities That Are Out of Whack

The Inescapable Fun Stuff

The arrival of the Year 2000 is a huge cultural event, chronicled in everything from TV sitcoms to doctoral theses. Let's see what kinds of priorities various people have set for how they're going to spend this once-in-a-lifetime evening.

There will be plenty of New Year's Eve mass weddings built into celebrations in various cities around the world. Dozens of couples at the Viva Las Vegas Wedding Chapel will be led through their vows by an Elvis Presley impersonator, who will turn over the service to an ordained minister for the final "I do." Less flashy but more historical will be the Philadelphia ceremony for 1000 couples, which will be officiated by Mayor Ed Rendell and his wife, Judge Marjorie Rendell. Alysia Henderson, one of the mass brides-to-be, downplayed the impersonal nature of saying "I do" in chorus with hundreds of others, saying, "I never really wanted the fairy tale wedding that most people want, with the church and the limo." In Thailand, a country still reeling from economic woes, a wedding consultant is marketing a New Year's Eve ceremony with 2,000 couples as a cost-effective way to get hitched. Wilmington, Delaware will award several dozen couples a "Millennium Marriage Certificate" at a group ceremony in a city park. Ken Boulden, Clerk of the Peace—who incidentally will perform his 2000th wedding ceremony that night—decided to stage the event after getting multiple competing requests to perform midnight ceremonies. Boulden intends to declare the 75 or so couples married exactly at midnight, after which city fireworks will fill the sky.

Also in the sky that night will be a jet (a 757) chartered by a Harvard museum to chase M-Day around the globe, with New Year's celebrations in multiple time zones and with informational lectures along the way. Although tickets went for a hefty $44,950 apiece, the flight not only is sold out, but has a waiting list.

There are thrill-seekers who are purposely choosing to put themselves in the path of a potential Y2K problem. I'm sure you know that some avid surfers make lemons into lemonade by flying to areas where hurricanes have just passed through and taking advantage of the monster waves that have resulted—in the summer of 1999, one such surfer, with a great deal of big-wave surfing experience, headed excitedly to the Southeast to surf in the aftermath of Hurricane Dennis, and ended up dying in waters that weren't quite as tame yet as they appeared. As we reach M-Day, there is a small percentage of people who have, for instance, purposely booked a plane flight that puts them in mid-flight as the year 2000 arrives. A couple of them are government officials trying to prove a point about airline safety, but the rest? Just building up stories to tell their grandchildren, I suppose.

Is an airplane a little too safe for you? There's a "millennium ballooning expedition" (scientific in nature, but marketed as an adventure) that will consist of balloon flights through rough Antarctic conditions to drop parachutists and cargo at the South Pole region as the new year arrives. You can sign on as either a balloonist or a parachutist, or you and a buddy can go and do both. It gets better—one of the goals cited by the Russian team leading the expedition is "to work out operations in Antarctica using new methods of transport and parachute technology." I'm not sure I'd attempt this with completely proven technology, let alone new technology; and I'm not sure I'd want to be doing it as M-Day arrives. Oh, yeah—did I mention the price tag? A cool $78,000 pays the way for one balloonist, one parachutist, and the transport of your hot air balloon. Gallons of hot cocoa, unfortunately, are not included.

As with most of the Y2K uncertainties we discuss, pulling off these "adventures" successfully is probably not going to turn out to be a problem, but why is doing something risky such a priority for these folks at a moment when Y2K computer problems will most likely be causing genuine grief for some people, somewhere? Beats me. I feel sorry for the Flying Elvii, though (the remarkable group of parachuting Elvis impersonators based in Las Vegas); they must be torn this year between either staying home and assisting with mass marriages in wedding chapels or plummeting from a hot-air balloon toward the ice-covered South Pole. Decisions, decisions.

Odd Preparations

One Y2K book wasted its time on this piece of actual advice about how the world might be when the Y2K crisis strikes: "In emergency situations, dogs are often hungry and frightened. Stay away from packs of roving dogs. Look for signs of rabies including frothing at the mouth and absence of fear in the dog." I saw many other pieces of less-than-urgent or less-than-relevant advice given to people during Y2K preparations:

- How to concentrate on sticking to one's diet if Y2K causes food supply disasters (of course, special dietary needs for a medical condition, such as the diabetic diet, deserve special planning, but this book was talking about how to make sure that in the clutches of Y2K chaos one would be able to continue working on dropping the extra ten pounds to feel better about wearing shorts in the summer of 2000)
- Learn to sing in multiple-part harmony because Y2K might eliminate TV and radio stations, forcing all entertainment to be provided at the neighborhood level "by a new crop of barbershop quartets, wandering troubadours, and storytellers"

- The need to stock up on spices because "Food need not taste bad just because you are operating in disaster mode"

Those and many other gems were dispensed, but didn't really help people to deal with the particulars of Y2K preparedness efforts that would matter most in the event of an actual crisis.

Generators have been in great demand, with the world's two largest diesel generator distributors seeing their orders increase at one point to more than eight times the before-most-people-ever-heard-of-Y2K level of demand. A diesel generator is an expensive purchase (the cheapest reliable one you can buy new is about $1500) and there's a very limited chance of needing it during any Y2K crisis that might occur or during any future emergency. Wise decisions about how to prepare have seemed to go out the window as many people could not come to terms with the idea that for a period of time up to as much as a couple of years, there are definitely ways to have all the essentials of life without any electricity. One can buy a lot of self-powered tools and extra batteries without coming even close to the cost of that sort of generator.

One couple has chopped up all the beautiful wooden fencing that surrounded their two-acre yard to store two years' worth of firewood because they think they won't be able to purchase gasoline to run a chain saw after M-Day. A man in the Northwestern US has bought a fairly large tugboat and filled it with enough gas to get the boat with his family on it all the way to Australia, where he thinks there will be fewer Y2K problems than most places. He has stocked seven months' worth of dried foods, and plans to fish for anything they need after that. I assume it's not just me who thinks that his actions sound an awful lot like he's taken it upon himself to build an ark.

Ellis Henican, a journalist, says that these sorts of people are all "headline seekers" and "irrational kooks." I won't go that far, because I agree to a point with many people's attitude that their preparations won't go to waste in so far as they'll eventually use up all the stored food, water, fuel, and so on. But preparation has to be in reasonable amounts and in carefully chosen ways, I think—beyond that, claiming you'll eventually use the stuff up is a wacky rationalization. Thousands of bottles of bleach-infused water, diesel generators you don't ever really need, 850 cans of Spam luncheon meat, etc. are not things anyone necessarily wants to have to use up or give away after M-Day. A couple dozen bottles, a couple dozen cans, and a less-expensive non-electrical heat source are must-haves as part of smart planning, but too much is too much.

At the end of August 1999, Reuters reported that manufacturers in Japan expect consumers to hoard certain goods in anticipation of Y2K-related chaos. Shiseido Co. Ltd., a leading cosmetics maker, is going to stockpile two months' worth of materials before M-Day. "We don't think more than two months' worth of stockpile is necessary," a Shiseido spokesman said. "If the problem isn't solved by then, people would be too frightened to buy cosmetics." Asahi Breweries, Japan's leading beer brewer, has taken extra barley into consideration to make sure beer production won't be impacted by Y2K. This baffles me a bit. I understand that each company has its own priorities, but where are the public priorities and government priorities? Japan is a country that's highly technologically advanced, where sophisticated public vending machines full of embedded chips sell a tremendous array of consumer products that are an important part of daily life, where the train system is perhaps more complicated and technologically-laden than any other in the world, where 51 currently operating nuclear power plants are completely digital and computer-dependent with no manual backup systems, and so on. With only about four months left until M-Day, Junichi Makino of Daiwa Institute of Research said Japan still lagged far behind countries like the US in solving the Y2K problem. I doubt its citizens are comforted by the fact that, no matter what else happens, they'll be able to get plenty of mascara and a six-pack.

Distractions from the Real Concern

Are you ready for a few examples of ways in which people have placed the Y2K computer problem at the center of something they were focused on, but haven't actually done a thing to help garner true understanding of the problem or to take steps toward overcoming it? In fact, if anything, these folks probably have had the opposite effect—making others treat Y2K even less like the potentially serious problem it is, because now they've seen it made light of so many times. I've pulled a random sampling for you out of the distractions file.

> Letter to the Editor: I wish everyone would stop abbreviating the Year 2000 to Y2K. Y2k is alright, as is y2k, but using K—with an uppercase letter—as the symbol for 1000 is wrong. By international convention it is "k," using a lowercase letter. ("K" is reserved for a unit of temperature on the Kelvin scale.) And isn't it ironic that if we had started programming computers just a quarter-century later than we did (mid-1990s instead of the late 1960s), we would never have had this problem? Somehow the electronic revolution came a few years too soon. DR. PHILIPPE P. BRIEU Los Angeles, Jan. 30, 1999

Okay, the points are taken—but what was the usefulness of that letter? It wasn't only Dr. Brieu who became fixated on what I consider to be insignificant details in the context of discussing the Y2K computer dilemma. Along with plenty of arguments in the media over whether the k should be lowercase instead of uppercase, there's been great uproar about the fact that the millennium actually begins with 2001 rather than 2000—in the context of tackling the computer problem at hand, 2000 is the key date, but some people have insisted on distracting attention from the computer problem with drivel about how the true Y2K problem is people's lack of understanding about when the new millennium actually begins. I wish they'd do something important with that expenditure of thought and energy.

The First Night Festival in the city of Red Deer in Alberta, Canada is being held on December 30 this year—a day early—to make sure partygoers won't miss out due to Y2K problems. "With the general level of [Y2K] uncertainty, a lot of people will feel the need to be close to their business and may not be free to participate in celebrations on New Year's Eve," said Red Deer Mayor Gail Surkan, although she hastened to add regarding the potential for Y2K computer problems, "We're quite confident nothing will go wrong." First Night Society president Cynthia Edwards was originally contacted by Red Deer's emergency services department and told December 31 might not be the best time to schedule a big party this year. "December 31st was not going to work for the city of Red Deer," Edwards said. "There are a lot of people with young kids who wouldn't come. What if something goes wrong?" In June, though, the Society received a letter from emergency services saying Y2K tests of the power grid had gone splendidly, and the town could hold the festival any night at all. With most of the First Night plans already finalized, Red Deer decided to keep the celebration on December 30. It's actually to their benefit—with entertainers being snapped up for other New Year's Eve gigs, the Red Deer folks planning for a party a day earlier were able to book some acts they otherwise couldn't have.

At online shareware download sites, Y2K software is available in abundance—you can get your hands on everything from fake system crashes for use as practical jokes after M-Day to Y2K screen savers with cute graphics of computers running amok, devouring money, and dropping important data.

This final item, I'm not even going to comment on; I'll just pass it along to you for your edification. Several sports books (companies that accept wagers from the public) have opened lines of bets on various Y2K-related disasters. Greg Champion, CEO of NASA International, a sports book that does business in Britain, Costa Rica, and Russia, said, "If it's of interest, we'll open a line on it. There are odds on everything." The available Y2K wagers include:

- Firearm Stockpiling: 200–1 that more firearms are sold in the US in December 1999 than December 1998.
- Bank Failures: 1,000–1 that a Y2K glitch will shut down the US Federal Reserve for 24 hours or more; 700–1 that Citibank, Hong Kong Shanghai Banking, USB, or the Dresdner Bank (major banking institutions in various countries) will close for at least 24 hours due to a Y2K glitch.

- Stock Market Crash: 30–1 that a Y2K event will cause the Dow Jones Industrial Average to drop more than 200 points on the first day of trading after M-Day.
- Utility Meltdowns: 20–1 that a "major" US utility or European telephone company (serving a certain minimum number of customers) will shut down for at least 48 hours.
- Airplane Trouble: 300–1 that a Y2K failure will down a commercial jet.

The company is also considering bets on a Y2K-inspired mass suicide or shooting rampage, as well as Y2K triggering a global recession. "Unfortunately, as morbid as some of them sound," Champion said, "There's a number that has got to be right." Other companies in Britain, like William Hill, are also doing brisk business in Y2K bets. Most of the bets William Hill accepts are roughly the same as the NASA bets, except this one that's uniquely their own:

- Second Coming: 1,000–1 that the Second Coming of Christ will occur in 2000.

William Hill also has accepted numerous bets that the world will actually end on or around M-Day; that particular bet is the only one where bettors are allowed to specify whatever odds they want.

Summary

Fons Kuijpers of the PA Consulting Group says that even companies which complete core Y2K compliance have to shrug off complacency, get back to basics, and analyze their businesses. "Organizations must ensure that they know exactly what is critical to the success of their business and then prioritize their effort on that basis," he explains. "They must focus on the real risks to their businesses, most of which will be outside their direct control, such as utilities or their supply chain." He says it's inevitable that there will be many small crises after M-Day, so companies should concentrate on those areas of their business which are critical to survival.

Establishing correct priorities for a corporation or for an individual requires gaining perspective first, and requires a willingness to filter through complexity to determine the most critical stuff and whatever else the critical stuff is connected to. It takes those and a bunch of other skills covered earlier in this book.

Many individuals and companies have mistakenly thought that finishing an in-house Y2K project of some sort and declaring themselves compliant is the only priority, but outside interactions can matter just as much. Are you keeping in touch sufficiently with those who mean the most to you? Are you doing anything to help those with whom you interact in your community? And are you testing to make sure you've truly achieved spiritual compliance and that you remain compliant?

Let's make sure that we have assessed and confirmed the priorities in our own lives, and that we remember the prayerfulness of the Lighthouse Movement and the determination of crusaders like Laurene West as we work on not only identifying what's essential in our lives, but on actively making it a priority, and keeping it a priority in all circumstances.

Let's enjoy the fun things of life when the time and cost and calling are right, but let's not allow too much utter fluff to fill our lives so that we're distracted from the essentials we've worked so hard to figure out. And whatever we do, let's not walk around with even the remotest thought that the end of the world is amusing. By all means, the next time we begin the Lord's Prayer, let's listen to exactly what we're saying, and allow it to resonate with greater meaning than ever before. All you require is available to you in any given moment. He lives in the most immediately accessible portion of your heart.

6

Knowing What You Don't Know

Y2K efforts have been full of surprises. These have included good surprises, like the delightful initiative and cooperation shown by certain key players in Y2K's public arena, as well as bad surprises, like unanticipated mistakes turning up during quite a few remediation and testing projects. It has been exciting and a real learning experience for just about everyone involved.

LESSON 46: INVESTIGATING THE VALUE OF INITIATIVE

Y2K work has shown us several types of initiative in action, not all of them good. Let's look at a few of the different forms of initiative that have been demonstrated.

THE INITIATIVE TO SELL US SOMETHING

One of the most obvious forms of initiative has been that of pushing Y2K products.

During 1999 a company named Masterminds of Fun launched an online comic strip for children featuring an evil orange bug (I know you can tell where this is going) who impacts all computers that aren't Y2K-compliant. This loathsome villain (yes, he's the Millennium Bug and his name is Y-Rus) may also steal millions of dollars from noncompliant ATM machines, name himself beneficiary on every insurance policy in the world, and steal people's investments. The strip, viewable at **www.hidenzeek.com,** features a hero named Zeek who bravely battles Y-Rus. Company officials say the intention is to have children join Zeek "in his mission to subdue the villain while having fun and encouraging Y2K awareness and preparedness." Besides the strip, their web site offers an interactive game, a screen saver to download, and various merchandise related to the strip. The idea seems to be successful; the characters can be licensed for merchandising, and the company has negotiated to have them featured in video games and animated cartoons. They won't disappear after Y2K, either; future topics tackled by the same set of characters might include environmental and other issues. Company officials say, "The ultimate purpose... is to educate youngsters by playing on a variety of problems which, like the Y2K crisis, [humans have] brought upon themselves."

In November 1998 the first of several brands of "Y2K Bug Spray" became available. The spray bottle, created by Dan Dyce and Dale Miller and initially moved into distribution for less than $1,000 out of their pockets, says on the label that it's the "Solution for Your Year 2000 Problems." The ingredients are more than 99.7% water, plus a touch of pine scenting. Dyce hopes it becomes the gag gift of choice for overstressed Y2K workers and watchers alike. If the $4.95 red and yellow spray bottle fails to deliver the suggested benefits, never fear—the product comes with a guarantee that it will still be a "solution" if used by Jan. 1, 2000.

There have been many software applications developed to analyze, fix, and test the completed fixes for Y2K problems—about 6,500 of them in all.

Many folks have jumped into roles as retailers of dehydrated foods, generators, wood stoves, and propane tanks, as lecturers or seminar leaders, or as creators of web sites offering Y2K content such as survival gear, videos, and books. Speaking of books, there have been about 300 of them on Y2K preparedness, even cookbooks for cooking in the midst of an extended crisis, such as *Y2Kitchen* and *The Y2K Recipe Book* (and so far just one book—the one you're holding—that doesn't teach how to prepare but instead talks specifically about Christian lessons garnered by having gone through the Y2K experience).

There have been several Christian novels about Y2K, and a few secular ones as well. R. J. Pineiro's *01-01-00: A Novel of the Millennium* was packed with heady descriptions of computer programming and other techie topics, as well as lots of ultra-hip references to modern life. The *NYT Book Review* said, "*01-01-00* isn't really about anything except the desire to plug into as many turn-of-the-millennium phenomena as possible." The publisher actually made that novel into a marketing machine; the book went hand in hand with what its publisher termed a "massive licensing program" for a 01-01-00 logo which was plastered all over various products through merchandising tie-in deals with partners as diverse as Bloomingdale's and Crunch athletic wear. From clothing to handbags to luggage, the date logo was meant to cause people captivated by the book (or even people who had never heard of the book) to crave millennium merchandise. As this book goes to press, much of that merchandise has recently been sold at clearance sale prices nationwide.

It wasn't only large corporations that cashed in with all these products as part of the preparedness craze; some individuals joined the fray. In late 1998, Buzz Nofal of Lawrenceville, GA put together a "Personal Preparedness Workshop," a three-hour video demonstrating tasks like long-term food storage and extracting emergency drinking water that's trapped in house pipes. By mid-1999, he'd sold an estimated thousand copies at $49.95 a pop.

Real estate in remote places was marketed using Y2K as a selling point. One ad for a $90,000 house in Washington state declared it a "self-contained Y2K retreat" and boasted of propane appliances and an outhouse dug in the yard.

Some people demonstrated initiative by promoting alternative energy sources to those worried about Y2K power outages. Trying to get a diesel generator has been increasingly difficult. China Diesel Imports, the largest US distributor of diesel generators, usually sells to rural customers who live where electric power lines don't reach. "With this Y2K thing it's gone crazy," the company president said. The company has cranked out more and more generators (prices start at $1700) to meet Y2K orders. Shipments of the most popular 8,000-watt model were already six months behind in 1998, up about 1000 percent since the previous year, and orders placed after Spring 1999 could not be filled by M-Day.

Some Y2K consumers not wanting to deal with a fuel supply at all have turned to hand-powered devices or renewable energy. Alternative Energy Engineering, Inc. hasn't been able to keep two particular products—hand-cranked radios and hand-dynamo flashlights—in stock. Laura Myers, a sales representative for Sunelco, which distributes solar equipment, said, "We're totally swamped by Y2K." Sunelco's 1998 sales were triple the previous year's sales because of Y2K. Even full-blown home solar systems, running from $2,500 to $25,000, got a boost from Y2K. "A lot of small installers around the country that have been struggling to make a living are now booked for months in advance," the publisher of *Home Power* magazine reported in 1998.

As far as electrical power is concerned, power auctions already take place regularly through power brokers. These are sales of excess electrical power by utilities that have too much available to other utilities who are undersupplied at the moment for one reason or another—it takes place on a regular basis, and prices of course go up in the event of any emergency need; brokers will likely see some of the most aggressive bidding ever if Y2K-related power problems arise in isolated areas. This might take place with not only power but any commodity needed following Y2K, and nobody knows what those things might be—perhaps water, perhaps batteries, perhaps propane, perhaps something completely unpredictable. After earthquakes in California, some people have sold bottled water on street corners for as much as $20 per gallon. We can expect more of the same in any other emergency circumstance we ever face.

WORKING TO OVERCOME SHORTAGES OF TECHIES

Jack Driscoll is a 10-year-old self-taught computer whiz who, just for fun, does things like setting up web sites so his classmates can do their social studies homework online. When he was at a daycare center in Irvington, NY (this was back when he still had not rolled over to a two-digit age himself, mind you) he solved a Y2K problem, saving the center's director hundreds of dollars that otherwise would have gone to a professional consultant. Not every company was lucky enough to have someone like Jack around, however, so most have hired high-salaried professional consultants to complete their Y2K work.

In 1981, Patrick Bossert (then a 12-year-old) co-created a guidebook for millions of people stumped by Rubik's Cube. In 1998, he used the same initiative to tackle a puzzle of greater importance, the Y2K problem. Bossert and partners at WSP Business Technology in Britain created a device, the Delta-T probe, to detect whether microchips are Y2K-compliant.

Two types of computer companies have really thrived: first, manufacturers who have sold updated versions or brand-new products that are compliant, or that simply have new labeling emphasizing compliance which already existed; and second, consultants that have come out of the woodwork like millennial cockroaches, seemingly always underfoot wherever people have turned for the past couple of years.

Ted Ulusoy, president of EDPS Inc., which does consulting related to Y2K, says all of this advice about information technology has been beneficial to many companies: "This forces them to modernize, and they will have the experience of handling the Y2K project, which is a large undertaking. Those who have done a good job will survive the Y2K problem and have a competitive advantage in the future."

Ulusoy himself is a study in initiative. He told CNN, "My company didn't exist nine years ago. But three or four years ago, I started talking to people at high levels about what they were planning to do, and they said, 'What about it?' Now there are lots of new companies and lots of previously existing companies providing Y2K services."

Consulting firms as a rule have had a lot of initiative. In a CNBC interview in May 1999, John Keane, CEO of Keane Corp., a complete software and services corporation which has gained renown as a Y2K solutions firm, discussed what Y2K has meant to his company, saying that his firm and others "certainly used Y2K to get a wind at our backs. Thanks to Y2K, we grew our company, added to our customer base, built our management team." Keane doesn't expect a slowdown in the market for his company's services following M-Day, because computers are permeating all aspects of our society; he notes that IT solutions are especially needed in areas such as e-commerce, data warehousing, the Internet, and so on, once Y2K work is completely finished and attention can be turned to other corporate needs.

Gartner Group, a consulting firm with thousands of IT clients, has ended up the Y2K adviser of choice for the business elite as well as foreign governments ranging from powerful nations like Japan to economically embattled nations like Russia. Gartner's Y2K prominence skyrocketed after a 1996 congressional hearing when a company representative estimated that American companies might spend as much as $600 billion on Y2K, making Gartner the first established firm to suggest a solid, startling price tag for Y2K remediation. The resulting publicity encouraged the firm to do additional Y2K research, and these days its reports and rankings inform much of the Y2K journalism that occurs. Even so, Y2K has stayed a tiny portion of Gartner's broader consulting business.

With all this talk about initiative, it's time to give you a better introduction to Peter de Jager. Until five years ago, de Jager was a computer systems manager for a textile company in Canada. He was one of the first computer experts to not only ring the Y2K alarm, but ring it loudly and clearly and incessantly; in fact, *The NY Times* has referred to him as "the Paul Revere of the Year 2000 problem." He created a web site with Y2K news, discussions of coding issues, and other information—it began as fairly technical, but quickly branched out to accommodate the broader audience that finally came around to start studying the problem. By being there first and relentlessly—it doesn't hurt that he's extremely knowledgeable and well-spoken—de Jager has been rewarded. More than 100 companies have paid $2,000 to $6,000 a year to advertise on his site, and he earns about $10,000 for every speech he gives to governments and businesses. He does 100 or so of these appearances per year, and has said publicly that for every engagement he accepts, he turns down at least two. He has earned the trust and respect of people from both the doomsaying and no-problem-at-all ends of the spectrum of Y2K viewpoints, which is a great accomplishment.

One big challenge has been the lack of programmers—by 1998 when the problem was finally being addressed on a broad scale in the US, we had about 300,000 job vacancies for computer scientists, programmers, and systems analysts. When you think about it, the gap between available talent and waiting jobs has been even wider during Y2K than the numbers show, because the crop of computer workers graduating and entering the workforce these days (who are counted as available talent) generally lack the skills needed by companies working furiously on Y2K remediation. So specialty retraining just for Y2K repair work has been necessary even for some of the people with brand-new college degrees.

How high have the worker needs been? Chase Manhattan has had as many as 200 full-time staff members tackling the Y2K problem. At certain points during their Y2K project, as many as 2,000 members of a total payroll of 69,000 members have been working on some aspect of Y2K. Chase has worked on about 200 million lines of software code. Citicorp, a smaller but more globally spread out competitor, has worked on about 500 million lines.

Some retired or laid-off programmers have gotten another chance. Randall Bart, 41, a California programmer specializing in Unisys mainframe software, could not get another programming job after being laid off in 1988, and worked odd jobs. "I had dead-end experience," Bart said. But for the last two years of the millennium, he was given work as a programmer again, fixing Y2K problems on a Unisys computer. "Come 2001, I'll still have experience that people don't want," he said. "But at least I'll have made some money by then."

In his first bold act as the government's "Y2K czar" in April 1998, John Koskinen won approval from the US Office of Personnel Management to hire back retired workers with appropriate skills to correct Y2K problems, and he secured for those workers a waiver providing a real incentive—they were allowed to simultaneously earn salaries for their Y2K work and continue receiving retirement benefits. Koskinen took the search farther three months later, getting AARP and the National Council of Senior Citizens to agree to conduct a joint recruitment campaign to bring retired computer programmers out of retirement to help with Y2K repairs.

Already steep technology worker salaries have gotten even steeper throughout the crisis, with programmer shortages pushing rates of COBOL experts to $90 an hour in some cities. To retain its best programmers, Bank of America at one point offered bonuses of up to $75,000, half not payable until May 2000. Keane Corp. offered $1,000 bonuses to employees who recruited friends or acquaintances to take jobs on Y2K projects. IT managers at some large firms have negotiated annual salaries from $400,000 to over $1 million. Outside consultants managing corporate Y2K projects have charged as much as $1,500 a day. The limited available talent and absolute looming deadline for making critical repairs by M-Day has made people with the correct skill sets highly valuable.

Some help has arrived from overseas, but not much, due to "high-tech visa" limitations in the US. The six-year high-tech work visas (H1-B visas) are difficult to obtain and require a pile of paperwork to keep. In 1999, Congress raised the number of H1-B visas from 65,000 to 115,000. All of them were used by June, leaving most jobs unfilled and frustrating US recruiters. The same number will be issued in the years 2000 and 2001 to allow Y2K projects to continue, and the allotment will drop back to 65,000 in 2002. An effort has been made to raise the number of visas to about 200,000 a year, but Michigan Senator Spencer Abraham says not to expect it, because organized labor and the presidential administration don't want to give additional jobs in one of America's most exciting, frontier-like fields to non-US citizens. Business and government leaders concur that the best solution is for US colleges to produce more high-tech graduates, but it will take years for scholarships and internships to really make strides toward solving the problem that way. British-born Julie Williams, who works at a software company in Seattle, told CNN in August 1999 that she wonders why the US won't allow more skilled immigrants to fill vacant high-tech jobs, saying, "The employer is stuck looking for American citizens and yet there are people who are dying to work but can't."

Quite a few US companies have taken the next logical step—shipping their projects overseas to be completed. India, Bulgaria, Ireland, Barbados, Israel—software jobs have been sent to these and other locations in the never-ending rush to overcome US talent shortages, visa limits, and outrageous labor costs. In the past year, software projects done in India alone have increased about 60%, according to India's National Association of Software Service Companies. That has meant nearly 200,000 jobs and has pushed annual Indian software exports to about $4 billion.

Much of the outsourcing boom began with Indian software firms making themselves available to do COBOL coding work related to Y2K, but has blossomed to include several other countries and many other types of work. A wide range of mission-critical projects such as real-time Internet applications integral to the functioning of giant corporations have moved offshore to third-party service providers or software development facilities, some of them even set up abroad by US companies. It's a lot cheaper. A company with 30 workers in the US and 90 in India pays a blended average hourly rate of about $37 per worker, compared with a rate of about $89 per worker if they were all in the US. Ever-increasing communications speed and reliability, along with steadily improving project-management discipline in several important countries doing the bulk of this farmed-out work have given US companies greater confidence to send more and more work overseas.

INITIATIVE TO GET THROUGH POTENTIAL PROBLEMS

During the Depression and wartimes and other historical situations when money wasn't plentiful, people found creative ways to get the essentials of life—they bartered, they kept an eye out for neighbors and relatives who needed help, and they gave whatever services or valuables they had if a particular family had a situation develop that required immediate help. During Y2K planning, some people have come up with creative ways to raise cash—finally rolled up those piles of change, finally cleared out the attic or garage and held a yard sale, or similar acts of ingenuity.

Y2K preparation has shown many examples of various types of initiative. Victor Porlier, a Y2K consultant, advised city dwellers to ask relatives or friends who lived in more rural areas if they would mind having visitors for the turning of the new year, and to take them up on it if they said you were welcome. Some experts advised that if you lived in an apartment building with three or more stories, you should request a move to an inside apartment on a middle floor in order to realize a slight heat advantage over those at the building's top, bottom, and edges. These and many other types of advice have told people to take the initiative to put themselves in the safest situation possible on M-Day.

Residents in more than 300 US cities have formed community preparedness groups to advise neighbors and work with local officials on contingency plans for everything from emergency food banks to neighborhood-by-neighborhood power generation. Many groups have passed out leaflets at shopping centers with checklists for Y2K supplies like batteries and first-aid kits. Imagine how important these groups as well as traditional community service providers like Red Cross, Salvation Army, and others will be if this turns out to be roughly equivalent to a bunch of small disasters scattered in various locations!

Michael Hyatt wrote in *The Y2K Personal Survival Guide,* one of his two best-selling books on Y2K, that people should consider contacting the leaders of every church in their local area, explaining the need for community preparations for Y2K and the opportunity for Christian evangelism. "If possible," he wrote, "try to arrange a time to meet with the pastor or even elders of the church and show them a video or read selections from this book."

Churches have been able to do so many things regarding Y2K: inform about the problem, encourage people to make balanced preparations, set themselves up to be able to provide food, water, shelter, medical assistance, and much more— or at least facilitate these things by offering space or volunteers or whatever's needed—in the event that problems occur. Very aware of their valued disaster-relief roles, some denominations have urged member churches to invest in generators and even consider converting extra building space to temporary living quarters for those caught without heat in winter if there are Y2K troubles.

Most books published from 1997 through 1999 on preparedness advised readers to push hard on their local authority figures (mayors, council members, etc.) to make sure that actions were taken to protect the public well-being. Ingenuity has been very welcome. Advocacy groups aren't always used to working in a non-adversarial relationship with industries, but that has been essential for Y2K. For example, some Y2K project teams might never have come up with the idea of installing good old-fashioned non-electric windmills at nuclear power plants for containment in the event of a problem that results in a leak. Yet that might be prudent, and it took a few people with tremendous ingenuity and initiative to prod regulatory agencies in various countries to look into ideas such as that as part of their Y2K projects. We've also seen some innovative recycling of existing materials. For instance, FEMA already had model programs for companies, plants, and communities to prepare for any sort of emergency; these were easily adapted to include Y2K preparedness and disaster mitigation. Many people and organizations have spent tremendous effort to put others in touch with relevant Y2K resources and expertise whenever possible.

Universities have been important for their attention and insights regarding Y2K, and some campuses have shown tremendous initiative during the years of Y2K awareness. George Washington University, for example, has co-sponsored a Y2K Symposium series with the *Washington Post* that has served as a wonderful forum for information exchange about the problem in its entirety.

Many companies have arranged for more employees than normal to be on duty in the weeks before and after the New Year, often to make sure a company can return to "unplugged" methods of business. Many vacations have been canceled. My wife, a night shift manager of critical care units in a hospital, needs to work New Year's Eve through New Year's Day, and at many other hospitals, managers will greet the new year the same way, being around just in case a Y2K crisis arises. Here are just a few representative examples of other preparatory activities to mitigate problems that might arise:

- Intel has begun installing extra power generators at factories in Asian and Latin American countries with questionable power grids. Intel purchasers have been visiting companies it currently doesn't buy from to "pre-certify" them to step in if a regular supplier fails.
- Humana added Y2K information to the standard disaster recovery plan for its regional service centers, making the plan increase from 20 to 66 pages.
- Kevin Rogers, an auto repair shop owner in Chattanooga, TN said, "I think the odds of there being a crisis is 100 percent. The odds of it being serious is impossible to predict." He decided to build a shed in his backyard to stock a three-month supply of transmission parts so that his business could continue uninterrupted.

Governments at all levels also have shown lots of Y2K-related initiative:

- The city of Lubbock, TX bought materials to make 1,200 stop signs all at once instead of its usual gradual purchase and replacement program for stop signs, to make sure they'll have about 800 stop signs on hand (instead of the usual 50) in case local traffic signals have troubles on M-Day.

- The State of Washington's National Guard plans to mobilize 3,000 soldiers (about half its ground forces) on December 31 and January 1 to be available to help deal with loss of utilities or other essential services, or to handle potential civil disorder. Other states plan to have units on standby. In New Mexico, officials plan to keep all 28 state armories open on New Year's Eve. In Rhode Island, the National Guard's adjutant general has chaired a series of meetings with state agency representatives to discuss contingency plans.

- California and some other states have even considered plans to position state employees in cities across the world to monitor possible regional computer glitches when different time zones hit midnight as M-Day arrives.

- In August 1999, official word came from the US Office of Personnel Management that it would be a bit easier for government employees who must stay on the job until the Y2K dilemma is fixed to carry over annual leave that they can't use this year. Normally, an employee would still have to schedule and then cancel their leave to be able to use it in a later year, but in light of the fact that "there is no possibility that an employee can be away from the workplace" because of Y2K work, they've made the carryover of this year's leave automatic.

The Government of Canada set up seven Y2K resource centers in Fall 1998 to help government agencies deal with various Y2K issues. Dr. Donald MacKenzie, head of the center that works with government laboratories across the country to make sure their lab technology is Y2K compliant, explained the benefits provided by his team, "We are providing a focal point for information and expertise.... With the large number of labs across Canada, all sharing the same issues, there is a lot to be gained by sharing what we know and what we learn."

In 1996, Canada launched its Student Connection Program (SCP), which hires and trains college students to provide customized, hands-on technology training to small and medium-size companies across Canada. In June 1998, they launched Year 2000 First Step, a new component of SCP to promote Y2K awareness, perform readiness assessments, and recommend action plans to businesses. As the name implies, First Step was only one of a number of stages a company might need to thoroughly prepare, but offered an economical way to get started. A one-day assessment, including hands-on evaluation of up to 10 PCs, cost about $130 (US). SCP provides services to about 90 urban communities across Canada, and has served an estimated 10,000 companies with Year 2000 First Step. Bennett-Gold Chartered Accountants was one of them, and spokesman Robert Gold stressed the usefulness of the Canadian government's initiative, saying, "As a technologically focused mid-size business we thought we were in good shape for the Year 2000. However, we decided to have our systems examined by a Year 2000 First Step student and learned we were not as prepared as we thought we were."

Let's examine just one more important case of initiative being required and demonstrated during Y2K issues. In September 1999 a top Pentagon official revealed that during August the US and Russia had found Y2K glitches in 6 out of 7 Cold War-era hotlines. The hotlines, put in place during the 1960s to guarantee immediate communication when needed, include direct links between the two presidents, a link between the US Secretary of State and the Russian foreign minister, and one connecting nuclear risk reduction centers on both sides. The two countries each still keep roughly 2,500 nuclear-tipped missiles pointed at one another on hair-trigger alert despite the collapse of the old Soviet Union and the end of the Cold War. The Dept. of Defense immediately took action, giving Moscow Y2K-compliant computers and software "to correct program deficiencies," according to congressional testimony by Asst. Secretary of Defense Edward Warner. In an even more remarkable example of initiative, to prevent any miscommunications during the date change, the US and Russia have agreed to set up a "Center for Y2K Strategic Stability" at an Air Force base in Colorado. Russian and US officers jointly staffing the post as M-Day arrives will be able to talk about any "defense-related problems that emerge," said Warner.

The Russian government's initiative regarding nuclear safety and Y2K didn't stop there. Forces of the 12th Main Directorate of the Russian Defense Ministry, responsible for the storage and security of non-deployed Russian nuclear warheads, have been ordered to maintain a "special Y2K monitoring and control center" at each of about 50 nuclear storage sites from December 1999 through March 2000.

Getting Information to the Public

The nation's largest PC manufacturers—including Compaq, Dell, IBM, HP, Gateway, and Acer—along with manufacturers of BIOS microchips formed an alliance and established a web site (**www.pcy2000.org**) to provide information to the public about Y2K issues.

Microsoft Corporation has always had a great deal of information available to consumers about Y2K, and in November 1999 the company decided to take an unusual step to help the home consumer in a more direct fashion. It released a 30-minute video with recognizable hosts such as Bill Nye, the Science Guy, explaining how to prepare PC hardware, software, and data for Y2K. The video is available for online viewing at the Microsoft Y2K web site, and also is carried in the Community Service section (the section of informational tapes which can be borrowed for free) at most Blockbuster video stores nationwide. When consumers check out the free video from Blockbuster, they're also provided for free the Microsoft Y2K Resource CD, which includes an assortment of Y2K tools and all the latest patches for key Microsoft products.

It has been very possible to increase community awareness through holding your own meetings (at church, at work, or anywhere else) or by participating in community meetings already scheduled and bringing your knowledge to add to the discussion. Yes, some people know more than others, and some are actually mistaken in what they think about various aspects of Y2K, but that's why God makes discernment available to us. If you believe you have figured out a thorny issue well and other people can benefit from hearing your opinions, it's not good to keep your ideas for only your own benefit as you watch others floundering to make sense of the same things you've already worked through.

Some people have made a concerted effort to convince one other person at a time to pay sufficient attention to Y2K issues. Mark Foster posted to online message boards regarding the need to take some initiative. Here's one of his messages:

> Message: 1028
>
> Subject: Y2K, as seen by a Father
>
> From: Mark Foster
>
> Date: Wed Sep 01 1999 09:03 CDT
>
> I've been in the computer industry for 18 years now. As I see it, and as I see my responsibilities as a father of two, there is only one suggestion: Do Something. I'm not suggesting that everyone turns their house into a mini Price Club or that we all buy guns. I'm merely stating that to continue towards this date and event without some precautionary provision is lunacy. The lack of understanding that the desktop PC represents a mere fraction of the overall problem suggests that many people and organizations have not begun to accurately measure the fiscal impact of this event, therefore leaving people to do for themselves what the agencies refuse to do for us. But really, isn't that the better way ? My advice: Do Something. Whatever makes you comfortable. However, in so doing, you may become uncomfortable in what you haven't yet done.

Many Christians, especially, got a lot of mileage out of their participation in online message boards and forums. Repeatedly, in topic areas as diverse as mutual funds and parenting and sports leagues and sewing, individual Christians spoke up and expressed their faith in God as a reason for courage in the face of whatever Y2K problems might develop. They didn't go out of their way to bring it up, but they often did step in with a faith-based response when they saw other posted messages expressing panic or any of a range of other viewpoints that did not coincide with the basic Christian viewpoint. It has been exciting for me to see those Christian responses being posted so confidently by so many people—

and to see the high numbers of times they've been read by others! It's wonderful that Christians have found ways to take a medium like the Internet, which literally welcomes every conflicting idea that the world can produce, and have used that medium respectfully and steadily to share a Christian viewpoint with the world about Y2K issues, giving Christians in the know great chances to be truly informative as well as uplifting.

Many people felt an early interest in Y2K issues but waited for others to figure out the details of what the problem meant for their family, church, workplace, community, nation, etc., rather than taking action on their own as soon as they felt a stir of consciousness to the importance of the problem. This is human nature, but shouldn't necessarily be a limitation you accept for yourself. Episodes of God calling people to do particular works did not end in Old Testament days, or with Jesus' commissioning of his group of apostles. God still calls people every day to pursue certain goals and accomplish certain tasks; it's tragic to not muster the courage and initiative necessary to do his will when he makes it known to us. If you've never felt called to take any special actions related to Y2K, that's fine, but it's wise to keep your eyes peeled for any future events or situations you encounter where God does set a special task before you.

A few people in the Christian community truly altered their lives for the sake of helping people face Y2K (examples are people like Shaunti Feldhahn and James Gauss, who not only researched the problem full-time and wrote books and gave lectures about it, but also opted out of their previous careers in order to focus entirely on Y2K from the moment they felt called to do so, all the way through M-Day—and probably beyond). I applaud the initiative and commitment that such a decision required.

That willingness to move forward with a full-time commitment to the task at hand reminds me of the occasion on which Jesus called two men to follow him, and they were willing to do so, but requested time first to go and wrap up some loose ends (burying a relative and saying goodbye to loved ones). Jesus told them not to return to finish up that other business:

> *Luke 9:62* Jesus replied, "No one who puts his hand to the plow and looks back is fit for service in the kingdom of God."

Forward movement is required when we commit to following Jesus. There's a small price to pay when following him, which is a willingness to move away from some of our prior concerns and take care of what we now realize is our highest concern, the calling of our Lord.

Other people have adjusted the work they've always done to incorporate chances to help people face Y2K (Pat Robertson, for example, has made sure that *700 Club* broadcasts regularly devote substantial time to news and views about Y2K from a good cross-section of Y2K authors and speakers; Larry Burkett, whose work focuses primarily on financial advice, has made an effort to include a fairly broad spectrum of Y2K information in conjunction with his ongoing work). These folks knew that their existing projects could not be entirely supplanted by Y2K issues, and they knew the limitations of their own research on Y2K, but they had the initiative to work on helping people achieve Y2K awareness to some degree.

There's another group of people who have been in a position to teach others about Y2K and how to prepare in sensible ways, but have done nothing at all to help anyone but themselves (I'm not naming any example names for this category of people, but they certainly know who they are), and their lack of initiative has been saddening.

An article in the Baptist Press (a news service of the Southern Baptist denomination) emphasized that Y2K offers "historic evangelism opportunities." Art Toalston, editor of the Baptist Press, says they've acted on this sort of initiative before: "Whenever there have been significant societal events, such as the Mississippi River flooding or Hurricane Andrew, Southern Baptists have been there to minister." Many prominent Christian voices, including Larry Burkett's, made the point repeatedly that Y2K could be a chance to win people for Christ in indirect ways as well, by giving non-believers a chance to see Christian reactions, preparedness efforts, and coping skills compared side by side with non-Christian reactions, preparedness efforts, and coping skills. The June 1998 *Money Matters* newsletter urged readers to "ask God to use the impact of Y2K—whatever it turns out to be—as a catalyst to awaken millions of people and turn them to Jesus Christ." Burkett was an excellent and early advocate for the church taking advantage of this potential crisis as a ministry opportunity.

Having Y2K serve as an invitation to Christ's kingdom is a wonderful goal, and as I write this very near the arrival of M-Day, there's still plenty of disagreement within the Christian community as to whether people and churches have truly worked toward the goal. In fact, some people are quite mad that more churches haven't risen to that challenge. Of course, any ill effects that occur from the Y2K problem throughout the year 2000 and subsequent years (remember that some countries and companies fully expect to see problems popping up in their systems for as long as four or five years beyond M-Day) might offer additional opportunities for individual Christians and entire churches to step forward and make a difference.

Remember the situation where Jesus saw large crowds of people coming to have diseases healed and to hear his teachings, but there were so many people helpless and requiring attention that he couldn't get to them all in a satisfactory manner:

> *Matthew 9:37* Then he said to his disciples, "The harvest is plentiful but the workers are few."

What Jesus did next is extremely important; two verses later, in Matthew 10:1, he "called his twelve disciples to him and gave them authority to drive out evil spirits and to heal every disease and sickness." The opportunity needed workers, and Jesus commissioned the workers so they'd be able to act on the opportunity. Let's always recognize harvest opportunities that we encounter, and let's pitch in to do some of the work if God wants us to. We might not be given the ability to "heal every disease and sickness" but we have ample ability to be of some level of service to those who are in need of assistance. Just because we can't fix everything doesn't mean we shouldn't make the effort to help in whatever ways we can.

> *1 Corinthians 15:58* Therefore, my dear brothers, stand firm. Let nothing move you. Always give yourselves fully to the work of the Lord, because you know that your labor in the Lord is not in vain.

Chapter 2 discussed faith, where it comes from, and how useful it is in our lives. All the faith in the world is unproductive, though, if it's accompanied by a selfish attitude that isn't willing to demonstrate that faith through actions.

> *James 2:17* In the same way, faith by itself, if it is not accompanied by action, is dead.

Just as in the big picture of God offering everlasting life to us we mustn't be complacent and take that grace for granted, but instead must live in such a way as to demonstrate God's grace in our lives, we also should feel that way about our individual situations on a daily basis, including in the context of Y2K. It's great to feel secure in the knowledge that God will take care of you, but don't let that sense of security so relax you that you don't take steps to take care of yourself and others along the way.

Chapter 7 will discuss helping others, but the *decision* to help others and the *attitude* with which you undertake a situation where you can help others are all about initiative. God wants us to give service, not just labor, in situations where our work is needed. Some people who pitch in to help others during Y2K might do it because they feel it's compulsory or they have a sense of obligation, but true service is voluntary and differs from dutiful labor. Let's continue to have a view to helping others, and a willingness to do so, long after Y2K, when everything's back on track and known to be going well. We should *serve* our fellow man as needed, not just act out of *duty* to him during problem periods.

Regardless of size or evangelical bent, every church can find opportunities to be useful during the Y2K problem.

Kennon Callahan, who has decades of consulting experience with congregations of many sizes and denominations, has written *Twelve Keys to an Effective Church,* a book emphasizing the "creative interplay" of evaluative, strategic, and spiritual factors in order to make a church as unlimited and as effective as it can be. To me, "creative" brings to mind the ingenuity and initiative that we've been discussing here. The book proposes to help church congregations focus on achieving the following things, which if you simply replace the word "congregation" with "business" or "person" might sound an awful lot like what businesses and individuals have had to do to tackle Y2K:

- Develop a realistic assessment of your present standing and stature in relation to other congregations.
- Study your congregation's strengths in relation to a successful model congregation.
- Address problem areas that are inhibiting growth.
- Make fundamental decisions about the primary direction of your congregation's future.
- Decide which strategic objectives will advance your congregation's long-range effectiveness in mission.
- Develop an effective program that is future-oriented, scripturally based, and primed for success.

Some friends of mine attend a church that doesn't have a very large budget, but their church still makes it a point to take advantage of chances to be of service to parts of the world far from their own doorstep. Each year, the church scrapes up enough money through various fundraisers to send a small group of congregation members overseas to help a country that needs volunteers desperately; this year the group is going to Honduras to help with recovery and rebuilding efforts from the natural disaster that occurred there a couple of years ago.

Medical professionals are very welcome if they ever want to volunteer for short mission trips to other nations where the need for medical services is drastic, and where both knowledge and equipment are sorely lacking. The same goes for teachers, engineers, and others with specialized skills. Down the line, once massive student loans are paid off and their lives are going according to plan, many of them notice and pursue service opportunities like that occasionally throughout their careers. Initiative of this sort doesn't have to arise as the result of a specific crisis only; there are many ongoing needs, and plenty of them exist closer to home. The people of the Appalachian region, for example, desperately need health care workers and school teachers to do stints there; the pay is not good and the setting is not glamorous, but the potential to be of service is tremendous.

LOOKING FOR LEADERSHIP

During any emergency, you need resources and the capacity to orchestrate those resources effectively. Anyone who has ever been early on the scene of a house fire or an automobile accident or a crime knows that often there's an initial period of chaos during which numerous well-intentioned people try to do helpful things but without any concept of where their efforts fit into the overall effort or how best the whole response should proceed. Usually, an established authority (fire department, police department, search-and-rescue team, or the like) comes along and starts steering and directing so that redundant or extraneous effort is weeded out. Likewise, the Y2K problem has needed leaders with the initiative to step forward and orchestrate successful ways to handle various aspects of the problem.

Many people with a leadership instinct stepped up to the plate early on in the Y2K situation. Remember that God's always leading—our best human leaders in all sorts of situations are those who allow God to inform their leadership.

> *Galatians 3:3* Are you so foolish? After beginning with the Spirit, are you now trying to attain your goal by human effort?

I'm glad that Christians have been among those willing to take leadership roles in many crises the world has faced. Religion is a stabilizer, affording us a steady confidence because we know that tomorrow, as today, we have God holding all things in his hands. Stable doesn't mean static, though—religion is also inspiring, providing dynamic power to enable action. No matter how big the problem, it's not as big to God as it seems to us at first, and with his help we can take on enormous tasks.

GETTING SOME ADDED ADVANTAGE FROM Y2K

During Utah's statewide Y2K project, Governor Mike Leavitt signed the "Digital State Act" directing state agencies to provide access to all of their services online within three years. So many systems were being revamped for Y2K reasons anyway, it seemed a logical time to do this and move Utah toward greater recognition as a high-tech state, one of the governor's goals. Welfare benefits, car registration, court documents, and every other state service eventually will be available online; even public schools are directed to work on allowing parents to exchange e-mail with teachers and principals and access lesson plans and students' grades online. About 2,000 software companies are based in Utah, along with other high-tech companies; the governor plans to work with some of them to help achieve the state's goal of providing services online. David Moon, Utah's chief information officer, said procedures and rules would have to be rewritten to enable certain services to be offered online. "We don't have all the answers yet," Moon said, but added with certainty that "we know what we're going to do after Y2K now."

Some politicians have tried to make Y2K a campaign issue. Ronald A. Faucheux, editor of *Campaigns and Elections* magazine, says Y2K was brought up in several state races during 1998, mostly by candidates simply saying they would do their best to fix the problem. The opponents usually agreed that Y2K work was a good idea, leaving nothing to debate about. Faucheux says there might be a better opportunity to "draw blood" with the Y2K problem after M-Day, noting, "This will be an issue in 2000 or 2002 if something goes wrong." In Connecticut, though, the state comptroller's race became feisty over Y2K. Nancy Wyman, the Democratic incumbent, considered a safe bet for re-election, discussed Y2K throughout her campaign and promised that the state would be able to send out checks in the year 2000. In August 1998, Wyman announced that by using her own staff, she would be able to convert her office's computers for just $750,000 instead of the $6 million one consultant had quoted. In September 1998, she announced she was creating a "municipal help desk" and web site that local government officials could visit for Y2K information, saying, "My agency could not keep our valuable year 2000 knowledge and experience to ourselves."

Christopher Scalzo, a state representative and her Republican opponent, decided to call Wyman's bluff on the Y2K card by holding a news conference to question her efforts to get her office Y2K compliant and to help local governments with their own conversions. Scalzo had obtained a consultant's report indicating that Wyman's office had not finished updating and testing its computers. "Either Nancy Wyman doesn't know what's going on in her office, or she doesn't understand what's going on in her office," he said. He implied she was the one trying to use Y2K as a political tool in the first place, not him, noting, "She's throwing the gasoline of political rhetoric on the fire of Y2K." Wyman responded to his accusations by saying that she had never claimed the job was completed yet, and pointing out that her office had well over a year left in their scheduled Y2K project. After that, the Y2K issue was allowed to slip into relative obscurity, as both candidates seemed to find other campaign issues to focus upon.

Throughout 1999 Dennis Grabow has been talking about the chance for "forward-thinking companies with strategies that embrace enterprise-wide compliance as a competitive advantage" to reap great rewards. He expects an entire paradigm shift in corporate strategy to an appreciation for complete Y2K compliance which will open doors for companies that are fully Y2K-compliant. Just as companies that invested heavily in technology and Total Quality Management strategies in the 1980s were rewarded in the 1990s with greater market share, better partnerships, and so on, companies that achieve complete Y2K compliance and successfully market their reliability might be rewarded in the "compliant economy" throughout the next decade or so. Non-compliant companies, he feels, will not only be hampered by an inability to compete but also face a decline in productivity, lower earnings, and reduced access to capital from investors.

Here's some advice that was given to small businesses early during the Y2K advising frenzy:

> Y2K is a chance to change ingrained processes, many of which you may have been better off culling from your company years ago. Have you made IT decisions you now regret? Perhaps you can eliminate the computer systems that haven't paid off by terminating a product line or service. Are you stuck in a data format that has added several steps to every customer interaction? Now may be the best opportunity to gut that format. The point is: Y2K is a systemic problem that, if you do nothing more than maintain your current system capabilities, by remediating, upgrading or replacing existing applications, will leave you back at step one as new competitive challenges arise in the next century. Think big, even for a few days (you have time), to see if there's a broader problem with the system or how you do business, before putting your Y2K plans in stone.

This was a call for businesses to have initiative to do more with this moment in time than merely endure it without setbacks, but to actually seek progress while others worked only on treading water to stay in place.

Starting in late 1996, Americans by the tens of thousands were convinced that there must be some way they could benefit on a personal level by making money from the looming computer crisis. An investment craze surrounded the stocks of companies with even the slightest Y2K connection. Bloomberg, Morgan Stanley, Peter de Jager, and others created indexes to track Y2K stocks. A Washington radio station began broadcasting a show twice weekly named "The Y2K Investor" targeted at individual investors interested in cashing in on Y2K stocks.

Some companies were quick to jump on the Y2K bandwagon. Zitel, previously just a maker of computer equipment, decided to resell Matridigm's Y2K-related software tools and to do Y2K consulting. Its share price soared from under $5 at the beginning of 1996 to almost $75 at one point less than a year later. Accelr8 Technology, a one-time penny stock company, announced in Fall 1996 it was entering the Y2K business and then raised a net $6.4 million by quickly selling a million shares of stock to eager investors looking for Y2K buzzworthy companies. You'll learn more about these sorts of companies in Lesson 48.

For an example of someone to whom the Y2K problem has brought added success, consider Roger Ferguson, Jr., who on August 6, 1999 was nominated to be the new Vice Chairman of the Federal Reserve Board of Governors, the first African-American appointee to that position. Ferguson is a technology expert who, among other achievements, is highly renowned for his leadership in helping the Fed in its preparations to avoid Y2K problems. That will forever be a highlight on an already illustrious résumé.

I've found that it's possible for most people to find some ways to use the potential adversity of Y2K as a benefit to their lives, even just while making the most basic Y2K preparations. As already noted, some people ended minor procrastination and reduced clutter and started getting some mileage out of items that held value, however limited, but had been just sitting around gathering dust.

My wife and I cleaned out a few closets that otherwise never would have been emptied so that we could store some extra food items in them. We also both took a renewed interest in our finances and in planning for the future instead of living paycheck to paycheck as we're prone to doing.

Preparation for possible Y2K problems in itself has required initiative. You've seen that not everyone has bothered doing something to get ready. For Y2K or any situation, don't worry about looking foolish for making careful, reasonable preparations. Do people feel foolish for choosing a car with an airbag, or any of a thousand other small preventative decisions we make on our own behalf all the time? Of course not. Fear of looking foolish keeps people from doing lots of things, including—to cite just one example—professing their faith in front of non-believers. Strive for greater initiative at times when it's really needed in your life.

Many of us make resolutions as each new year arrives. I hope that for folks reading this book—or others doing self-directed reflection on the meaning of the Y2K computer problem in their lives—a steadfast resolution following M-Day will be to pinpoint some of the Christian lessons available from having gone through the experience of preparing for and dealing with Y2K issues, and to retain those insights for a lifetime.

In a store parking lot recently, I heard one woman say to another, "All I know is, I look forward to Y2K being over, so I can stop living at the Sam's Club." In preparation for Y2K, Americans stockpiling supplies have spent a great deal of time at Sam's Club and other warehouse-style bulk shopping clubs. Now that Y2K is arriving, I want to invite you to take a visit with me to another Sam's Club, one where no one checks your membership card and no purchase is required. Let's just take a minute and socialize with Samuel of the Old Testament, a prophet and judge who spent his whole life telling people about the greatness of the Lord, opposing the Philistines, and advising earthly kings Saul and David. On one important occasion, after the ark of the Lord had been passed through the hands of enemies because Israel was out of favor with God and the Philistines had gotten the better of them for many years, the people of Israel finally rid themselves of false gods and committed to returning to the Lord with their whole hearts.

Samuel had all of Israel assemble at Mizpah to pray to the Lord for repentance, and while they were all gathered in one spot, the Philistines figured it was as good a time as any to attack. The Lord assisted Israel to achieve the seemingly impossible by defeating the Philistines, and Samuel was extremely grateful to God, but for him it wasn't enough to feel warm and fuzzy about it. He needed to take action, and did so this way:

> *1 Samuel 7:12* Then Samuel took a stone and set it up between Mizpah and Shen. He named it Ebenezer, saying, "Thus far has the Lord helped us."

He erected a memorial pillar and wrote "Ebenezer" on it, commenting, "Thus far has the Lord helped us." Many people use the end of each year as a chance to review blessings bestowed by God, and to mirror Samuel's action. We each ought to raise Ebenezers of gratitude for perpetual providence and grace, for life and health, for resources provided, for protection from danger, for the privilege of serving, for strength and understanding. All these things deserve our gratitude, and I've seen them all in abundance in the context of the Y2K problem. We all should do this in various ways at important times in our lives, and whether we survive Y2K completely unscathed or actually experience Y2K difficulties, this moment of millennial mania and computer problem concerns is as good a time as any. Each of us in his or her own way, however private or public, might want to grab this chance to set up an Ebenezer and write on it in exuberant, sprawling letters, "Thus far has the Lord helped us."

Samuel had a way of recognizing chances to mark important moments. When Saul was being established as the head of Israel, Samuel rallied all the people to go to Gilgal (1 Samuel 11:14-15) where they could take stock of the importance of the occasion, and where they could throw a huge celebration in recognition of God's greatness and care for them. It was a gathering where they reaffirmed their convictions, became united in a cause, and evaluated their own initiative and adherence to God's standards. Y2K has been the same sort of opportunity for us as the worldwide church to assemble and focus the attention of many scattered lives on a central issue in both celebration and evaluation of our purposes and of the work yet to be done, of renewing our convictions, and of seeing great examples of how our commitment to Christ can lead to tremendous initiatives just waiting for church congregations to recognize and pursue them.

Lesson 47: Every Good Siesta Must Give Way to Work

Julian Gregori wrote in *What Will Become of Us?* that he believes during whatever the Y2K computer problem brings, "each community will see otherwise obscure men and women rise to the occasion in heroic ways." We discussed a few such heroes in the previous lesson. There have been as many people, however, demonstrating laziness during the entire Y2K event.

Laziness is hard to understand; it's rarely in our best interest to be lazy, but it sure seems characteristic of human behavior. According to surveys conducted by the Small Business Administration and professional polling organizations, three out of four sole proprietorships and other very small businesses hadn't done anything about Y2K by December 1998, and more than half still hadn't done anything by October 1999.

In perhaps the most glaring example of laziness I've seen throughout Y2K work, some small software firms that produced custom software solutions for

> ### Is Reuse of a Prevalent Idea a Form of Laziness?
>
> Almost every Christian book, TV program, or radio program that addressed Y2K issues went right for a couple of old favorites—the parable of the lamp oil (I've used it, too—see the end of Chapter 1) and the story of Joseph making sure that sufficient food was stored in advance of the famine which he knew would be coming, so that an entire nation not only had plenty for its own needs, but enough to help neighboring countries as well. Those were reasonable biblical examples to use, with comparisons that were clearly appropriate for discussions of Y2K preparations, and for some people those two passages alone formed the full extent of what they did in the way of searching for a Christian outlook on Y2K.
>
> Just because those examples were used by many others, they weren't off-limits for repetition by anyone else who wanted to make the same points. To repeat things when they're excellent things isn't laziness, but to not bother to seek additional insight or avenues to accomplish a task set before you *is* laziness. Make sure you always get real mileage out of any concepts you hear and repeat, and expand them as necessary to be even more useful to your exact needs. It's not laziness when people planning a wedding borrow concepts from other people's weddings to make their own marriage special, or when young parents adapt parenting techniques from other parents who have more experience—it makes sense to save time by reusing what you can in the way of information and innovations to get through this world in a good way; just don't ever let the large body of work that has already been done by others rob you of your own initiative and willingness to take steps to form your own opinions, make your own decisions, and forge your own direction during important events.

clients during the 1980s and 1990s decided to go completely out of business in 1998 once Y2K became a widely recognized problem that was going to be addressed in a comprehensive manner by most large companies. They found complete dissolution of their companies preferable to the thought of coping with the overwhelming technical support demand flooding in from their former clients asking about their products' compliance. It's shameful that their laziness went past mere refusal to work on a problem and extended all the way to unwillingness to do the work necessary to be accountable for their own past actions.

In July 1999, US Secretary of Education Richard Riley wrote a letter to most college and university presidents and chancellors in the nation, complaining that only a small number of schools had taken advantage of a government test to make sure computer systems handling student financial aid are Y2K-ready. $50 billion in loans and grants from various federal programs assist nine million students each year, but of 5,800 institutions involved with federal financial aid programs, only 22 had successfully used the Y2K test to make sure their systems can exchange crucial data with federal computers after M-Day. The Department of Education's 14 mission-critical systems were made ready by March 8, 1999 through the work of 20 full-time employees and around $45 million. A few unexpected problems had cropped up; for instance, three new systems bought from vendors who swore their computers were Y2K-compliant turned out to have problems requiring correction. Still, the DOE had worked hard on becoming Y2K-ready, and once it had done so, was understandably dismayed that its partners (educational institutions) didn't work as hard as was hoped. Riley was disappointed that colleges didn't do the voluntary test that they had been asked to do, and suggested in his letter that if more institutions didn't get over their laziness, he might need to make the tests mandatory.

Edward Yardeni, chief economist at Deutsche Bank Securities, did an analysis of the disclosure statements of 372 of the 500 companies in the S&P 500, a widely followed stock index. He found that just 44 of the companies—under 12 percent—had spent 75 percent of their projected Y2K budget by the end of 1998. "This doesn't mean that the others are not going to get the job done," said Yardeni. "It does mean that they aren't leaving themselves much time." Y2K experts worry that companies who are too lazy too long and then must rush to catch up are more likely to:

- Make mistakes during repairs
- Prepare flawed contingency plans
- Take dangerous shortcuts while testing

Most Y2K teams, though, haven't put a wholehearted effort into the discovery phases of their projects, but instead have worked in a fashion that requires pouring on the steam later. This laziness in terms of acting on Y2K projects is just "typical information technology" according to Leon Kappelman, a software management expert and professor at a university in Texas, who says, "You don't get any recognition until the last 30 days that your project is going to be late."

I'm categorizing laziness as something different than just the absence of initiative. I think of it as something arguably worse—not merely the act of doing nothing, but actually choosing a direction to avoid the task at hand. Laziness is knowing that something needs you to become motivated and take action, but specifically choosing not to do so.

Laziness is a relative thing. When compared to a group like small businesses, our federal government agencies can hardly be called lazy. And the Congress, which in the most basic sense propelled all the Y2K projects of the federal agencies via budget approvals and the institution of reporting deadlines, was hardly lazy—I've already praised Congress for recognizing what a high priority the Y2K problem deserved to be. Some individual federal agencies, though, certainly seemed lazy in their own ways, and as an end result, nearly half the federal agencies failed to meet the March 1999 deadline to have their most critical computers fixed.

Now, that wasn't the end of the story for them, by far—they got their acts together much more as time went on, and as this book goes to press at the very end of 1999, over 96% of all of those critical systems within the federal agencies have been declared ready for 2000, but many observers feel outright laziness was a factor in the widespread failure by agencies to meet the March deadline. They just hadn't made up their minds to take action yet. So, what harm did that cause? For the most part, it caused a great deal of unnecessary worry for those watching and waiting for the agencies to achieve compliance (all the citizens who need government services, all the other governments at the state and local levels who do business with the federal government, and all the private sector businesses that are regulated by, or report to, or in one way or another rely upon certain federal agencies in order to continue their own business as usual).

The Bible urges us not to be lazy:

> *Proverbs 6:10-11* A little sleep, a little slumber, a little folding of the hands to rest—and poverty will come on you like a bandit and scarcity like an armed man.

Hold it, you're thinking. *Didn't you tell us back in Chapter 3 that we need to make sure we rest?* Yes, but there we were talking about the need for actual sleep and physical revitalization. This verse from Proverbs metaphorically uses "sleep," "slumber," and "folding of the hands to rest" (three descriptions of catching some zzzzz's) to represent a slackened attitude by someone who simply chooses not to work. The outcome inevitably is that something ends up wanting in the person's life. Circumstances of want often attack people who are sitting still; it's harder for such circumstances to overtake someone who's working wholeheartedly at something worthwhile.

You might be wondering how to overcome laziness if it's something we're all prone to feel. I like the following suggestion from 2 Timothy about how to get all your necessary work accomplished:

> *2 Timothy 4:5* But you, keep your head in all situations, endure hardship, do the work of an evangelist, discharge all the duties of your ministry.

This doesn't only apply to evangelical work. Keeping your head in all situations isn't easy, especially in one that's as fraught with uncertainty and chaos as the Y2K problem. But if we can manage to do that, we'll be keeping ourselves in shape to be able to "discharge all the duties" of whatever types of work we're taking on.

> *2 Thessalonians 3:10* For even when we were with you, we gave you this rule: "If a man will not work, he shall not eat."

If Christians are lazy and don't put in the effort required to attend to practical matters, the example they set isn't a great one, and their ability to serve as a good witness to others is diminished.

> *Romans 12:11* Never be lacking in zeal, but keep your spiritual fervor, serving the Lord.

Sometimes comfort is a reason we're lulled into laziness. To take only one of many examples, there are plenty of Sunday School classes that never move beyond studying the same few books of the Bible. Admittedly, there are books that contain much more to work with than other books (a 16-week study on Obadiah or Jude, for example, is inconceivable, while books like Acts, Ezekiel, Romans, Jeremiah, and several others offer plenty of material to allow much longer studies). Class leaders should think about overcoming the temptation to retread old ground constantly. Tackle the minor prophets or a set of epistles or a study on the Holy Spirit or the Group of Twelve or any of dozens of other important topics that often get very little concentrated attention.

In many ways, it's easy to be a lazy Christian. Sitting in a pew week after week is a great core for your worship life, but if it's all you ever do, there may be much potential going unrealized. Outside of church, you can increase your fellowship with God through devotional time, through joining a Bible study group, and so on—but those actions require you to overcome laziness. Within the church, you can increase your usefulness by not only contributing your prayers and financial offerings and willingness to occupy a seat each Sunday morning, but by giving your presence more often in more ways, and by accepting some of the service opportunities that abound in most churches. Joining a committee or participating in a fellowship program of any sort requires you to overcome laziness. Becoming a lay speaker or someone who participates in community outreach efforts or who volunteers to help with hospital visitation or any other activities your church carries out requires you to overcome laziness. Laziness might be preventing you from going to additional services (many churches have morning services, services on one or more weeknights, plus all the occasional and seasonal services such as prayer vigils, revivals or church renewal sessions, Advent services, Easter sunrise service, and so on). Acolyte, usher, greeter, chair folder, flowerbed weeder—the jobs you can do to help your church are probably unlimited, if you don't allow laziness or comfort or inertia or whatever you want to call it to prevent you from taking action.

Laziness is choosing not to bring to the table whatever you have to contribute in the way of energy, ideas, prayers, or even simply your presence. Don't fall into the laziness trap that seems to snare so many people in so many situations.

LESSON 48: ENSURING QUALITY IN THE FACE OF ADVERSITY

Despite the mammoth tasks and chaotic schedules of Y2K projects, there has been a welcome insistence on quality by certain individuals, groups, and governments. The Y2K Steering Committee of Transport Canada, which regulates safety and security for all forms of transportation that come under Canada's federal jurisdiction, has retained the right throughout Y2K preparations to limit or shut down any company processes that it deems unsafe. While each company is responsible for its own Y2K readiness, according to André Morency, chair of the committee, "Y2K or not, all companies must meet normal safety standards. A computer failure is not an acceptable excuse today for failing to meet safety regulations, and it will not be an acceptable excuse at any time in the future."

Real estate appraisers (especially those handling commercial property) have started to diminish appraisal value of real estate if they identify Y2K problems or noncompliance in systems belonging to the property.

By now you've probably seen that construction and building metaphors have been natural throughout Y2K discussions—Peter de Jager compares facing global Y2K issues to building the Panama Canal, while others compare the Y2K challenge to building a new home. Not only Y2K remediation but the basic construction of computers and the software that runs them is a lot like the process of constructing buildings. Some experts expect our experience with the Y2K problem to lead to changes in the way software is written, just as earthquakes sometimes lead to stricter building codes. Y2K has increased the debate about whether programmers should be required to obtain professional certification similar to that required for certain engineers. Marsha Woodbury, chair of Computer Professionals for Social Responsibility, a group concerned with technology's social consequences, said, "You don't want an unlicensed engineer working on a bridge, but you have unlicensed computer programmers working all the time." In 1998, the Computer Society of the IEEE (Institute of Electrical and Electronic Engineers) took a step in the right direction by creating a new software engineering code of ethics; among other things, it mandates programmers to act in the public interest and "promote an ethical approach to the practice of the profession."

Evidence of a greater commitment to quality software projects is already visible. Sometimes Y2K consulting firms haven't helped companies that have asked too late. Many firms during mid-1999 began refusing to take on Y2K projects for certain companies, even if those jobs were going to be extremely profitable, because the consultants realized it was too late for those companies to fix everything in time and still achieve quality work.

Sometimes we must insist on quality, and that includes eliminating potential bad results in advance. Quality control in factories doesn't take place when a customer brings back a faulty product—it's too late then. If the Y2K problem causes trouble for particular companies or government agencies, it's a given that heads will roll—but firing a corporate exec or removing a politician from office won't do a thing to solve the problem. It's been far more important to help people in leadership roles to complete their Y2K remediation and contingency planning efforts well, thereby preventing problems from occurring.

While we're enthusiastic about the example that Christians can set by the way they handle any possible Y2K disruptions, we should be on guard against trying to spin any Y2K fallout into an attempt to swoop in and rapidly convert everyone in sight. Like computer conversion projects, the best kind of Christian conversions don't take place out of fear and don't take place in haste during a crisis. The most effective conversions take place with deliberation and determination, and for the purpose of moving toward something wonderful instead of away from something terrible. Think of the history of religious conversions. Were the Crusades perfect conversions? No, they were massive, sweeping, brutal attempts at conversion by force and the results of any such conversion by any religion throughout history has been eventual resentment and retraction by those who were converted in such an awful fashion.

If you're a relatively new Christian, don't rush things. It's better to steadily work on effectively purging certain lifestyle choices from which you are escaping than to force yourself to make complete and instant changes that you'll eventually come to resent and undo. Slow and steady wins the race. If you're the type who actively seeks to convert others to Christianity, don't make the same mistake there, either—hurrying and pushing to attain the short-term result you want does not always secure the desired long-term result. Your approach should be diligent, consistent, Spirit-led, and with the specific goal of people progressing toward God rather than just fleeing that which isn't God.

You can gain tremendous benefit from an honest assessment of your level of quality as a Christian, a spouse, a friend, a relative, a church member, a citizen, and so on.

My friend Frosting taught me a lot about achieving quality. In college, he was a math major struggling with his few mandatory computer programming courses and I was a computer science major struggling with my mandatory series of advanced calculus and discrete mathematics courses. He spotted quickly that we each had strengths that the other lacked and weaknesses that the other could fix, and insisted we become study partners, which took care of both of our Achilles' heels. Moreover, Dennis (his real name) and I came from fiercely different mindsets about the purpose of attending a university. My father had convinced me that friends during college were to be avoided, because students need to concentrate only on studies in order to get everything possible out of their educational experience. Dennis' family had taught him that you go to school to grow into the fullest person you can be, which includes not only book learning but a broader participation in campus life. So just as he insisted we become study partners, Dennis also insisted we become friends.

I got to know his family and he'd often ask me for help figuring out what to give his young daughter for her birthday and similar decisions which increased my world view a hundredfold from what it would have been if I'd kept my nose buried constantly in my textbooks. Initially, I fended off his invitations to take an occasional break from studying and go hit the student life center for some Ping Pong or go to hear a standup comic who was visiting campus or go to a basketball game, by quoting him one of my father's views: *There's a time for plain-old cake and there's a time for frosting—and during college, friends are frosting.* Dennis laughed every time I said that, and by the time we truly had become friends, it was a running joke with us. Whenever we introduced ourselves to a new classmate, I'd say, "Hi, I'm Chris" and he'd say, "And I'm Frosting."

By the time we graduated, I always called him Frosting, and when he was one of my groomsmen several years ago, I happily introduced him to everyone (even the minister) as Frosting. To this day it takes me some effort to remember his real name when I address a letter to him or tell someone a tale about our college hijinx. I give tons of credit to him and to several other people I met in my freshman year who taught me the benefits of increasing the quality of college life through participation in social activities as well as studies. I also give Frosting credit for increasing the quality of our academic lives by realizing the need for both of us to get outside help on particular skills that weren't our own strongest suits—he now knows a great deal more than he ever thought he would about computer programming, and I know a great deal more than I ever thought I would about differential equations, thanks to Frosting's insistence that we improve the quality of our study methods. During college, I grew tremendously as a person thanks to extracurricular as well as curricular life, and somehow was never overly distracted from my studies—I graduated with a high GPA with a double major and a minor, and went on to complete a master's degree. My life is far fuller, though, for having had plenty of friendships along the way. As for Dennis, he doesn't work strictly in mathematics, because jobs in his specialized area of math are few and far between. Instead, he got a job right out of college working for a large company as, of all things, their quality control manager. I think that's fitting.

Poor Quality Will Be Revealed Eventually

After the devastating earthquake and aftershocks in Taiwan in September 1999, officials issued arrest warrants for builders who had used newspaper and Styrofoam as part of the structure of certain buildings, in places where they had claimed to use concrete. This deceit was only discovered because of the disaster, of course. Standard inspection and quality control efforts by government officials hadn't discovered that shoddy work until it ended up being responsible for devastating injuries and tremendous cost during the earthquake.

Rest assured that shoddy work or even shoddy advice will be revealed eventually. There were some advisors who scared me on the subject of raising cash for Y2K—some Christian advisors actually recommended cashing in IRAs as a source of cash, being willing to take any necessary tax penalty in order to liquefy those funds. That's dangerous for your future if there's no need for the money due to Y2K trouble, but it emphasizes the conflicted viewpoint of many advisors during the early days of general Y2K awareness. They told people essentially: The future matters more than you think it does (therefore you must prepare in order not to be slammed by Y2K) and yet at the same time the future doesn't matter as much as you think it does (so don't worry about what you're doing to your long-term nest egg by losing money with a costly switch to gold or a penalty from cashing an IRA). I'm content with all the individuals who took enough initiative to get *some* spare cash and have it on hand for M-Day, but I have to resent the poor advice that some pundits gave out, telling people to prepare for Y2K in drastic ways without keeping a reasonable view of the bigger picture.

The Defense Special Weapons Agency, the agency responsible for managing the nation's stockpile of nuclear weapons and helping to cope with nuclear weapons accidents, was criticized by government auditors checking the quality of various agencies' Y2K work, because they had listed three mission-critical computer systems as completely Y2K-ready without having any independent testing done, and had accepted assurances from software vendors about certain products rather than directly testing the products. The Defense Special Weapons Agency was not alone in failing to hire outsiders for independent testing and for conducting what the auditors felt was inadequate testing; the auditors ordered several agencies to retest equipment under a revised federal Y2K policy. Robert Lieberman, Assistant Inspector General of the Department of Defense, felt the problem resulted from not having enough guidelines in place early enough. He said, "A lot initially was left up to the discretion of whoever owned and understood each system. It was felt that, given the sheer magnitude of systems, it was necessary to decentralize the whole operation, to give people a lot of latitude as to what they did. In retrospect, everybody agrees that that approach was a mistake."

Let's take a moment to very briefly revisit some of the acts of initiative praised earlier in the chapter.

Those Who Farmed Out Projects

The Gartner Group warned in July 1999 that contractors and programmers hired by companies to make Y2K fixes may have left "trapdoors" to move money between accounts, steal confidential data, or conduct malicious attacks on corporate systems, and that Y2K remediation projects might result several years from now in at least a couple of electronic heists, espionage, or data destruction to the tune of billions of dollars. Gartner issued a statement saying, "The likely perpetrator would be a highly skilled software engineer who has worked on Y2K remediation efforts and understands both computer systems and the underlying business processes... who feels unrecognized or unappreciated." According to Gartner, the largest opportunity for such a trapdoor being included arises when a system crashes during Y2K testing at a critical moment in a tight schedule and repairs need to be made by a single software engineer without the usual oversight and review process.

These trapdoors are possible in some farmed-out work, as well, where quality control can't always be done as tightly as with projects that are kept in-house. Some experts have recommended that projects completed in other countries be scrutinized carefully for any possible trapdoors once they're returned, prior to implementation by the companies that sent them overseas to be done.

This shows that initiative can simultaneously earn you congratulations and scrutiny, because the foreign countries that stepped forward and made a name for themselves in the software industry thanks largely to Y2K have also ended up being slightly mistrusted to do quality work, and those that made the decisions to farm out the projects have gone from being praised for ingenuity to being eyed suspiciously at certain companies.

Those Who Provided Information to the Public

People who took the initiative to bring Y2K information to the public have often been very helpful. Sometimes, though, there has been an ulterior motive. Here's just one little example: Pat Boone stepped forward as a spokesman for Y2K issues and recorded a series of announcements for Y2KNET (the Year 2000 National Educational Task Force). He said in statements, "I want to help bring Y2K to the family dinner table" and that Y2KNET offered "the best coverage of any site I've seen."

What he didn't say was that the "Educational Task Force" getting him to pitch their information was created by a precious metals and rare coins dealer,

Swiss America Trading Corporation, which made sure that the "educational" offerings at their site about Y2K finances suggested that people defend against Y2K problems by investing in—you guessed it—precious metals and rare coins. Apparently for Boone it was an easy step from recording heavy metal to accidentally promoting precious metals, but only those who carefully evaluated the quality of the information being handed to them could realize the underlying motives that influenced the material from that and many other sources which on the surface appeared to be completely objective and helpful.

Those Who Invested Heavily in Y2K Stocks

Plenty of people thought investing in Y2K stocks was a great idea, and many investment advisors promoted the idea to thousands of individual investors. If you knew what you were doing and got in and out at the right times, you could have made a fortune with such investments, but you also could have lost a great deal of money trying to hit it big.

The party was over for Y2K stocks long before M-Day was anywhere in sight. The Bloomberg Year 2000 Index rose strongly through the latter part of 1997 and beginning of 1998 (though still not outpacing the S&P 500) but plummeted starting in about February 1998. Bloomberg's and other major Y2K indexes declined for most of 1998 and 1999.

The luster was so far gone from Y2K-related stocks that even large consulting firms like Gartner Group with significant work in areas outside of Y2K ended up slumping in stock price as investors tried to figure out what might happen to all IT consultants after the Y2K frenzy ends. Gartner's stock went down 37 percent from July 1998 to July 1999, when investors for the most part were completely exiting the Y2K mania.

While some companies actually made a great deal of money thanks to Y2K, not all were big winners or even did what they claimed they would do in the way of Y2K work. Charles Morris, fund manager for the T. Rowe Price Science and Technology Fund, said, "In the year 2000, like in any other segment of extreme potential, you get some players and some pretenders."

Many companies for which hype, stock price, and investor expectation had escalated astronomically due only to Y2K—such as Viasoft, Zitel, and Data Dimensions—ended up fizzling and losing a lot of money for a lot of investors. Data Dimensions kept hitting new highs for a while, and was so overvalued at one point that its market capitalization was 275 times the company's prior year profit (far above the average for a company with a solid future, even a high-flying tech stock).

Many people invested in a company named ZMAX because it had a Y2K tie-in, without realizing that before Y2K came along, it had been an unsuccessful oil company, and even earlier had been an unsuccessful gold company—

changing its stripes as often as needed to try to ride the latest market trend. After it changed its name to ZMAX and started saying it was in the Y2K business, even though it didn't provide financial data to the SEC about its new corporate Y2K "strategy," its stock soared from $2 to $20. It later declined steadily and the entire gain dissolved, of course.

Investment advisors tried to warn individual investors to check out key details like company history, management, number of employees, and whether it seems more interested in really conducting any business or in simply selling its stock. Many were simply so convinced that they had spotted an exciting field full of potential profit and huge winners that they invested foolishly.

Then there's Accelr8 Technology, which came out of total obscurity and announced it was entering the Y2K business, quickly sold a million shares of stock for over $6 million, and had top company executives sell some of their shares to the tune of $1 million. The company kept issuing information to the press about its expected revenue stream related to Y2K, always something that sounded remarkably profitable. Sales and earnings figures for the company generally proceeded downward, and investors who watched their money evaporating in this company's stock didn't have a lot of places to turn for objective information about it; only one supposedly independent analyst maintained coverage on the stock and advised investors about it, but a little digging revealed that he was the son of an Accelr8 director. The fine print in his research reports stated that his friends and members of his family might own shares in the companies he covers, but that tiny confession aside, he didn't hold back from telling attendees at Y2K conferences, people in online chats, and so on, that Accelr8 was a good value and should be considered for purchase.

All of these sorts of stories *do not* mean that initiative and clever problem-solving and innovative approaches are always dangerous. Most of what I celebrated during Lesson 46 in the way of people's initiative during the handling of Y2K is still applaudable. Don't shy away from appreciating ingenuity or accepting creative solutions, but realize that you must be careful (and of course prayerful) so that you won't buy into shabby solutions.

LESSON 49: PARTIAL SOLUTIONS AREN'T PERMANENT SOLUTIONS

Many people feel that Y2K is finally serving as some comeuppance for an "industry that shrugs off errors" which is what computer hardware and software manufacturers have been called by columnist Stephen Manes. He has criticized "the 'good enough' standard that allows companies to ship products with known problems while planning to fix them in the next release." Other critics call this tendency by software manufacturers the "BVAF bug" (meaning they're shipping a Beta Version As Final). Indeed, patches have been more common on software applications in the 1990s than on faded blue jeans in the hippie heyday of the 1960s.

One of the things that has made initial Y2K-related analysis of systems tedious is the fact that many software packages had been modified, renovated, and patched over and over again since they were originally written, often by different people at each update. Therefore any actual problems were buried further and further within what appeared on the surface at all times to be fully functioning code. It's as if someone decided that it was critical that all the lead paint needed to be removed from homes that had been painted with it decades ago, or we would face an imminent health disaster. Some of the lead paint would be easy to find, but some of it would be hidden under many other layers of fresh, safe paint that would need to be torn away to get at the bad stuff. Some other lead paint might be hidden behind wooden paneling instead of new layers of paint, and some of it might never have been directly covered by anything, but might be inaccessible because it was trapped behind a new firewall that was added when an addition was made to a home, or because a drop ceiling was installed, or any of thousands of other reasons that might not come readily to mind if someone doesn't have a very specific, thorough documentation of the changes that took place to that entire house since the days when the lead paint was the only thing covering the walls. Now imagine this entire remediation needs to be done to millions of houses around the world all within a couple of years. That's essentially the challenge Y2K has posed.

Patching some things in our lives is inevitable—when you get a small tear in a pool liner, it's foolish to replace the entire cumbersome liner, so you patch it. If you have a puncture in your car tire, it's often practical to patch (or plug) it rather than replacing the whole tire. There are some things, however, that get exponentially complicated and dangerous if they're patched and modified in ways that are only good enough to barely fix a problem without making a wholesale improvement—for instance, if you discover you have an electrical system that contains mostly frayed wiring, you shouldn't just put one new wire in where one of the frayed ones has shorted. When you're aware of the overall problem, you should replace all of the faulty wiring in order to avoid a more catastrophic problem (like a house fire) occurring later.

Despite history's lessons in partial fixes not serving the complete long-term needs of software users, some clever folks have tried to confront the Y2K reprogramming task from a different angle instead of head-on. They've found that there are some neat ways to pack additional information into the same two digits already used for storage in non-Y2K-compliant systems, and by packing that additional information in there they can create four-digit year *awareness* in most existing software and databases without really switching over to four physical digits. This saves them from having to rework many stored data files where dates are already saved as two digits, saves them from revising certain other software systems that are used to access dates as two digits, and so on.

෴ Note

If you're technically-minded, you might want to do an Internet search on the term "Berner digits" (a.k.a. "bigits") and read about the details of this method for handling Y2K fixes.

But does this sort of clever solution truly fix the problem? If doing the job any way other than switching over to a full four digits sounds like trouble to you, you're right! Cutting corners and saving effort were the behaviors that caused the Y2K problem in the first place. Clever approaches like the bigits approach can save a huge amount of work during Y2K remediation efforts, but doing the job in another less-than-ideal way is simply laying the groundwork for additional recoding being needed later, as programmers decades from now might need to revamp software and stored data to bring it from a bigits solution into compliance with a true four-digit solution (because bigits solutions will only last another 100 years or so at most). Moreover, think about the implications of sharing data between a system that has had a bigits Y2K solution with another system that's had a full-blown, four-digit Y2K solution—any time one company merges with another, or needs to start sharing data with an outside partner for one reason or another, its bigits solution might need to be reworked to agree with the more thorough Y2K work done by the partner company. A bigits solution might be a fine thing to do if a company were an island unto itself, but as you learned in the chapter about interconnectivity, very few companies can claim such a status anymore.

The fundamental cause of some patching and other partial solutions is that companies sometimes are not willing to abandon older applications completely even when they know something better is available, because they want to ensure backwards compatibility with the existing apps (often to avoid retraining or the time required to switch over administrative and user processes, or because they're unwilling to convert all their current data files). Therefore a great opportunity to completely fix the problem is purposely bypassed in favor of sticking with what's familiar and comfortable and still works to some extent. Sometimes we make our lives backwards-compatible the same way, when in fact we need a complete revision.

Jesus on one occasion spoke out against patching and trying to make older systems keep working beyond their usefulness:

> *Matthew 9:16-17* "No one sews a patch of unshrunk cloth on an old garment, for the patch will pull away from the garment, making the tear worse. Neither do men pour new wine into old wineskins. If they do, the skins will burst, the wine will run out and the wineskins will be ruined. No, they pour new wine into new wineskins, and both are preserved."

With these two metaphors, Jesus was expressing the complete overhaul that religion was undergoing. Wineskins were quite pliable and soft at first, but over time became prone to bursting if they tried to stretch and hold new wine. The old garment (or old wineskins) that Jesus spoke about represented traditional Jewish religion, unable to hold the new cloth (or new wine) of Jesus and the new covenant of salvation being made available to all people through him.

Lesson 50: It's Kinda Sorta Mostly Pretty Important to Be Accurate

In early 1999, some motorists in N. Carolina received notices that their next emissions test would be necessary by 1910. In November 1999, the City of Philadelphia sent letters to at least 400 people telling them to report for jury duty in the year 1900. Minor amusements, but indicative of the sorts of surprises possible with increasing frequency following M-Day, some of which may be much stronger inconveniences. You know by now that most Y2K problems will hinge on inaccuracies being treated as accurate.

All Y2K work has been permeated with concerns about levels of accuracy. Many people have referred to things that aren't at all accurate in the context of Y2K, such as "the Y2K virus." The Y2K problem is not a virus and won't cause any viruses. It's also not a bug according to the accepted industry definition of a bug. It's not just a programming-related problem, and it's not just capable of appearing on M-Day, as you learned in Chapter 4. Many of the explanations given out during discussions of the actual computer problems have been either overly simplified or outright inaccurate. Even when they've been correct they're sometimes lacking an awareness of the broader complexity of the issues. People have to scrutinize details in order to notice inaccuracies, though, and not many people are great at scrutinizing the details of anything these days.

Computer programmers use the term "black box" to refer to any section of code (an entire program or a piece of a program) into which you pass one or more pieces of data, and out of which you get some particular type of output, but where you don't care about the details of what goes on inside the black box. In other words, you don't care exactly how the input turns into the output. To take a very simple example, a programmer using a black box procedure to raise a number to the third power knows it needs specific input—a number. And he knows it creates specific output—the input number raised to the third power. Sending in the number 2 gets the number 8 as output, sending in the number 3 gets the number 27 as output, and so on. Inside the black box, however, might be only one line containing a specialized **CUBE()** function if the programming language has such a function that already knows how to raise numbers to the third power. Or there might be several lines of programming code that multiply the number by itself, then multiply that result by the number again. Or a different set of mathematical steps might be used to raise the input number to the third power. All that matters to the programmer is that what he sends into the black box ends up coming out the way he expects it to.

I don't bring this up just to bore you with another computer programming concept; I bring it up because we've all been trying to make most things in our lives into black boxes. We might buy a lawnmower recommended by Consumer Reports because we trust their output (their recommendation about which lawnmower to buy) and never investigate the mower in detail ourselves. We don't know exactly how CR goes about the testing, but we feel that we can trust the results. No big deal—that's a fine way to make decisions and take actions as we all live busy lives in an increasingly busy world.

Think about other areas that some people treat as black boxes, though. They drop their young children at day care and don't scrutinize the details of what happens while the children are there, and pick them up at the end of the day assuming they've come out all right. They assume that the kids will not only be healthy at the end of each day, but at the end of a couple of years will come out ready to smoothly enter school because the innards of the black box (the day care program) are working correctly. There are many other black boxes throughout our lives, and as long as we put in and get out what we expect, we don't spend a great deal of time examining the details of what's going on inside the black box. That's why individuals and communities are always so surprised when there's a scandal involving a Cub Scout leader molesting members of his troop, or a church treasurer caught embezzling funds, or any of thousands of other unpleasant surprises that occur now and then all over the world. Some black boxes that seem very trustworthy have incorrect things taking place inside of them.

A major Y2K challenge has been accurately examining everything to the necessary extent—prior to Y2K projects, most people in business, even the IT people, didn't know enough about the innards of how their systems had been built from the ground up. This is the result of several things, most notably:

- Turnover in personnel
- Advances in languages and equipment bringing more and more "black box" situations
- Interconnectivity among departments (and whole buildings, and eventually whole companies) that each began with an independent system, but were "bridged" to each other; people who build hardware and software bridges to make these connections often learn only enough about the older systems on both ends to facilitate the merger, and don't necessarily spend any time revising code and incorporating total consistency at the original code level

Knowing What You Don't Know

You probably know less than you realize about even the most important systems in your life. Say you own a house that's now around 40 years old, have lived there for 20 years, and have done an average amount of repairs and renovation during those years. First of all, do you have access to a complete set of blueprints for the original construction of the house? Next, can you say with certainty that you can remember every new part that's been added to the plumbing system or electrical system (the location, the supplier, and the date it was added) and that every component of both those systems as well as every appliance in the house conforms to today's building codes, and where all the underground utilities are buried, and the date that each tree in the yard was planted (and which nursery it came from), and any number of other details which are comparable to the types of details IT managers had to nail down when they undertook the assessment phase of their Y2K efforts. Most likely, all you know for sure is that as each repair or improvement was done to your home, you or other family members or any hired experts completing each job made sure that the new stuff worked well enough with the existing stuff, and then left it at that.

In Y2K work, where accuracy was essential, certain people held the standard of exactitude at remarkable levels. Judi Worsham, data processing manager for the Medicaid program in Oklahoma, kept track of her work with great precision even before all the Y2K concerns about accuracy of information had come to the forefront. Here's one of her actual statements to the press back in 1998: "As of November 5, we have completed 55.07 percent of the work to be done by June 30, 1999, and we have used 56.51 percent of the days available since we started on January 1 of this year."

Huge companies with the most complicated array of potential problems were sometimes the most diligent about pursuing accurate assessment. Some members of the Y2K team at PSE&G, a large utility, spent much of 1998 trudging through a program consisting of 7 million lines of code. That was just one program! In its overall Y2K effort, PSE&G had to work on over 700 programs with a total of about 46 million lines written in more than two dozen programming languages.

Our personal challenge is examining ourselves as thoroughly as businesses conducted the Y2K assessment phase. Find out which of our systems (faith, ethics, emotions, desires, goals, and all the other things that make up a functioning person) are inconsistent with the others, have flaws, or could simply use a replacement part to make sure they keep functioning well. Find out which of our systems interface with other systems that are corrupted or riddled with incorrect data, and decide what we can do to prevent that external influence from causing bad results in our own system. Lastly, once we've figured out that something does need to be fixed or replaced, we should conduct a remediation effort within ourselves that's as rapid and rigorous as possible.

Another term I want to spring on you is "blind spot" which as I apply it to Y2K is slightly different from the way you know it in the context of automobile mirrors. Even when a computer problem is recognized and addressed, things that occurred during the problem aren't always remedied. Think about a price at the grocery store ringing up incorrectly, which happens all the time. You notice and bring it to the cashier's attention—he fixes the charge on your order (at some stores, even gives you the product at a discount or free), and as long as it's an honest store they immediately find and correct the computer flaw that's making the price ring up incorrectly, so that no future customer will be overcharged. What they don't do (have no way of doing, and feel no sense of obligation to do) is figure out which previous customers were also overcharged for the same item, and refund their money. Those customers have therefore paid too much because their transaction with the store took place in what I call a blind spot, a period during which neither party to a transaction was aware that the transaction was flawed. Whenever a Y2K problem is found, there's the potential for business activity or data transfer or important decision-making to have occurred during the blind spot, and not everyone will realize there's a need to go back and rework everything that took place while the Y2K problem was in place before its discovery.

You know that many companies have a "Fix it on Monday" attitude about Y2K, figuring that most problems are going to be of the inconvenience-causing variety and can be remedied once they're discovered on January 3, 2000. So some things might go on a little too long when January 1, 2000 arrives and get fixed two days later. At first that doesn't sound very problematic, but what if that traffic accident or speeding ticket which has been preventing someone from getting auto insurance at reasonable rates never drops off his record as it was supposed to after three years, because the three-year anniversary date happens to fall into that small blind spot? What if thousands of other inconvenient things fall into the blind spot and aren't ever discovered?

It's often sufficient to notice and correct problems after a while, but there will be companies that don't realize (or don't care) that to fully correct the impact of the problem, they need to dig into the details of what took place during that blind spot when no one yet realized that anything was wrong, and find all the transactions or activities that seemed on the surface to go correctly during that timeframe, and undo and then properly redo those things. Moreover, any transactions or activities that were supposed to be done during that timeframe but were mistakenly left undone need to be identified manually and then completed. When scattered Y2K problems arise in 2003 or 2006 or whenever, will all the necessary corrections actually take place? It's anybody's guess at this point.

There are several areas of Y2K concerns where accuracy doesn't seem to have been taken to the greatest possible level. In August 1999, New Zealand

Y2K specialist Jocelyn Amon spent part of one workday searching Internet web pages for Y2K errors and "was easily able to find over 300." She found examples of date-related errors in code written in several languages, including C++, Perl, and Java. Some web programmers don't realize that they can create the same sorts of date-related problems as "traditional" programmers. The problem-riddled web pages Amon found were written in the past year or so, and several were at online tutorial sites offering code for other programmers to learn from or reuse.

"Because of the changing nature of computing," Amon points out, "we are frequently only beginners in whatever language we are developing in." She contends that web programmers often don't learn from textbooks and manuals, preferring to learn from each other or by borrowing code from other web sites, and are also sorely lacking in peer review processes. She has received a lot of criticism from the programming community for being so outspoken on Y2K problems. She has been flamed (had an onslaught of angry messages directed at her) in newsgroups and has gotten into arguments online during which other coders claim some of the date-related problems she's discussing aren't strict Y2K problems, but rather regular bugs based on flawed logic that just happen to cause problems starting on M-Day, which they feel somehow don't qualify to be called "Y2K problems." Amon is unyielding, saying, "Programmers should know by now. There is no excuse—we've been hammered with information about Y2K."

There have been mistakes in Y2K monitoring; as a minor example, Gov. Jeb Bush's Team Florida 2000 web site has taken jabs from journalists for affiliating some medical facilities with the wrong counties and other mistakes which don't necessarily sound important on the surface, but which could be significant if they ever led to critical systems falling through the cracks because some Y2K team responsible for certain systems wasn't told about a problematic system within their purview. There also have been mistakes in the distribution of information about Y2K; for example, a description of an online course named *Is Your PC Ready to Face the Year 2000?* contained numerous errors, and I certainly wasn't going to pay the tuition to find out if the course materials were also error-prone.

One amusing inaccurate item I stumbled across during Y2K research was the Y2K countdown clock offered on the web site of one of the leading Y2K consulting firms (a company whose name you've seen several times in this book and in many other Y2K discussions), which had been written incorrectly in JavaScript and was off by one hour. No big deal, really, except that the countdown was ticking off every second until M-Day arrived, and this consulting company was making millions of dollars promising its clients that it would be thorough, precise, and not miss a single detail of necessary Y2K remediation. I sent the company an e-mail message suggesting that they might want to reprogram the countdown clock to be as accurate as possible, and received a thank-you message after they adjusted the clock the next day.

Here's a fascinating example of inaccuracies circulating during Y2K work. In June 1999, the Federal Aviation Administration made a point of telling consumers not to believe some US airline representatives who were blaming Y2K systems testing for flight delays. Paul Takemoto, an FAA spokesman, said, "I have no idea why airlines would say that. It's completely false." Michael Motta of the Seattle branch of the National Air Traffic Controllers Association suggested that the reason was simply airlines hoping to use Y2K to deflect blame from themselves for certain delays. The incident in June that triggered the FAA comment was that despite the fact that all such testing had been completed the previous March, American Airlines agents in Chicago told some passengers that nationwide stoppages were being caused by Y2K testing, a claim completely refuted by an FAA public affairs representative. John Hotard, a spokesman for American asked about the incident, told reporters that agents at gates sometimes seek convenient answers to give to frustrated passengers, and said, "Y2K testing can be an easy answer to give for delays when they really don't know. We need to do a better job of giving accurate information to agents."

Insiders at the FAA told CNN and other news outlets about a similar incident in May 1999 when FAA head Jane Garvey was told by US Airways agents who didn't know about her high-powered connections that a flight delay had resulted from Y2K testing of air-traffic control systems. Garvey checked with her own people and discovered the excuse was inaccurate; lo and behold, US Airways officials soon issued a statement acknowledging the importance of agents being accurate with customers.

Remember Accelr8 Technology, the company that came out of nowhere claiming it was a Y2K solutions provider and ended up having its stock price soar as a result? On November 16, 1999 the death knell pretty much sounded for the company when the SEC charged the company and three of its executives with misrepresenting the company's Y2K software and using questionable accounting methods. The company's legal counsel disputes the charges and will take proper avenues of defense. David Zisser, the company's lawyer, said the SEC might be "trying to take some things out of context."

The SEC complaint alleges that Accelr8 and its two top officials made false claims in press releases and SEC filings from 1997 to 1999 about the capabilities of its Navig8 2000 software, claiming it could analyze programs for IBM, Unix, and Windows NT machines, whereas according to the SEC the software was created to only analyze programs for VAX/VMS machines. It also alleges that Accelr8 filed false financial statements with the SEC from April 1998 through

April 1999, counting revenue from contracts that actually went unfulfilled and other accounting discrepancies. After the SEC charges, Accelr8 shares dropped to less than $2 again for the first time since the surge of publicity two years earlier fueled in part by their own agents and officers.

It doesn't matter what the outcome of the Accelr8 court battle is—the damage is done, M-Day is practically upon us, and investors were seduced long ago into pouring millions of dollars into the company. The inaccurate claims about what their software can test might at the very least have ripped off investors, and also might have caused certain naive businesses to wind up with incomplete or incorrect Y2K remediation projects.

Lesson 51: You Can't Let Down Your Guard

In late 1998, President Clinton praised the Social Security Administration for completing its basic Y2K remediation ahead of schedule. On September 3, 1999 the agency acknowledged that it had unknowingly sent out letters to more than 32,000 people informing them that certain benefits they were currently receiving would end on January 1, 1900. This minor glitch is one of many that have proven that even those ahead of the game can still have problems occur, and that everyone needs to stay alert rather than become complacent and feel assured that their work is both finished and flawless.

Resource planning has been crucial. Many consulting firms have been overwhelmed with requests to have on-call resources available during the last two weeks of December 1999 and the first few weeks of the year 2000. Many corporate clients are prepaying for resources that they hope never to use, just to make sure someone will be available in case of Y2K failures. A very common practice to help companies be as alert as necessary has been disallowing vacations to ensure that people will be at work in the event of Y2K problems as the new year arrives.

A Fall 1998 survey from *CIO Magazine*, a publication aimed at top executives of large corporations, indicated concern among business leaders. 56 percent of the executives they had surveyed believed the Y2K problem would not be resolved by M-Day, and some of them envisioned true trouble on the horizon. 10 percent said they would be stockpiling food, 11 percent said they'd be buying generators or wood stoves, and 13 percent had decided to upgrade their personal security "with alarm systems, fencing, and firearms." Abbie Lundberg, the magazine's editor-in-chief, said those execs weren't going overboard: "They're not thinking about building bunkers and learning how to tan hides." They simply had decided to be on alert and have basic plans in place in case problems such as power outages happened to arise.

As individuals and governments and churches, we know how to rally around a cause. Unfortunately we so often do it after a problem of some sort has already occurred. We kick into a state of high activity once something big is underway. I'm glad we can do that, but I'd like to see us stay in a higher gear on a more constant basis if at all possible. Religion tends to be more or less seasonal, with churches having times of relaxation and times of intensive effort, and in the course of a typical year most congregation members in any given local church know when to expect lulls and when to expect the church life to take on a frenzied feeling. The worldwide church works this way, too, coming together in a whirlwind of activity once in a while when there's a tremendous cause to focus upon—Y2K has been one such cause. It won't surprise me at all if there are plenty of other situations beyond Y2K that manage to mobilize and stir the passion of the worldwide church. As individual churches, though, let's try to maintain our passion for serving and outreach and community involvement whether the universal church as a whole seems to be on full alert or not, and as individual congregation members, let's try to maintain our enthusiasm for sharing our faith and our overflowing grace with others whether our local church as a whole seems currently to be in or out of season.

The chance for trapdoors was discussed in Lesson 48. Those and other possible problems with Y2K repair work have provided reasons for managers of Y2K projects to stay on alert not only through M-Day but well beyond it.

Members of the early church received numerous warnings to remain alert:

> *1 Peter 5:8-9* Be self-controlled and alert. Your enemy the devil prowls around like a roaring lion looking for someone to devour. Resist him, standing firm in the faith, because you know that your brothers throughout the world are undergoing the same kind of sufferings.

RELATED VERSE:
MATTHEW 10:16-17
1 THESSALONIANS 5:8
1 PETER 1:13

About four years ago, I considered throwing my hat in the ring along with other consultants and doing nothing but Y2K remediation jobs until the year 2000. Every consultant knew that there'd be big bucks available during 1999 to everyone who had proven themselves knowledgeable in the field by that point. I did what my heart told me instead, and devoted time to general church computing issues and to helping computerize small churches, with Y2K preparation work a full-time interest and occasional side job. On a personal level, I'm glad that I didn't plunge full-time into Y2K-related work. It has been hard on the people who have done so. I'm a perfectionist and would have been prone to year after year of 90-hour workweeks that wouldn't have allowed me to work on many other important things I've been proud to be involved with for the past few years.

We not only need to be alert to dangers and problems we might encounter, but in general we need to be alert to the correct things to do and the correct time to do them. How often do we evaluate ourselves that thoroughly, though? Most of us don't, and instead are happy with the overall person we are, content to glide along in a state of contented bliss without actively seeking chances to identify and improve anything about ourselves or our chosen paths. For many people, the task of honest, thorough self-evaluation proves as difficult as the Y2K analysis phase was for many businesses. My wish for all individuals in today's world, Christian or non-Christian, is to strengthen their awareness of their own internal "systems." Document (at least make mental note of) certain things that are unique or excellent or weak about your own system so that those things never surprise you when they crop up in your daily interactions with the outside world. Decide if anything needs remediation, and if so, fix it as promptly as you can so that it never gets a chance to undermine your overall functioning. Above all, stay alert to the types of traps that might exist because your own system isn't completely fixed, as well as the types of outside influences that might come along and mesh badly with your own system.

LESSON 52: SO MANY MISTAKES, SO LITTLE TIME

When January 1999 arrived, minimal Y2K problems were reported by some systems that were dealing with year 2000 dates for the first time:

- Government computers in Washington, DC and several states couldn't sign people up for unemployment benefits because forms couldn't recognize a date in the year 2000 as the ending date for the benefits.
- Taxi meters had plenty of problems, with some in Singapore unable to run for several hours on January 1, and some in Stockholm (to the pleasure of passengers) unable to switch to higher fares on January 1 as they were supposed to.
- Some accounting software produced incorrect invoices or proved unable to issue correct ones.
- A company named Environmental Systems Products found that some of its equipment could not produce a 00 windshield sticker for indicating that vehicles had passed inspection. Instead of the 00 sticker that should have started appearing December 22, the faulty equipment printed out

stickers saying 91 and many inspection stations unwittingly put them on cars, causing some drivers to get tickets for being apparently eight years overdue for inspection. The problem cost the company a lot of money as well as mild embarrassment.

Ian Hayes, president of Clarity Consulting, cautioned at the time that "there are a hundred problems for every one reported" and numerous experts warned that companies with systems creating bad data might not realize it for some time. John Koskinen, head of the President's Y2K Council, expressed concern that the relatively smooth entry into 1999 might encourage local governments and small businesses to adopt a "wait until it breaks" policy which would be a bad approach to dealing with Y2K concerns during the final year before 2000.

Many times people think that it's okay to leave certain little mistakes uncorrected, without realizing what huge problems they can grow into. Each year, enthusiastic tourists to Florida, knowing they shouldn't do so, purchase baby alligators and bring them back to their home states because they can't resist how "adorable" the tiny animals are. Inside of a couple of years, most of these folks request help from zoos, professional animal handlers, or other authorities to undo the mistake they made by bringing the small gator home with them.

Think of all the other examples you've seen of people leaving small mistakes in place so long that they became much larger ones. Early negligence has led to increasingly severe problems in the case of kudzu, the Japanese plant which was brought to the southern US for decorative purposes by a few people who didn't foresee what would happen in the US without the same natural opposition to kudzu spreading that exists in Japan. Kudzu has now steadily spread its way across large portions of several states, killing many other plants and trees that it covers, and establishing roots that can become as thick as two feet in diameter. About three years ago, I saw an abandoned house completely swallowed by kudzu in a matter of months, until just one row of bricks at the top of the chimney poked through at the top of the house-shaped kudzu patch to indicate that a home had once stood in that spot. Dow Chemical and other companies have been working in conjunction with government agencies on solutions to the kudzu problem, but that small, original mistake has grown into something completely unwieldy and difficult to overcome.

We all recognize the truth housed in the Bible example of the seed sown among the thorns which eventually is strangled and never realizes its potential (Matthew 13:7). You reap exactly what you sow according to where it's sown, and only if you choose well-prepared ground and eliminate any encroaching weeds and maleficent plants can you have a great crop of whatever good stuff you're trying to grow, whether it's a good computer system or a good Christian produced by the sowing of the word of God. Do your sowing carefully, and along the way keep an eye out for mistakes you might be allowing to take root in your life or in the life of your church, realizing that they're liable to become more damaging and more difficult to do away with the longer they're ignored.

Mistakes During Preparation

Paul and Christina, a couple in Florida, were worried about the Y2K problem, so as one of their initial preparation steps, they got $20,000 in cash from their bank accounts and buried it eight inches below ground in their backyard, then placed a doghouse over the spot. They planned to use the money for a generator and other Y2K supplies. They woke up one morning, however, to find that the doghouse had been moved and the money had been stolen.

Some other people haven't stored their Y2K water, dried food, and other supplies correctly, and have lost a major investment due to poor preparations, such as cans that could rust, containers that weren't insect-proof or rodent-proof, and so on.

Mistakes During Repair Efforts

With huge teams of programmers working on Y2K solutions, sometimes they took actions that contradicted each other, and sometimes they found new errors that other members of their own Y2K solutions team had introduced.

On average, for every 1000 lines of code programmed, over 50 new errors are introduced—don't forget that there are both syntax errors and logic errors, and several subtypes of each. With brand-new programs being written completely from scratch, those errors are easier to debug than with revisions of existing programs. When you're injecting new code into an old program or simply revising a section of old code, your ability to find and resolve new errors is usually dependent on the consistency of the original code you're working with.

You know by now that older programmers aren't completely to blame for the Y2K problem. For quite some time, many end users have been entering two-digit dates in spreadsheets, databases, and other applications that require dates to be input. Most application software uses some rule of thumb to determine the century for two-digit dates that are entered. Some software assumes the years 24 and higher are in the 20th Century, while the years 23 and lower are in the 21st Century. Other software uses 31 and above as the 20th Century, with 30 and below as the 21st Century. Any such rule of thumb is nothing like a comprehensive solution that allows every four-digit date to be used. So, those of us who have gladly entered two-digit dates in our applications as a way to speed up input for the past several years might have to update a lot of data now to make sure all dates match up with the correct centuries; otherwise, we might have mistakes buried deep within our data files.

Shaunti Feldhahn's Y2K book contained a section called "A Few Encouraging Facts" and the first item listed was, "New automatic techniques are being invented and adopted to speed the fix. While none can ever be the single, longed-for silver bullet, they can assist the process enormously."

In the past couple of years, in fact, several companies have developed new diagnostic and recoding tools that could partially automate the tedious process of locating and repairing outdated code involving dates and date calculations. Well, in some cases this is even scarier than not having any automation at all. Any of us who have used computers for decades know that there are limitations to the flexibility and intuitiveness of all software, and some situations arise where all the programming logic in the world doesn't cover the complexities and particularities. Humans (sometimes one human taking ten seconds to discern how something needs to be approached, but sometimes entire teams of humans taking years of study) are required to figure out the necessary solutions in those situations.

The importance of human involvement can't be overemphasized in Y2K situations and many other troubleshooting situations. All the computer diagnostics in the world can't handle every problem your automobile has, for example, because while the computer display says "Check A, B, and C to determine cause of stuck belt" a human mechanic will hear the mews of a frightened stowaway kitty cat (or any other bizarre possibility D) and reach up there to remove the claws—er, cause—of the stuck belt. Anytime you take a new piece of software and have it renovate old software that you haven't personally inspected with human insight, there's a likelihood that at some point or other, the repair software is going to run across a chunk of the old software that it doesn't know what to do with, or worse yet, misinterprets. If the repair program throws an exception and calls for human assistance at that point, things are probably okay, but if the repair program for some reason feels it understands the code it's reviewing and makes incorrect changes, then quickly the situation turns into the blind leading the blind, and one mistake in one location of a program that's several thousand lines long can easily cascade into dozens or hundreds of related mistakes.

Sometimes a mistake is just misperception; for example, to fix date fields you have to first identify them as date fields, but not all programmers name date fields the same way, and not necessarily in ways that make sense.

The tragic reality that some Y2K fixes themselves have been partially or entirely wrong is spoofed in a popular joke memo circulating on the Internet since 1998, which pokes fun at misunderstanding what Y2K compliance really means and doing something wrong as a result:

A worker sends the following memo to his boss:

TO: Mr. Dunphy

FROM: Bruce Blodgett

RE: Date conversion you requested

I hope that I haven't misunderstood your instructions because, to be honest, none of this "Y to K" conversion effort has made much sense to me. At any rate, I've had my team go through all the databases and application files, analyze every line of programming code in all current and archived systems, and revise the online scheduling calendar as well as the printed office calendars. I'm happy to report that we've completed all necessary modifications and enhancements to correctly reflect these month names:

Januark

Februark

Mak

Julk

Also, the days of each week have been changed to Sundak, Mondak, Tuesdak, Wednesdak, Thursdak, Fridak, and Saturdak.

Your entire operation should now be fully Y to K compliant.

There truly have been misunderstandings by staff members that have led to mistaken fixes (in ways far more subtle than this Y-to-K joke, of course). There also have been plenty of mistakes made in terms of incomplete fixes. The 1972 fix described earlier in the book as acceptable for some people's purposes (for instance, to keep your home VCR on the correct weekdays during 2000 if it only accepts two-digit years and you don't want to buy a new VCR) has been used in some programming situations as a temporary fix to keep things running on a very limited basis until more substantial reworking of code can be done. That becomes very dangerous for any systems that do calculations—all it takes is one overlooked calculation that you don't adjust back from 1972 to 2000 by addition of years (or minutes, or months, or whatever units the context requires) and you've got a big mess with potentially faulty data.

One of the most inconvenient and costly examples of a problem caused by a Y2K conversion project took place in England. London Electricity PLC, a major utility serving the London metropolitan area, has a system named Powerkey that allows customers to prepay their electricity bills at stations in stores around London, then get credit for the payment by running their "key" (a smart card) through a reader. At home, each customer inserts the key into his or her electricity meter, which monitors the amount of prepaid electricity. After the company's software had been upgraded for Y2K and some customers had been given new keys designed to be Y2K-compliant, some of the new keys caused glitches or complete shutdowns of certain older home meters. Of about 8,000 people who got the new keys before London Electricity realized the problem and stopped distribution of the new keys, around 2,000 had problems at their home meters which caused the power to go out completely, and around 2,000 more had less severe problems.

London Electricity has about two million total customers, so the percentage of customers that experienced problems before the bad keys were stopped was tiny, but the overall event really rattled people. According to *This Is London*, a daily newspaper, some of the customers with outages went without sleep for a few days because they worried about missing the utility's engineers whenever they came by to fix the problem (the utility had warned them that they might have to wait another 24 hours for the next service technician if they missed the first one). After two weeks, there were still about 200 customers having problems with their meters, but eventually all the troubles were resolved and the utility reworked and relaunched the upgraded Powerkey program later in the year.

Mistakes During Testing

Even if Y2K fixes didn't cause problems, sometimes Y2K testing did:

- A Y2K test of a satellite orbiting the earth in 1998 caused 90 percent of the world's pagers to be nonfunctional momentarily.
- The well-informed industry grapevine still asserts that it was a Y2K test in June 1997 that caused Smith Barney (a huge financial firm) to momentarily place an additional 19 million dollars in numerous customer accounts (causing over $10 trillion in erroneous balances), although the company has never publicly acknowledged the cause of the error.
- During a Y2K test, an inventory control system for the US military wrongly marked 90,000 items for removal from the inventory system.

∽ Note

Computer-induced mistakes are not unique to Y2K, of course. On one of my books about programming for a large computer book publisher, an editor doing a spelling check on the book's front matter (the title page, etc.) was in too much of a hurry, and when my last name was questioned because it wasn't in his spelling checker's dictionary, he accidentally agreed to accept the computer's suggestion for a corrected spelling of my name. So take it from Chris Hairdo, there are plenty of ways that attempts at polishing and improving things can actually introduce new errors.

Some Y2K testing programs available for downloading free from several Internet sites, including Survive 2000 and YMark 2000, have proven useful to tens of thousands of people for testing their desktop computers. Using those sorts of tests with particular system configurations, however, has caused some applications to lose data or expire.

These are isolated incidents and the inconvenience they caused was debatably negligible, but they're representative of exactly what the overall nature of Y2K problems is—namely, that it's impossible to know whether or not *all* at-risk systems have been identified, and that there are likely to be small things popping up for years that catch even the most sophisticated and successful remediation teams off guard.

On June 16, 1999 a Y2K test of an emergency system at a sanitation plant went wrong and spilled about 1.2 million gallons of untreated sewage into part of the Sepulveda Dam Recreation Area. The accident happened after power was cut to simulate an electrical failure during testing at the Tillman water reclamation plant. A backup generator was slow to kick in, causing a computer controlling the sewage gate to malfunction as the result of a programming error from the mid-1980s. The spill was not due to a date-related Y2K computer problem; in fact, the Y2K program managers for the site weren't called in when the trouble occurred. The Y2K test simply uncovered a problem that would have happened on any occasion when power went down unexpectedly at that facility. In this regard, Y2K testing might have been helpful to certain organizations by revealing weaknesses even outside of date-related problems, but to most media covering the sewage spill, and certainly to the people who lived near the site, more than a million gallons of spilled raw sewage amounted to a Y2K testing problem that was unarguably inconvenient and won't easily be forgotten.

A goofy testing problem occurred in early April 1999 when securities traders were conducting a Y2K test. A device that controls phone traffic to computers at the National Securities Clearing Corporation was faulty going into the test. It delayed entries of trades and bookkeeping information for an undeterminable number of firms for several hours. The NSCC couldn't get all the incoming phone traffic promptly transferred to its backup phone lines, and eventually found the reason—Bell Atlantic had those backup phone lines tied up to do a different batch of Y2K testing!

Sometimes there has been an inability to test despite a desire to do so. Many companies have been so pressed for time that they've had to shortchange the testing portion of their projects. Those with thorough testing plans seek to involve business partners because computers so often interact with outside systems, but the partners aren't always available for (or willing to engage in) cooperative testing. Bell Atlantic, for example, is responsible for wires that carry billions of dollars in financial transactions, and reported having many more banks request to test with it than could be accommodated.

The need to continue daily operations has precluded testing in some situations; one water treatment plant in China, for instance, supplies two-thirds of Beijing's water and to date has never been allowed to be shut down for testing, so it has not been possible to determine if computers there are vulnerable to Y2K trouble. Experts agree that water would still flow if computers at the plant malfunctioned, but it might not be purified as usual.

Mistakes in Thinking Compliance Has Been Achieved

On March 6, 1999 work slowed down at the US Agency for International Development after a computer that officials believed had already been fixed failed testing. Officials at the time had to announce that five of the agency's seven mission-critical computers would not be fixed by the March 31, 1999 federal deadline.

Hardware and software vendors can test their products comprehensively, but still might not address all the ways they're used by customers. A director of Y2K testing at Zurich American reported that his company had problems with software even from large vendors like IBM (which has been widely recognized as doing great work on Y2K issues), saying, "We have found 10 major Y2K problems with applications vendors told us they had tested and found compliant." He added that even with big-name business partners, each company worrying about achieving Y2K compliance with its own systems and the particular ways they're used has to take "a 'trust nothing, test everything' attitude."

The Ultimate Mistake: Fixing Only Ourselves

Shaunti Feldhahn wrote about a problem with some Christians today, "As our unsaved friends, neighbors, and coworkers have gone further and further astray, we Christians have followed—either in practice or through our silence."

As of October 1999, according to information from Gartner Group and Cap Gemini, 82% of Fortune 1000 companies had encountered a Y2K problem during their testing and remediation efforts. Many times those mistakes provided information which could prove useful to subsequent Y2K repair efforts by many other companies, and it's wonderful that some of the companies encountering the mistakes had the courage and sense of cooperation and responsibility to share information about the problems they'd encountered with the rest of the world.

Computers that are fixed well will recognize bad data coming in and ignore it. To be of real service, though, they would not simply ignore it, but actually repair it and notify the sender of the faultiness of their output. We face the same thing in daily life—when people interact with us with evildoing or false teaching, I feel we have three choices:

- Accept it (BAD)
- Ignore it (BETTER)
- Respond and try to repair the problem at the source and any other locations where it exists besides just our own location (BEST)

LESSON 53: MOVING FROM KNOWLEDGE TO WISDOM

The one and only thing that remains constant in Y2K discussions all the way up to M-Day is uncertainty. Indeed, this book doesn't give a definite analysis of problems that have occurred due to Y2K problems, because its writing is purposely finalized just before the new year arrives. Nobody has been able to say—or can say now—exactly how many systems might experience Y2K-related trouble, because many review and remediation efforts carried out in haste could eventually prove to be fallible. Moreover, once all the mission-critical items are taken care of, there are millions of lines of code making up less-important applications, and millions of embedded chips serving as part of less-important systems, which will be corrected over the next few years if companies decide those systems are worth spending the money to fix.

"If you're not losing sleep at night, you don't understand the problem," said Timothy Scudder, a vice president at Gartner Group, at one point. "Year 2000 is not a tech-weenie problem. It's a business problem."

Despite prompting like that, there has been far more uncertainty than understanding about the Y2K problem. Uncertainty is what has made many people frustrated and confused about Y2K, and it's what makes many people frustrated and confused about Christianity also. Just as people felt "if you'd only tell us exactly what will go wrong, we'd take the necessary actions to make sure we avoid Y2K problems," there are many people who feel that if someone could explain to them in logical terms that fit their human understanding exactly what future benefit awaits or what future disaster can be avoided by becoming a Christian, then they'd consider doing it. But in the absence of such proof for how things will go, they'd just as soon err on the side of disbelief and inaction.

I've seen over and over again that Y2K information inspires action. People on the fence about the importance (or lack thereof) of the Y2K problem haven't done much to prepare—until learning enough about the potential problems to realize that there were credible reasons to prepare, at which point they've whizzed into action. Surely those who aren't willing to make a commitment to Christ would be willing to plunge rapidly into action if they had enough information to make themselves believe that the result of not doing so could be disastrous. Well, the results *can* be disastrous, and that's why many Christians feel such pressure to share the Good News of Jesus Christ with those who don't know it yet.

In terms of raw knowledge, we've learned some amazing things during Y2K planning. We've learned that diesel fuel is an oil, so it keeps longer than gasoline (which spoils after about a year). The longevity and fuel economy of diesel has made many people preparing all-out for Y2K decide to spend upwards of $1,500 for a diesel generator rather than just $400-$600 for a gas generator. We've also learned that matches have a shelf life of roughly one year. If you're like me, you've kept some matches around for many years and they still work, but the match manufacturers make a point of letting us know that we shouldn't count on them lighting after they've been stored beyond a year.

We've also learned to do math in ways we never quite realized we'd do—for instance, it turns out a team of goats can provide the same milk as a single cow for much less initial cost and maintenance expense, plus the goats are more effective at mowing the yard. If it hadn't been for Y2K, many of us would never have encountered such varied bits of knowledge.

All the detailed information we've gathered about Y2K issues, however, has not changed the fact that no one knows exactly how the problem will play out, what impact (both negative and positive) it might have on individuals throughout the world, and so on. Only God knows where Y2K fits in the overall scheme of things. In fact, it's foolish for humans to think we've gotten a handle on much of anything. Our earthly knowledge is so insignificant in the face of eternity.

People do tend to get puffed egos because of knowledge, and we constantly applaud those who excel at earthly knowledge—it's why game shows like *Jeopardy* and *Who Wants To Be a Millionaire?* are hugely popular, and why people think membership in an organization like Mensa means something. Having large quantities of knowledge supposedly makes you elite. The Bible makes it clear, though, that the elite group to truly be desirous of joining is that group of people who achieve greater understanding through God's wisdom, not man's.

Among the most central Christian tenets are two that relate to knowledge:

- The concept that salvation is based on faith rather than knowledge
- The concept that biblical history and wisdom are sufficient to guide the lives of Christians

1 John 3:20 ... God is greater than our hearts, and he knows everything.

God more than makes up for whatever we don't know. We can be at ease knowing that he's available to help sort out the details of issues that baffle and overwhelm us. We have to not let our hearts work against God by leaning toward our own predrawn conclusions, or by feeling doomed to failure instead of trusting in God.

> **RELATED VERSE:**
> 1 TIMOTHY 6:20

1 Corinthians 13:8 mentions that "where there is knowledge, it will pass away," referring to human knowledge. That's a distinction I want to draw—there's human knowledge and then there's true wisdom which supersedes human knowledge—a set of knowledge derived exclusively from God.

> *Ecclesiastes 12:12* ... Of making many books there is no end, and much study wearies the body.

The context of this verse from Ecclesiastes is realizing that true wisdom is limited to a certain collection of knowledge, all ultimately available from God, and that to try to add more to what he has given us or try to learn more than what he allows us is foolish.

Prior to Jesus' crucifixion being imminent, even he didn't know what the timing of God the Father would be:

> *Matthew 24:36* No one knows about that day or hour, not even the angels in heaven, nor the Son, but only the Father.

> **RELATED VERSE:**
> ACTS 1:7

Proverbs 19:11 teaches that wisdom is one of the things that can provide patience. Here are some other examples of the many things the book of Proverbs says about wisdom:

> *Proverbs 4:7* Wisdom is supreme; therefore get wisdom. Though it cost all you have, get understanding.

> *Proverbs 13:16* Every prudent man acts out of knowledge, but a fool exposes his folly.

> *Proverbs 28:26* He who trusts in himself is a fool, but he who walks in wisdom is kept safe.

> *Proverbs 3:5-6* Trust in the Lord with all your heart and lean not on your own understanding; in all your ways acknowledge him, and he will make your paths straight.

The last two proverbs presented here assert that the mind having knowledge is secondary to the heart trusting God. Refer to Chapter 3 for a broader look at how God guides our steps and helps us determine which paths to follow.

Wisdom requires understanding combined with a strict adherence to the truth. There's a clear method outlined in the Bible for obtaining true wisdom—it must be done through God:

> *Job 32:7-8* I thought, "Age should speak; advanced years should teach wisdom." But it is the spirit in a man, the breath of the Almighty, that gives him understanding.
>
> *1 Corinthians 2:14* The man without the Spirit does not accept the things that come from the Spirit of God, for they are foolishness to him, and he cannot understand them, because they are spiritually discerned.
>
> *James 1:5* If any of you lacks wisdom, he should ask God, who gives generously to all without finding fault, and it will be given to him.

To reiterate the point, Colossians 2:3 tells us that Christ serves as a storehouse of wisdom for us, mentioning that in him "are hidden all the treasures of wisdom and knowledge."

People who poke fun at Y2K issues and downplay their importance bring to my mind the scoffers mentioned in 2 Peter 3:3 who "will come, scoffing and following their own evil desires"—there have been plenty of scoffers about Y2K and its importance as a learning experience or an opportunity to reach out to others. There are people who have believed the entire Y2K problem is a hoax or has a particular political agenda. You shouldn't let their arrogance distract you from your openness to God's wisdom.

> **RELATED VERSE:**
> PROVERBS 9:12

> *1 Corinthians 3:19* For the wisdom of this world is foolishness in God's sight. As it is written: "He catches the wise in their craftiness."

One of the best ways we see the progression from relying on human knowledge to accepting God's wisdom played out in the Bible is in Nathanael of Cana, who is infamous for his response to Philip after the latter tells him that the Messiah has been found, and it's Jesus of Nazareth. Nathanael wonders whether anything good can come out of Nazareth (John 1:45-46). Nathanael didn't necessarily have a personal grudge against the town of Nazareth, but since he had studied scripture and prophecies thoroughly, he knew that The Coming One was going to come from Bethlehem. Nathanael's concern was in line with the skepticism that certain Pharisees had about Jesus (John 7:40-52), wanting to make sure that whenever the Messiah appeared, he could be proven to be a true fulfillment of the prophecies of older scripture. Their foolish certainty prevented them from investigating enough to see that Jesus actually satisfied their rigid requirements.

Jesus knew that Nathanael had this goal of recognizing the Messiah when he met him, and saw that Nathanael was a man of sincerity hoping to discover the truth. The integrity of Nathanael's seeking enabled him to be fully illuminated by Christ upon their meeting, and Nathanael's willingness to be shown the truth helped him to recognize it even though it contradicted his preconceived notions completely. Once Nathanael saw the truth, he said to Jesus "You are the son of God" (John 1:49). He's the first person in the gospels to confess awareness of that fact. Philip and Andrew previously had acknowledged Jesus as the Messiah, but not explicitly as the Son of God. Nathanael added something even more important—he called Jesus 'the King of Israel.' Everyone who chose to become a disciple of Jesus during his lifetime wanted a king to establish the Jewish kingdom and help them restore their nation to its rightful glory, but remember that they all expected it to be an earthly kingdom, a palace and a temple right down the road somewhere to be a seat of power there on earth. They expected the Messiah to be the king in that earthly kingdom, so once they recognized that Jesus was the Messiah, they called him King of the Jews. Nathanael, on the other hand, specifically called him King of Israel rather than King of the Jews, recognizing Jesus as the Son of God sent to have *spiritual* sovereignty over the *spiritual* community of the people of God, rather than someone who would have earthly political power. This was a distinction that didn't sink in with some of Jesus' other closest followers until after Jesus' death and resurrection.

> *1 Corinthians 8:1-3* We know that we all possess knowledge. Knowledge puffs up, but love builds up. The man who thinks he knows something does not yet know as he ought to know. But the man who loves God is known by God.

As you think about this verse, remember that Jesus essentially *is* love. His message, his ministry, his purpose—all are centered on love. At the time he met Jesus, Nathanael might have been a scholar and perhaps was fully *puffed* up, but was not yet fully *built* up in the way that the love of Jesus could build him up.

Nathanael had a somewhat hard demeanor when first presented with the notion that Jesus might be the Messiah, but once he progressed from the realm of his own knowledge to the wisdom he found through Jesus, he softened completely, demonstrating the following biblical notion of the improvement that can come from attaining wisdom:

> *Ecclesiastes 8:1* ... Wisdom brightens a man's face and changes its hard appearance.

Lesson 54: This Is Undoubtedly Far and Away the Best Lesson Ever Written

Some law enforcement officials are going to play it extremely safe around M-Day. One small section of northeastern Ohio offers a case study of the sorts of differences in outlook that exist. Summit County Sheriff's deputies have had all vacations from December 20 through January 9 canceled so a full staff can be on hand in case of Y2K emergencies. But some police departments are doing nothing special to prepare for Y2K, believing efforts made to update computers have eliminated the possibility of problems. The Portage County Sheriff's Department, right next door to Summit County, is one of several departments not doing anything out of the ordinary. With most departments, of course, off-duty personnel are expected to report for duty in the case of *any* major emergency, and New Year's Eve is no different.

Police Major Don Diamond of Canton, OH (where police have no special Y2K-related plans) went so far as to tell a reporter from the *Akron Beacon Journal* that he thinks the Y2K problem is "a big bunch of hooey—it's all about a computer glitch that was recognized two years ago and it's been corrected."

Jim Brown, who testified in April before a Senate special committee on Y2K technology, teaches emergency preparedness to law enforcement officers, and has placed his own research on Y2K on the Internet to serve as a resource for others, felt that sort of cockiness was unwarranted. Brown doesn't view canceling vacations and taking other preparatory actions prior to M-Day as going overboard, but as merely sensible precaution. In his capacity as police chief of Hudson, OH, Brown has decided to schedule his full department to work 12-hour days from December 30 straight through January 4 with no days off. He said, "The problem with law enforcement is that people tend to want to wing things," and stated that from his point of view, "You have to have plans in place and be ready to rock and roll, regardless of what happens."

Apple Computer was accused of arrogance by some of its most loyal users after a commercial aired during the Super Bowl which suggested that "only the Macintosh was designed to work perfectly" and left many viewers with the impression that owning a Mac meant there would be absolutely no concerns about Y2K readiness on their desktops. As we've already covered in this book, Mac users still need to pay attention to software concerns, including not only noncompliant software but also data files that have resulted from the practice common among Mac users as well as IBM-style PC users of entering two-digit date data in spreadsheets and databases, then using that data as the basis for complicated charting, presentations, and other business processes.

As trivial and scattered as most Y2K problems might be, the people affected by those problems are likely to be angry at any companies or government bodies that they believe have allowed the problems to occur or to have a more severe impact than needed. Organizations that don't prepare adequately for Y2K or don't provide the correct sorts of information about Y2K might face serious repercussions, because wherever there turn out to be actual problems, the failure of certain organizations to prepare properly might earn them long-lasting distrust from the public.

Still, there's a "millennium shrug" among plenty of organizations domestically and overseas. In the final few months before M-Day, in fact, some entire industries and even entire countries—such as Hong Kong, Singapore, Australia, and the United Kingdom—have come across as being especially confident that they've got potential Y2K problems under control.

When I think about arrogance, I often think of what happened with Moab:

> *Jeremiah 48:16* The fall of Moab is at hand; her calamity will come quickly.

The people of Moab had been prosperous and peaceful for a long time, and had become vain and secure that they were free of all the problems of the day, like pestilence and war, that affected other countries around them. From their conceited state arose not only a rotten attitude, but also plenty of the usual sorts of corruption and sinfulness that often take hold when people have had things too easy for too long and take it all for granted. The Lord saw how the people of Moab, completely insolent and defiant, were boastful and laughing at their troubled neighbors. The entire 48th chapter of Jeremiah serves up a harsh blast of words from God sounding like a trumpet to announce that the people of Moab needed to wake up from their arrogance and slothfulness.

Any people who give in to worldly concerns or push God out of the driver's seat in their lives are deserving of the same sort of wake-up call. Let's allow the Y2K scare—and it truly has been a scare in certain ways for many people—to serve as a trumpet awakening us so that we notice the carelessness to which we in a prosperous and technologically advanced world can so easily succumb.

It's always a challenge for those who are comfortable to truly empathize with what's happening in the lives of those less fortunate, and to truly let their hearts rest with God instead of the things of the world that they've grown accustomed to having:

> *1 Timothy 6:17* Command those who are rich in this present world not to be arrogant nor to put their hope in wealth, which is so uncertain, but to put their hope in God, who richly provides us with everything for our enjoyment.

> *Proverbs 27:1* Do not boast about tomorrow, for you do not know what a day may bring forth.

James warned about the very same problem, an arrogant presumption about how the future would go, instead of a regard for God's sovereignty:

> *James 4:13-15* Now listen, you who say, "Today or tomorrow we will go to this or that city, spend a year there, carry on business and make money." Why, you do not even know what will happen tomorrow. What is your life? You are a mist that appears for a little while and then vanishes. Instead you ought to say, "If it is the Lord's will, we will live and do this or that."

> *Proverbs 16:18* Pride goes before destruction, a haughty spirit before a fall.

See how David declares that his way is perfect:

> *Psalm 18:32* It is God who arms me with strength and makes my way perfect.

I don't feel David is being arrogant here. He is honest about the importance of the work he's done and how far he's come and the victories he's gained, but he gives credit to the Lord for all his success. Honoring God in that way turns what might be viewed as bragging into instead an acceptable appraisal of the achievements that David has managed to carry out with God's help.

We're a know-it-all society and want to figure out everything, including whom to blame for Y2K. In mid-October 1999, America Online had a special feature area with a survey asking users, "Who do you blame for the millennium bug?" and an article suggesting that Grace Hopper, a true computer pioneer, might be at least partially to blame. Many other media outlets at different times have blatantly or subtly nominated other possible candidates to take the rap for the overall problem. I don't blame any individual or group of programmers, because as explained elsewhere in this book, various aspects of the problem were established in different ways over time by many people, and numerous chances to curtail or correct the problem were ignored by thousands of people prior to the late 1990s.

Grace Hopper herself, however, deserves momentary attention in our lesson on arrogance, because she believed mightily that computers were under human control and couldn't have conceived of the full panoply of problems cloaking the computer world as M-Day arrives. Hopper was an accomplished woman well-known for her achievements in the field of computer science, even nicknamed "Amazing Grace" by some people because of her tremendous problem-solving ability. She was also a spunky character who spoke her mind—for a few years, she was a memorable occasional guest on *Late Night with David Letterman*. Hopper helped develop the language COBOL in the late 1950s, and to save much-needed memory, she and her partners incorporated the two-digit year strategy. In 1945, it was Hopper who found a moth in the Mark II, an early supercomputer—the discovery widely acknowledged to be the origin of the term "bug" which to this day is still used to describe programming problems. Hopper extracted that moth using tweezers and taped it into her journal. Photographs of that journal page appear in many computer textbooks (including several that I read as a student during the early 1980s and several that I worked on as an editor or developer during the early 1990s), and the entire journal is in the Smithsonian Computer Museum. Hopper did more than find that bug and co-create COBOL; she also created the first code compiler and had a distinguished Navy career—there's even a vessel named after her, the USS Hopper.

She was belligerent in her belief that computers would do more than people ever thought they could, and felt that pioneers like herself had achieved a mastery over machines that would extend into the future in limitless ways. She had faced a lot of skeptics in the early days of computing, and was proud of how computers had outperformed everyone's expectations. Indeed, Hopper wanted very much to live to the year 2000 to be able to celebrate what she was sure would be a high moment of triumph for computer technology. We see now how loaded with irony it is that she once told an interviewer who asked her why she wanted to see the year 2000, "I have two reasons. The first is that the party on December 31, 1999, will be a New Year's Eve party to end all New Year's Eve parties. The second is that I want to point back to the early days of the computer, and say to all the doubters, 'See? We told you the computer could do all that!'"

I'll share just one more story about computer upgrades and arrogance. A press release from the Bank of Scotland's web site on August 16, 1999 said "As part of a programme to improve the availability of customer services, Bank of Scotland has invested £21 million in computer upgrades [to] become the first financial institution in Europe to deliver services from a synchronised pair of central computers. The Bank is now able to remove one computer from service at any time for maintenance or to fix a problem with virtually no impact on customer service." The press release went on to quote the bank's Managing Director as saying, "Changing lifestyles and changing banking patterns have promoted a growing requirement for reliable banking services 24 hours a day, 7 days a week. This investment not only allows us to offer constant service to meet this demand but also keeps us at the forefront of banking technology."

Less than two weeks after the highly-touted new system was installed, the London Bureau of IDG's News Service carried this story, "The Bank of Scotland admitted today that it has been experiencing computer problems for at least ten days that have delayed [thousands of] transactions. The problems are with a new system that has caused problems with international payments..."

There has been no room for arrogance in terms of anyone thinking they've achieved full mastery of the complicated computing challenges facing them, no matter how much they spend or how careful they think they've been.

Summary

Initiative is great, but you must remain alert to any situations where acts of initiative might house inferior quality. It's also important to understand what occurs within the black boxes of your life, and work on finding ways to notice everything that takes place in your blind spots. Through an accurate awareness of what's happening around you, you can make sure that you're taking care of everything you need to.

When you notice a tiny problem, realize that it might eventually grow into a much larger problem if it's ignored rather than headed off while still small. In all situations, whether hoping to spot mistakes or to confirm successes, strive to make the transition from a reliance on earthly knowledge to a humble openness to God-given wisdom.

7

Getting Everyone to Work for the Team (and Vice Versa)

The Y2K problem in a sense has been a giant emotional X-ray machine, often revealing the size of people's hearts, their spirit of cooperation, and the true nature of their actions.

Lesson 55: The Benefits of Working Together

Decisions about Y2K preparedness at home have needed to be made with other family members who share a household—in particular, with spouses. You cannot be unequally yoked in terms of your faith or your viewpoints on major life decisions. Y2K has been another great opportunity for couples to take note of and work on smoothing out differences between their points of view. It's critical to practice the fine art of compromise, and maintain a prayerful willingness to do what God wants the two of you to do.

A truism is expressed in one of the most frequently cited Bible verses:

> *Luke 11:17* Any kingdom divided against itself will be ruined, and a house divided against itself will fall.

By working together in an open and honest way on Y2K issues, companies and other companies, or companies and their customers, have been able to make better progress toward Y2K solutions than by working individually (as a bonus, sometimes it has been quicker, cheaper, and more accurate with partners involved). Some companies and even entire industries were great examples of this type of transparency and teamwork from the start. Some others needed a nudge, so Congress passed legislation encouraging businesses to share information about how to overcome the Y2K problem. Sen. Robert Bennett and other supporters issued a joint statement explaining that the legislation was meant to overcome a "stony silence in the sharing of essential information about such remediation efforts" arising from fears that any information corporations made available might eventually be used against them in court.

The bill provided limited protection from lawsuits for businesses that shared information about the computer problem which they believed to be true at the time but later turned out to be incorrect, and provided that information given confidentially by corporations to the federal government wouldn't be released to third parties. It also established a government web site to serve as a clearinghouse for Y2K information for businesses, consumers, and all levels of government.

The teamwork required to handle Y2K concerns has included large and small roles, learning and teaching roles, hands-on and hands-off roles. The people who know the most about fixing the Y2K problem are not the sort who have management and leadership positions, not the sort who go on press junkets—and not the sort, I dare say, who write books. This doesn't mean that many of us who are in the public eye discussing the problem quite visibly and quite frequently don't know a great deal about it—most of us do—but we aren't the people who know the most about specific systems that are impacted by the problem, and we aren't necessarily the type of ingenious thinkers who will derive the most effective solutions. It takes all sorts of team players to take on an opponent like Y2K.

With Y2K as with any significant challenge, we've needed some people to steer, some people to build, some to repair, some to forge ahead, some to beware of dangers along the way, and so on. The effort made during Y2K remediation efforts and contingency planning, in fact, has mirrored the way a smoothly functioning church should operate—distinct talents and interests all working tirelessly in tandem, united by a common central cause, all the diverse abilities fitting together to create a tremendous force moving en masse in the right direction.

Steve Cochrane, exercise training officer for the Federal Emergency Management Agency in Cheyenne, WY is pretty confident heading into New Year's Eve. "We've been working very closely with all the counties," he said. "We feel pretty good about preparations in the state." The only difficulty he foresees is if two or three separate areas within the state should happen to experience problems simultaneously.

The same holds true for families or churches or any other teams that rely on the well-being of numerous individual members. One person being ill in a household doesn't cause too much trouble, but if an illness suddenly strikes several members of the same family at once, the household might really suffer and have to struggle to recover. If a church body has a couple of members in trouble at a time, it's able to keep functioning, but if multiple members fail at once, the entire church is at risk of not being able to cope. The more members there are experiencing a crisis, the more that crisis damages the collective body. The early church in the New Testament is a great model for how to survive crisis and continue functioning as a successful team:

> *1 Thessalonians 5:12-15* Now we ask you, brothers, to respect those who work hard among you, who are over you in the Lord and who admonish you. Hold them in the highest regard in love because of their work. Live in peace with each other. And we urge you, brothers, warn those who are idle, encourage the timid, help the weak, be patient with everyone. Make sure that nobody pays back wrong for wrong, but always try to be kind to each other and to everyone else.

The Teacher in Ecclesiastes, who was practical despite his occasional pessimism, also acknowledged the advantages of teamwork in facing life's difficulties:

> *Ecclesiastes 4:9-12* Two are better than one, because they have a good return for their work: If one falls down, his friend can help him up. But pity the man who falls and has no one to help him up! Also, if two lie down together, they will keep warm. But how can one keep warm alone? Though one may be overpowered, two can defend themselves. A cord of three strands is not quickly broken.

He was talking about facing a world full of troubles, and suggested that along with reliance on God, there's another coping mechanism—having friends to help with life's trials. The more challenging life is, the more important friends are. It's too late to seek friends and partners only at the point when you need them, of course—you must have friends and partners before times of crisis because you truly want to share life with them, not because you're building up a pool of favors owed to you so that you can invoke them later.

> **Related Verse:**
> **Galatians 6:2**

Lesson 56: Perhaps Some People Think Jesus Taught Us to Prey

Earlier in the book we focused on the excellence of praying; let's spend just a moment looking at the horrors of preying.

There have been examples of businesses planning to prey on their enemies. Some Y2K consultants, in fact, have only managed to convince certain companies to undertake a Y2K project by using one key motivating concept: *If Y2K projects are done well, they'll allow your business to take advantage of your competitors' Y2K problems and steal some of their customers.* Web sites of certain Y2K consultants were riddled with innuendo that businesses could use Y2K to defeat their competitors. Apparently those consultants and the businesses that bought into that line of thinking aren't adherents to this biblical suggestion:

> *Proverbs 24:17* Do not gloat when your enemy falls; when he stumbles, do not let your heart rejoice...

There also have been software vendors trying to victimize businesses—especially mid-size companies that have sizable budgets but not a lot of extra in-house resources—by forcing them to pay outrageous amounts for repairs or upgrades to their mission-critical systems, knowing those companies felt an urgent need to bring their systems to a state of Y2K compliance. Government agencies and truly helpful advisors had to constantly inform businesses that they needn't feel they were at the mercy of software vendors. One such piece of advice told companies not to be afraid to threaten to take legal action if necessary to avoid being bilked by software vendors: "If you can show damages, including exorbitant upgrade costs, you probably will win a case against a vendor. That doesn't mean you should head to court. Just call the vendor's bluff when they quote a price for the upgrade. Tell them that you'll find someone else to buy from, and that you'll call your lawyers—then, hang up. If vendors are concerned with maintaining their customer base, they will likely call back with a better price."

Ripoff prices of goods and services should not be tolerated during a crisis just because demand can be manipulated through fear tactics. While the Bible endorses a free market system, it specifically speaks against gouging and usury in a number of places:

> *Proverbs 11:1* The Lord abhors dishonest scales, but accurate weights are his delight.

> *Job 5:12* He thwarts the plans of the crafty, so that their hands achieve no success.

> **RELATED VERSE:**
> ISAIAH 10:3

Do you remember when John the Baptist called a crowd listening to him a "brood of vipers"? Various people who sought baptism asked him how to straighten our their corruption and behave in ways that would please God.

Luke 3:11-14 John answered, "The man with two tunics should share with him who has none, and the one who has food should do the same." Tax collectors also came to be baptized. "Teacher," they asked, "what should we do?" "Don't collect any more than you are required to," he told them.

> RELATED VERSE:
> DEUTERONOMY 24:14

There's also been some accidental negative consequence caused by Y2K-related financial maneuvering. In August 1999, several major US corporations, a few foreign countries, and even the US Treasury began to accumulate huge amounts of cash just in case something Y2K-related might go wrong somewhere. They raised it in various ways, but corporations most often did so through huge debt transactions in the markets, the sort of activity that can raise rates on certain types of business and consumer loans as liquidity in the overall market dries up.

Y2K also has made many lenders and investors pull their money out of developing-nation markets, especially those where significant Y2K problems are considered much more likely. Some economists say that Y2K has seen the overall amount of foreign cash available to emerging markets drop to the lowest levels of the past 15 years or so. Since as a fundamental rule the amount of foreign investment available to a developing (or recovering) nation determines that nation's ability to develop (or recover), investors who have chosen to pull their investments from these countries realize they're setting these fragile nations up for additional economic distress.

For now, though, let's concentrate on activities where the victimization is fully intentional. In another part of the preying arena, there have been plenty of examples of out-and-out criminal activity. Realize that it's not uncommon these days for criminals to take advantage of technological turmoil and complicated software systems to facilitate their wrongdoing. At the height of Y2K repair projects in Summer 1999, the General Accounting Office released a report revealing that at least 7 of the 58 Medicare contractors had been using technology tricks to steal from the federal health care program. Employees of the sneaky contractors had deleted claims from processing systems, falsified claims documents that normally would have been rejected because they related to services not medically necessary, and tampered with software by deactivating checks that should have flagged and prevented questionable claims. Rep. John Dingell expressed how far software-based crimes had come, saying, "The record suggests that we may have gotten state-of-the-art private-sector efficiency in fleecing the taxpayer."

As computer technology conducts more and more of the world's high-dollar transactions, there will be a corresponding increase in the willingness of thieves and embezzlers to find ways to use software and the regularity of software problems in devious ways.

And the scams—oh, the scams! Police departments from Chicago and other large cities with prevalent Y2K scams have released numerous community alerts warning residents about the scams. Swindlers and "entrepreneurs" appear with just about every potential or actual disaster, hoping to cash in. It's among the worst of crimes, in my opinion, to prey upon vulnerable people in the worst of times.

The Australian National Securities and Investment Commission wanted to test the fear levels and gullibility of the public, so it set up a fake online company in March 1999 named Millennium Bug Insurance that would supposedly offer insurance to protect businesses against losses caused by Y2K glitches. The web site solicited investments in the phony company from individuals visiting the site; of the over 10,000 people who visited the web site, more than 200 offered to invest in the company, and were ready to hand over a total of over $4 million to the bogus company. On April Fools Day (appropriately enough), those willing to invest were told the site was an elaborate scam meant to teach investors to be more careful.

The US Better Business Bureau has identified over 100,000 web sites selling Y2K survival products, many of which have hawked "survival" products that are ordinary household items sold at nearly 10 times their true value. That type of predatory practice capitalizing on some people's paranoia about Y2K is bad enough, but there have been actual con artists working overtime as well. Con artists thrive in climates of uncertainty, so the Y2K problem has been a perfect opportunity for them. Here are some common scams that have caused problems:

- Callers posing as bank representatives say they're going to transfer customers' money from checking or savings accounts into "Y2K-proof" accounts just for safekeeping during the date transition. Of course, to prove you're the right person, you must provide them your account and PIN numbers.

- Callers or e-mail messages tell you that banks are unprepared for Y2K and you should transfer all your funds to a certain other investment—often gold, silver, unreliable bonds, stocks, or other assets. Of course, they don't tell you that you'll likely lose money when you try to liquefy those funds again later, if the investments exist at all.

- Callers say your current credit card won't work after M-Day but the company will gladly send you a new magnetic strip or sticker to bring it into compliance. Of course, you must provide them your credit card number.

- Callers offer completely bogus insurance that supposedly pays benefits in the event of false billings or faulty accounts due to the Y2K problem. Of course, once you've paid them for the coverage, they're nowhere to be found.

- Repairmen claim appliances (or vehicles, or computers, or other items) need upgrades to continue functioning after M-Day. Of course, the repairs are completely unneeded and often very expensive.

> *Psalm 12:1-2* Help, Lord, for the godly are no more; the faithful have vanished from among men. Everyone lies to his neighbor; their flattering lips speak with deception.

Then there are industries that have profiteered by capitalizing on fear. Lee Johnson, an earnest young man from Atlanta, said in an interview for ABC's *World News Tonight*, "I'm stocking up on ammunition, because I don't want no one breaking in my house. I don't want no looters." The gist of the news story featuring Johnson was that playing to many people's sense of panic about Y2K had become big business for certain industries, including the gun industry. The report showed footage of a happy gun store owner commenting on his daily interactions with customers who told him they were stocking up on ammo and other items specifically because of Y2K concerns. The gun industry, slumping a bit in recent years because of a few critical lawsuits and gun control laws, has gotten a windfall from concerns over the Y2K problem. Many manufacturers didn't waste any time swooping in on the opportunity—Bushmaster listed a Y2K Limited Edition weapon. Tapco described one of its rifles as "Y2K-ready." *American Handgunner* magazine had an article on Y2K accompanied by pictures of rioting and looting, asserting that when anarchy breaks loose, people will be grateful to have handguns.

Some of the predatory actions that relied on scare tactics were more than just financially damaging. 42-year-old Rodney Allen was arrested in Ontario on August 20, 1999 and charged with multiple counts of sexual assault and assault with a weapon. His victims? Teenage boys (at least three that police know of so far). His method of luring them? Y2K fears. He promised the boys refuge in a blast-proof shelter after terrifying them with claims that the world would explode on January 1, 2000 because of computer-induced mayhem. Several similar episodes have been reported throughout North America on the national and international newswires to which I've had access, and since such news often remains at the local level, it's reasonable to assume other incidents of this sort have affected particular communities here and there.

Earlier in the book we characterized those who have tried to pay sincere attention to Y2K concerns and to diligently work on preparations as hard-working, focused ants. These people who engage in various forms of predation must therefore be considered the antlions in the Y2K scenario. The antlion, for any of you who don't know, is an insect whose larva digs a pit in the sand where it lies in wait for other insects—particularly ants—to come along so that it can attack and devour them.

Of all the scams and schemes I've witnessed during the years leading up to Y2K, I've resented most of all the people gouging or swindling others who have used Christianity as a lure. We see this all the time in certain ads in the Yellow Pages and so on—there are people who later reveal themselves to be anything but Christian once people do business with them, but who use a dove or church or cross in their advertisements to promote a sense of trustworthiness. Y2K has brought out this tendency in excessive quantities, because from the beginning of Y2K awareness in the US, Christians as a rule have been more likely than non-Christians to actively seek information on achieving Y2K preparedness. It not only sets back the legitimate Christian business people who would like to include Christian symbols in their own ads and have them well-received by people, but also strikes a blow at Christianity as a whole.

The exploitation of the name of Christ or of Christian symbols without truly meaning the things you claim to mean is despicable. In 1 Timothy 6:3-11 (especially the beautifully inspiring charge in verse 11 that we all should use as a goal), Paul specifically warned Timothy not to try to use godliness as a means to financial gain. Many of the things we must pursue as Christians—faith, patience, godliness, compassion, and so on—stand directly in opposition to greed, so a stand-off takes place between greed and the things of God on many fronts. Y2K has been just the latest of many situations where you can easily notice this.

LESSON 57: FINDING THE GOOD SAMARITAN IN ALL OF US

Back in 1998, all Y2K preparation was based on the premise that problems would strike everywhere, so there might be a need to survive on one's own for weeks without help. One Y2K book offered this advice, "We do not recommend telling people you are storing foods for the long term... If the Y2K problem creates a major crisis, they'll be at your door, asking to take from your supply." I saw several Y2K experts on TV echoing the same sentiment, but that's ridiculous; nothing in the Bible endorses hoarding. Even the tremendous storing effort in Egypt done by Joseph was not an act of reliance on the sufficiency of the actual food that was stored, but an act of compliance with God's wishes, which eventually put Egypt in a position to help not only itself but the rest of the world as well.

Steve Farrar has written about people who have a hoarding mentality, "If you come along with a need, they will more readily give you a bullet than share from their storehouses. People who hoard are self-centered, and they will eventually fall into the pit that they dug for someone else." The Bible captures the same sentiment with slightly less venom:

> *Proverbs 11:26* People curse the man who hoards grain, but blessing crowns him who is willing to sell.

In mid-1997, the Chinese government directed its ministries to demand free Y2K repairs, stating that suppliers which refused would no longer be allowed to sell products to the government. The head of the Chinese government's Y2K effort has eased up on that directive since then, saying China realizes it can't expect vendors to bear the entire cost of repairs. "The question is, how much should they pay? Chinese users have already paid a lot," she said, but then added realistically, "As we know, big companies like IBM never do anything free of charge."

Beijing wasn't the only place that the notion of free software repairs crossed people's minds. Milberg, Weiss Bershad Hynes & Lerach in New York and several other law firms have filed lawsuits against software companies that required customers to pay for Y2K upgrades, claiming the companies should have been willing to provide free upgrades for their short-sighted software.

The Defense Department, the federal agency expected to be on the front lines of responding to potential crises caused by the Y2K problem, revealed in August 1999 that it does not plan to comply with all requests for help from state and local civilian authorities. DOD adopted that position in a message sent to all branches of military service by the Army's Director of Military Support (DOMS) at the Pentagon. The DOMS is charged with providing military support to civilian authorities under the DOD Y2K Consequence Management Plan. The message sent out in August was consistent with earlier guidance from Deputy Secretary of Defense John Hamre emphasizing that the first priority for military units engaged in any sort of Y2K crisis management must be their mission of defending the nation. Hamre outlined this basic principle: "Commanders will not compromise military readiness in providing support to civil authorities."

The DOMS message gets more specific, pointing out that even if civilian authorities require help, they might not get it: "It should be anticipated and publicized that not all requests from civil authorities will be filled." The DOMS also has decided to limited what the Pentagon will disclose about the status, location, and quantities of its Y2K-critical resources, including food, generators, and a variety of engineering equipment. According to the DOMS message, "any request for inventory levels of DOD resources from non-DOD activities will be denied." That sounds a lot like the attitude of the Y2K book quoted earlier—in essence, don't tell anyone what you've got, or they might want some of it.

The US Navy's Y2K consequence management plan calls for centrally managing at the national level all requests for help that come from communities near naval bases. Local base commanders can only engage in "unilateral emergency actions that involve the saving of lives, prevent great human suffering or mitigate great property damage, only when time does not permit approval by higher authorities." Y2K problem researcher Jim Kerrigan expressed doubt, though, that any military bases would actually ignore problems in nearby communities if they occurred, saying, "When it comes right down to it, I suspect bases will be able to help local communities. They can't do their own jobs if the local community is up in arms."

Hopefully no one anywhere will need to see whether or not the planned selfishness by certain agencies and individuals would give way to compassion should an actual crisis strike. The plans themselves, however, are a sad reflection of the selfish mindset that many have fallen into.

Perusing the online consumer Y2K information from one of the telecommunications companies I deal with frequently (a company with which I've been very pleased when they've handled several jobs for me in the past), I ran across a page telling customers, "It will be your responsibility to ensure that telecommunications-related equipment that was not provided by us is Year 2000 compatible." It was a quick bit of jargon meant to cover the company as much as possible in the event of trouble with telecom equipment in certain homes or workplaces. The message was simple: *If it isn't ours, we don't know anything about it, and don't want to know or need to know, and you can't make us care at all about that other stuff, because we're informing you officially that anything we don't bear direct, provable responsibility for is your problem.* It was just like a thousand other pages I'd read in a thousand other companies' web sites and printed materials, all making essentially the same statement, but for some reason that line rubbed me wrong that day, and made me start reviewing the extent to which each company in the Y2K melee was doing the same sort of covering itself. I know that's typical business behavior, and I know they're just playing it safe, but I also know that when you boil that behavior down to its essence, it's selfish.

I realize that many of us cover ourselves the same ways as we go through life, being noncommittal at all the right moments, leaving some of the nastiest decisions up to other people whenever possible so that they'll bear the responsibility of having made them instead of us, and so on. The most common occurrence of this is probably in terms of noticing physical tasks that someone else has neglected to do. As long as we've pulled our own weight in a particular situation, we often don't feel the need to go the extra mile and help out anybody else with their share—after all, we took care of our own, didn't we? No one came along and helped us, did they? We're well-practiced at doing this on the job and with our family members and in our church life—we delineate our own obligations from other people's obligations, and then avert our gaze from troubles that don't fall on our side of whatever line we've drawn to limit our responsibility. I understand that we can't solve everything for everybody, and that each person needs to do his best to bear his own load in this world, but there are plenty of times that we could step out of our safe boundaries and work on helping in some area where we have the capability to help, even though it isn't an area of mandatory responsibility for us.

This applies to small stuff that happens to everyone now and then. For example, you see an empty parked car with its headlights on in the parking lot. You know the driver has forgotten to turn them off, and you can see that the driver's door is unlocked. Your options are several:

- Ignore the problem completely
- Go inside and ask a store clerk to make an announcement about the car
- Search for the car owner yourself to let him know his lights are on
- Open the car door and turn off the headlights and not tell anybody

Ignoring the problem is a valid option to those people who strictly delineate their responsibilities from "other people's responsibilities"—after all, your own headlights are your problem to deal with, and if you're ever stupid enough to leave them turned on while you're in a store, you'll have to deal with the consequence, whether it turns out to be no problem at all or a weakened battery or a completely dead battery. And you don't expect anyone to go to any extra work to turn off your headlights for you, so no one should expect you to do any extra work to turn off theirs. Right?

Well, maybe. I agree with the part about not expecting anyone to cross over into your realm of responsibility and take care of the things you should be taking care of yourself. I don't think, however, that this means you can't still cross over and do things for others despite the fact that in an ideal world everyone would be able and willing to take care of his or her own responsibilities. What I'm urging is that when you delineate in your mind the absolute areas for which you're convinced you bear responsibility versus the areas for which you're convinced you don't bear responsibility, you shouldn't envision the boundary lines using the double line marking seen on highways meaning no one's allowed to cross over from either side. Instead, envision double lines with a dashed line on your side and a solid line on the other, so that even if you won't let anyone cross over and help you with your responsibilities, you realize it's possible to cross over and help them with theirs. Or, better yet, think of the boundaries as only dashed lines and no solid lines, so that you feel it's also possible for someone to cross over and help you out occasionally, although you don't expect them or require them to do so.

I have seen some businesses choose to delineate their own responsibilities using dashed lines instead of solid ones, and then do remarkably unselfish acts for their clients or even for other businesses. In the small downtown area of Harriman, TN there were two competing florists on opposite sides of the main thoroughfare for a number of years, but just a few weeks before Easter one year, a fire broke out on one side of the street and gutted one florist's shop. Easter is one of the biggest income-producing times of the year for those who sell flowers, and when I heard about the fire I immediately felt sorry for the florist who had suffered the fire loss, assuming that she'd be out of business through the upcoming holiday. I was amazed and delighted, however, when I learned that the florist on the other side of the street, her direct competitor who hadn't suffered any setback due to the fire and could have used this as an opportunity to cash in at the other's expense, instead had done the nearly unimaginable—she had given the competing florist cooler space, storeroom space, and table space in her own store, and they both were filling their orders for Easter out of the one store that had been located on the fortunate side of the street when the fire occurred.

I hope that during any moments in our lives when we get to decide how far we're going to go to help someone else in a moment of need, we don't think like the majority of businesses and individuals in the world today who don't step out of the safe boxes they've created for themselves, but instead try to think like the wonderful florist who decided it was appropriate to share her store with just about the last person in the world anyone would expect her to be willing to help.

You know about the Good Samaritan, of course (Luke 10:25-37)—he's a great example of someone giving aid even in a situation where most wouldn't expect him to give aid. The Bible repeatedly tells us to help those in need in all circumstances, in as many ways as possible. Don't forget the message Esther 9:22 (discussed in Lesson 8) contains—that helping others is an act of appreciation and celebration for your own blessings!

All earnest giving pleases the Lord:

> *2 Corinthians 9:7* ... God loves a cheerful giver.

Conversely, anyone who's overly selfish displeases the Lord. The word of God given to Ezekiel at one point cited the sins of Sodom. In God's view, the people of Sodom "were haughty and did detestable things" and these are some of the particulars:

> *Ezekiel 16:49* [Sodom] and her daughters were arrogant, overfed and unconcerned; they did not help the poor and needy.

God finds it highly offensive when his followers are unconcerned with the plight of others.

Once we make sure we've taken care of the homefront, it's selfish to care only about ourselves. Most days on most roads in America, you can find a few drivers embodying this selfishness—if all lanes are full, they zoom up within a few feet of someone's bumper and pressure him to get over so that they can pass; if it's bumper to bumper, they swoop into the shoulder and try to move forward at least a few car lengths; they dart out in merging situations without looking—or worse yet, proceed after they've looked and learned it's unsafe, forcing others to brake and make their piglike actions successful; when someone else is slowing down to exit or turn, they dash around that vehicle and then cut back in to make the same exit or turn.

These drivers are infuriating, and their actions indicate that they mistakenly believe that whatever they have going on in their life is more urgent than whatever's going on in everyone else's lives. We'd have safer roads and more cooperation among drivers and less road rage if everyone accepted the fact that they're not the only one anxious to get home to their family, they're not the only one needing to get to work on time, they're not the only one with a child waiting to be picked up or running late for a doctor's appointment or on their way to a date with the person of their dreams or whatever the thing is that makes each bad driver think that he or she has got the most important life of anyone on the road.

There has been much talk of the dreaded "spillover effect" that might occur with Y2K problems, in which a failure within one system—such as a portion of the electrical grid—causes load transferal to other "helper" systems that in turn might fail because of the new load. Hearing that terminology in the context of Y2K has amused me for the past couple of years, because I've often talked to fellow Christians about a "spillover effect"—and it's a *good* thing the way I've always used it. My opinion is this: God's grace and provision in our lives is so abundant that for those of us who recognize all that we've been blessed with, there is much more than we'll ever need for ourselves. It's fairly obligatory, then, that we notice other people in need, and allow God's grace to spill over from us to them so that our own overflowing cup doesn't merely result in waste.

We who are given so much should pass along a portion of the mercies that we receive, in turn giving to others a share of the goodness that has been given to us by God Almighty. The amount we give demonstrates God's grace at work in us. There are numerous Bible passages touching upon the same theme—that the grace of God is so unlimited and abundant that it can overflow from us and reach others:

> *2 Corinthians 9:11-12* You will be made rich in every way so that you can be generous on every occasion, and through us your generosity will result in thanksgiving to God. This service that you perform is not only supplying the needs of God's people but is also overflowing in many expressions of thanks to God.
>
> *1 Timothy 6:17-18* Command those who are rich in this present world not to be arrogant nor to put their hope in wealth, which is so uncertain, but to put their hope in God, who richly provides us with everything for our enjoyment. Command them to do good, to be rich in good deeds, and to be generous and willing to share.

In a Y2K-related crunch or in any other time of need, should you only help your friends and family? Only help the neighbors you know? Only help people from your own country? Only help Christians? With limited resources, these questions seem appropriate for some people to ask. The answer to all of them is a simple "No"—you're called to help anyone who requires help:

> *Proverbs 25:21* If your enemy is hungry, give him food to eat; if he is thirsty, give him water to drink.

Jesus followed right in line with this older scripture, teaching his disciples to love their enemies as much as they loved anyone, and to show mercy and kindness in all situations. Best of all, Jesus lived and died in unflinching demonstration of his teaching, giving literally everything he could for the sake of all humankind.

In the Great Depression years, it was common for men to wander from town to town seeking work and food; the "hobo" arose from that crisis, feeling there was no option left but to trust in the kindness of strangers. Some sociologists and others watching the countdown to Y2K have actually anticipated a resurgence of hobo activity if there are any segments of society hit especially hard by Y2K problems. I see a possible name already—this new generation of hobo might very well be called the "millennibum" by the media—but all the clever labels in the world wouldn't mask the fact that he'd be as wounded in his pride as the original hobo was during the depression years. Let's be on the lookout for anyone we encounter who needs a helping hand during whatever localized Y2K problems do occur or at any other point later in our lives; help your fellow man in the light of Christ's love, without the slightest hesitation or condescension. This basic principle of right living has been around since the time of Solomon:

> *Proverbs 3:27-28* Do not withhold good from those who deserve it, when it is in your power to act. Do not say to your neighbor, "Come back later; I'll give it tomorrow"—when you now have it with you.

You learned in the last lesson about Y2K predators who have been the antithesis of generosity, taking advantage of Y2K fears or supply shortages to scam or gouge vulnerable people. The ideal solution in overcoming these actions would be not merely to get people to stop the ripoffs, but actually get them to move on to engage in acts of charity. Consider this verse:

> *Ephesians 4:28* He who has been stealing must steal no longer, but must work, doing something useful with his own hands, that he may have something to share with those in need.

This simple verse lays out Paul's suggested four-step system for us as individuals and for society overall to be stable and well-functioning:

- Unwavering Honesty ("must steal no longer")
- Hard Work ("must work")
- Careful Stewardship ("that he may have")

- Unrestrained Charity ("share with those in need")

The ultimate good turnabout that Y2K troubles could bring would be in line with that verse from Ephesians—people who were previously greedy and conniving seeing the reality of others' difficulties, abandoning their prior schemes, and finding it within themselves to practice kindness and generosity.

LESSON 58: DO ALL REQUESTS FOR SERVICE DESERVE US?

Here's a quick anecdote about Y2K and an unlucky customer service representative. In early 1998, when a woman asked to open a CD at a branch office of Comerica Bank, a bank employee warned her about possible Y2K problems, saying, "I don't know that I would do that, because this CD goes past the year 2000, and this bank is in trouble. We may not make it." Unfortunately for the service rep, the woman opening the account was married to the CIO of Comerica. From that day on, the bank worked hard at training its service reps not to say negative things. The last thing any business has wanted during Y2K preparation is to have an uncertain customer, already wondering about the Y2K readiness of their organization, deal with a service rep who sounds alarmist, less-than-confident, or unencouraging about the future of the company.

Christian churches and individuals also have had to decide how to provide service during the years of Y2K awareness to anyone who might need some form of outreach. The Y2K problem has provided a great chance for many ministries to extend the embrace of their current range of services farther and wider throughout the community. There are weak and searching people who have sought leadership during the time leading up to M-Day as they've heard about the need for Y2K preparations. If churches haven't made the effort to share objective and soundly-reasoned information with people like that, some other source has, and that other source could be given a leadership role in the lives of those people that might prove more harmful than good.

Paul urged fellow believers to make the most of every chance to proclaim the mystery of Christ:

> *Colossians 4:5* Be wise in the way you act toward outsiders; make the most of every opportunity.

The greatest possible disaster for any person is to never come to know God and his plan for us, and therefore to experience eternal death as opposed to eternal life.

Sometimes you get a chance to help others in their walk of faith, but sometimes you only get a chance to minister to their physical or emotional needs. Either way, you're doing as Jesus did—he often did the physical care first, then later confirmed for people who he was and *why* he was there for them.

Remember that we'll be refreshed if we refresh others (see Lesson 26). It's important to serve tirelessly:

> *1 Peter 4:11b* If anyone serves, he should do it with the strength God provides, so that in all things God may be praised through Jesus Christ.

> *Galatians 6:9* Let us not become weary in doing good, for at the proper time we will reap a harvest if we do not give up.

Now, back to Comerica Bank. Becky Siewert, the company's Y2K communications manager, has told her customer service reps to keep the core messages simple: "The Y2K challenge is our top priority. The safest place for your money is in the bank. Your funds are FDIC-insured." Comerica is stressing each employee's responsibility to get the Y2K message right. Each employee must take a 25-minute Y2K training course, pass a test, and sign a statement saying he understands the bank's Y2K message and is accountable for what he says. Employees certified as "Y2K Champions" go around asking other employees Y2K questions and rewarding those who give correct answers with encouragement and small prizes. Siewert said, "Employees are no longer getting into these hour-long conversations with people. We've provided them with the confidence to say, 'We can speculate for days, but this is what you need to know.'"

We can take some guidance from her propensity toward directness and the sense of responsibility she insists on fostering in each person doing service. As you notice opportunities for meaningful service in your life, be equally straightforward and succinct in your messages and your actions. If you choose to share information about Christ with others who don't know about him, stick to fundamentals: "Faith is a top priority. The safest place for your life is in God's hands. Your salvation is already insured if you don't choose to withdraw from it." And when you feel comfortable in your role as a "Champion for Christ," you can help fellow Christians confirm their own response systems and can provide them with some encouragement.

∽ Note

You learned earlier in the book that a non-compliant system sending faulty data to a compliant system can cause problems. It's also true that if Y2K problems are severe, a compliant system sending correct data to a non-compliant system can cause a malfunction, misinterpretation, or complete crash in the non-compliant receiving system. Make sure your Christian outreach doesn't cause your nonbelieving friends, colleagues, or relatives to "shut down" because you're sending them too much stuff they don't yet understand or aren't ready to handle.

Maggi Williams of Belnexxia, Inc. works on providing help desk services for half a million Internet service subscribers. She's had many people calling her service center with irrelevant questions about Y2K or with questions that should go to a hardware or software manufacturer, not an Internet service provider. She is not thrilled by people's tendency to call even with requests that aren't appropriate, and comments wryly that when M-Day arrives, "Even if things go great, people will call and say, 'Nothing happened. What do I do?'"

Williams has worked hard to deflect as many questions as possible from her customer service reps, using an automated help desk on the web, followed by an automated voice-response phone system, and then finally some call center operators to deal with the few customers who outmaneuver the automated systems. Her outlook on the slew of inappropriate calls she expects after M-Day if there turn out to be any widespread Y2K problems is intriguing. "If the worst comes true," she reflects, "there will be no phone service, and we'll have no problems."

I urge you to see if you've done the same thing in any aspect of your life, setting up buffers to keep out the trivial and irrelevant service requests and prevent them from bogging you down. With school programs and church programs and civic activities and regional and global needs and family obligations, we all could easily have our individual service capabilities overwhelmed if we tried to respond to every request that came along, but sometimes when we're trying to preserve our time and energy for the most important jobs by deflecting the huge onslaught of service requests headed our way, we might accidentally turn a deaf ear to some people or groups who really need what we have to offer. If you have taken steps to limit your involvement in service work to preserve your own sanity and to keep a balanced life without running yourself ragged trying to do everything that every person and group in the world might ask you to do, just make sure the screening process is careful so that you don't end up hiding from any chances to serve that you might really want to take.

> *Colossians 3:23* Whatever you do, work at it with all your heart, as working for the Lord, not for men.

There's a limited amount of energy and time for everyone, but remember what you're ultimately working for. It's easy to get wrapped up in career, for example, and shut out service opportunities that compete for the same personal resources you possess. But as this verse from Colossians expresses, the greater calling is living a life that carries out God's will. Some of the people who excel at what they do, but never find any time for family, friends, strangers in need, or service work of any kind should learn from this.

Let's see one more perspective from another Y2K customer service expert. Bruce Calhoon, Contact Center Practice Director at Answerthink Consulting Group, knows that many companies are doing nothing special to prepare their service centers for Y2K, but he advises companies to at least consider several special questions to decide if they're prepared to successfully handle a sudden dramatic increase in service requests due to Y2K problems or questions. Here's a sampling of those questions, which I've reworked slightly to leave out industry specifics:

- Who is likely to contact you and why?
- What information will you need to handle the calls?
- Can you qualify calls and answer the simple ones, forwarding the rest to a few experts?
- Does your system have the capacity to handle more requests?
- Can you triage service, offering the best service to the most profitable customers?

As you can tell, I'm having fun comparing Christian service to Y2K service, even if the comparison's a bit of a stretch. So, let's see how you can answer Bruce's questions. A little thought will tell you exactly the sorts of people who might contact you with service requests, and the information you need is probably all available from the living and learning you've done. You probably *should* think about outsourcing or referring some of the service requests that are out of your league (we all get those from time to time) to someone else—a minister, a volunteer who has more time or more appropriate skills, a professional service organization, or whomever—whenever you know you'd be floundering trying to fulfill a particular service request yourself. An honest self-assessment is needed to determine if you have the capacity to handle any more service requests on a regular basis, or possibly just in an emergency.

By all means, though, don't triage whatever service you're giving in your life by prioritizing your "customers" according to how much they can give back to you later. Even the least among us here on earth matter greatly in God's sight (this is discussed in Lesson 60) and whatever you do for the least of people is being done for God. Strive with all your energy and the greatest possible enthusiasm to make the most of every opportunity, and don't just act on the ones that will bring you some sort of reward! The true reward lies simply in the chance to do the service.

Lesson 59: All Parts Matter

It has been critical for people in business and government to realize that all voices in the Y2K dialogue matter (think about the obscure people whose stars have risen rapidly thanks to their insights about Y2K, and think about even the most extreme voices of fringe thinkers which we've needed to pay attention to if only because they influence a certain segment of Y2K watchers to behave in certain ways) and all hands willing to help in the execution of Y2K remediation projects matter (think about the unprecedented partnerships that have taken place during Y2K, between some competing companies, between some consumer advocacy groups and the manufacturers they typically oppose, and so on). Recall the joy among chief information officers in certain large corporations who, thanks to Y2K, have been given their first opportunity to really join in the directional management of the entire corporation.

There are groups of people that many Y2K project managers ignored at first, but that later were considered invaluable. Customer service representatives weren't included in many projects, until it became clear that they're on the front lines of influencing what customers feel about the Y2K preparedness of each particular company—immediately they became part of the Y2K team.

End users (the people who actually work with software applications on a daily basis) weren't included in many projects at first, because most managers thought the end users simply needed to be given repaired or upgraded programs to work with once the Y2K projects were over. The smartest Y2K project managers, though, have included end users from the start, because these users are the ones who need to know that everything might not proceed normally at the beginning of the year 2000, who need to be on the lookout for the appearance of glitches that weren't eliminated successfully during Y2K remediation, and who need to be counted on to report crucial information about Y2K problems to the team members that can actually fix the problems.

End users, in fact, are among the most important members of any software team even when there isn't a crisis like Y2K looming—on a regular basis, these users have to cope with bugs, upgrades, downtime, performance problems, processing bottlenecks, and so on, so they can be expected to handle Y2K issues with much aplomb. Moreover, they're the ultimate testing tool and often are the people who must carry out contingency plans if there are any problems, so they've definitely deserved to be included in Y2K projects and given due credit for the important role they play in successfully handling the arrival of Y2K.

Remember that 1 Corinthians 12:26 teaches "If one part suffers, every part suffers with it"—it doesn't just say that if the most important part suffers, every part suffers with it, but that if *any* single part suffers, *every* part suffers with it. This doesn't mean that all church members are identical in interests or abilities—but all are equally vital to the church as a whole.

Paul says to look at oneself with "sober judgment" (Romans 12:3) and realize that each of us has been blessed by the same grace of God in different ways:

> *Romans 12:6-8* We have different gifts, according to the grace given us. If a man's gift is prophesying, let him use it in proportion to his faith. If it is serving, let him serve; if it is teaching, let him teach; if it is encouraging, let him encourage; if it is contributing to the needs of others, let him give generously; if it is leadership, let him govern diligently; if it is showing mercy, let him do it cheerfully.

> **RELATED VERSE:**
> 1 PETER 4:10

Paul is outlining various roles that people have in the early Christian church, but of course it's possible to apply this same sort of analysis and come up with a realization of how you can work in the most effective ways in *every* situation. Notice that encouragement merits separate mention in this verse; a later lesson discusses the benefits of encouragement as a way to serve others. The most important thing to realize here is that although people have various abilities, there's a common driving force behind those abilities:

> *1 Corinthians 12:6* There are different kinds of working, but the same God works all of them in all men.
>
> *1 Corinthians 3:8* The man who plants and the man who waters have one purpose, and each will be rewarded according to his own labor.

God makes everything grow if we're willing to put our efforts toward achieving his purpose. Keep in mind, of course, that you aren't pigeonholed into only having and exercising one gift—many people have numerous gifts that all must be used wisely, and Paul later adds that Christians should "eagerly desire the greater gifts" (1 Corinthians 12:31) and work at taking on additional roles and as great a responsibility for doing God's work as our abilities will allow. No matter what your particular talents are, as long as you're aware of them and remain on the lookout, you'll spot opportunities for your particular capabilities to match up with some of the world's particular needs.

LESSON 60: THE LEAST... YOU SHOULD DO

God watches over everything and extends his care to everything, including things which might to us seem insignificant or unnecessary to watch over.

> **RELATED VERSE:**
> MATTHEW 10:29-30

The Bible makes it clear that the shelter God provides for man is not limited to a select group of people:

> *Psalm 36:7* How priceless is your unfailing love! Both high and low among men find refuge in the shadow of your wings.

God makes great success stories out of people with humble beginnings.

> *Isaiah 40:29* He gives strength to the weary and increases the power of the weak.

In the Old Testament, God made prophets and leaders out of common men, and chose a group of people with no particularly outstanding qualities to be his chosen people. In the New Testament, God chose a peasant girl to be the mother of Jesus, and Jesus during his ministry made apostles out of a very motley crew of ordinary men.

> *1 Corinthians 1:26-29* Brothers, think of what you were when you were called. Not many of you were wise by human standards; not many were influential; not many were of noble birth. But God chose the foolish things of the world to shame the wise; God chose the weak things of the world to shame the strong. He chose the lowly things of this world and the despised things—and the things that are not—to nullify the things that are, so that no one may boast before him.

Since God's provision and appreciation for people has always included even the least likely people, we also must not shun the insignificant or lowly things of this world. Unfortunately, many people have a tendency to do so. The following verse lets people know that they shouldn't consider others to be "beneath" them, but must appreciate and serve everyone:

> *Romans 12:16* Live in harmony with one another. Do not be proud, but be willing to associate with people of low position. Do not be conceited.

On certain occasions, Jesus explicitly stated that there would be consequences to not attending to the needs of *all* our fellow men:

> *Matthew 25:45* "He will reply, 'I tell you the truth, whatever you did not do for one of the least of these, you did not do for me.'"

Moreover, he expects us to be willing to humble ourselves in all situations. When an argument started among the disciples as to which one of them would be considered the greatest (Luke 9:46-48), Jesus used a small child to demonstrate the need for them to be willing to serve all others, and told the disciples "he who is least among you all—he is the greatest."

> RELATED VERSE:
> MARK 9:33-37

We must aspire to be unaspiring. In my view, that isn't too much for God to expect of us. We are exalted so greatly through him and lifted so high by his love, there's no need to exalt ourselves in any circumstance. As you go through life and occasionally achieve things considered highly honorable by human standards, or find yourself in any situations where it would be easy to draw comparisons between your own status and the status of others, be wary of the temptation to lift yourself unnecessarily in your own eyes or in the eyes of others. The elevator of grace that drops people off at the eternal penthouse suite only lets people get on at the basement level.

The parable in Matthew 13:31-32 compares the kingdom of heaven to a mustard seed, which is a tiny seed. This doesn't mean that God's plan is somehow progressing from trivial to substantial; the gift of making everlasting life available to us has always held the same huge importance. The parable speaks specifically of the church when it talks about the difference between the tiny seed that gets planted and the fully grown tree it eventually becomes. With a determined effort by all of us who tend to the church and contribute to its growth, the domain in which God's will is done can expand to its maximum potential despite its humble beginnings in Galilee and Judea. As people spread the gospel, it's always sown as the smallest of seeds and begins as a very small part of the lives of the people who hear it, but with humble dedication, great patience, and the right conditions, it grows into a tremendous (you might even say "tree-mend-us") thing.

LESSON 61: CONCERN FOR THE WEAK

Hand in hand with the need for humility goes the need for concern about those who are weak.

> **RELATED VERSE:**
> JAMES 1:27

There are concerns about the potential damage Y2K might do to entities that are already considered relatively weak by comparison to the rest of the world. Third-world or economically-troubled countries (as opposed to countries like the US), impoverished communities (as opposed to cities like Los Angeles, able to spend over $75 million to prepare for Y2K), the smallest businesses (as opposed to corporate giants like IBM), and the most infirm individuals (as opposed to those who are young and healthy with no special needs) are all considered to be at greater risk. People are worried about the "last straw" factor—Y2K may break some people and companies and even entire troubled nations that previously were already weakened in various other ways.

People worry, and rightly so, about the potential impact of Y2K on those with special needs. One "payment management system" in the US that wasn't able to be fixed by its target deadline of April 1, 1999 worried a lot of people, because that one system alone is responsible for disbursing about $165 billion per year through 10 federal agencies, including grants for the federal school lunch program, highway construction projects, and health care benefits.

Although it jumped to conclusions, one Y2K book correctly identified some key areas of concern when it noted, "The impact of Y2K on medical service will severely affect the sick, the elderly, the handicapped, and infants. Because poor people rely on government help, they will feel the impact of reduced medical services more than the rich." Substitute "might" where they used "will" and you've got a reasonable starting point for an important Y2K issue. Indeed, people with conditions requiring medication, special diets, or particular equipment have been strongly encouraged to do Y2K planning that takes their special needs into account.

The medical community worldwide has in no way put in place effective barriers to all negative effects from the Y2K problem on the quality of health care that people will receive following M-Day. Even here in the US, where thanks to plenty of information and resources we've at least had a fighting chance at preparing well, we've already seen Y2K take a toll on certain aspects of health care for certain groups of people. In one sad example, about 18,000 Massachusetts Medicaid patients were forced out of the Tufts Health Plan because Tufts concluded it couldn't reprogram its computers to handle recent Medicaid changes while completing the work necessary to resolve Y2K problems. "It was a very difficult decision for us because serving the Medicaid population is part of our mission," said Richard Shoup, Tufts' CIO. "But this is about business survival." It's impossible to say what disruptions and inconveniences might result for individual patients or groups of patients once the bulk of problems kick in when M-Day arrives.

The elderly have also been on many people's minds, especially of course the organizations that have senior citizens issues as their primary concern. The AARP web site, as part of its Y2K disclosure, has reassured viewers that it's being realistic but positive about the massive challenges posed by Y2K and their ability to continue serving their members despite the challenges:

> Given the magnitude and complexity of the problem, it would be imprudent to unequivocally guarantee 100% Y2K compliance as of December 31, 1999. However, AARP has devoted considerable resources to the problem and are confident that we are making significant strides towards compliance. We have also communicated our Y2K concerns to those contractors and companies upon whom AARP relies very heavily for services, or who provide AARP members with services.

Randy Johnson, chairman of the county commissioners board in Hennepin County, MN, said about services being administered at the county level, "I'd be surprised if there was not some dislocation and some interruption of services. We are trying to work with our clients, many of whom are elderly or frail, to make sure they know how to reach us if they have problems."

The Social Security system in the US appears to be fixed, but what about other countries that have government pension plans which form the total fixed income of many seniors? Some of those countries have federal agencies which are highly computerized but which aren't expected to be anywhere near fully prepared for the arrival of M-Day.

And what about social services for groups other than seniors? Here in the US, the viewpoints of county and state officials are considered valuable because many federal benefit programs are administered at the county and state levels. In the words of John Thomas Flynn, CIO for the State of California, "If social services are disrupted, you'll have more than computer problems. You could have civil disturbances. That's why this issue is a high priority for us."

Most state governors have recognized the Y2K problem as a priority for their administrations, but John Koskinen said at the end of 1998 that the President's Y2K Council was still "concerned about some states where it's not a priority of the governor and it's viewed as merely an information technology problem, off on the side."

The media has been pretty rough on Alabama, for example, which at the end of 1998 reported to the public that it had done only small percentages of the work required for certain key social services computer systems, including less than 10% of the necessary work on the computers for tracking child abuse and neglect cases and less than 20% of the necessary work on the computers for issuing food stamps and welfare benefits. The deputy commissioner of the Medicaid agency in Alabama thought she was putting people's fears at ease by saying, "Our existing computer system is not being touched. We won't upgrade it. We'll put in a new one on Oct. 1, 1999." Instead, many people since then have cited her as an example of inexcusable risk-taking, since large conversion projects like the one her agency planned are rarely completed on time and typically require significant time for testing after installation to make sure that no flaws exist. In mid-December 1999, Alabama was in the national news again after a study declared it to be the state most likely to suffer Y2K computer problems.

To end this topic on a positive note, Washington, DC is an interesting example of a government working hard at getting provisions in place for its needy and at-risk citizens. The government there has been hammered by some Y2K researchers for not doing enough to guarantee readiness for certain of its agencies' computer systems, but has been praised by many for its preparations that are specifically aimed at addressing people's physical needs. For instance, the District will be able to manually operate its subways, which are critical for poorer residents to be able to get to work and other appointments, and will have large, well-equipped warming centers open after M-Day for any people who find themselves without heat due to utility problems.

Things That Aren't Always Given Great Consideration

A bunch of actions related to Y2K have tickled me because they show that while during any crisis or preparation for a potential crisis most people direct all their energy and attention toward the major areas of concern, there fortunately are always a few people who notice the needs at the outer edges and direct their energy toward areas of concern that might otherwise go unnoticed and unattended to if it weren't for them. These are people who realize that all parts truly do matter, even the smallest and weakest and least central parts.

For instance, the environment wasn't at the top of everyone's list of Y2K concerns. At the end of August 1999, PTI, the technology arm of the National League of Cities, National Association of Counties, and International City/County Management Association, released a wonderful report to help local governments plan for Y2K-related environmental problems. It addressed specific issues such as what people should do in the event of sewer backups or drinking water pollution. The report was crucial; the environment hadn't been paid enough attention to early on, because other industries like banking, manufacturing, airlines, and communications, received the focus of most Y2K research efforts and information campaigns. Ronda Mosley-Rovi, director of environmental programs at PTI, said, "There was a lot of conversation here about telecommunications and public safety, but not a lot about the impact on the environment. There's a real need for documentation from the environmental [aspect]." Possible environmental effects associated with Y2K were discussed in the report, and advice was given about public education, waste and wastewater handling, contingency planning, hazardous facilities management, and more.

Now it's time for a quick fish story. By June 1999, Washington state agencies were almost completely Y2K-ready. A statewide risk-assessment report examined the state's vital services and found that only one agency, the Fish and Wildlife Agency, still had projects considered at high risk. Julie Boyer, program manager at their Y2K office, said the agency had established a target date of June 30th for full Y2K readiness and was confident they'd be done "on time or close to it." The most intriguing thing she said, however, is that the wildlife agency has already established Y2K contingency plans in case their systems aren't all upgraded properly by M-Day. For example, if any of the state fish hatcheries is unable to use the alarms that let workers know there has been a change in water quality, there's a contingency plan that requires manual monitoring of the water, so the fish won't be in any danger.

It truly warmed my heart when I learned about the backup plans for the care of those fish and each time I learned about all sorts of other things the average person would never think of off the tops of their heads as Y2K concerns. Many people who worked thoughtfully and relentlessly on those relatively obscure concerns have kept a lot of important things in our world from experiencing Y2K-related problems, and we should treasure their numerous contributions every bit as much as the contributions of those people who have worked full-time on making sure that banks get themselves into good shape and nuclear weapons programs remain safe and all the other large, central concerns are addressed. People have to watch out for all of the other people, animals, and systems in this world that can't take care of themselves, and Y2K has been a fine reminder of that fact for those of us who sometimes take certain of these things for granted.

The Unfortunate Status of Small Businesses

Indulge me by reading another joke that made the rounds on the Internet during Y2K preparations. It's a mock press release that says:

> McDonald's signs now stand at 99 gigaburgers (GB). Within months or even weeks, the corporate giant expects that number to roll over to 100 GB. The signs were designed years ago when the prospect of selling 100 billion burgers seemed unthinkably remote, so they have only two numeric places. This means that, after the sale of the 100 billionth burger, the signs will read "00 Billion Burgers Sold." Experts predict this will alarm the public and cause them to think that no McDonald's hamburgers have ever in fact been sold, spawning a loss of consumer confidence and eventually leading to complete bankruptcy of this corporation which has led the fast food industry for so long.

All right, the bit about the signs is funny and the whole notion of a large corporation like that being obliterated by the Y2K problem is out-and-out hilarious—but for anyone watching Y2K progress carefully for the past few years, that joke hits close to home concerning an unfortunate fact: Some small businesses are expected by government officials and industry analysts to be bankrupted by the Y2K problem.

It isn't going to be McDonald's, but it's going to be some mom-and-pop operation that never has realized how reliant they are on a particular computerized system outside their own doors, or it's going to be some one-doctor clinic that's the only medical facility in a small rural town in the deep South, or any of thousands of other businesses that are extremely vulnerable. Some small companies in the software field already *have* gone out of business just to avoid the overwhelming costs of coping with the problem, and other companies in a wide range of fields are expected not to have the necessary resources to cope with whatever negative surprises the problem socks them with early in the year 2000. A lack of readiness could cause a business to miss deadlines or fail to meet contractual obligations, destabilizing the business and hurting its competitive position. In the worst cases, these troubles could result in a complete shutdown of the business.

According to an Industry Canada study in mid-1999, 31% of Canadian businesses with five employees or less that own or use technologies susceptible to the Y2K problem had not taken *any* preparation steps whatsoever. The Canadian government's web site included this statement:

Many small and medium-size business owners mistakenly think that the Year 2000 problem only affects large companies with complex networks and customized software packages. The reality is, whether a company has three PCs or 300, the millennium bug can potentially cripple the business' computers, operating system, software, and networks as well as jeopardize vital links with customers, business partners, and suppliers.

Small business is the largest segment of the economy, but the least prepared for the Y2K problem, according to surveys by Ziff-Davis Computer Intelligence, Gartner Group, and others. Government leaders haven't been shy about mentioning the severity of the problem. Canadian Industry Minister John Manley said, "My message to businesses in Canada, particularly to small ones that have not yet addressed the problem, is simple and direct: Take action immediately." John Koskinen, head of the President's Y2K Council, told a reporter from the *San Francisco Chronicle* in October 1999 that almost 800,000 small businesses in the US are still vulnerable to Y2K failures, and said bluntly, "If you're a small company that decides to wait and fix it and does not get it fixed on time, our position is, 'That's life.' It's a great, free country and you have the freedom to fail." These statements have never generated a great deal of media attention, though, perhaps (the cynical mind says) because small businesses aren't the ones buying the bulk of advertising in print periodicals and on TV networks.

It's unquestionable that the smallest operations are generally the least prepared. Geoff Forage, partner at management consulting firm Ernst and Young, said that business continuity planning for Y2K (that's fancy talk for spending loads of money on backup plans and strategies to enable survival in the event of significant problems cropping up) is being done mainly by the biggest companies, adding, "That's not to say it shouldn't be done by smaller firms, but they tend to fly by the seat of their pants. They hope there won't be a problem or if there is, somehow they will struggle through."

There's general evidence to show this is true in several industries that haven't had a great deal of Y2K research conducted, and there's statistical evidence to show it's true in industries that have had such research. Here are a couple of examples:

- In early August 1999, reports came out showing which banks had been categorized as unsatisfactory by the FDIC, which banks had been told they were not fully satisfactory yet and needed some more improvement, and which banks had been categorized as satisfactory. According to *American Banker*, the unsatisfactory banks had average assets of $47 million, the banks which were told they needed improvement but were expected to achieve Y2K readiness had average assets of $152 million, and the satisfactory banks had average assets of $630 million.

- A small collection of the largest communications companies is serving the needs of almost all individuals and businesses in the world. In the US, for instance, less than two dozen leading companies provide local phone service to more than 97% of all US customers. In mid-1999, the FCC praised the Y2K preparedness of those companies, but expressed worry that some small- and medium-size companies were behind on Y2K efforts because they lacked technical expertise and money to make the necessary changes.

- The leading online service provider, America Online, which has 20 million subscribers, confidently claims full preparedness for Y2K, because it's a huge company that has had plenty of cash and personnel to undertake remediation and contingency planning. In stark contrast, however, Prodigy Communications Corp., which at the end of 1998 had a total of about 650,000 subscribers to its two online services, notified subscribers to its Prodigy Classic service in the third week of January 1999 that it would have to shut down its Prodigy Classic service, citing the Y2K problem as the reason. Prodigy told customers that it could not avoid the effects of the problem on its older proprietary systems that ran the Classic service and therefore had to shut down what had been one of the earliest and most beloved cyber-communities. While the company encouraged the more than 200,000 Classic subscribers to migrate to its newer Prodigy Internet service (which is considered Y2K-ready) there was no requirement or guarantee that the subscribers would do so, meaning that the acknowledgment of defeat at the hands of Y2K by the already weakened Prodigy, a company that had steadily lost subscribers to AOL and a variety of ISPs over the past few years anyway, took the company from 650,000 subscribers down to 433,000 in one fell swoop, and left them in the position of simply hoping that some of those customers would believe in their small company enough to subscribe to its newer service.

These vulnerable smaller businesses are often the strong foundation of local community, and do many things (like sponsoring junior sports leagues and public broadcasting and local school events) that help to hold the community together. Long after M-Day, we as a society should be willing to notice and do something about remedying any negative impact this computer problem has had on small businesses, because before Y2K even came along, many of these little guys were already at risk due to tremendous pressure from volume discounting, massive advertising, and other tactics available to their larger competitors.

Because smaller companies often sell a limited range of products or offer one specific service into a limited marketplace, they're much more vulnerable to an all-out catastrophe than large corporations which sell multiple products and services into many different marketplaces. It's not all doom-and-gloom for small businesses, though. Thankfully, many of them can still use their brains, adapt, and do things manually because their workloads aren't as large. Also, because they tend to be less dependent on technology than larger companies in the first place, they might have fewer internal Y2K problems.

In addition, some organizations have been kind enough to specifically look out for the little guys. Small-business owners confused about the Y2K problem have been able to get a free Y2K video and workbook through a Penn State University outreach program. Many other programs have offered checklists and other literature, counselors to do one-on-one strategizing about Y2K difficulties a small company might face, and other services especially for small businesses. A number of online sites offering Y2K information have included specific collections of resources for small businesses, including information on special loans and tax incentives available through various programs.

The Small Business Administration not only has had a web site but also a toll-free help line where businesses could get step-by-step assistance about assessment, remediation, and contingency planning. In March 1999, the Congress approved legislation allowing the SBA to guarantee loans for small businesses either trying to fix their own computers or in some way endangered by Y2K problems with their suppliers, customers, or their usual lenders. The SBA is willing to guarantee about $500 million in loans through the end of the year 2000. A sad continuation of the tendencies discussed earlier in this book to put things off as long as possible, and to take precautions only when it's clear they're going to be absolutely necessary, shows up in the fact that applications for the loans, originally expected to flood in by the thousands during the first few months of the program, ended up trickling in only by the dozens. SBA officials feel that many small business owners are simply waiting to see if a specific event will force them to request such a loan following M-Day.

Lesson 62: The Nature of True Support

We've seen riots in Los Angeles, massive train wrecks in India, and other events completely shift the resources of a city or an entire region to try to cope with that one episode. Now what if there are multiple events at once? People from other areas usually pitch in to help an affected area recover from natural disasters. In fact, this is one of the most heartening things about our world—our capacity to recover. Honduras suffered mind-boggling hurricane damage in 1998, and their *whole* infrastructure was gone, but they've steadily made progress in their recovery efforts with the help of many people from the rest of the world.

With Y2K, people have worried that if there are enough small independent problems simultaneously, resources won't exist to be able to be transferred to all those locations and help out with whatever messes have occurred.

> *1 John 3:17* If anyone has material possessions and sees his brother in need but has no pity on him, how can the love of God be in him?

Remember the unfortunate irony already mentioned of churches and community service organizations often being negatively impacted during a crisis in two ways (directly through their own disruptions and also indirectly through a reduction in contributions) at exactly the moment when those churches and organizations may be very much needed. Furthermore, many of the biggest hearts are found in small organizations, so they may be among the institutions least able to endure severe setbacks. True support makes sure it has a storehouse in place to cope with crisis.

> **RELATED VERSE:**
> ACTS 4:32-35

I read a Y2K book during 1999 that told readers, "It's very likely that most hospitals will be overwhelmed and understaffed during Y2K, so *you may not be able to get any attention at all, even if your condition is life threatening*" (italics theirs). This is terrible fear-mongering, and producing fear in people is not true support. All panic ever did for anybody in the Bible was to get them a lecture. There is absolutely no scriptural basis for panic. Constant demonstrations of love and faithfulness are what earn approval from God.

Software companies for the most part went so far as to identify and categorize potential problems with various versions of their software products. They supplied patches for newer versions, but if your version was fairly outdated, they often didn't go any extra mile for you, but simply expected you to pay for an upgrade to the latest version of their product. Incomplete support is not true support.

One of the ways to help others is by getting together for companionship and encouraging one another. The needs of believers are often met through other believers.

> *Ephesians 4:29* Do not let any unwholesome talk come out of your mouths, but only what is helpful for building others up according to their needs, that it may benefit those who listen.

> **RELATED VERSE:**
> 1 THESSALONIANS 5:11

True support includes encouragement in any form.

Mitch Ratcliffe in a column on August 13, 1999 took a look back at some 1998 predictions of pre-Y2K events, finding the non-occurrences of many predicted events "illustrative of how ill-conceived most pessimistic Y2K scenarios really were." He gleefully bashed John Westergaard, Mike Adams, and others representative of the whole "doomer" mentality that had been proven overly pessimistic to that point. Ratcliffe wrote that Gary North had stayed "sound asleep and wrapped in his nightmare." He called Adams "a master of addled logic" and concluded with the opinion that "Some people just never learn. I only wonder what loopy stories these guys will be hawking next year." Ratcliffe felt it important not only to give the public accurate information about Y2K from his own viewpoint, but also to bash the inaccuracies of others.

Proverbs 10:18-21 teaches that the tongue can be beautiful and of great benefit or can be wicked and poisonous. I feel offering words of encouragement rather than an "I told you so" should be your goal concerning Y2K and all other situations in life where you happen to be ahead of the curve and others aren't as well off.

> ## Note
>
> I hate to use one day's work by one particular person to point out the "I told you so" tendency during Y2K discussions, because the same behavior occurred regularly by people at both ends of the spectrum of Y2K problem predictions. I've chosen that Ratcliffe column to mention, though, because it's a particularly striking example of how easy it has been during Y2K dialogue for meaningful idea exchange to degrade into name-calling and finger-pointing, and also because I've mentioned elsewhere in the book several of Ratcliffe's ideas that I like very much and completely agree with, so I hope my book represents a more objective, embracing form of criticism than the form I've considered less than ideal when I've seen other people taking jabs back and forth at each other.

Look at the wide gulfs that have developed between perspectives on Y2K, and think about those between Christians as well—we have heaven-pushers versus hell-threateners, we have touchy-feely-loving God depictions versus wrathful-tired-of-your-human-rebellion God depictions, and various other differences standing between large numbers of believers, some of whom truly delight in finding fault with the logic or beliefs of those on the other side of an issue.

The author of Jude wrote to warn against people who didn't strive to support Christianity through study of and teaching of its core beliefs, and who instead stirred up dissension and misled others through faultfinding and false teaching:

> *Jude :16* These men are grumblers and faultfinders; they follow their own evil desires; they boast about themselves and flatter others for their own advantage.

While we're on the subject of fault, let's focus on the fact that most companies have hated to admit any fault. Some lying vendors have deceived plenty of clients about the compliance of their products, some lying companies have deceived stockholders and government agencies about testing results, some lying suppliers have deceived clients about the certainty of their ability to supply goods after M-Day, and so on.

A July 1, 1999 *Orlando Sentinel* story suggested that as many as 50% of vendors may be lying to their clients about Y2K compliance. I feel most of the lying that has occurred is rooted in problems of pride—how often do we in our daily lives also not want to admit weakness or mistakes? We'll usually make corrections or even make amends if we've done wrong, but we'd just as soon do it behind closed doors rather than under the scrutiny of anyone else. A willingness to admit fault is essential, though, if we're to move through life maturely and in a spirit of cooperation with the rest of the world. True support is honest and not only relies on finding out what others know, but also shares with others what is already known, even when it takes courage to share the truth.

In my view, true support also includes compassion whenever that's appropriate. Compassion is essentially a deeply felt sympathy for someone else's misfortune. Y2K has shown us some simple acts of compassion from sometimes surprising sources. The Internal Revenue Service, for instance, not renowned in most circles for being a compassionate agency, felt sympathy for companies that had to cough up unexpectedly large amounts of money to complete Y2K projects, and decided to allow full tax deductions in a single year (rather than the usual three years) for the amounts that businesses have spent to repair or convert existing software to fix the Y2K problem. It's generally advantageous to fully deduct costs in a single year because the entire deduction becomes immediately available for other purposes. Several other countries provided similar Y2K-related tax relief to businesses.

To understand more about what compassion is, simply look to the life and works of Jesus, who was unfailingly compassionate. The Bible in several locations urges us to mirror that behavior:

Ephesians 4:32 Be kind and compassionate to one another, forgiving each other, just as in Christ God forgave you.

> **Related Verse:**
> **Philippians 2:4-7**

Jesus is the ultimate conveyor of love, and love is an integral component of compassion, and of true support.

Tim Wilson, frequent lecturer on Y2K issues (and firm believer that numerous problems will result), has gone out of his way for over two years to convince people that Y2K deserves their serious attention. He is genuinely concerned about people making sure they take action to avoid having problems, but is also frustrated that people in general haven't been as concerned as he feels they should be. He was mostly but not completely kidding when he talked about wanting those who have said there'll be no Y2K problems to get just a little taste of the inevitable problems that some people will have to endure. About possible Y2K disaster, he said on a radio program, "I'd really like to see nothing happen. Actually, I've got a list of about 60 people I'd like to see it happen to, just for a day or two." I'm sure you know without a great deal of commentary from me that true support avoids being spiteful or mean-spirited even toward those who reject and refuse it.

1 Peter 3:8 Finally, all of you, live in harmony with one another; be sympathetic, love as brothers, be compassionate and humble.

Mark 12:31 is where Jesus taught his disciples "Love your neighbor as yourself," easily recognizable as the fundamental underpinning of the Golden Rule (Matthew 7:12 and elsewhere) which more broadly promotes always behaving toward others the way you'd like people to behave toward you.

At the meal where Jesus predicted his betrayal by Judas Iscariot, he took the same concept about love a step farther by giving his disciples an important commandment:

John 13:34 A new command I give you: Love one another. As I have loved you, so you must love one another.

The ten commandments handed down from God earlier through Moses remain in place, and Jesus added one—to love others as he loved us, which is to say, utterly and completely. This is more than just loving others as ourselves— it's a higher goal to try to match the boundless love of Jesus. This new commandment accompanies the new relationship we establish when we accept Christ into our lives. The passage goes on to emphasize that by accepting this one new commandment, we can demonstrate to all men that we're Jesus' disciples—thus, it sets forth one extra step that allows people to make the huge leap to actively demonstrating their Christian faith to the world.

Reading this passage where Jesus lays out the new commandment often reminds me of a moment in the secular film *This is Spinal Tap*, in which a rock 'n' roll guitarist proudly explains that his amplifier's volume control goes beyond the industry standard of ten volume settings. "Mine goes to eleven," he says proudly, with all the confidence of someone who carries his commitment to loud music farther than anyone else does. When I reflect upon Jesus' parting guidance for his followers, I feel pride in knowing that in terms of having a set of commandments that will make my life fully pleasing in God's sight, "Mine goes to eleven." This principle of love set out in the "new command" is critical on a daily basis, not just in and around a crisis such as the Y2K problem, but at all times. True support in the form of love is given universally and constantly.

Whenever you put on the "love garment" discussed earlier in the book for patience and humility (refer to Lesson 18 or turn to Colossians 3:12-14 for its full description), keep in mind that compassion and kindness are two other components of the outfit, and that love is what holds it all together.

Summary

We've seen that the Y2K problem or any other significant challenge can bring out a broad range of behaviors in people, from the very best to the very worst imaginable. Don't pride yourself on always being a single strand, but instead strike a harmonious "cord" with others who can team up with you in supportive relationships. It's important to be a non-stop participant in the spillover effect, letting the blessings and grace in your life pour out into the world around you, and choosing to help rather than harm in all circumstances, no matter how much sacrifice that might require from you. One of the greatest things you can do is to appreciate that all parts matter, and attend to the needs of even those which on the surface seem weakest and least significant.

8

Imperfect World, Perfect God

Sometimes the problems of the world seem too overwhelming for people to handle. Times of crisis or the mere anticipation of crisis can make it even harder to stay certain of our coping abilities. After all, some people point out, we're only human, none of us is perfect, and the wide-ranging challenges of modern life are tremendous. This chapter will explain, though, that by not feeling burdened or broken, and by acknowledging our connections with God, with Scripture, with other people, and with history, Christians can function as effectively as possible in all times and all situations.

LESSON 63: MAINTAINING COHESION AND A STRENGTHENED SENSE OF COMMUNITY

The church is inextricably part of the broader community. I've long been disappointed in Christians—and there are plenty—who refuse to associate with non-Christians in their business or private lives. You can't learn about the needs of others and be of service to others unless you are willing to overstep your comfort zone and deal with a wide variety of people, each in his or her own setting. It's not a principle of truly energetic church-building to sit back and wait for the masses to gravitate toward the church. The church must actively go out and bring the Good News (and associated good deeds) to the world. Y2K has provided a backdrop for noticing this principle in action among certain groups of Christians once again. Many churches have been key in helping their entire local communities (and sometimes those far beyond their local communities) to learn about and overcome potential Y2K-related problems.

In every community, no matter the size, churches often play a central role in providing shelter and relief in times of disaster. Not only is a church building a place of rest or protection for those who are without a home or without adequate protection or supplies at home, but the people of the church provide companionship and reassurance as well. Even in a community teeming with people with different opinions on matters of politics and business and so forth, churches often are the main places where groups of people can come together in cooperation and compassion.

Many churches have decided to hold prayer vigils for the world on New Year's Eve so that exactly as midnight of M-Day arrives in various parts of the world, prayers are directed toward those specific regions. This would have been a nice idea any year, but with the Y2K problem it has felt even more important to many congregations. Those churches feel a sense of cohesion between themselves and the world, and work on furthering that cohesion through their own actions. I want to spend this lesson talking about cohesion between individuals and churches and nations, and the sense of community that can be derived from a united spirit and shared experiences.

Examples of cohesion have been everywhere, because so many of the required Y2K remediation efforts are massive in scale and require unique partnerships. In 1998, the US Justice Department granted antitrust exemption so that members within the Securities Industry Association and the National Association of Manufacturers could cooperate and exchange data about the Y2K problem, although similar cooperation between some of those companies is normally disallowed due to concerns about anticompetitive effects. Other countries also allowed their leading companies to work together in ways previously unheard of, just so that Y2K could be overcome.

There have been many decisions by those doing well in the battle against Y2K problems to send expertise to other places to make sure others' Y2K projects are done as well and as quickly as possible. Here are just a few examples:

The huge majority of Indian and Inuit programming at the Canadian Department of Indian Affairs and Northern Development (DIAND) is usually managed by the First Nations communities themselves. Just like municipal and regional government officials, the First Nations administrators have had to assess and inventory their administrative systems to minimize potential disruptions due to Y2K problems. DIAND has stepped in and offered assistance to help First Nations chiefs and councils with their infrastructure inventories and Y2K assessments for the more than 900 inhabited reserves in Canada.

In August 1999, Hong Kong decided to send assistance to neighboring countries, because although Hong Kong itself is ready for Y2K, it risks fallout from less-prepared Asian trading partners. Roy Ko, a Y2K expert at Hong Kong's Productivity Council which oversees Y2K readiness of some 300,000 firms, said that China, Thailand, and the Philippines are viewed as vulnerable and any havoc there could mean problems for Hong Kong, and could hurt its status as a thriving business hub.

In late summer 1999, the US Pentagon turned its focus from preparing domestically to preparing its overseas military bases and the communities that house them, because half a million US troops and military dependents overseas might face problems with local power, water, or phone service. By September 1999, only about 40% of 130 key bases worldwide met the Pentagon's standards for readiness, and Deputy Defense Secretary John Hamre said about the rest, "We anticipate there will be some disruption. . . . We are concerned about what happens to dependents living on the economy overseas." The Pentagon has sent teams of Y2K experts to Europe, the Middle East, and Far East, and has sent large quantities of backup equipment to certain bases.

Even with a very late start, some countries have made wonderful headway in overcoming potential Y2K problems through tremendous cohesion and teamwork. The United Nations in December 1998 hosted its first summit for all member nations on the Y2K problem. More than 200 representatives from 120 member-states convened to identify the critical points in solving the computer problem and forming contingency plans. Ahmad Kamal, Pakistani ambassador to the United Nations and chairman of the UN's working group on information technology, noted "there will be problems" but appealed for an international spirit of teamwork.

The outlook expressed by some at that point was, "We have at least two years' worth of work to do in a year's time." Acknowledging that some failures would be inevitable, the group spent lots of time discussing how nations could develop contingency plans. One suggestion was to set up "SWAT teams" that could move swiftly into the hardest hit areas with technical assistance. Six months later, another international conference took place, and the reports were encouraging. Kamal at that time was able to announce, "Action is under way everywhere, by and large on schedule." From that point on, the inevitable disruptions from Y2K problems were deemed likely to be less widespread and less serious than had been feared six months earlier. The second meeting had delegates from 173 countries, up from the original 120 countries.

The benefits of this effort will extend beyond the year 2000. Regional sessions related to the series of international conferences have created bonds that are likely to foster international cooperation on technological issues long after the Y2K challenge has passed. John Koskinen commented, "The amount of cooperation going on is fascinating. A lot of the worry about international preparedness a year and a half ago was because no one could imagine putting all these people together."

Some tensions, though, did serve as stumbling blocks for cooperation on Y2K efforts. Cooperation between the US and China was slightly impaired by tension over the accidental Chinese Embassy bombing by US troops in Belgrade and by fundamental disagreements between the two countries on certain hot-button topics. The same tension arose between the US and Russia. After the US and Russian governments had established their plan to jointly staff a Y2K monitoring center at the end of the year to avoid misunderstandings in the case of Y2K glitches in weapons detection systems or other defense systems, the NATO military action began against Yugoslavia, a Russian ally. At the end of March 1999, along with an announcement that it would send relief aid to Yugoslavia, Russia announced that as a punishment for the "criminal US-led war" against Yugoslavia, Moscow would no longer cooperate with the US on work related to the Y2K problem.

The cooperation they abandoned primarily consisted of advice from the US to Russia on how to prepare computers and missiles. To emphasize Russia's official anger, the Russian military chief, Gen. Anatoly Kvashnin, refused to pick up the phone when he received a call from Gen. Henry Shelton, head of the US Joint Chiefs of Staff. After the situation in Yugoslavia shifted, Russia announced it would cooperate with the US on Y2K work again, but because of the political tiff that took place in March, several weeks were lost from an already inadequate supply of time to cooperate on Y2K remediation.

In another glaring example of tensions getting in the way—this time deep-seated historical ones—Morocco, which organized the regional meeting for North African and Middle Eastern nations, refused to allow Israel to participate in that regional meeting. When the head of the UN's Y2K committee suggested that perhaps Morocco had only excluded Israel because it had found that Israel had no "shared problems" with its neighbors, reporters accused him of covering up the real reason, the tremendous religious and political tension pervading international relationships in that part of the world. The UN representative said in response, "We can't force people to invite people they don't want in their homes."

Those and several similar incidents have saddened me throughout the years of working on Y2K. We all need to stop letting things divide us, at the international level and at the individual level. In our own lives, people sometimes even manage to let good things divide them (career advancement, weddings, and other supposedly happy events have caused squabbling among certain people) so we're of course all the more vulnerable to letting genuinely troublesome things divide us. Identify the key relationships in your life—spouse, church, other family members, friends, connections with various parts of your community, and so on—and work on making those relationships impervious to divisive influences.

Some think the entire issue of Y2K has never deserved attention, but it baffles me how anyone could think that. Hundreds of billions of dollars, several thousand news stories, and millions of discussions around the water cooler haven't added up to nothing. They have formed a group experience for all of us, and an individual experience for each of us. The crisis has brought our world somewhere different than where it was before the average person had heard of the Y2K problem. Shared experiences are what truly create cohesion for any set of people, from a pair of newlyweds taking a honeymoon trip or law school classmates whose experience forges lifetime friendships, all the way up to the scale where entire nations are drawn closer together because they've been involved in a global war or a global cooperative effort such as the effort to tackle the Y2K problem has been.

Strong relationships with neighbors are essential not just for Y2K but for other times as well—crime watch, safety patrols to make sure the elderly or infirm are doing okay, and information sharing about any issues of current concern are great things to have in place at all times, but have been especially recognized as needs during Y2K. Sharing tools and talents is important, too—most neighborhoods have a mixture of people with varying abilities and interests, and you can either end up with everybody lacking individually or with everybody coming together to complement one another and form a complete team with everything it needs to take on whatever comes its way.

I've given Y2K advice to some other communities that might not occur to you at first when you think about community, including orphanages, prisons, group homes for mentally challenged individuals, and assisted-living residences for seniors. Since people live there and administrative programs are in operation, those places usually have faced the double burden of doing all the preparations required for a business as well as all the preparations required for a home. The Y2K problem has been very useful for teaching me to expand my personal concept of community. The role of the church in the leadership and support of communities holds true for all segments—rural as well as urban, poor as well as wealthy, and so on. And the need for this broad understanding of community doesn't end once we've gotten through Y2K—it's ongoing, and I hope we'll manage to keep in place many of the feelings and strategies for reaching out to everyone.

Many experts have framed the Y2K problem by saying that the impact will be localized and therefore everybody needn't worry, but I think it's a mistake to think that way. Sure, the concerns about preparation are mostly local, but odds are that any negative impact is likely to be somewhere away from you, so it's not enough to think only about yourself, your church, your job, and your community. We can't celebrate that we're okay if it turns out that others aren't. When the odds work in your favor and you get through M-Day completely unscathed, is that the end of it for you, or will you put the same effort into caring about someone else from someplace else who does have a Y2K-related problem that you would have put into solving your own problems if you'd suffered from any?

One Y2K book wrote, "Part of the 'American way' is to expect people to stand on their own two feet, and if someone else has a problem, we think it's the person's own fault." The book went on, though, to express hope that "Y2K might be the catalyst for the most revolutionary tearing down of walls between neighbors since the Berlin Wall was breached."

Liza Christian, a community organizer working on Y2K preparedness in Oregon, credits the experience with strengthening relationships between neighbors. In her words, "Y2K shines a huge spotlight on the fact that, as integrated as we are to technology, we have become unintegrated to each other. The view in our community has shifted toward getting to know one another and recognizing we really do need each other. Technology has created a veil in some regards, and this crisis has lifted it."

The same sort of distance many people place between themselves and the problems of other countries is sometimes also placed between themselves and the problems that exist in certain areas within their own country, state, or locality. I'm not naive enough to think that solutions to all social ills will result if people from different socioeconomic situations simply meet and interact with each other more. I do think, however, that the tendency for many people who are better off to turn a blind eye to the needs of people who are worse off than themselves or different than themselves is a tendency that Christians must avoid.

Why does it usually take a crisis to bring people together? We haven't just seen this with Y2K, but with every isolated natural disaster (think of various tornados, floods, and so on) or horrible crime (think of the Columbine shootings and others) that unites a previously laid-back community of strangers and makes them feel tremendous bonding. It's nice that it happens after a problem is in the works, but why does it take a problem to kick off that type of togetherness? How about we all get together for a *lack* of a crisis sometime? I propose that in 2002 we stage an event to do that. We'll call it Y2K+2 (that will please those who love acronyms and symbols), and we'll all make a big hubbub about the fact that nothing is going to go wrong with any of the things that we rely upon for daily living, but we'll take the opportunity to improve friendliness with our neighbors and meet with fellow citizens and government officials and decide how we can help the most fragile members of society and make an extra effort to keep in touch with our loved ones. Let's try to learn from our preparations for M-Day, whether we're directly affected by problems or not. If we get just one thing out of this experience, let it be: It shouldn't take the threat of something going wrong to make us all act right.

LESSON 64: ONLY IN SPELLING SHOULD JESUS END WITH US

The Y2K experience will be simultaneously global and personal, different for everyone and yet in some ways the same for all of us. It potentially matters to everyone in the world. As explained in Lesson 44, it's always important to make sure you're living up to your responsibilities on the homefront, but it's also unforgivable if you never expand the scope of your awareness and concern.

How we'll fare here in the US on M-Day is all that matters to many Americans. Consider this line from *The Y2K Family Survival Guide* (Harvest House, 1999): "It is almost certain countries in Asia will be hard-hit, and that will no doubt create financial disturbances in the United States. However, we also believe in American ingenuity and in our unique ability to adapt and survive hard times. More than that, we believe most Americans will want to get things going again in this country and will work overtime to reestablish many of the things we've come to take for granted—like television, telephone connections, and the speedy resumption of commerce. And we believe in the gracious providence of God."

To me, this comes across as somewhat ethnocentric. We *should* care about Asian countries or countries from any other continents that are hard-hit, whether or not they cause negative ripples in our own economy. I dearly love the US, but I have to wonder what "unique ability to adapt and survive hard times" some Americans think we have. It seems to me that many other countries have faced more difficult circumstances than we have, not only in recent years but throughout recorded world history. The US, for the most part, is a place of relative comfort and luxury, and the very fact that television is the first example cited for services we'd want to reestablish is indicative of how cushy our lives have become. I, too, believe in the "gracious providence of God," but the Bible tells me that it's not a selective providence. God's care rests upon America, but our country doesn't rate special care above and beyond that which rests upon any other country of the world. Through Jesus' sacrifice for all of mankind, God's everlasting grace became universally available to all who would partake of it.

Many people mistakenly have thought the US was the singular world leader in Y2K awareness and remediation. In fact, a couple of the Scandinavian nations were well out ahead of our nation in terms of information, nationwide initiative, and accomplishments regarding Y2K early on.

While many African nations matched up with the general American stereotype of being behind the times and lacking in technology and therefore insulated from Y2K's negative effects, some surprises could be found by studying Y2K efforts of countries on that continent. The Kenyan government, for example, launched a task force to look into the Y2K problem in October 1997, far earlier than several European nations. Botswana is another great example—it has significant technology infrastructure and has led the way among African nations in terms of Y2K preparedness, achieving a state of full readiness for its heavily computerized utilities months before M-Day. Botswana Telecommunications, the national carrier, started to prepare in mid-1997 and by August 1999 was giving demonstrations to the media and other national governments of its preparedness.

We often are so ethnocentric that we forget the brilliance, talents, and dedication of people in other parts of the world, and Y2K has been a good context in which to realize that we in the US certainly don't have a monopoly on knowledge and achievement. Gartner Group reported at the end of September 1999 that besides the US, the "lowest risk" category includes Denmark, Sweden, the Netherlands, Switzerland, Bermuda, Britain, Canada, Belgium, Israel, and Australia. Gartner projects that 15% of businesses and government agencies in these countries will suffer at least one failure that significantly disrupts operations. There are intermediate risk ratings, and then the "highest risk" category, which includes over 30 countries like Russia and China—Gartner projects that at least 65% of businesses and government agencies in those countries will run into at least one major problem.

> ### Note
> Some countries that are far less developed will feel less of an impact—first, because they're not as dependent on computers in as many aspects of life, and second, as unfortunate as it is, because they're used to more discomfort and more things not working. Vietnam is one of these, Indonesia another. China believes itself to be less vulnerable than many industrialized countries due to its relatively low level of computerization. At the end of February 1999, Sen. Robert Bennett's subcommittee sent a team to Russia to evaluate Y2K preparations. Bennett said they returned with the conclusion that "they are going to have real problems" but that "no one is going to notice because they said nothing works over there right now."

Still, there are expected to be significant disruptions overseas. Jacquelyn Williams-Bridgers, US State Dept. Inspector General, said at the beginning of March 1999, "It is becoming increasingly clear that there will be Y2K-related failures in every corner of the globe, some of which could prove harmful to US interests." By July 1999, John Koskinen said, "Many more countries are going to have problems than not." Let's look quickly at a random sampling of the preparedness status of various nations.

The Middle East

Most Gulf Arab states have been working hard. Public concern has become high in the region, with local newspapers during the latter part of 1999 filled with tips, updates on the compliance efforts of companies and government departments, and reports from seminars on the problem. Most of the six Gulf Cooperation Council states—Bahrain, Kuwait, Oman, Qatar, Saudi Arabia, and the United Arab Emirates—have created government task forces dedicated to raising awareness and monitoring remediation. Among the least prepared sectors in the region are health care and education.

Saudi Arabia, the region's biggest economy and the world's largest oil producer and exporter, has done great at preparing its utilities and banking sector. Most oil companies in the Middle East and North Africa region began tackling the Y2K problem by 1997, and are in good shape heading into M-Day. Some Middle Eastern countries are at risk, though, from potential computer problems at desalinization plants that could lead to unsafe water and health problems.

Italy

A government committee finally began dealing with the Y2K problem in early 1999; no national campaign to raise public awareness was launched until February 1999. Weak points there include hospital equipment and other public services. Starting late is costing Italy dearly—expenditures to achieve readiness are expected to exceed $30 billion—and many Y2K projects there can't be finished by M-Day.

Japan

The Economist reported in August 1999 that Japan lags in Y2K preparedness behind even much poorer countries like Thailand, yet Japan is possibly more reliant on technology than any other country in the world. The same month, Tokyo newspapers reported that major banks had ordered thousands of extra futons for management to stay overnight on New Year's Eve in case of trouble.

Ziff-Davis reported that according to a survey of vendors it had conducted, "Japan really doesn't get this problem." Most Japanese PC makers hadn't even offered Y2K information about their products or Y2K links on their web sites. *The Economist* did note that because Japan computerized many sectors much later than the US, a lot of software there has always been Y2K compliant.

Terrie Lloyd, publisher of *Computing Japan*, says the lack of government concern is largely cultural: "In Japan, the society is so much more ordered [than in the US] that the government doesn't care enough to spend 60 billion dollars to make sure everything is compliant. The Japanese government doesn't actually care whether people are without food and water for a few days. The Kobe quake proved that." Workers in Japan cannot tell their bosses when a system has problems, because confrontation of any kind is still practically unheard of.

Australia/New Zealand

This part of the world overall is in great shape, and has done thorough preparation. New Zealand's plans even included delivering a checklist of preparations to every house in September 1999. A report by the Australian Bureau of Statistics has shown that around 44% of Australian companies do not intend to undertake any Y2K work. A government official presenting the report said, however, that the level of Y2K awareness is so high, it appears that the businesses deciding to do nothing "have made informed business decisions."

Latin America

Gartner Group analysts predict half of all Latin American companies and state agencies in Argentina, Colombia, the Dominican Republic, Guatemala, Panama, and Venezuela will see at least one critical failure. In even worse shape are Costa Rica, Ecuador, El Salvador, and Uruguay. Social unrest and paralyzed commerce are tangible fears. In Latin America, said Ian Hugo, deputy director of Britain's Taskforce2000, "the public doesn't protest with phone calls and letters—it riots and destabilizes the government. There's lots of potential for that."

Venezuela, the world's third largest oil exporter, has given hardly any public attention to the problem. A US Senate panel included Venezuela on its "shortlist" of the eight countries seemingly least prepared. "We're going to have a food-supply shortage," predicts Alejandro Bermudez, the government's information systems manager. He estimates 40% of Venezuela's food-processing plants will have trouble when faulty computer chips in automated factories disable production lines. Another anticipated failure is the halting of 2,500 elevators in the capital city of Caracas. "We know it's going to happen," said Bermudez.

Venezuela fears creating runs on banks and food shortages if it follows the lead of the United States in advising citizens to prepare for possible disruptions, said Hugo Castellanos, head of the Venezuelan Y2K agency. In October 1999, just 10 weeks before M-Day, Venezuela unveiled a presidential task force to fight the Y2K problem. Its head announced that they'd already been working on systems for a year and that critical systems such as public services were 90% ready for the date rollover. He said unspecified "non-critical systems" were 65% ready. Airlines, utilities, and state-run oil company Petroleos de Venezuela have announced completion of Y2K upgrades.

"For us [Y2K] could be like a volcanic eruption," said Hernando Carvalho, a Colombian civil engineer. Analysts say Latin and Caribbean governments have been able to do little more than focus on preventing disasters brought on by the Y2K problem. "They're only focusing on critical systems and contingency plans," said Rafael Hernandez, a World Bank information specialist. Nearly all Latin American governments rely on computer systems, but at precisely the moment they should have been investing heavily in Y2K fixes, cascading effects of the Asian financial crisis pounded most of their economies. Colombian civil aviation officials say their radar systems will fail without repairs costing over $11 million, which the federal government cannot provide. Without radar, controllers will rely on voice communications and keep planes spaced more widely apart, delaying flights.

Not every nation in the region is in trouble. Mexico and Chile budgeted explicitly for Y2K starting in 1998, and Mexico has had even stricter reporting requirements for financial institutions than the US. On the whole, though, Latin American Y2K officials have divulged few details of their countries' progress because international investor confidence has been at stake.

India

Missiles in India have been declared "Y2K-proof." The airport authority has asserted compliance in the Delhi and Mumbai air traffic systems. Leaders were late to realize the extent of the problem, and as of Spring 1999, only 20% of industries had initiated action. At least 50% of all computers nationwide may be affected, an Indian computer industry executive has predicted.

Our Challenge Is Expanding Our Thinking

US citizens for the most part have grown quite cynical about social unrest in foreign countries. So much news of civil war, rebellion, martial law, and rioting has reached our ears about dozens of countries in recent decades that most such reports now merge easily with our general mindset of "yeah, that's a mess" rather than striking us with immediacy and evoking true concern. Many Christians say an immediate prayer for the people in those situations when they hear such news, which is a wonderful thing. In some cases, people lend a hand or contribute money or supplies to help with the needs that exist in overseas situations. There's definitely a sense in our country, though, of being protected from those sorts of problems. We've been too comfortable for too long, and in today's culture of "pay *too much* attention to something and then forget it completely and move on to something different" the ideological tensions and civil unrest we've experienced in the history of our own nation seem far more remote to the average American today than you'd expect based on the relatively short amount of time elapsed since some of those events.

Our thinking definitely can stay too localized. Let's make sure that whatever Y2K problems strike, we genuinely feel concern for those affected, wherever they are. Let's also make sure that the challenges of the universal church are felt in our home churches, wherever those are. The church is a global collection of local bodies. We all should feel a meaningful connection to the worldwide church, not just when we sponsor a missionary or participate in a World Communion Sunday or similar event, but on a daily basis as we all work collectively on our shared goal of living and spreading the Good News.

> *Philippians 2:4* Each of you should look not only to your own interests, but also to the interests of others.

A couple of books (including *Facing Millennial Midnight*) mentioned India and Pakistan as nations "on the brink of nuclear war" and claimed that those nations were "among the least prepared for Y2K" and thus a threat for accidentally touching off nuclear war. As far as I can tell, those concerns are ill-informed, as the Y2K problem has made neither of those countries more likely to launch a nuclear attack now than they were prior to the Y2K problem. I'm concerned about the fact that some people might use the Y2K event to renew or further entrench their latent prejudice against certain countries, such as Japan or Russia or Pakistan.

Simultaneous with this concern about Americans resenting other countries, this crisis also might give residents of other countries reason to resent the US. Much of what the rest of the world does in the way of computing is bought, borrowed, or reverse-engineered from our country's technology. We assume for ourselves in many ways a leadership role on the international scene. With the assumption of leadership comes responsibility as well. Is computer programming going to be considered just another "decadent and destructive" American product given to the world along with products such as fast food and steamy TV shows that glamorize immoral lifestyles?

One last topic I want to touch upon while we're discussing Y2K's impact on other countries is the fact that for some developing nations, this is a severe setback on their path to technological advancement of even the most basic sort. International development agencies increasingly view technology as an essential part of modern life, critical for young people to have access to and experience working with, no matter where they live. Many people have made it their mission to help bring more technology to countries that don't have broad access yet. Let me share just one representative example of Y2K setbacks in this effort.

Glenn "Jeep" Holthaus is a retired US Marine who has made it his mission to teach computer skills to underprivileged street kids in Thailand who otherwise face a future of garbage collecting or begging and an inability to enter the mainstream working world. During the past few years, he had managed to piece together donations of new and used parts to set up over 200 computers throughout Thailand for street kids to use. Unfortunately, just as his project was gaining great momentum, the Y2K problem slammed the entire effort. In an e-mail message at the end of August 1999, Jeep acknowledged, "We are going to have major problems with Y2K, since most of the boards are quite old." As it turned out, *all* of the systems needed Y2K fixes, and for many of them replacement of the flawed components would have cost more than the entire systems were worth, and therefore wasn't done. After M-Day, his "lucky" systems will be able to handle only certain non-date-sensitive programs, and the "unlucky" systems will instantly become archaic pieces of junk that no longer function at all. Most of the kids from the streets of Pattaya and other Thai cities where Jeep's computers had been placed won't know exactly what they're missing out on, but Jeep and many others who care about expanding those children's future possibilities *will* know and regret the setback.

LESSON 65: LEARNING EXTENDS FROM ONE GENERATION TO THE NEXT

Peter de Jager, the preeminent Y2K consultant, has said, "It's an adventure I'll be able to talk to my grandchildren about." Even for those of us who haven't had Y2K consume all our time, there's the potential for it to provide us fodder for future tale-telling. Think about what you want future generations to remember about this event; they'll only remember what you package and preserve for them.

> *Psalm 103:15-16* As for man, his days are like grass, he flourishes like a flower of the field; the wind blows over it and it is gone, and its place remembers it no more.

> **RELATED VERSE:**
> PSALM 89:47

Y2K is unarguably a once-in-a-lifetime (OIAL) event. Of course, many seemingly OIAL events turn out to happen more than once in our lives. Accepting Jesus into your life seems on the surface like a OIAL event, but there may well be one or more times later in life when you come to know him again, either because you've drifted and are returning to him anew, or preferably, because you've come to know some part of his love which you hadn't known before, and that OIAL thrill is yours to enjoy all over again.

Even when things don't repeat in exact ways, there are often cycles of similar experiences. Remember that human beings have thousands of years under our belt. Innovation and survival have been necessary time and again for many generations before ours. The problems we face today have different facets than the problems faced by people sixty years ago, or six hundred years ago, but disasters have come and gone, including famines, wars, plagues, and many more. People throughout world history have endured and bounced back.

> *Genesis 26:18* Isaac reopened the wells that had been dug in the time of his father Abraham, which the Philistines had stopped up after Abraham died, and he gave them the same names his father had given them.

We often have to revisit tasks from previous generations and meet the shifting challenges of a new era, re-digging older wells. The legacy of faith from our ancestors can lay the groundwork for meeting the responsibilities and challenges of the present. Life is an ongoing process of cycles of renewal, and an awareness of this lets us enrich the power of the present and the hope of the future using the lessons of the past.

> *Jeremiah 6:16* This is what the Lord says: "Stand at the crossroads and look; ask for the ancient paths, ask where the good way is, and walk in it, and you will find rest for your souls."

When I first confronted the challenges of Y2K repair work, I immediately thought of Nehemiah's efforts to complete the rebuilding of the city wall of Jerusalem, which had been left in ruins when Israel fell to the Babylonians in 586 BC. If the Jews didn't rebuild, they faced danger from enemies as well as disgrace for Jerusalem, their leading city (it would be evidence that God was displeased with them). Allow me to zip through the story from the book of Nehemiah, noting particular similarities between chapters of that story and what has occurred during Y2K repair projects.

Nehemiah conducted an inspection of the ruined wall in secret (Y2K parallel: companies and governments which didn't disclose much about their assessments of flawed systems) so that spies and enemies wouldn't have anything to use against him and so that he could develop a clear plan. The Jews were so frazzled and uncertain at that point that to try to unite them to rebuild the walls without a definite plan would have resulted in skepticism instead of cooperation (Y2K parallel: skepticism resulted in some people who were given too much conflicting information without a clear plan of action). Nehemiah was mocked and ridiculed by a variety of officials, and various groups of people refused to help with the work for a variety of reasons (Y2K parallel: those most feverishly tackling the problem were mocked and ridiculed, and various people refused to help for a variety of reasons).

Okay, from here onward, you can supply the many Y2K parallels yourself based on previous lessons you've read in this book. In Nehemiah 4, the strength of the laborers was giving out, and the rubble and complicated leftover layers from the previous wall made it difficult to rebuild. In Nehemiah 5, bickering occurred between the poor and the wealthy despite the cooperation required to complete the wall. Usurers took advantage of the neediness of the poor, but Nehemiah intervened and did his best to make sure that all people were treated fairly.

Nehemiah 6 tells about a situation in which Nehemiah could have been extremely fearful, but he realized it would be unfaithful to not trust in God. That chapter is wonderful, because it gives us an outline of the solutions for fear:

- Awareness of one's duty and willingness to do what's critical and avoid distraction (verse 3)
- Not following incorrect thinkers (verse 8)
- A sturdy faith and turning to prayer (verse 9)
- Personal character and integrity (verse 11)
- Knowledge of facts to understand the circumstance (verse 12)

In Nehemiah 8, the people were told by Nehemiah to find joy where they previously had felt only grief. They were told to refresh themselves with "choice food and sweet drinks" and "send some to those who have nothing prepared."

Once the wall was completely rebuilt, other nations were awed by the accomplishment, and realized that the God of Israel was tremendous. Realize that when you tackle a challenge that's visible to your local community or to the entire world, and you are clearly faithful to God and obey his commandments to help the needy and trust him to oversee the uncertainties, you end up showing people not only that you as an individual Christian (or a group of Christians or the entire universal Christian church) have achieved something, but that God has achieved something. Recognize projects that need your effort, give it wholeheartedly, and let the results stand as a tribute to God who has provided all your talents and resources.

The details of the effort from Nehemiah's day are still relevant today when looking at Y2K and any number of other challenges that a church or community might face. Nehemiah put excellent teamwork into action. He demonstrated great leadership. He figured out how to make do with extremely limited resources. When physical trials threatened the workers' spiritual well-being, he encouraged and reassured them. He assigned most workers to start building near their own homes, thereby employing the principle that everyone should take care of their own area and then go on to help others later if possible. They built the wall at a steady pace, without much selfishness, and with lots of prayer.

For the rebuilding of the wall, God brought an interesting blend of people together in Jerusalem—a unique mix of talents, attitudes, and backgrounds that was suited to the monumental task at hand. The Y2K problem likewise has been a situation where God has assembled a specific mixture of people—religious and non-religious, and with a tremendous diversity of talents, backgrounds, motivations, interests, and needs—to result in not just a successful repair project, but also the potential for future relationships, ongoing work, and a spirit of cooperation that doesn't evaporate. The real victory of Nehemiah's project wasn't simply that the wall was rebuilt—it was the time following the rebuilding when people were able to achieve tremendous things, when the city could get back on track and make progress again. In the post-Y2K years, may our modern world and the arena of technology which we've been renovating be blessed with the same sorts of progress.

I hope all who have worked hard throughout the latter half of the 1990s on this "wall-building" task of correcting and protecting the world's systems from potential Y2K problems will take time—once the wall is fully built and our systems have been fortified—to stand upon the wall and reflect upon what has been learned and achieved, and to look forward to the more promising outlook that awaits us. Knowing that God oversees the efforts of all generations provides comfort for anyone who recognizes that each generation gets only a few steps in the ongoing march of history.

Steve Farrar, who holds the outlook that under the roof of their own loving family home is the best place for kids to learn to deal with adversity, has been such a fine proponent of hope that he sees some promise even if Y2K problems should result in the absolute worst-case scenario. He writes, "Instead of reading about God's miraculous provision in the life of someone on the mission field, you will experience his provision firsthand. And you will never forget it and neither will your kids. In a hundred years, if the Lord Jesus hasn't returned, your great-grandchildren will still be talking about the greatness of God in the year 2000."

Remember the assurance of Romans 15:4 that "everything that was written in the past was written to teach us." You're part of the eternal chain. It's essential to keep track of the times God has provided for you, steered you clear of danger, or helped you find solutions. Remember the specifics, and in small doses at appropriate times, share those stories with people who matter to you—children, relatives, friends, and sometimes even strangers can all benefit from your ability to discern God's presence in your life and summarize it for them so that your history is a witness to the unfailing grace and unsurpassable greatness of God.

> *Psalm 22:30* Posterity will serve him; future generations will be told about the Lord.

> RELATED VERSE:
> PSALM 145:4

LESSON 66: THE NEED TO GET THE WORD OUT

On March 13, 1998, most people in Germany had a lack of interest in Y2K, thinking it a trivial problem. Then came a test at the Hanover city power company, led by a confident data processing manager. A few minutes after simulated "midnight," the computer began spewing thousands of error messages, then froze entirely, and its monitors went blank. For a few minutes, it was impossible to trace equipment breakdowns or monitor the electrical grid, which astounded all the local media that had been invited to watch. It took seven months to eradicate all the problems from that test. "I really thought it would be fine," said Juergen Rehmer, the manager who led the event. "We had made a lot of changes already, and I was quite certain that a full-system test wouldn't present any great difficulty." The embarrassment of that test was badly needed in Germany; it disrupted widespread complacency about the Y2K problem. German airlines and airports had recognized the danger earlier and were well on their way to readiness, but an estimated 60% of German companies hadn't even started a comprehensive Y2K assessment by 1998. "We believe there will be a substantially higher rate of bankruptcies in the year 2000," said Walter Schmitt-Jamin, a managing director of Hermes, a German insurance company. He said a doubling of the usual bankruptcy rate is entirely possible. If the test in March 1998 hadn't fired such a distinct warning shot, it's likely that German companies would have been in even worse straits come M-Day.

In April 1999, Beijing, China also held a dry run for M-Day. Their test resulted in three computer crashes in the city: the reservations system of a luxury hotel, the network of a major corporation, and the board that displays exchange rates at a bank. "I've been telling people, 'This is a tiny version of the Y2K issue,'" said a Chinese computer consultant at the time. "It was like an alarm."

In August 1999, San Francisco Mayor Willie Brown held a press conference to disclose results of a study showing that 36% of San Francisco's small-business owners had no plans to combat Y2K problems. The results, Brown said, could be a major disruption to the city's economy.

Issuing warnings has been a large part of getting the word out about Y2K. That's why those who have informed the public about Y2K have been labeled using such names as Cassandra and Paul Revere (by those deeming most Y2K warnings necessary and beneficial) and such names as Chicken Little or The Boy Who Cried Wolf (by those deeming most Y2K warnings unnecessary and damaging).

It has taken courage to discuss Y2K openly, since there are many strong opinions at all points on the ideological spectrum. Certain "camps" of Y2K experts have been in complete disagreement on individual points, and those walking a middle road were often assaulted from both sides.

In summer 1997, White House OMB Director Sally Katzen mentioned that there was much work to be done, then said, "we are confident that we will finish that work so that the year 2000 computer problem will be a non-event." The same summer, though, a *Computerworld* article suggested, "The problem is far worse than even the pessimists believe."

Pat Sajak opened the *Wheel of Fortune* show that aired on December 31, 1998 by saying, "This is the last day of 1998. Just one more year until our computers crash, we're living in hovels, and eating tree bark." At the 1999 Emmy Awards on September 12, 1999, David Hyde Pierce closed the show with the line, "We'll see you in the next millennium—if your televisions are still working." It was voguish among many public figures to make flippant jokes about Y2K problems to demonstrate disbelief in the doomsaying hype.

Meanwhile, Paula Gordon, an adjunct professor at George Washington University, was saying to reporters quite seriously, "How many Bhopals and Chernobyls do you need?" She has compared Y2K to Apollo 13 and WWII, among other events, and has called it "one of the most serious threats facing mankind ever in our recorded history." She has tracked the time remaining to M-Day by hours, not days (9,045 hours were left when I first heard of her, and something like 95 hours were left when this book was finalized). She feels hardly anyone in the government is willing to admit how much of a problem exists.

Internet Y2K newsgroups in existence during 1999 ranged from **alt.y2k.is-no-problem** to **alt.y2k.end-of-the-world**.

Michael Hyatt, full-time follower of Y2K issues and author of two best-selling books, was still amazed by the contradictory info at the end of September 1999. He wrote, "After years of intense effort and billions of dollars spent by corporations and governments, I expected that as we stood on the threshold of the new millennium a clear picture would finally emerge. Boy, was I wrong." After citing some of the many extreme differences in outlooks between those who think Y2K will be a brief "bump in the road" and those who think we're headed off a cliff, Hyatt concluded, "It is now painfully clear that we simply are not going to get to the bottom of this issue between now and Jan. 1. The only prudent response, therefore, is to err on the side of caution.... Don't let all the conflicting and confusing information keep you from taking action." There have been credible experts pushing both ends of the spectrum—doom and lightness—but no credible expert has ever said that there would be no problematic effects at all from Y2K.

This entire experience tells us first and foremost about communicating: No matter what your message is, don't expect to reach everyone. Adopt the "He who has ears to hear, let him hear" outlook expressed by Jesus throughout his teaching, realizing that those seriously seeking the truth can hear and accept whatever valid information you share even as others choose not to hear and accept it.

Frank Hayes wrote this advice to IT professionals at the end of August 1999 about coping with the major discrepancies in Y2K information: "Do any of these people know what they're talking about? Well, yes—some of them, some of the time. And if you can slice through the contradictory predictions for your top management, you can provide a real service." On certain of the trickiest issues, he said it's "better to pass all the predictions along to your top management. They'll draw their own conclusions. But whatever you do, make sure they know.

Gather and winnow all the Y2K information you can get.... Shoot down myths. Point out which claims are supported. Give your executives the best, most conclusive evidence you can. If IT doesn't explain Y2K to them, who will?"

Many computer professionals have felt a great sense of responsibility for making sure they're getting the word out correctly about Y2K topics. "I don't know if we're going to be the heroes or the goats of 1999," wrote Allan Alter, another *Computerworld* columnist, but "we must accept our inevitable public role; what the world wants from us is level-headed, trustworthy guidance in a scary time."

I appreciate the sense of responsibility by both men in not wanting to let those who aren't insiders make wrong assumptions based on limited knowledge. Don't we see this with Christianity all the time? Some non-Christians latch onto a small event—like Rev. Jerry Falwell's slight gaffe over Tinky-Winky which was belabored in various media—and extrapolate erroneously that most Christians are narrow-minded and go around picking on trivial aspects of secular life. It's important to make sure that you help bring a careful, informed presentation of Christianity to the world, because there *are* extreme and misinformed views of Christianity coming from a variety of sources. If Christians don't responsibly explain Christ's love and purpose to the world, who will?

As a nation, we think it's uncool to take things too seriously. My wife and I watched a national beauty pageant recently, and during the interview round, one contestant was asked something about the tremendously devastating earthquake in Turkey that occurred in mid-1999 and another was asked something about the impact of episodes of school violence in America such as the tragedy in Littleton, Colorado. Both girls gave sober and thoughtful answers, full of as much compassion and sincerity as the short answer period allowed. At the end of the round, the off-stage commentator told the TV viewers that those girls probably wouldn't score very well, because they hadn't found a way to make their answers "light and enjoyable." Think about the absurdity of insisting that even when we focus attention on tragic events, things must be kept "light"—yet that's what many people these days feel compelled to do. We could learn something from looking at the nation of Finland, where most residents are so somber as to be thought unfriendly by tourists. That's not necessarily the best solution either, but surely there's a middle ground where it's okay to be concerned in all situations that merit concern, and it's okay to be joyful in all situations that merit joy.

Because our needs have been met in our Lord and Savior, we Christians are in a better position than almost anyone to exhibit a steady, healthy range of emotions that's grounded ultimately in the knowledge that all things work together for God's purposes. White House "Y2K czar" John Koskinen wasn't completely in Pollyanna mode, and gave some honest assessment of things that wouldn't be ready in time, but his job (and an important one) was to help the average citizen keep his/her head and react sensibly to the arrival of M-Day rather than fly into a panic and behave irrationally. I see the presence of a soothing voice sometimes as a very good thing, but quite a few Y2K experts bristled at how often the official picture that was painted didn't show much of the potential negative stuff.

In fact, from 1996 onward, as book deals and interview schedules and consulting work defined the set of several dozen people who were renowned as worldwide "Y2K experts," there was a lot of posturing and confrontation between various camps of these individual experts. At times, for those of us who followed the activities and information output of many of these people on a daily basis, it was a lot like the world of professional wrestling, with caricatures being drawn and insults occasionally being hurled in various directions. The "Gary North is a Big Fat Idiot" web site and the special version of the song "Don't Worry Be Happy" that the folks at Y2KNews Radio recorded to poke fun at Koskinen are just a couple of examples.

Koskinen has been a fascinating study in how difficult it is to be a consistent voice, which most of us admittedly aren't great at doing in any aspect of our lives, let alone when the media is recording 80% of what we say. He's had surges of alarm-sounding, then lulls, then more alarm-sounding. In 1998 he warned "We need to avoid creating panic and precipitous, counterproductive activity" and decided to help industries spotlight success stories rather than glitches or testing difficulties.

Liza Christian testified before a US Senate hearing in May 1999, however, that she felt Americans were being lulled by "an orchestrated public relations campaign." She cited statements by Koskinen and spoke of a concerted effort to "tranquilize" the American people, explaining, "The reasoning is that if you provide full disclosure, people will act irrationally and panic....While some of the 'positive' statements about Y2K progress are grounded in fact, others are 'window dressing' covering truly serious problems."

Koskinen said in September 1999, "Our basic strategy is give people information—they have a lot of common sense and they will respond appropriately. If we're going to win this battle, we're going to win it with information. We're not going to win it with slick PR campaigns." Less than a week later, Koskinen expressed worries that Americans had become too complacent about the potential impact of Y2K problems, saying, "We can't surprise people. There *are* going to be Y2K failures on New Year's Day." The same week, Tim Wilson stated his feeling that White House officials have "created this cloud of confusion over [the Y2K problem] and have not allowed the people to understand. If people would have understood Y2K a year and a half ago, straight up, we could have handled it."

Cliff Kurtzman, president of Tenagra Corp., publisher of the Y2K Information Center web site, said about Koskinen, "The general mood in the Y2K community is that he's extremely quiet, not as visible as people would like him to be," and added "He's not making it as big of a problem as it is."

The consensus among many Y2K consultants was that the technique of Koskinen and other White House spindoctors was four-pronged:

- To "embarrass the media off of Y2K" and make it socially unacceptable for the average citizen to be concerned about Y2K
- To shift focus to the international lack of preparedness to reassure people that we "smarter" Americans will be relatively okay
- To lay groundwork so that if anything happens, it can be blamed on "those loonies" who were doomsaying about possible Y2K disasters enough to create a self-fulfilling prophecy
- To move final responsibility from the federal level to states and cities

Over 70% of US companies had already experienced Y2K-related failures by August 1999, according to an ongoing Cap Gemini America survey of IT executives at 161 companies and government agencies. Only 2% of the companies polled actually suffered business disruptions because of those glitches, as they were able to either fix the problems quickly or enact workarounds. Few of the failures were made visible because they didn't cause significant business disruptions, and companies didn't have many reasons to make them public.

Communications experts have said it's vital to plan for Y2K calamities and deal honestly and quickly with the public, the media, and business partners, but most companies aren't concerned about that. Bill Patterson, president of Reputation Management Associates, has talked to "dozens and dozens" of companies, and none had any interest in a public affairs contingency plan for Y2K glitches. "I gave up trying to convince them," he said. "We will see who's right."

Silence has been the preferred communication method for many people. Some heads of state, such as the presidents of Colombia and Argentina, have chosen not to even mention the Y2K problem publicly for fear of causing bad reactions by citizens. The US government has gathered a lot of data about the preparedness of the private sector, but mostly on the condition that it not identify individual companies. From July to September 1999, US embassies worked to collect data from countries perceived as lagging. 76 nations fully complied with the survey, and another 56 nations shared information with the center but did not permit its release to the public.

Misinformation or lack of information became such a problem that corporations started sending their own people to visit suppliers to verify that Y2K work was being done correctly. Executives at GM's Opel subsidiary, for example, found they couldn't trust the word of vendors about certain products' Y2K compliance. Even some industrial robots they'd bought in 1997 which were supposed to be Y2K-compliant turned out to have Y2K glitches. By August 1998, Opel started sending its own Y2K team on assessment visits to key suppliers "to ask questions that indicated whether the suppliers knew what they were talking about," according to Roger Aze, Opel's Y2K coordinator. Questions such as "Do you have a person in charge of Y2K?" and "Do you have a program and a schedule?" revealed whether the suppliers were bluffing or were legitimately addressing the Y2K challenge.

Some companies like NIKE have had the courage to put out info admitting bluntly that they couldn't even get responses from their suppliers, and without that information, couldn't possibly conclude anything about the true picture for how Y2K might impact them overall.

Sometimes it seems politics can take precedence over the truth. The US consular reports giving Y2K travel advisories for 190 countries list Russia as "moderately prepared," for example, but the Ukraine (right next door and in roughly the same shape) is listed as "unprepared." Italy is widely acknowledged as being terribly underprepared, but the diplomatic way of saying this in the consular reports is that Italy "could lower their risk... by making greater progress." The reports are blunt, though, with some countries that they don't fear offending, such as Belarus, for which the travel advisory says that there's a good chance of power, heat, and water shortages lasting several days or more during cold winter weather.

Companies within some industries have shared lots of inside info with each other about faulty equipment and the status of upgrades and so on, but much of that info is not made public, so we're not fully aware of where all the true concerns lie. It's difficult to get accurate info, so what can we look for to really gauge the problem? Almost everyone has participated in the silent treatment at some point.

Last May, the National Security Agency classified a Defense Department Y2K database as "highly sensitive," prompting the military to yank it from the Internet. The Readiness and Disclosure Act in Fall 1998 which limited certain Y2K liability to encourage companies to share information included a key provision barring the public from attending meetings of the Y2K council and its subcommittees, saying the federal open-meeting act "shall not apply to the working groups established under this section." Jack Gribben, a White House spokesman, said, "There's a certain necessity, to a degree, in having private meetings. We want to encourage people to be candid about their progress, and opening the meetings up to the press and the public doesn't always encourage candor."

Maine officials on September 30, 1999 blocked the release in report form of an expensive independent consultant's Y2K study about the state, fearing that people would get their hands on it under a state "right-to-know" law. The explanation was that they were afraid criminals would find out about the status of certain police operations and other things which might give the criminals some sort of advantage over the police, but most Y2K watchers sensed that Maine officials were worried that average citizens would react badly to the report in general. One Y2K advisor said about the decision, "Don't you think that this sort of nonsense is going to cause fear where fear is not even an issue?"

Global 2000 Coordinating Group, a group of international banks, securities companies, and insurers from 46 countries, planned to publicly rate the readiness of more than 30 nations and publish its findings in February 1999. The goal was to impel lagging countries to work harder and put pressure on all countries to disclose more information about their progress. Many Y2K consultants praised the planned publicity as an example of cooperative information-sharing for the public good. Immediately after the announcement, though, critics began suggesting that the financial group's ratings might create more problems than benefits, fearing they might inadvertently cause a flight of capital and destabilize some large developing countries, so the ratings weren't released as planned.

Certain groups and agencies haven't found the courage to tell the truth about Y2K issues because people might react in harmful ways. Likewise, it takes courage to tell God's truth—you might not always get a great reaction. You might scare people or might see them go into denial, but you can't shy away from telling the truth.

Proverbs 15:23 A man finds joy in giving an apt reply—and how good is a timely word!

A timely word is often essential. Not everyone who spoke of the Y2K problem in years past was listened to, but their word of warning was persistent and finally got the attention it deserved. Even after M-Day, the season for timely words is not over in the context of the Y2K problem. We still have the need for timely words of information, explanation, sympathy, apology, encouragement, and congratulations.

One of Y2K's many uncertainties has been whether there will be any decrease in our ability to communicate. We now have a lightning-fast mentality. We're all used to being aware of what the rest of the world is up to in an instant—think of CNN's coverage of the Desert Storm military operation—that communication speed has somehow made us think we have greater control over events. It's not true, though—the fact that natural disasters or crimes or wars are shown to us in real time doesn't mean that they're any less shocking or devastating to those involved with them. A last-minute sense of panic or reassurance about Y2K is possible. Americans are watching to see if problems pile up in the 17 time zones that reach M-Day ahead of the US. Some government officials in California have said they feel they have an advantage because they're nearly 18 hours behind Australia, which they think is like having an early warning system. The *Wall Street Journal* in mid-December 1999 reported a huge surge in the purchase of equipment for satellite-based communications by corporations and government agencies wanting to ensure rapid communications capabilities are in place on M-Day.

A widely distributed e-mail hoax in 1999 told PC owners that they needed to set the Regional Settings date format in Windows to a four-digit format. The implication that your PC is not Y2K compliant unless you make this adjustment, or worse yet, that your PC becomes compliant just by making this adjustment, is incorrect. The date settings there merely control the display of the date and have nothing to do with how dates are stored internally. Because information travels amazingly fast in today's world, unfortunately misinformation travels just as fast. The best Bible quote I know about that sort of misdirection of attention and mistaken belief that someone has a handle on a simple fix is the one and only occasion on which you might say Jesus identified a "bug" in someone's logic:

> *Matthew 23:24* "You blind guides! You strain out a gnat but swallow a camel."

Jesus was lecturing teachers of the law about their legalistic ways and explaining to them the need not only to practice tithing and other acts that are a surface fix, but also to have true, comprehensive solutions—love, mercy, justice, and faithfulness—permeate their actions.

We have seen lists of possible Y2K vulnerabilities and solutions become commonly available on web sites, in books and periodicals, etc. Many places of business have put out information for customers about Y2K compliance. There has been too much media saturation, perhaps, but at the grassroots level the Y2K problem has been one of the most amazing examples of excellent communication I've seen in my lifetime. People gathering and disseminating information with the sole purpose of helping to spare others from misery and give them a way out— sound familiar? Yes, this has been a sort of secular evangelism. In fact, credit unions and utilities and public libraries and other groups have distributed billions of small pamphlets (think tracts!) explaining what the problem is and that they've already gotten a handle on how salvation from the problem can be attained.

Typically those spreading the word about Y2K have been most effective working directly with one person at a time, addressing that person's specific concerns and questions and helping him to really understand the issues surrounding Y2K. Remember when you practice your own evangelism that it doesn't matter how small an audience you're working with. Philip the evangelist's encounter with the Ethiopian eunuch (Acts 8:26-39) was much different for Philip than the large crowds he was used to talking with, but Philip was grateful for the chance to offer guidance and explanation to this unexpected audience of one, and the end result was a successful conversion and a baptism.

Bumper stickers I've seen in the past two years include *Year2Kneel*, *Yes2theKingdom*, and *Yield2theKing*. Some Christians have thus sought to transform "Y2K compliant"—the label that's everywhere now on packaging, web sites, and so on—into a Christian message. Such effort isn't necessary—as Christians, we already have our own pervasive labeling systems in place. The "Y2K compliant" labels remind me greatly of the Christian fish that many people place on their vehicles, a declaration that "I've been successfully converted." Lesson 35 discusses the need to not oversimplify our faith through such symbols, but in some regards it's thrilling that so many people are willing to advertise to the world that their own personal conversion is complete. And it's not just fish—crosses, angels, or other overtly Christian symbols mean the same things—you can trust me to work for good, you can count on me to be the product of quality workmanship, and I've got an instruction manual (the Bible) that will tell you everything you need to know about me and the way I behave. Such a symbol also immediately tells people what things you're incompatible with.

We don't all need to show off a label (my wife, for example, wears a cross on a pendant around her neck tucked out of sight—it makes the same sort of statement, but merely to provide satisfaction for herself rather than to make a pronouncement to the world), but it's great for any Christian who wants to do so to use a symbol like a cross, a fish, a dove, or something similar as jewelry or as part of their home's or automobile's decor to gladly profess their "Yes 2 the Kingdom" compatibility. Far more importantly, it's great to live in a way that actually demonstrates that state of readiness.

In the world of Y2K, terms such as "Y2K-ready" often have taken on particular political and legal meanings (especially when used constantly and casually for PR purposes) rather than holding any sort of specific technical or operational significance. Make sure you're not just a political or legal "Christian" wearing the term loosely, but instead make sure that being Christian has a fully operational meaning in your life.

I love Y2K because, unlike some less complex issues, it has caused Christians to discuss it biblically using a breadth of passages from both the Old and New Testaments (Old for judgment and warnings and God's faithfulness to us, New for God's ultimate promise to us fulfilled through Christ, and both Testaments for lessons on practicing compassion and enduring hardship, etc.—moreover, in turning to the entire Bible, we see generational lessons that hold equally true for people at different points in time).

You know by now that two leading Christian organizations that worked hard at informing people about Y2K and the vital role that the church could play in the entire event were named after Old Testament figures: The Isaiah Project (**www.isaiahproject.org**) and The Joseph Project (**www.josephproject2000.org**).

> ### ∽ Note
>
> Almost all Christians discussing Y2K felt very comfortable using the story of Joseph and the famine from Genesis 41 as an example of beckoning to responsibility and diligent preparation so that we're unfazed and prepared for service in our own and others' eventual times of need. There were a few notable exceptions, like Dave Hunt, who in his book *Y2K: A Reasoned Response to Mass Hysteria* took issue with the use of this example.

I like the namesakes for these leaders in the Christian Y2K preparedness movement. In fact, it's easily possible to point to other figures in the Bible whose foresight, faith, unselfish thinking, obedience to God's leading, and other laudable behavior brought them to situations where they were able to provide solutions as others fumbled desperately amid chaos. For a brief time I considered creating my own Y2K group and naming it in similar fashion, after Amos or Micah or somebody else with God-given foresight, but then I decided I'd prefer my group to actually be a "non-prophet organization." (Sorry—those who know me realize I can't resist making a bad pun like that.)

Why turn to the Bible to figure out Y2K or any other event in our lives? Because in any situation, it's the Christian's central source of truth. Y2K has shown us better than most human predicaments how complex and contradictory people's opinions can be. I've seen many web sites and books claiming to be the "ultimate source on Y2K"—how can any person or set of people ever truly think they're the ultimate source on anything? For Christians, the ultimate source of instruction and information doesn't change, regardless of the circumstance we're trying to understand:

> *2 Timothy 3:16-17* All Scripture is God-breathed and is useful for teaching, rebuking, correcting and training in righteousness, so that the man of God may be thoroughly equipped for every good work.

Anyone willing to be a believer rather than a perpetual doubter, willing to rely upon God's eternal authority rather than human speculation, should search the Scripture. While Christians have needed to "get the word out" during the Y2K event, we've also needed to "get the Word out."

I participated in one community group meeting about Y2K where they discussed plans to ask local store owners to stock extra quantities of particular types of foods that might be needed in a crisis. They drafted a letter to the mayor to try to get him on board with their plans, then crafted an information campaign for local schools, then carefully planned how they'd be able to ask neighbors, without being too intrusive, about specific medical needs or other special concerns so that hospitals and police departments could be asked to prepare in appropriate ways. Next, the group divided into pairs and practiced approaching strangers to discuss Y2K issues. This was typical of similar Y2K planning sessions all over the world—much of the work involved spreading the word in one way or another.

Much of the work of the church in all times boils down to that simple task, also. The early and modern church both have struggled with spreading the Word. The problems faced by the early church included direct opposition, a rigid adherence to an outdated religious system, overreliance on magic, and so on. The problems faced by today's church include information overload, cynicism, overreliance on science, lack of personal contact, and so on.

2 Timothy 4:2 Preach the Word; be prepared in season and out of season; correct, rebuke and encourage—with great patience and careful instruction.

LESSON 67: THE RELENTLESS PURSUIT OF PERFECTION

Some leading Christian voices in the media suggested that God probably would use Y2K as a test for many people. Even if that doesn't turn out to be the case, I recommend we use it as a chance to test ourselves. We've mentioned earlier in the book the idea found in James 1:2-4 that trials can lead to perfection and completeness.

You probably know the term "trial by fire" as it refers to the refining of metal in a crucible—Zechariah 13:9 and 1 Corinthians 3:15 present the same concept in terms of God testing man. Although the Lord's love for us surpasses any human love, the Lord still might refine us throughout our lifetime through various testing situations. We ourselves also must test the quality of our entire lives and the efforts we put into the work we do for God. The wrong work humans do will be destroyed and the right work will survive the flames.

God told Ezekiel to give this message to the king of Tyre:

Ezekiel 28:12b You were the model of perfection, full of wisdom and perfect in beauty.

The rest of Ezekiel's message was an unfortunate one. The king had blown the perfection he'd once had (when in a good relationship with God) through sins and dishonesty and pride, and thus would come to destruction and a horrible end.

The king was an example of someone who moved from perfection to brokenness. Now let's look at someone who relied upon God to move from brokenness to perfection. David had reached a point where he had enemies conspiring against him, had lost the respect of his friends, and was living in primitive conditions as a fugitive afraid for his life. He felt that those who had once viewed him as something wonderful had come to see him as something shattered and useless:

Psalm 31:12 I am forgotten by them as though I were dead; I have become like broken pottery.

David went on to explain that God cared for him even though people didn't. God mended the broken pieces of David to make him something whole and wonderful again. If God cares even for broken pieces of pottery, which can only be used for basic tasks as a scoop or a scraping tool or a landscaping ingredient (but more often are simply discarded by people as having no obvious value), then God surely cares for and can mend any broken aspect of our lives, just as he mended David's life.

I don't think God dislikes computers or any other modern technology—if I thought so, I wouldn't head up an organization that provides free computer hardware and software to churches and those doing missions work. I don't think God allowed Y2K to snowball to high anxiety levels for certain people and to the massive worldwide complexity of effort required for remediation efforts and so on in order to condemn and threaten all of us directly with punishment for particular behaviors we've demonstrated in recent history. I think that all the stuff discussed earlier in this book—short-term thinking, tendency to procrastinate, selfishness, poor priorities, laziness, greed, and many other factors—have made Y2K just another (albeit very large) example of the types of things that can result when certain wrong factors influence our daily decisions about how to live and act.

I do believe that God wants us to show good stewardship over that with which we've been blessed. Not ruining things (like the planet's resources) and not squandering things (like money) and not ignoring things (like the worth of every person) are essential if we are to have those things around and working well when we need them.

> *James 3:2* We all stumble in many ways. If anyone is never at fault in what he says, he is a perfect man, able to keep his whole body in check.

There is no perfect man without God. We can try to improve ourselves through all the self-help books and good intentions in the world, but we'll never be fully fixed until we're in solid relationship with God. Patched-up systems are okay, but eventually need a total fix. Turning a flawed computer system into one that's fixed, fully functioning, and Y2K-compliant has required a full-blown Y2K "conversion" project, and of course when we're saved as Christians we also use the terminology of being "converted" into something that's fixed, redeemed, whole, and compliant with God's will.

We all have the fatal flaw of sinfulness, and none of us know exactly what problems will or won't result from our own imperfection as human beings. But we know that God gave us the solution—Christ died for our sins to make sure that all our systems wouldn't fail unexpectedly, and that we could have a successful future, as long as we believe in him.

As you saw in Chapter 6, Y2K fixes haven't always been right and the people discussing their "knowledge" of the problem haven't always been right. The ways of man are prone to mistakes in judgment and execution. The only solution in this world that's always right is the way of the Lord. Proverbs 30:5 tells us "every word of God is flawless" and Psalm 12:6 explains in more detail that "the words of the Lord are flawless, like silver refined in a furnace of clay, purified seven times." In 1 Peter 1:19, Christ is called "a lamb without blemish or defect."

Do we have any right to expect that sort of perfection in our own lives? Absolutely! The 24th verse of Jude mentions that God is able to "present you before his glorious presence without fault."

> **RELATED VERSE:**
> PHILIPPIANS 2:14-16

There's an undesirable thing we could do to prevent our own perfection through God's love, explained in this verse:

> *1 John 4:18* Perfect love drives out fear, because fear has to do with punishment. The one who fears is not made perfect in love.

The worst thing we can do is to fear things and not trust God, to let worry and unfaithfulness creep in rather than accepting God's love and all its power. We must fear God in the ways discussed in Lesson 12, but not fear the things of the world and whatever they might do to us.

Paul tells the Corinthians as he ends his second epistle to them (2 Corinthians 13:11), "Aim for perfection." Like Paul, I believe that God wants us to progress toward perfection, and that he gave us the means to accomplish that through the precious gift of his son to die from this world so that we could come to live eternally. We as individuals will not be perfect while we're on this earth, and we as churches will not be perfect in all circumstances. Christian individuals and churches have something perfect living within them, though. Jesus Christ is an embedded system, a flawless one that perfects us from within. Through God's grace alone, we who are inherently imperfect can be brought to perfection.

When requiring something of us, God doesn't expect perfect people to show up. By finding everlasting life through acceptance of God's new covenant for us through Jesus Christ, though, our flawed selves become positioned to achieve perfect works through him. He can locate our hidden flaws instantly, and remedy them instantly. You have to *hope* that computer-related flaws are able to be correctly fixed, but our personal flaws, on the other hand, are undoubtedly able to be perfected by God. Once we accept Christ into our hearts, our prior flaws are forevermore rendered powerless. We're meant to strive for perfection, to work at being Christlike in everything we do. Perfection is not a pompous goal, but a necessary goal if we're each to become and remain the best person we can be.

> *1 Thessalonians 2:4* ... We are not trying to please men but God, who tests our hearts.

> *Psalm 139:23* Search me, O God, and know my heart; test me and know my anxious thoughts.

Let's put the same type of thorough examination and preparation that we've seen during Y2K compliance efforts into making sure our hearts are fully compliant, so that when God tests them he finds that they are. If anyone has a heart that isn't pure, isn't content, or isn't filled with the proper feelings, God can perform a complete system overhaul in only the time required to confess to God the desire for such a conversion:

> *Ezekiel 36:26* I will give you a new heart and put a new spirit in you; I will remove from you your heart of stone and give you a heart of flesh.

God can replace your non-compliant heart with one that's spiritually alive and functioning as it should.

> *2 Corinthians 13:5-6* Examine yourselves to see whether you are in the faith; test yourselves. Do you not realize that Christ Jesus is in you— unless, of course, you fail the test? And I trust that you will discover that we have not failed the test.

There is tremendous reward in complying with God's commands, but we don't always notice all of our own failures and glitches. God's examination of us sees even the most subtle, most hidden aspects of our lives, and overcomes any ignorance or carelessness that might occur during our own examination of ourselves. We must count on him to forgive and correct even those problems we miss when we search our own internal systems:

> *Psalm 19:12* Who can discern his errors? Forgive my hidden faults.

God has a perfect program for us. Let's get with the program.

Summary

It's reassuring to me that, no matter what particular events come to pass as a result of the Y2K problem, and no matter which organizations or companies or governments find themselves constrained from business as usual following M-Day, every church in the world can conduct worship and other activities pretty much as usual. Regardless of the availability of computers, electricity, banking, telecommunications, and a variety of other luxuries to which we've grown accustomed, the church can remain intact and capable of ministering to people's needs at every level.

If you ever catch your thinking remaining too localized, please expand its scope to include all of God's world. With the glory and assurances of God sustaining and empowering you in the same ways that previous generations have been sustained and empowered, you can confidently tackle whatever critical tasks you encounter. Once you've undergone the Yes 2 Kingdom conversion, Jesus is your embedded system, and you can steady yourself at all times in the knowledge that he is flawless and will never fail you.

As Hebrews 6:1 explains, once the foundation of basic Christian lessons has been established, we should progress from elementary teachings to a full Christian maturity in all matters through diligence, discernment, and practical and constant application of our faith. Every new year, especially this one, offers the chance for reflection and a fresh beginning. Carrying with us everything we've learned from the Y2K problem, let's move forward to life's highest possibilities.